BEVERLEY NICHOLS

Sketch of Beverley Nichols by Cecil Beaton

Beverley Nichols
A Life

Bryan Connon

TIMBER PRESS
Portland, Oregon

Publisher's Note: This volume is a reprint of the work first published in 1991 by Constable. The reader should note several minor differences between the two printings. The selection of photographs and illustrations has been revised and expanded, as have the bibliography and author's conclusion. In other respects, the two printings are identical.

First published in 1991 by Constable

All photographs and illustrations are the property of the Bryan Connon Collection.
Frontispiece drawing of Beverley Nichols by Cecil Beaton.

Published in 2000 by
Timber Press, Inc.
The Haseltine Building
133 s.w. Second Avenue, Suite 450
Portland, Oregon 97204, u.s.a.

Printed in Hong Kong

Library of Congress Cataloging-in-Publication Data

Connon, Bryan.
    Beverley Nichols : a life / Bryan Connon.
        p. cm.
    Includes bibliographical references (p.) and index.
    ISBN 0-88192-444-X
      1. Nichols, Beverley, 1899– 2. Authors, English—20th century—Biography.
  3. Gardeners—England—Biography. I. Title.
  PR6027.I22 Z6 2000
  828'.91209—dc21
    [B]   99-046819

To the memory of
Elliott Graham
mentor and friend

Contents

Illustrations

All the photographs came from Beverley Nichols's own collection, now in the possession of the author. Photographs follow page 112.

John Nichols and Pauline Shalders in 1890
Beverley, aged three
Beverley, aged sixteen
Beverley at Oxford in 1917
Beverley in 1918
Manuscript fragment of a Beverley Nichols song
The Nichols men, circa 1920: Paul, John, Beverley and Alan
Dame Nellie Melba
King Constantine of Greece
Syrie, Liza and Somerset Maugham
Publicity photo for *Twenty-Five*
Beverley at the piano
Beverley with the British ambassador to the United States in 1928
Beverley in New York, 1929
Beverley circa 1930
The garden path
Beverley gardening at Glatton
The dining hall at Thatch Cottage
The sitting room at Thatch Cottage
The cottage at Glatton in the 1930s
Arthur Diamond
Beverley with his jet-black half Siamese cats
Sheet music title page, 1930
On the Elstree set of *Glamour* in 1931
Dame Edith Evans
Sheet music from *Floodlight*
Frances Day and Beverley
Beverley at London Studios, November 1938
In the Hampstead garden, late 1930s
The garden at Beverley's Hampstead house before work done to his design
Cyril Butcher
Passage to India, 1943
The 'secret' door at Merry Hall
The music room at Merry Hall

Acknowledgements

I am indebted to Beverley Nichols who invited me to write this biography and who supplied much of the material and information it contains.

Following his death, I was further assisted by his executors – his brother, Canon Paul Nichols, and Mr Cyril Butcher – who could not have been more helpful and frank in supplying information of a personal nature. I am most grateful also to Mr Nichols's nieces, Mrs Jill Tatem and Mrs Judy Williamson, and to those connected with the Nichols and Shalders clans: Mrs Margaret Chidson, Mr Peter Fitzgerald-Moore, Mary Lady Fuller, Mrs Nancy Meggs, Mr John Nichols and Mrs Margaret Vance.

I should like to thank the following individuals and institutions who have all helped in a lesser or greater degree, and I trust that I have not, by an oversight, omitted any names.

Miss Amanda J.E. Arrowsmith (County Archivist, Suffolk County Council); Mr P.J. Bottrill (Area Librarian, South Devon Area); Mr John Brennan; Various officials of the British Broadcasting Corporation; Mr Rex Bunnett; Mr Peter Burton; Mr M.A. Carpenter; Mr Alan Chapman; Mr John Cooling; Mr Tom Corbett; Mr Peter Cotes; Mrs Rose Kyffin Crossfield (*née* Evans); Miss G. Denton; Mr Arthur G. Diamond; Mr Larry Drew; Mrs Kathleen Edmunds (*née* Mohan); Mr Vivian Ellis; Mr Gervase Farjeon; Mr Eric Glass; Mr Elliott Graham; Mr John Hawkins (Hoddell Pritchard); Mrs A. Helme; Miss Eileen J. Hose; Dr John Jones (Dean-Archivist, Balliol College); Mr E.G.H. Kempson (Archivist, Marlborough College); Mr Geoffrey Langley (County Reference Librarian, County of Avon); The Law Society Services Ltd; Mr David Machin (The Bodley Head); The Raymond Mander and Joe Mitchenson Theatre Collection; Miss Joan Mason-Martin; Mr Alec McCowen; Sir John Mills; Mr Billy Milton; Mr Alan Neve (Performing Rights Society); Mr Patrick Newley; Mrs Joan Nicholson; Miss Joyce Packe; Mr Steve Race; The Royal Agricultural College; Sherborne School, Dorset; Mr Alfred Shaughnessy; Mrs Susan Shaw; Mrs Betty Spillane (*née* Hicks); Miss Gloria Swanson; Mr Len Thorpe (Warner Chappell); Mr Hugo Vickers; Mr Dick Vosburgh; Miss Undine Wiggins; Mr Emlyn Williams; Mr Sandy Wilson; Mr M. Winn; Mr Peter Yan; and Mr George M. Young.

I am grateful to Bachman and Turner for permission to quote from *Twilight* and to W.H. Allen for allowing me to quote from various Beverley Nichols works. In addition, I thank Mr Peter Burton for permission to quote from a letter written by Robin Maugham and Mr Sheridan Morley for permission to quote from *The Noël Coward Diaries*.

I am indebted to Mr Geoffrey T. Roberts for research; to Mr Andrew Harvey for general assistance; to Mr Derek Harmer-Morris for his invaluable help in preparing the manuscript and for his criticism and advice; and to Prudence Fay, my editor at Constable. Finally, I must express my appreciation to Mr Eric Glass for his patience and encouragement.

B. C.
1990

Preface

When Beverley Nichols invited me to write his biography he promised that there would be no inhibiting constraints; 'You must tell the truth as you see it, however unflattering it may be.'

On most aspects of his life he was frank and informative but he refused to discuss his father, John Nichols, except to denigrate him as he had done in his horrifying *Father Figure*, published in 1972. Then, a few days before his final illness, he unexpectedly spoke in kindlier terms of him and promised he would tell me 'the real story' at our next meeting. What he intended to reveal will never be known but I was prompted by this to investigate his account of events rather more thoroughly than I might otherwise have done. The result has been the rehabilitation of John Nichols and of several other members of his family whom he also defamed. Indeed, what Beverley wrote was so at odds with the facts that the unravelling of the real story has become a central theme of this biography. Not all of the truth has been discovered; there remains a family mystery which extensive research has failed to resolve. Perhaps the answer lies in a bundle of old letters or in a dusty file?

From an early age, Beverley was driven by a compulsive desire to be famous, even great. If greatness eluded him, fame did not. With it came financial reward, but that did not satisfy the hunger for recognition by his peers as a serious author which persisted until he died. In studying his prolific output, published and unpublished, I have been consistently delighted by its substance and depth, its felicity of style and wit, and often by its prescience. I have also been disappointed by its lapses into sentimentality, self-pity and melodrama. Try as I may, however, I can think of no other writer who, while pursuing a long and successful career as a journalist, also succeeded in the contrasting fields of, among others, the novel, drama, revue, detective stories, travel, political commentary, religion, gardening, biography and children's books.

In attempting to illuminate the personality behind the often contradictory facets of the Beverley Nichols façade, I have been aware that the evaluation of a character, however conscientiously undertaken, can only be partially accurate and never complete. The many people to whom I spoke had firm ideas about the type of man they thought he was, or imagined him to be. Whether they loved, admired or heartily disliked him, they all agreed that his potent charm was the main constituent of this façade. In an early self-portrait he wrote: 'In my heart of hearts I know – how bitterly I know!

– my weaknesses, my stupidities, my vices. But I am not going to parade them before you.' Towards the end of his life, however, this is precisely what he decided to do.

In case readers may consider I claim undue familiarity by the use of his Christian name throughout the book, I should explain that it avoids confusion with other members of the Nichols family and it is how he was known to his friends and acquaintances. For the spelling of other names I have relied on several sources, including contemporary press accounts. In the case of Noel Coward, I have followed the example of his biographer, Cole Lesley, and ignored the diaeresis. I have deliberately avoided footnotes or an appendix of sources because I find them irritatingly interruptive in biographies. The source reference is in the text; if it is not, the information comes from material in my possession or from my discussions with Beverley himself.

· I ·

Family Reputations

1790–1890

IT is difficult to imagine a family as vile as the Nicholses who, if Beverley's account in his autobiographical *Father Figure* is to be accepted, vied with the Borgias in almost everything bar murder. If they lacked this vice, Beverley tried to make up for it by three self-confessed attempts at patricide. According to him, the Nicholses were a worthless lot, the family tree twisted and thorny. Grandfather was a drunken sadist who beat his sons unmercifully; Uncle George was grasping and mean; Uncle Arthur was a swindler and womanizer who died riddled with syphilis. John, Beverley's father, was the personification of evil, an alcoholic who revelled in destroying his wife and children.

By contrast, he saw his mother's family, the Shalders, as creatures of charm, generosity and wit. His mother Pauline, graceful, sweet and kind, kept to her marriage vows with misguided integrity until death released her from a life of torment and humiliation.

With these, as with so many of Beverley's strongly held opinions, there were no shades of grey, only black or white – but those opinions could alter. Black could metamorphose into white or white into black with the speed of light. One day he was a passionate follower of Jesus Christ, the next an agnostic; now a dedicated pacifist, then an advocate of war. It was the same with friendships: one moment he was a lover, the next an enemy. But however volatile his attitudes might be, his hatred of the Nichols family, once established, remained unalterable.

Beverley, however, had every reason to be proud of his Nichols blood. The Nicholses were Gloucestershire yeomen farmers who could trace their history back for many centuries. Over the years, they spread across the west of England in a tangle of clanship so intricate that it is impossible to construct a comprehensive family tree. If every Nichols had lit a lantern at midnight on the day Beverley was born, the West Country would have been a blaze of light.

When Thomas Nichols, Beverley's great-grandfather, married Maria Greenland in the village of Almondsbury in 1828, the wedding certificate described him as a yeoman. If anyone had prophesied then that by the end of the century the yeomen of England would be extinct, along with the system they represented, he would have been locked away as a lunatic. Yeomen were the backbone of the nation, below the nobility but above the labouring peasantry. Yeomen might be very prosperous or comparatively poor, but they took pride in their status and achievements.

Thomas and Maria settled at Sundays Hill Farm in Almondsbury. It was a hard-working life, simple in its pleasures and serene in its insularity. Maria had three servant-girls to help in the house and dairy, and Thomas had no shortage of labouring men and boys to work the land. Five children survived beyond infancy, three sons and two daughters. It was taken for granted that the boys would become farmers, as generations of Nicholses had done before them.

Like his brothers, George, the second son, grew to be a fine physical specimen and was particularly noted for his good looks and charm. When he was eighteen, he attracted the attention of George Gibbs, an important landowner. The story goes that Gibbs was out riding when he saw George ploughing with a team of horses. Every farmer's lad learned this skill as a matter of course and the finer points were hotly contested in competition at local country shows. Gibbs was impressed by George's expertise and, in conversation, was beguiled by the boy's manner and intelligence. He proposed to Thomas that he should take George under his patronage and send him to the college at Cirencester which he had helped to found. The college, the first of its kind, was dedicated to improving knowledge of the 'Science of Agriculture' and was enthusiastically supported by Albert, the Prince Consort, a friend of Gibbs. George's benefactor was not disappointed for, at the end of two years' study, his protégé was awarded a diploma with honours, an achievement recorded on a plaque which still hangs in the college dining-hall.

George and his patron remained close friends and their association became increasingly important to George as Gibbs and his family rose in power and influence. With his help, George started on his own at Charlton Farm, a holding of some 500 acres at Wraxall, a village near Bristol, where he employed upwards of eighteen men and a groom. Almost from the beginning he assumed the role of gentleman farmer. An excellent horseman, he loved hunting, racing, hare-coursing and shooting, and was invited to join the Duke of Beaufort's hunt. But he was not a gentleman farmer in the sense of being an absentee who left the running of Charlton to others, for he kept a tight control on the day-to-day affairs of the farm and made a success of it. In 1855 (describing himself as a yeoman, like his father before him) he married Mary Natriss, the daughter of a well-to-do confectioner with a business in Wine Street, Bristol. Like her husband, she was socially ambitious. They were to have one daughter and five sons, one of whom died when he was only a few months old.

The policy of Free Trade at the time stated that unrestricted imports would be balanced by the value of exports. Farmers dreaded the effect of cheap food imports and many diversified their capital into other enterprises. Several of the Nichols clan pursued sidelines, in particular auctioneering, and George himself decided on this as a second career. In 1860 he laid the foundations of the firm which was to carry his name for almost a hundred years. If all he had offered was exuberance and charm, his new venture might easily have fizzled out, but he had a shrewd business brain and, from the outset, he was a financial success, helped by his widespread contacts in agriculture and the valuable support of the Gibbs family. Within a few years, he took into partnership an experienced auctioneer, F. J. Alder, who brought to the venture a knowledge of fine arts which George lacked. Their auction rooms and offices at 59, Broad Street, Bristol became a city landmark, with the huge figurehead from SS *Demerara* dominating the exterior. (When the firm eventually joined forces with Alonzo Dawes and Hoddell in 1959, the ship's figurehead was taken down for repairs but it was found to be in poor condition and quite beyond renovation.)

George moved his family to Parsonage Farm, Long Ashton, so that he could be nearer the business and the boys a short journey from the city schools. Mary wanted them to go to public school to be brought up 'like proper gentlemen' but George refused. His sons were not to be softened by such effete influences. They had to prepare for life the hard way and he underlined what he meant by flogging them soundly for any misdemeanour and for failing to do well at school. He also expected them to be all-round sportsmen and athletes. This worked well enough except in the case of George junior who was a sensitive child with a passion for beautiful things and for music. When he joined the family firm, his good taste brought a new dimension to the business but, in sharp contrast to his father, he was a private man with a quiet charm. George H. Young, whose father Edward was in partnership with George junior for twenty-eight years, said of him in November 1985: 'He had a reputation for his knowledge of antiques and their value. He was of a somewhat nervous temperament. He was always well dressed in check tweeds. It was said he always went to the same tailor and that the cut and pattern never varied. He had a good singing voice and I remember hearing him sing solo at St Stephen's Church.' His widow Blanche left his collection of antiques to the Bath Preservation Trust and the National Trust, to be displayed in his memory.

In the mean time, George senior went from strength to strength. He was in demand to conduct auctions from one end of England to the other and he and Alder were frequently engaged as arbitrators under orders of the Court of Chancery. He continued his country sports, joined the council of the Royal Agricultural College and was invited to judge at county shows for miles around. He led in the establishment of the Bristol Whit-Monday Horse Parade and he also started the annual Bull Show which he modelled on the famous show in Birmingham. He and Alder acted as honorary secretaries to the Royal Show and the Bath and West of England Shows and, in his spare time, he took up bell-ringing, eventually becoming Master of the Society of Bell-ringers of St Stephen's, Bristol.

In the 1880s the controversy surrounding the Free Trade policy came to a head when America began dumping cheap grain on the British market. Agriculture was thrown into chaos. Thousands of workers were sacked and farmers desperately switched to livestock instead of grain, a measure which was doomed when New Zealand and other meat-producers exported cheap frozen carcases to England. Many of the unemployed, forced out of the countryside, flocked to the new manufacturing areas which were hungry for cheap labour, while others emigrated to America or to the Colonies. In a comparatively short time, the elaborate structure of British agriculture, built up over hundreds of years, had collapsed and a way of life disappeared for ever.

George the yeoman farmer may have suffered, but George the auctioneer enjoyed a boom. His popularity, reputation for fairness and his shrewd judgement were sought by bankrupt farmers selling their assets, who believed he could be relied upon to give them a fair deal. He celebrated his new financial success by moving into a handsome house, 13 Pembroke Road, in the select area of Clifton in Bristol and by making several sharp investments in land and property. He was now fifty-five years old but he worked and played as hard as ever. He acquired a place in Wiltshire for hare-coursing; at one stage he controlled land totalling over 1,600 acres and employed sixty men. Not surprisingly, he was often approached to take an active part in local politics but though he was a staunch Conservative he refused.

He may have had some setbacks in his triumphant progress, but none compared to the bitter disappointment he suffered at the hands of his favourite son Arthur who, in many respects, was a duplicate of his father, though a flawed one. He had charm and good looks, but he was a drinker, a gambler and a womanizer. Every time he got into trouble, George bought him out of the consequences. He was either blind to Arthur's faults or confused them with the rip-roaring masculinity he so admired. He indulged Arthur's sudden whim to go into the theatre and financed a production of *Hamlet*, with his son playing the lead. Undeterred by Arthur's total lack of stage experience, George took the Gaiety Theatre in London for an afternoon to launch him and to show off his abilities. The whole affair was a shambles for there was no talent, nothing but an overweening ego. George then attempted to set Arthur up in business ventures but they failed. Somewhere along the way, Arthur had acquired a share of the property in

Wine Street which his mother's family owned and George, rather than lend him more money, bought this from him to help pay for a new start in Australia. Once there, Arthur married and did reasonably well, ending up in politics, but even there George had to come to the rescue when he became entangled in a shady financial deal.

By comparison, the other sons were exemplary: George and Herbert went into the family business and John, Beverley's father, into the law. He was admitted to the Roll in July 1887 and received his first practising Certificate in August of that year.

During the last six years of his life, George suffered several heart attacks and was forced to take things more easily, but, by comparison with most men, his was a hectic life. Still very much a friend of the Gibbs family, he was deeply honoured when asked to act as a guide to Edward, Prince of Wales, when he paid an official visit to the area. In November 1895, though ordered to rest at home, he insisted on going down to the drawing-room to receive friends and to discuss business. The following February he suffered a fatal heart attack, dying on the 18th.

The funeral, in keeping with his status, was a splendid affair. The cortège, with the coffin on an open carriage piled so high with floral tributes that all people could see was a mountain of flowers, consisted of eight carriages for the family and close friends, followed by other mourners in their own vehicles. It made its way over Clifton Suspension Bridge and through Ashton Park which his friend, Sir Greville Smyth, had opened for the occasion as a mark of respect. The service at Long Ashton church was conducted by three clergymen, and as the coffin was carried to the grave, which was lined with yew and white narcissi, the organ thundered out the Dead March from *Saul* and church bells in Bristol and Long Ashton rang muffled peals in tribute.

This was the man Beverley later dismissed curtly in *Father Figure*, and yet his achievements are well documented. The local newspaper described him as one of Bristol's best-known citizens and said: 'He had the rare gift of making many friends and his bright and cheerful disposition and kindliness of manner were among his prominent characteristics.' Beverley said of him that he liked to be thought of as a gentleman but that there was little evidence of gentility.

The bulk of George's considerable personal estate went to his wife, and there were bequests for the children. Everyone, with the exception of Arthur, did very well, and even better when Mary Nichols died some years afterwards. By the time of George's death, his son John had married Pauline Shalders and they had had their first baby. There was a wreath from their son, 'little Paul', somewhere on that mountain of flowers on George's coffin.

The Shalders were a fenland family from Norfolk, whose name means 'dwellers by the rushes' – although some of the family believe they originally crossed from the Continent. Beverley's maternal great-grandfather Noah was a pawnbroker from Norwich, where he was born in 1790 and baptized at St Stephen's Sepulchre Church. In 1817 he married a local girl, Mary Norton, and they had ten children. Alfred, Beverley's maternal grandfather, was born in 1830. When he married at the age of twenty-two he was a warehouseman: his bride Rebecca, just nineteen, was the daughter of John Todd, a cloth merchant. Her mother Rachel was a Reaney, a fairly well-to-do family judging by the quality of their silver which is now in the possession of a descendant. This collection includes a set of eggcups said to come from Jane Austen's family with whom the Reaneys believed they were connected. Beverley once wrote that, much as he would like to believe that he had a touch of the Austen blood, he had to concede that there was no truth in the story. There was a Jane Austen in the family but, as far as he could see, it was not the lady who wrote *Pride and Prejudice*. This discovery was slightly embarrassing as the story of the alleged connection had already appeared in the press and he was being invited to speak to literary societies as a descendant of the great novelist. It became rather more embarrassing when people began to see evidence of the Austen influence in his work which, they concluded, was proof of the connection. Beverley had to admit that, if the influence was there, it was because he was a devoted reader. 'I hope', he said, 'I have some of her ironic detachment.'

Alfred Shalders was even more successful in business than George Nichols. He took his young wife to Bradford and set up on his own as a merchant dealing in cloths of various kinds. They lived initially at 44, Stoughton Place but as he prospered they moved to a large house called Oaklands, near Oak Avenue, which was demolished only a few years ago to make way for a housing development. They had four children: Paul, who died in his teens, Julian, Catherine, and the youngest, Pauline, Beverley's mother, who was born on 22 October 1865. Alfred became more and more affluent and bought another house, Elmleigh, this time in Ilkley. It was a vast place with large conservatories filled with semi-tropical trees and plants, with extensive grounds and massive hothouses. Rebecca, revelling in her wealth, became a noted hostess and patron of the arts. It was at Elmleigh that Oscar Wilde stayed one December while lecturing in Leeds. Rebecca made a great fuss of him while casually drawing his attention to the luxury of the surroundings and mentioning the advantages to be had from vegetables and fruit grown in one's own hothouses. The following morning, Oscar declined the elaborate dishes ranged on the sideboard and said that it would be perfection if he might have a handful of raspberries, 'pale yellow raspberries'. This unfulfillable request momentarily disconcerted Rebecca but, with presence of mind, she decided that it was one of the witty remarks to be expected of Oscar. The story was told, with variations, for years afterwards. As Beverley put it, 'The Shalders enjoyed dining out on Oscar's breakfast.' The anecdote was promptly dropped from the family repertoire when Wilde was disgraced. Polite society then went to extraordinary lengths to eliminate the memory of Wilde, and if his name was mentioned at all, it was spoken with a shudder of revulsion. It was as if the man and all his works had never existed. The Wilde affair and its aftermath were later to play a part in Beverley's own story.

Rebecca and Alfred spoiled their children outrageously; whatever they wanted, they had, provided that money could buy it. It was a happy family, with none of the stuffiness usually associated with the middle class of the period. Possibly because they had made money so quickly, they had no time to acquire snobbish inhibitions. They were ostentatious and a little vulgar, but they never lost a kind of innocence, or their children an open-mindedness. It might be going too far to say that it was a Bohemian household, but it was very like one. Rebecca shared her pleasures with the children; she loved taking them to theatres and concerts in Bradford and Leeds and they met a wide cross-section of creative people at home. They were given a good education and the girls were sent to France to learn the language. Pauline went to a convent outside Paris, where she was amazed and amused by the nuns' complicated stratagems designed to prevent the girls from seeing each other's bodies. The girls had to take baths wearing linen shrouds, and dressing and undressing had to be achieved without a centimetre of flesh being revealed.

As far as running a house was concerned, the girls' education was limited to dealing with staff rather than with acquiring any practical knowledge, because Rebecca could not envisage any circumstances in which it might be useful for her daughters to know the rudiments of cookery or household chores. This was to be a disadvantage in the case of Pauline's sister Catherine, who married William Spence, a penniless country doctor, and had to learn housework the hard way. The poor girl could not even boil an egg and despaired of ever learning to light a fire. One of her grandsons, Peter Fitzgerald-Moore, remembered her well, for she did not die until 1943 at the age of eighty-six. 'She was a broad-minded woman, far in advance of her time.' He also said that she always kept in close touch with his great-aunt Pauline. Both he and Margaret Vance, another of Catherine's grandchildren, had a clear impression of their great-uncle Julian. When Alfred died in 1895, Julian took over the running of the business which he managed from the London office in Golden Square near Regent Street. He was something of a dandy, an extrovert character with a sense of fun. By all accounts, Pauline was as broad-minded and as fun-loving as her brother and sister.

· 2 ·

The laughing child

1890–1912

I T is not known how or where Pauline Shalders met John Nichols. Family legend has it that John, who practised alone, had a client with business interests in Bradford which involved her father, Alfred. It was love at first sight. A photograph taken at the time of their engagement shows her gazing serenely into the camera while he stands, a bull of a man, staring fixedly ahead. They made a handsome couple, and from each family's point of view it was a highly suitable match. Alfred was particularly pleased with his new son-in-law who was not only a success professionally but also a noted athlete: he had played rugby for Somerset and had been a champion long-distance runner. In short, he was a 'man's man' – and as time would show he was also a man for the ladies.

They were married in Ilkley in 1890, spent their honeymoon on the Isle of Wight, and set up home at The Mead, a pleasant house in Long Ashton, Bristol. Paul was born on 23 November 1891, by which time John, the junior partner in Benson Carpenter of Corn Street, had a reputation as a brilliant solicitor. He was particularly noted for his facility with words and the commanding charm of his presence. He followed his father into the Society of St Stephen's Bell-ringers and in 1895 became Master. In the same year, his son Alan was born and John joined Bevan Hancock as third partner at their offices in Baldwins Street, Bristol.

Over the next few years, the young couple became prominent in local society. For Pauline there was the busy life of a hostess, organizing 'At Home' and dinner-parties with the help of her domestic staff. The children, Paul and Alan, naturally had nannies and nursemaids, but Pauline spent as much time as she could with them. John, heavily involved with his work, also became increasingly interested in municipal and political affairs. A staunch Conservative, he took on the duties of agent to the local Tory organization. The family moved to a more spacious home, The Woodlands, in Bower Ashton, Bristol, where a son was born on the evening of 9 September 1898, 'when the lamps were being lit', as his mother told him years later. He was named John after his father, but it is not known why he was given the middle name of Beverley. It does not feature in either the Nichols or the Shalders families – perhaps it was a whimsical reference to the character in Sheridan's *The Rivals*? To avoid confusion with his father, he was always addressed as 'Bev'.

To the local community, the Nicholses must have appeared an ideal couple, the epitome of Victorian middle-class virtues. But, behind the façade, something was wrong.

From his earliest years Beverley sensed an unease between his parents, indefinable but always there. Sometimes he caught a scattering of harsh words, and when his mother hugged him to her he felt it was more for her comfort than for his. Looking back, he concluded that they were incompatible, with father a brutish man and mother a gentle, passive woman. As he grew older this opinion hardened; his mother was cast as victim and father as tormentor. Paul, by contrast, described his parents as a perfectly normal married couple, devoted to each other, but with the problems to be expected from any relationship.

In 1899, John was elected Conservative Councillor in the Corporation of Bristol. The Law Society Papers show that he also became a Freeman of the city although there is no indication of this in the Bristol records. He made no secret of his political goals: a combination of hard work for the Tory party, his charm and his influential contacts gave him high hopes of a full-time career in politics. Paul remembered his father as being convinced that his ambitions would be recognized and fulfilled: 'I want a title I can pass on,' John said. In order to free himself from daily routine, he resigned from Bevan, Hancock and Nichols in 1901 but, although he had amassed enough capital to be financially independent, he continued to renew his certificate as a solicitor for a number of years. He now devoted himself wholly to the Tory party and Paul recalled his frequent visits to London on political matters. Such was the esteem in which he was held in Bristol that he was offered the Mayoralty of the city but, to the astonishment of his fellow Tories, he declined it, considering that it would be unfair to commit himself to such high office when at any time he could be called upon to serve as a Member of Parliament.

Suddenly, in the following year, 1902, John announced that he and his family would be leaving Bristol to settle in Suffolk. Before he left, there was a series of functions to wish him farewell. At one of these, a dinner given in his honour by the local legal fraternity, a long piece of doggerel verse in his praise was read out and he was handed the scroll upon which it was inscribed in impeccable script. In the nature of these things, the verse was banal, but the sentiment was clear. According to Paul it concluded as follows:

He built friendship
In the hearts

Of his fellow men
And this was the house
That Jack built.

By the end of 1902, the Nicholses were settled in Wissett at The Red House, a rambling place with fifty-four acres of land. What has never been explained is why they left Bristol and whether there was any significance in the choice of Suffolk. The obvious reason might have been that John expected to be selected as candidate for a Tory seat in the county, but if there is any evidence for this, it has been lost. Alternatively, John might have changed his mind about politics and decided to become a farmer – but there is no evidence that he took any interest in his Suffolk acres. On the contrary, Paul remembered John as spending most of his time away from Wissett, ostensibly on business in London. What becomes increasingly clear as events unfold is that the departure from Bristol marked a significant change in John's life.

Beverley remembered Wissett with happy affection. With John off on his trips to London and Paul and Alan away at school, Pauline had little to occupy her apart from managing the indoor staff and doing some lady-like gardening, so she concentrated her attention on her beloved baby son. Beverley recalled idyllic summer days spent helping Pauline in the garden and exploring the richly beautiful countryside, and cold, hard winters crouching in front of a blazing fire toasting muffins for tea.

After only two years, John decided to leave Suffolk almost as suddenly as he had gone there. The family had no connections left in Yorkshire, since after the death of Alfred Shalders Rebecca had moved from the overblown grandeur of Elmleigh to a London flat in Great Russell Mansions, Bloomsbury, where she died in 1900. It is surprising that they did not move to London, the city having much to offer both parents and, for Pauline, the added attraction that her brother Julian, with his family and other relations, had settled there. However, from the many options open to them, they selected Torquay, the 'Queen of Resorts' which had been developed by the wealthy Palk and Cary families to cater for the upper ranks of society. In other words, it had been created by gentlemen for gentlemen.

Torquay owed its initial discovery partly to the Napoleonic wars when fleets of warships anchored in Torbay. As they might be there for months awaiting action, officers often sent for their families, and favourable reports of the coast and its temperate climate began to spread. Napoleon himself saw Torbay from his prison ship, the *Bellerman*, in 1815 and was reputed to have exclaimed, '*Enfin, voilà un beau pays!*' Torquay was frequently compared to the Italian Riviera because of its sunny climate and luxuriant growth of trees and plants, and the Italian illusion was sustained in the architecture of the villas, cunningly laid out on the wooded hills, so that even the smaller houses set in their own grounds seemed individually important.

When the Nichols family took Rockwood in St Matthews Road, Torquay, in 1904, the Queen of Resorts was at the height of its popularity and prosperity, although upper-class residents complained that it had 'gone down' since boarding-houses had been opened for the lower ranks of the middle class. A local guide, praising the exclusivity of the resort, warned that anyone seeking the garish pleasures of Blackpool or Margate would be disappointed, and observed, with approval, that there were no Punch and Judy shows or 'nigger minstrels' on the sands. There was, however, much entertainment of a refined character: the Royal Italian Band played programmes of high-class music in the Princess Gardens and military bands sounded forth on the pier. Famous artistes and orchestras gave concerts in the Pavilion and the Bath Saloons, and there were plays at the Theatre Royal. Golf, cricket, rugby, fishing, sailing and tennis were catered for, the shops reflected the quality of the clientèle, the hotels were splendid, and spiritual needs were satisfied by over thirty places of worship.

By the time Edward VII ascended the throne in 1901, the population had grown to 33,000, and a high proportion of the residents provided services to the well-to-do. Today it is almost impossible to imagine the gulf that existed between the different classes, or to conceive the innumerable subtleties within the class categories, the whole enshrouded in a web of snobbery. Although Edwardian England was becoming more relaxed in its attitudes, a wealthy man could still be referred to scornfully as 'being in trade' and therefore not a real gentleman: true gentlemen came from the professions or, better still, from the land-owning aristocracy. When Pauline went shopping, she did not leave her carriage unless it became absolutely necessary: tradesmen were expected to come out to her to show her their wares and to take her orders. Mrs Kathleen Edmonds, whose father owned a linen shop in Torwood Street, remembered him going out to see a lady customer and inadvertently resting his hand on the carriage door: he was sharply commanded to remove it. Religious observance was then socially essential for most people. Holy Trinity Church was one of the more fashionable Sunday meeting-places; coachmen and footmen waited patiently outside while their betters worshipped.

Behind the façade of respectability there was a racier, merrier Torquay. The parties and sexual shuffles, either aboard the yachts which dropped anchor in the harbour or up in the secluded villas, were common gossip among the servants. The Edwardians had nothing to learn about permissive behaviour but it was all very discreet: the chase and the intrigue were half the fun.

At Rockwood, Pauline gave parties, luncheons and dinners, but the centrepiece of her social activity was the 'At Home': her own 'day', engraved on her visiting cards, was 'First Wednesdays'. The preparations for the afternoon ceremony were time-consuming for the household. Apart from the staff making the house sparkle more than usual, there were flowers to be arranged, the piano to be tested to guarantee that it was in tune and music to be sorted, but most important of all was the preparation of food. China or Indian tea was freshly prepared with water drawn from the elaborate silver kettle which hissed gently over its spirit lamp. When Pauline was not herself 'At Home', there were reciprocal visits to be made almost every afternoon. Her household staff was headed by cook, who earned around £20 a year, a parlourmaid and a tweeny, all three of whom lived in, 'all found'. Other workers came in every week to do the laundry and the rough jobs. The boot-boy, who arrived very early every morning to chop wood, fill the coal-scuttles, and clean the boots and shoes, earned a few shillings a week. The outdoor staff varied in number but there were two regular gardeners. They were expected to bring their own food with them but cook might provide a jug of tea if she was in a good mood.

When Beverley was six years old, a governess was added to the household. She occupied an uneasy position between master and servants, being neither one thing nor the other in the social structure. Miss Meig Herridge was a lady-like creature, more than capable of instructing a small boy in the basic three Rs and the piano. She was very fond of plants, teaching him to recognize those in the gardens and the hedgerows, and starting his collection of wild flowers and grasses. Beverley later called her a saint: a devout member of the Plymouth Brethren, a Calvinistic sect, she had her own brand of faith for, as far as she was concerned, everything illustrated God's goodness. If men were evil, it was a sign of His forgiveness that they were not immediately thrust down into the fires of hell. Suffering was a device to test mankind. Years later, when she had cancer, she praised the Lord for pushing her to the limits of endurance. She said to Beverley, as she lay in the bleak ward of the old Charing Cross Hospital, 'I am oh so glad!' It was her favourite utterance, her praise to God in all circumstances. No one could have been a better exponent of all the saintly virtues, but whether her stark version of Christianity, with its constant references to hell-fire and salvation through blood, were appropriate for a sensitive and impressionable child is open to question. On the one hand, Beverley had the devout Miss Herridge, and on the other his indulgent mother who had no strong religious belief.

John Nichols found Torquay very much to his taste. At home with the family he was often withdrawn, but outside he was a different person. A fine figure of a man, always impeccably groomed, wearing expensive clothes, a flower in his buttonhole, his eyeglass firmly in place and exuding an aroma of toilet water and cigars, he cut a fine dash in the bars of the Royal and the Grand Hotels and, for the price of a few drinks, bought the camaraderie available in such places. It was not long before he was part of the racier life of Torquay and acquired the first of a series of mistresses. The women he liked, and who found him irresistible, were 'ladies' and usually respectably married – not for him the lower classes. Apart from the Royal and the Grand, his favourite rendezvous was the Queen's Hotel, an elegant establishment run by a discreet Swiss hotelier. John's longest-lasting liaisons were with the wife of a leading Torquay businessman, and with a lady who was always seen about with her King Charles spaniel. All those involved maintained a conspiracy of silence, but there was gossip, and some devout Christian tradespeople were outraged by the flouting of the Commandments by their social superiors.

In *Father Figure*, written in 1972, Beverley spoke of his father's taste for low-class prostitutes before his marriage, but made no mention of his extra-marital affairs. He admitted in 1980 that he had omitted any reference to them because some credit might reflect on John, if only on account of his sexual prowess and personal magnetism. It might also have suggested to the reader that Pauline was deficient in their sexual relationship, and the purpose of the book was to vilify his father.

Beverley opens *Father Figure* by stating that his first memory of John was seeing him dead drunk on the dining-room floor. Around this 'first memory' he weaves a story calculated to arouse sympathy and horror. In a scenario worthy of the silent screen, cook and the servants are in the kitchen, Pauline is in bed with some undefined illness, the two older boys are downstairs, and Beverley is asleep. Father is in the dining-room alone, finishing his meal. He reaches for the port decanter and collapses, falling from his chair, the decanter breaking and cutting his wrist. As he falls, he pulls the tablecloth with him and fruit, silver and glass are scattered across the carpet. To put what follows into chronological order, we cut to Beverley's bedroom. Alan rushes in, wakes him up and carries him downstairs to the dining-room where Paul is binding his father's wrist with a table napkin. John lies groaning, his eyes 'rolling to and fro'. To Beverley, he seems a dangerous animal who might get up and stagger about 'again' and bite and claw and kill. John's eyes focus on the child and he spits out a couple of obscene words – we are left to imagine what they might be. Beverley struggles out of his brother's arms, runs into the hall and down the long corridor to the kitchen quarters, pursued by Alan who cannot prevent him from shouting hysterically, 'Daddy's drunk.' He then falls to his knees praying to God to 'make Daddy better and not let him hurt mother'. We now cut to the hall where Pauline, enfeebled by her illness, is making her way slowly down the stairway, one hand clutching the banister, the other clinging to the arm of Paul who is entreating her to go back to bed. She wears an 'old' dressing-gown over her 'cheap' nightdress. Enter Alan with Beverley, who runs to her. She comforts him and then walks slowly to the dining-room where the guttering candles light the dramatic scene. She tells Paul she has no further need of him and shuts the dining-room door behind her. Beverley goes back to bed.

We now cut to next morning when the brothers are eating breakfast alone. Alan describes going to fetch the doctor and Paul explains how they all helped to get father up to bed. 'He said awful things all the time and he was sick on the stairs. Cook put ashes on it.' He then announces that there is to be a family conference in the billiard-room at ten.

In the billiard-room, Beverley, in a sort of waking nightmare, sees his father's face, with its wine-drenched moustache, in the mirrors, in the pictures and even on the moose head which hangs over the fireplace. Mother leads the boys out into the garden where she forbids them to mention the incident of the previous night to anyone. She will tell the governess herself. She explains that father was not himself, he was ill. 'He was drunk,' observes Alan. 'You must not say that,' she chides him. 'But he was, he was,' say Paul and Beverley in chorus. She goes on, 'It's his heart. The doctor says it's a disease. We must not think unkindly of him.'

It is a curious story, told with melodramatic passion by someone who had brooded about it for decades. Paul dismissed Beverley's version of this incident but admitted that there was a violent quarrel between the parents which shocked him profoundly: 'That awful evening at Rockwood when I was fourteen was a sort of explosion from which I never really escaped.'

In his version of 'that awful evening', Beverley goes out of his way to enlist our sympathies for Pauline. It is not enough that she is ill and has to cope with a drunken man, but already she is forced to make personal sacrifices, hence the 'old' dressing-gown and the 'cheap' nightdress. Until she died, in fact, Pauline always dressed expensively. Beverley made a great point of the sort of genteel poverty in which he said they already lived: in an earlier version of *Father Figure*, he had included an episode set some six years later in which some visitors who are renting the house inadvertently see in the larder the family supper, a plate of tripe. He is so ashamed of this that he explains it away to them as being 'for the servants'. In the published version, he omits any mention of the family income and the reader, left to imagine Pauline struggling to keep up appearances while her husband pours most of the housekeeping money down his throat, is bound to assume that there was not much money. In reality, however, the family income was around £2,000 per annum and, as tax was only pennies in the pound, they were left with a great deal to spend. Pauline could have afforded a dozen nightdresses in pure silk, if she had cared to. A man could buy a dozen shirts for £3 or so; if he smoked cigars, they cost 16s per hundred, while champagne cost £3 for twelve bottles.

Beverley also avoided the subject of the houses they lived in. All the Torquay sequences in the book are set in Cleave Court, the other two houses, he tells us, having faded from memory. This conveniently fudges the issue. In fact, each home they moved to was grander than the last, a curious progression for a family allegedly getting poorer. Beverley's only reason for speaking of economies being made in the early 1900s was to build up the case against his father. Similarly, he tells us of his own misery which, if he is to be believed, was almost constant, and leaves us in no doubt of his state of mind after 'the awful evening'. The scene is the drawing-room, but instead of playing the piano as he usually does he sits drawing a picture with trembling hands, terrified as he hears the sound of his father's steps on the stairs. The steps come nearer and the shadow of a rose falls across the paper. His father lays it on the paper, with dew still fresh upon it. 'I thought you might like this,' his father says.

This appears to be a rather touching moment, an act of propitiation, a plea for forgiveness or understanding. That, however, is not the point Beverley is making: he tells us that the incident was like a curse, for he was never able to grow roses thereafter. Even when he was famous and a rose was named after him, it failed. In his last garden, at Ham Common, he claims that the few roses that exist are pale and sullen, seeming to shrink from the sunshine into the shadow, and that when he walks towards them, they look away. Whether in Beverley's mind they looked away or not, the roses, in fact, made a fine show, rambling in profusion over the garden walls as they had done in the garden of his cottage at Glatton. When asked why he did not have roses in the beds (this was before *Father Figure* was published) he replied, 'They are not right for this garden. I love them when they are in flower but otherwise they look so ugly, particularly standard roses. But I do have some tucked away out of sight just to cut for the house.'

In 1908, the family left Rockwood to move to The Grey House in Old Torwood Road, in the exclusive residential area below Warberry Hill. The house is still there but it has been converted into flats. Beverley had said farewell to Miss Herridge who went to take charge of other small children but, as she visited for tea, she was presumably in the neighbourhood. He was now a pupil at the grandly named Wellswood School for Gentlemen. This was run by E.P. Oldfield, known to the boys as E.P.O. Beverley was already showing a flair for English but, like many children, he loathed maths. Surprisingly, he liked sports which included rugby, cricket and a fierce version of hockey. Unfortunately, he was bedevilled by an old injury to his leg, which had occurred when he was four or five and had fallen out of a bedroom window on to the stone-paved terrace below. He later described this as an attempt at suicide born of childish despair for which, predictably, he blamed his father. The effects of this injury remained with him into adult life.

He had also developed into a gifted pianist under the initial guidance of Miss Herridge and later of a Miss Rossiter, and his singing voice was pure and pleasing. He remarked, after hearing Dame Nellie Melba at a local concert, 'She sings just like me.' He was in great demand in the drawing-rooms of Torquay, and when he was older he also appeared at local concerts. These public and private performances were to become a feature of his life for many years and it is not too far-fetched to suggest that his popularity with audiences gave him a taste for theatrical presentation which was to prove valuable later on. He was not the only star turn in the family: Alan's voice was also good and, when it broke, it settled into a better-than-average light baritone, good enough for him to go into the professional theatre. Paul, too, had theatrical flair which he was to use to good effect as a preacher.

Both parents encouraged their boys' musical abilities. In a letter written from The Grey House, Beverley tells a friend that 'Daddy bought a lot of new records' after having his gramophone repaired. He did not specify what the records were, but they were likely to have been fairly middle-brow, in contrast to Beverley's taste which had been led to Mozart and Chopin by Miss Herridge. Chopin was like a God to the boy pianist, and it was not long before Beverley began to compose in imitation of his style. This remained one of his greatest pleasures and it was only when he could no longer play that he gave up composition. He left behind a box of music carefully written in his own hand.

John liked to show off Beverley's expertise to guests, but expected piano pieces such as 'The Rustle of Spring' which his son considered vulgar. The climax of the entertainment was always a series of improvisations on a theme. John would prop against the music-rest a triptych which depicted a river, first at its source, then flowing through countryside and finally through an industrial area. The caption read, '*Men may come and men may go, but I go on for ever.*' Beverley admitted that he enjoyed showing-off and the guests always appeared suitably impressed by his mixture of musical fireworks. Later, at parties, he would illustrate musically the character of one or two guests or of unpopular public figures. It is said that he could be extremely witty and ingenious when doing this.

Unfortunately, John did not detect that, to Beverley, music was more than just a pleasing social accomplishment. The boy dreamed that one day he would play 'real' music, preferably his own, to adoring concert-goers just like those who packed the Bath Saloon or the Pavilion. In this ambition he may have been encouraged by Pauline who, hungry for musical entertainment, took him to all the concerts she could.

Once Beverley had got over the initial shock of school discipline as compared with the indulgent atmosphere of home, he seems to have enjoyed his schooling. His brothers were now both at Sherborne School in Dorset, but Beverley was not lonely for he quickly made new friends among his fellow pupils. His best friend was Cedric, the son of Dr Todd who lived and practised in the Torquay end of the Babbacombe Road. The boys became inseparable, and were constantly in and out of each others' homes for tea. Todd is not mentioned in *Father Figure*; instead, Beverley goes to some lengths to explain that he lost friends because he was unable to invite them casually to the house for fear that his father might be at some stage of a drinking bout. This fear, he says, remained with him even when his father was long dead – as he turns the key in his own front door, his heart beats faster: 'He' may be waiting on the other side. But there is no hint of this in the diaries, where 'tea', as apart from the formal 'At Home', seems to have been something of a domestic industry with open house more common than not.

On the other hand, it is not impossible that Pauline may have stopped visitors during John's drunken bouts. These, Beverley tells us, followed a set pattern: a week of whisky at the rate of half a bottle a day; a second week of a full bottle a day, augmented by brandy and ale; then bed in a semi-coma, coming round only to top up the alcohol level from a bottle by the bed. When he had finally sobered up, there would be three or four days during which he was remorseful, tearful, penitent; then he would often be kind and cheerful, before starting off once more on his half bottle a day. Beverley's account is prefaced by the unequivocal statement that this happened every month of John's life.

It is clear, even allowing for exaggeration, that, at some stage, John became an alcoholic in the clinical sense and then, from time to time, went well beyond his average capacity. Beverley mentions very emphatically the effect that too much whisky had on John, when his bad temper flared to the surface and his verbal treatment of Pauline became worse. It might be expected that, with the dreadful example of his father's drinking, Beverley would be bitterly opposed to alcohol, but he was not. On the contrary, he could be a formidable drinker himself, who thought nothing of finishing a bottle of sherry before lunch when he was working on a book. At bridge-parties in his own home, he frequently left the table to go to the downstairs lavatory. New guests found the apparent weakness of his bladder something of a surprise, but the old hands knew that he had a bottle of gin tucked away en route, in addition to the drinks available at the card-table. He never quite forgave a friend who found the hiding-place and developed a sudden, similar bladder deficiency.

In both *Father Figure* and the later autobiography *The Unforgiving Minute*, Beverley dwells on his unhappy childhood to such an extent that it was a surprise to learn from Paul that Beverley was a happy, laughing child, only likely to make a fuss if he did not get his own way, which for most of the time he did. Unlike many children, even allowing for the tension between his parents, aggravated as it was by his father's drinking, he had, apparently, little to be miserable about. He did not lack material comforts and, most of all, he did not lack love. If anything, he was overwhelmed by the possessive and indulgent love of his mother and by the knock-about love of his brothers who, typically, teased him unmercifully, although he was not slow in hitting back. He was also admired by friends and neighbours for his abilities, good looks, the Nichols charm and his sense of humour. His father loved him in his own way and, despite the conflict which intensified between them as they grew older, John also tended to spoil him and was most generous.

From the entries in Beverley's schoolboy diaries, it is difficult to imagine him as the trembling, terrified creature he afterwards liked to portray. He records his sports interests: hockey three times a week, rugby and cricket ('got 58 not out'), tennis and the craze for roller-skating. There were long cycle rides with Todd and a catalogue of teas, theatres, concerts and parties: all these he rates as 'not very nice', 'fairly nice' or 'very nice indeed'. He and Todd shared a love of stamp-collecting, and his intense interest is reflected in the meticulous details of swaps and purchases: 'Two penny blacks from Knight for sixpence, rather a bargain.' He sends off regularly, sometimes twice a week, for 'stamps on approval' as well as catalogues, and he receives a monthly journal from Stanley Gibbons of London. He also notes his visits to the local cinemas, sometimes as often as three times a week, accompanied by Todd, very often by Pauline and, on occasions, by 'daddy'. Kathleen Edmonds, a year younger than Beverley, was surprised at this because she and her brothers were not allowed to go to the Electric Theatre, it being considered an entertainment for the servant-class and somewhat common. But Miss Undine Wiggin, one of Beverley's contemporaries, remembers that she and her brother Lancelot, who was also at E.P.O.'s school, went to the picture-house on an average of twice a week, and that this was by no means exceptional among the well-to-do.

In a piece he wrote in 1961, Beverley reminisced about the people he knew in Torquay, mentioned Lancelot and Undine Wiggin and asked whatever had become of them. Miss Wiggin was happily living in Torquay, and was still there twenty-five years later. She recalled Beverley vividly, especially on his visits from Marlborough and Oxford. 'I quite lost my heart to him, he was so charming and good-looking.'

Among his large circle of friends was Rose Evans who became Mrs Kyffin Crossfield. She confirmed the richness of Torquay life before the First World War, and the alarm with which her parents and their friends watched its character change as the elegant homes became private hotels and flats, and as day-trippers and holiday visitors turned it from a winter to a summer resort. 'We escaped in my father's yacht – he always preferred steam yachts.' The Nicholses also escaped to quieter places along the coast and let their house during the height of summer.

Rose described John Nichols as 'always very affable', and Pauline

Nichols as 'delightful, but rather a quiet person.' The Nicholses appeared to be an affluent family, without any indication of the financial problems Beverley emphasized in *Father Figure*. Paul was rarely in evidence, except when on holiday. Alan was an outstandingly handsome man who 'set all the girls' hearts a-flutter'. She remembers the sensation he caused when he arrived on leave from the Gordon Highlanders in his regimental kilt. Although John's drinking was kept a secret and, as far as she was aware, nobody ever saw him drunk at home, there were stories of his leaving the Queen's Hotel in an incapable condition and being helped into a taxi. There was no doubt about Beverley's distress at the behaviour of his father during his bouts: 'He used to confide in my mother and myself and tell us how unhappy he was at the way he treated Mrs Nichols. The sad thing was that Beverley seemed to be his father's favourite. He was so proud of him when he began to make a name for himself.'

During the 1930s, the Evans family lost contact with Beverley and it was not until the 1940s that they met again. 'A taxi driver arrived at the front door with a message from a Mr Nichols. He had been taken ill and would we go to him? We could not think who Mr Nichols might be, but we went into Torquay in the taxi and found it was Beverley, very weak and sick. We brought him home and put him to bed. He had some sort of stomach upset but he was over it in a few days.' Beverley had arrived in the town and taken furnished rooms in the shopping centre, but the Evans family never discovered why he had come. When he was better, he returned to London and that was the last they saw of him. There was not even a thank-you letter. As Mrs Kyffin Crossfield confirmed, Beverley was always something of a hypochondriac.

Miss Wiggin tells much the same story about the Nichols family: 'He was a very nice man but, of course, Mrs Nichols was not as flamboyant as he was.' She and her family were quite unaware of John's drinking but, as she said, such a subject would never be broached within earshot of children.

The Nicholses' social set included Sir Vincent and Lady Hammick who lived nearby, and Violet Tweedale who lived in a grand house called Villa Maggiore and wrote romantic novels. She was a great favourite with Beverley, who was fascinated by her belief in the existence of goblins and ghostly creatures. She had the disconcerting habit of claiming to see people's 'auras' and once proclaimed loudly to John Nichols that his aura was deep purple. She was also given to statements such as: 'I see two elves climbing up your foxgloves.' Beverley could barely suppress his giggles on these occasions, expecially when everyone else received her pronouncements with polite solemnity.

There was also Madame de Runkel who shared her home with two other ladies and was thought to be a little 'peculiar'; Miss Faithful, who lived in a house abutting upon the Nicholses' grounds and intruded into their lives in an odd manner, for she kept sixteen laughing jackasses whose shrill and lunatic cackles could be heard across the gardens; and Professor Oliver Heaviside, who dressed in the Japanese manner, painted his long finger-nails bright red and was given to writing letters in the third person describing himself as 'His Wormship'. To the amazement of his neighbours, he once refurnished his house with lumps of granite. Beverley claimed that Miss Faithful, Professor Heaviside and, to some extent, Miss Tweedale, frightened him and added to the horrors of his childhood, but in fact they were figures of fun to the young people who frequented the Nichols home.

Both Pauline's and John's indulgence of Beverley is reflected in his diaries; for example, they accepted his slightest excuse for missing school. One morning he stayed away because he had a cold, but he recovered sufficiently to go to a tea-party in the afternoon. On another occasion he walked out of school when he ought to have been in class for algebra, one of his pet hates, but John wrote a note excusing him. The next day Beverley noted that his form master, Mr Mills, was 'pretty angry'. It is possible to detect a hint of satisfaction when he noted laconically a few days later, 'Mr Mills hurt his leg.' The diaries also mention father's 'illnesses', but the entries suggest these happened four or five times a year, rather than monthly. The abbreviation he used for his father was P.H., short for 'Pet Hog' – a nickname used openly by the brothers and accepted by John Nichols, who was rather proud of his prodigious appetite and thought the nickname amusingly described his gluttony. Pauline also had a nickname, 'The Ma Bird', usually written as 'The M.B.'.

In New Year 1912, Beverley and Pauline went to London for a week. He was later to describe this as his first visit and his reason for mentioning it was simply to underline his lack of cultural education as a boy. He won an essay prize for writing on the French Impressionists, but, he declared, that was because he had studied a selection of picture postcards bought from a gift shop in Torquay which otherwise specialized in 'Presents from . . .' These, he says, were a revelation, his very own private art gallery which included works by Renoir, Monet, Pissarro and Degas. He stuck two of the postcards inside the lid of his desk at school: Monet's picture of spring flowers, and Cézanne's 'Les Baigneurs'. The dreaded Mr Mills, seeing these and indicating the Cézanne, asked him if he liked looking at the bodies of naked young men. In passing, Beverley tells us that on his 'only' trip to London his 'cultural' excursions were confined to the Zoo, Madame Tussauds and the Tower, all of which he detested because he dimly realized they were 'monuments to human cruelty'. If that trip in 1912 was his only visit to London, then he did not mention in his detailed diary account any 'monuments to human cruelty'. What he did describe were six days crammed with activity: two visits to the Coliseum (then a variety theatre), the second visit because there were 'house full' notices at *Peter Pan*, an evening at Drury Lane to see the pantomime *Hop-o'-My-Thumb*, dinner at a Soho restaurant called La Rocheyn, and trips around the big department stores, Selfridge's, Harrods and Whiteley's of Bayswater – the last, in 1912, being highly fashionable and its surrounding area very desirable.

Selfridge's was a high spot of the holiday. It had only been open for three years and was the brainchild of Gordon Selfridge who introduced the latest American marketing techniques and dazzled his customers with specially designed window and internal displays, concepts new to London. It had its own corporate identity, another new idea, with everything from carpeting to packaging and even string carried out in 'Selfridge' green. Beverley and Pauline spent hours browsing there, and he bought a supply of peanut brittle, a sweet he had never seen before. It was his first introduction to American know-how and razzle-dazzle.

They stayed with Cornelia and Tom Thorne at 1, Ascott Avenue in Ealing. Torquay may have been the Queen of Resorts but Ealing was the Queen of the London suburbs. Like Torquay, it had been developed by shrewd speculators to cater for the various categories of the middle class. Despite its many changes, it requires very little imagination today to see what it must have been like in 1912. Indeed, Ascott Avenue, which was built in the early 1900s, is as exclusive now as it was then and Number One, a splendid detached corner house, is typical of Edwardian affluence. Cornelia, or cousin Cornie, as she was called, was a Reaney, the same Reaney family who claimed the Jane Austen connection. Cornie was to become one of Beverley's closest friends and confidantes. It is surprising that she is not mentioned in any of his books because he discussed many personal matters with her, and their correspondence lasted until her death in the 1930s.

Staying in Ealing meant travelling into the centre of London every day and Beverley details these journeys on tubes, trains and trams with typical schoolboy enthusiasm. He notes proudly that on two of the days, when 'The Ma Bird' stayed in because of a bad cold, he found his way around on his own. There are several mentions of 'cousin' Monty, Montague Chidson, who, several years later, was to become the first British pilot to shoot down a German plane in the 1914–1918 War. One day Monty met him at Dover Street tube station (now replaced by Green Park station), took him to St Paul's, right up into the golden ball at the top of the dome, to see the view, and they lunched at one of the many Lyons teashops which dotted the city. On another afternoon, Beverley took himself to the Picture Palace in Ealing Broadway, which was also known to the locals by its earlier name, the Cinematograph Theatre. The entry for the last day, 6 January, reads: 'Taxi all way to Paddington to catch 10 to 12, very fast train. Alan met us. Daddy had been very bad indeed and male nurse called Richards came yesterday by

Dr. Walker's orders. He slept in my room so I slept in Alan's old room. Daddy out when we arrived home but R brought him back. Mother persuaded him to take sleeping draught and go to bed.' The sparseness of this entry is somehow more telling for its lack of dramatic decoration than the florid style he employed years afterwards to describe his childhood.

Later in 1912, the Nichols family moved from The Grey House to the much grander Cleave Court on the Lower Warberry Road. Today it is known as Riviera Court and the extensive grounds which surrounded it in the Nicholses' time have been reduced by the erection of two bungalows. The coach house in which John garaged his car has been converted into a home called Cleave Cottage.

· *3* ·

Schoolboy emotions

1912–1916

B EVERLEY never understood why his father chose to send him to
Marlborough instead of Sherborne where his brothers were educated. Both schools were equal in reputation and there was very
little difference in their fees. Both practised the then popular brand of
muscular Christianity, a mixture of God for the soul and games for the
body. Academic attainment came third, and ex-pupils of both schools (Alec
Waugh in the case of Sherborne and Beverley in the case of Marlborough)
were to say later that each school's syllabus was largely irrelevant to the
needs of the modern world. It was generally accepted that Marlborough
was rather tougher and this may have influenced John Nichols's choice.
Whatever the reason, Beverley arrived at the school without the benefit of
being Nichols Minor, 'the brother of . . .'. For the first time in his life he was
on his own, with no indulgent mother or father to sympathize or write
excuse notes for him.

The darling of the Torquay drawing-rooms soon found that his new
audience was either indifferent to his precocity or regarded it with disdain;
the right to be idiosyncratic had to be earned and new boys who behaved
without due humility were put firmly in their places. In addition, Beverley
was too pretty and, by their standards, too effeminate. The shortest route to
acceptability would have been as a sportsman, but he failed to impress his
peers, however hard he tried. As he had not been a duffer at games in
Torquay, it suggests that the standards at his prep school were rather lower
than they should have been, because in the competitive atmosphere of
Marlborough he was well below average.

He was horrified by the peculiar system of toughening up and discipline.
New boys were expected to perform a series of gymnastic exercises
gripping metal rings let into the ceiling of the dormitory. If they failed to
reach the standard required by a certain time, they were given ten strokes of
the cane on their pyjama-clad bottoms by a prefect. Prefects also had the
authority to punish for misdemeanours, and very popular with them was
'turfing'. This consisted of making a boy run down the stone steps to the

basement and up again as many times as the prefect thought fit; a hundred 'turfings' were not unusual. Boys could also be punished for failing to observe the correct ceremonial for carrying the Kish, a large, flat cushion in which books were contained under the arm when pupils went from one place to another. In his first year, a boy had to display exactly six inches of the cushion in front, for to display more or less was regarded as an offence.

As Beverley found himself shunned by the boys whose admiration he would like to have won, he was forced to make his few friends among other outcasts, a situation he found humiliating. He wrote home begging to be taken away, but the only response was money and parcels of expensive food from his mother. He used these delicacies to try to bribe his way into favour with those he admired but, with the cruelty of schoolboys, they accepted his gifts and then turned away from him.

Beverley was forced to think out a strategy to make life bearable and sensibly decided to get down to hard work in the classroom. Like many gifted children, he was bewildered by what he saw as the stupidity of his peers and angered by the failure of his teachers to perceive his brilliance with the clarity with which he saw it himself. He soon began to impress them with his facility with the written word in English and history, although maths still eluded him. He was quick to pick up languages, but his ability to mimic a cultured French accent was regarded as affectation. He also discovered that, despite his old leg injury, he was one of the fastest sprinters in the school, and a series of successes put him into a new category; suddenly, his humour and charm became acceptable. As he had tactically dropped his effeminate mannerisms, he was seen as physically attractive, and by his second year at Marlborough was actively involved in the first of his schoolboy affairs. He also discovered that he was attractive to men older than himself and this gave him a sense of power which he was to exploit with considerable success.

According to him, his first experience of adult seduction was in Torquay. His seducer, Egerton Edwards, usually known as Egie, lived with his parents at Warberry Court nearby. He was in his late twenties, a homosexual of the most blatant kind, so blatant that Torquay society in general and John Nichols in particular refused to believe that he could be what he so obviously was. They found his outrageous behaviour highly amusing and were convinced that this sophisticated young man must be a devil of a fellow with the ladies. His parents indulged his aesthetic tastes to the full. It seemed to escape everyone's attention, except Beverley's, that the male staff at the house were extraordinarily beautiful and usually imported from countries where homosexual behaviour was accepted with a shrug. It also seemed to be casually accepted that Egie's 'friends' in local pubs were not the young men someone of his class would normally mix with. The Nicholses encouraged Egie's interest in Beverley; indeed, they seem to have been flattered by it. Pauline accepted the outré clothing, artificial hairstyle and Egie's make-up without thinking too much of it, although, referring to his rouge, she once remarked that he 'touched up'.

The seduction took place at a dinner carefully planned by Egie. When Beverley arrived in his newly acquired, first dinner jacket, hair carefully brushed and his mind echoing with parental admonitions about behaviour, he found that the dinner was to be tête-à-tête, and not, as he had expected, a family occasion. Egie received him in his own sitting-room which was heavy with the scent of tiger lilies and lavishly decorated with photographs of sun-tanned young men who, Egie explained, were fisherboys he had met on his travels in Greece. They were, Beverley noted, mostly in the nude. Dinner, served by an astonishingly picturesque footman, was a lavish affair accompanied by several wines and ending with a choice of liqueurs. Beverley realized, as he sipped yellow Chartreuse, that he was intoxicated. Egie, judging his moment, made the final moves in the ritual of seduction. How far he got is a matter of conjecture but his technique was apparently very different from the masturbatory mechanics of schoolboy sex.

Egie lavished attention upon him after that first night. There were more dinners, outings to local concerts, expeditions into the country and long evenings in the great drawing-room of Warberry Court with Egie besottedly watching as Beverley played Mozart and Chopin. When Beverley returned to Marlborough, Egie pursued him with love-letters full of quotations from homosexual authors whose sentiments expressed his own. In his account of this episode, Beverley claims an innocence of the implications and, indeed, explains that he avoided a physical relationship with Egie. His innocence is difficult to accept, but he may well have avoided further sexual contact after the first encounter. Most boys in their teens, whether ultimately heterosexual, homosexual or bisexual, find the sentimental posturings of older men faintly ridiculous. Beverley could have avoided Egie if he had wished, but, as he explained, he was a sympathetic companion with whom he shared a love of music and whose sound artistic judgement helped to mould his own. All in all, Egie did Beverley little, if any harm, although it could be said that he introduced him to the adult homosexual world of which, from choice, he was soon to be a part.

The Nicholses' blindness to Egie's real nature is surprising, but relationships, sex aside, between a younger and an older man were not uncommon at the time. Perhaps, in his *naïveté*, John Nichols assumed that the sophisticated Mr Edwards, who had a baronet in his family, was introducing Beverley to the world of the gentry. He never budged from his belief that Egie was a hell of a fellow with the ladies.

Egie was so befuddled by his infatuation that it never occurred to him that there was anything unusual in his giving his young friend an expensive edition of Oscar Wilde's *The Picture of Dorian Gray* for his birthday. Beverley claimed that, at the time, he was ignorant of Wilde or the scandal still surrounding him, though he had the instinctive good sense to read the story in his bedroom with the door locked. Whether such ignorance is credible is for the reader to judge, but it was Beverley's defence to his father who demanded to be let into the bedroom and then behaved as if he had caught his son in an illicit act. 'You pretty little bastard,' he shouted at him, 'you pretty little boy,' enunciating the word 'pretty' in a shrill parody of a homosexual voice as he hit him across the face. Then he spat on the book and tore the pages with his teeth. 'Oscar Wilde! To think that my son . . .' Beverley protested that he did not know what Wilde had done. This apparently halted his father's rage and disconcerted him. 'What did he do? Oh, my son, my son!' – and he collapsed on the bed and burst into tears. Beverley, in his account, does not attempt to explain this odd reaction. He adds that, at dinner that night, his father was amiable and kept winking at him as if they shared some secret joke. Early next morning, he was awakened by his father who presented him with a sheet of paper on which he had written, 'ILLUM CRIMEN HORRIBILE QUOD NON NOMINANDUM EST', which Beverley translated as '*The horrible crime which is not to be named*'. 'That', said John, 'is what the man did.'

In another version of this story, a tearful Pauline is involved as the book is ceremonially burned on the sitting-room fire. In both versions, Beverley says he did not name Egie as the person who had given him the book, so Egie's standing with the Nichols family is unimpaired. And in both versions, Beverley asserts that he was no wiser about Wilde than he had been before. It was, he commented, a curious introduction to the problems of homosexuality.

As we now know, he was no stranger to homosexual behaviour by then but he may not, until that episode, have realized the problems surrounding it. In *Father Figure* he tells us that the incident compelled him to form a judgement on the subject of sexual abnormality. On one side was Egie, on the other was his father, one 'abnormal' and the other 'normal'. The 'normal' was acceptable to society, the other was not. If this was the verdict of society, says Beverley, he would take the liberty to differ. It was, he says, an 'adult judgement'. Bearing in mind that homosexuality was a criminal offence, it was not only an adult conclusion but an early realization by Beverley of his own nature. Whatever misery or happiness this was to cause him in the years that followed, at least he did not have to undergo the mental tortures which haunt so many men who cannot come to terms with their sexual inclinations. It is pointless to speculate why Beverley was a homosexual. As far as he was concerned, he was, and that was that. In his book of verse published in 1982 he included a poem on the subject; the final lines are a footnote to his acceptance of his condition.

So sigh no more, my friend;
What you have done has long been done before
And will be done again.
And yet, do not forget,
There is no refuge in the storm
For those who dare to differ from the norm
And in the end, you pay the price, in pain.

Shortly after the page-tearing, book-burning episode, Beverley decided to kill his father. He tried twice. His own account in *Father Figure* is so theatrically melodramatic that it is difficult to believe that it was not written tongue-in-cheek. It is the horrifying tale of a boy driven by his own frustrations and an inordinate love for his mother, but Beverley, whose sense of humour was never very far away, lets his story slip into black comedy with elements of farce. Even at his most earnest, there is a feeling that he is standing to one side with a twinkle in his eye, mocking the events he recounts and the schoolboy character at the centre of them.

Having made his decision to kill, he coolly assesses the means. Poison seemed the best bet, but which one? The problem was solved by the family doctor's warning to John Nichols against taking too much aspirin. Here was the means, and the opportunity posed no difficulty: John Nichols, recovering from one of his drinking bouts, could only take soup and Beverley was often deputed to take up the tray. As a footnote Beverley adds that the family was going through a financial crisis and the staff was reduced to a single maid.

In his account, Beverley cycles over to Newton Abbot to buy a bottle of aspirin. He chooses market day when the town is crowded with shoppers and he finds an 'obscure' chemist. To avoid later identification, he holds a handkerchief to his face as if his nose was bleeding and turns his head away as he hands over the money. Home again, he crushes eighty grains of aspirin tablets into powder and mixes it in water ready for use. That evening, as he takes the tray with his father's bowl of soup upon it, Pauline remarks how cheerful her boy seems, for he is whistling the opening bars of an intermezzo by Brahms and he goes on whistling, as he carries the tray upstairs, pausing only to stir in the deadly mixture. He is calm, almost disinterested, with no trace of guilt; does a man feel guilt when he strikes at a snake slithering towards the one he loves? The one he loves in this case is his mother. It did not seem to occur to Beverley that, if his plan succeeded and there was a post mortem, Pauline would be the prime suspect, having the opportunity, and a motive in John's blatantly adulterous behaviour.

Up in the bedroom, John Nichols is in a maudlin mood. 'I'm a bad father. You'd be better off without me.' Beverley hands over the tray. 'You are too good to me,' moans father. 'Better than you guess,' thinks Beverley grimly as he watches John drink the soup from the bowl, his loose lips closing over its edge like some questing slug. When John has licked up the last drop, Beverley swills out the bowl at the washstand. For a moment, he contemplates watching the death throes but decides it might be all rather unpleasant; instead, he goes to the drawing-room and plays to his mother the 'Moonlight Sonata' followed by some transcriptions of César Franck's organ chorales which seem appropriate to the occasion.

Suddenly there is a cry in the distance, then another. Pauline starts to her feet but Beverley insists on going to investigate instead of her. As he speeds up the staircase, he prays to God to let his father die. Hopefully, he flings open the door. Instead of seeing a corpse, he sees his father out of bed and getting dressed. Thinking it is his wife at the door, John snarls, 'Clean up that bloody mess,' then, seeing his son, his tone changes: 'I'm afraid I have been rather ill.' He had been, all over the bedroom. Instead of killing him, the mixture had made him vomit, purging his system. The next day John is as bright as a button, eating hugely and even mowing the lawn for exercise. So the first attempt ends in ignominious failure.

A few weeks later, Beverley tries again. The boys are away and the staff now consists only of a cook-general. Somewhat surprisingly, Pauline also decides to go away for a short holiday, leaving her beloved son at the mercy of a drunken monster of whom he is frightened. Before she leaves, she instructs Beverley what to do if his father starts on one of his bouts – send her a telegram, call the doctor and put a bottle of whisky she has hidden in the grandfather clock by his father's bedside so that he can drink himself into a coma. Above all, stop him from going out. It seems a heavy responsibility for a schoolboy and, to forestall any such thoughts on the part of the reader, Beverley emphasizes that it was the only time his mother ever went away and that, in any case, his father had been behaving himself since the soup episode. This makes her decision all the stranger – but, for purposes of plot, she has to be away and off she goes.

No sooner has her cab turned out of the drive than Beverley hears a whimper. There in the front hall is a pretty little puppy. Bearing in mind that the nearest house is some distance away, where has it appeared from? Beverley does not ask; it cannot have appeared from nowhere, like Alice's Cheshire cat, but he simply accepts its mysterious appearance and decides to keep it. This instantly presents a problem because his father hates dogs. The boys, Beverley tells us, have never asked to have a dog because they knew what the volcanic reaction would be. Quickly he hides the puppy in his jacket and carries it to the old coach-house where he makes a bed of sacking in an old box. The puppy promptly goes to sleep. He then takes the cook into his confidence. 'Lord help us, Master Beverley,' she gasps, 'what will he say?' and drops her rolling-pin in her agitation. 'He must never know,' replies Master Beverley gravely.

A few days later, father embarks on another drunken spree and within a short time has taken to his bed. Beverley puts the spare bottle of whisky by his bed and, as 'the days sped by', spends all his time with the dog, days of bliss running through the country lanes. Knowing his father as well as he did, it seems highly optimistic of him to assume that the bottle would last for very long, but apparently it held out until the 'last evening'. Beverley takes the dog along the cliffs at Babbacombe Bay and when they return home, it is nearly dark: ominous clouds scud across the sky and the wind howls. He puts the dog away for the night into its bed (now a little straw-lined basket rather than the box of sacking) and goes into the house 'in search of father' – who, we may recall, is supposed to be in bed, comatose. The house is deathly quiet for, Beverley tells us as an afterthought, it is cook's night off. He runs upstairs. To his horror, the bedroom is empty and so is the bottle of whisky. He runs from room to room calling for his father but there is no sign of him and no reply to his cries. His father must have gone out for more whisky. Now anything might happen! He has betrayed his trust! If only he had bought another bottle! He decides to go in search of him, grabs an old mackintosh belonging to his father which is far too big for him, and sets off into the stormy night, a grotesque figure with the voluminous folds of the mac 'rattling in the wind'. Down in the centre of the town he searches the bars: what he intends to do if he finds his father we are not told – beg the drunken man to leave the demon drink, in the manner of a temperance melodrama, one supposes. But there is no sign of father. In one bar, a sailor clutches his arm and asks him to have a drink but he pushes him away, continuing his quest from pub to pub, seeing the faces of blowsy women and leering sailors through the fumes of tobacco smoke. The bars are 'the seven circles of hell'. Worn out, he at last gives up and catches the last tram home to 'the haunted house on the haunted hill'.

He does not go indoors: instead, his first thought is of the puppy who might be frightened by the howling wind. The dog has gone, vanished as mysteriously as he had arrived, but there are signs of disturbance: the straw from his basket, 'his little bed', is scattered over the floor and garden tools lie around as if they had been thrown. Somebody has committed this 'final monstrosity', but who? Can we be surprised, Beverley asks us, if he assumes it was his father? He has two fierce emotions: the first a bitter grief that the dog has gone, and the second an even more bitter hatred that, at long last, has crystallized into the compulsion to kill. This comment seems to ignore the fact that the compulsion to kill has already resulted in the débâcle of a few weeks before, but that is how Beverley expresses it.

Still in the flapping folds of the old mackintosh, he goes once more in search. Suddenly it occurs to him that father might be in the garden and, sure enough, there he is, lying dead drunk on the lower lawn. Conveniently above him, on the edge of the grassy slope, is the heavy roller normally used for the tennis court. He remembers his father complaining about the odd-job man leaving it too near the edge and remarking that one day it would be the death of somebody. Now Beverley decides it will be the death of him. He manoeuvres the roller into position, using as his target the loathed head of the man whose eye-glass glitters in the moonlight. He pushes, and the roller begins to move, very slowly at first, then leaping from his control and charging down the slope. There is a strangled cry and then silence. Beverley goes to bed convinced that father's skull has been crushed. Next morning, the cook finds the Master lying on the grass with only a broken leg. On hearing this bad news, Beverley has hysterics. The man is indestructible, immortal – 'He will be with me through life and beyond life, for ever and ever, amen.'

The story of this second attempt at murder is certainly more questionable than the first. Apart from the curious appearance and disappearance of the dog, there are lapses of logic. Why did he not search the garden before searching the bars? Where was father while Beverley was searching the house and calling out for him? If he had stumbled and fallen in a drunken stupor, how had he got rid of the dog? If we assume he went to the coach-house and scared the animal away by throwing garden tools at it, where did it go? It was never heard of again. There might be answers to these questions but Beverley did not supply them. The biggest flaw in the story is the assertion that the boys were not allowed to have a dog: Alan had one. Beverley writes of it in his diary and there is a photograph of him with the dog in his arms.

This dark, nightmarish interlude of bungled attempts at patricide curiously resembles the stage thrillers that chilled audiences in the 1930s. It was little wonder that the critics of the 1970s were sceptical of Beverley's confessions when they appeared.

It is a relief to return from all this to the reality of the day-to-day life of Cleave Court when the Nichols family lived there. In the grounds, the gardeners are going about their business; in the house the cook supervises the preparation of luncheon. Perhaps John Nichols is sprucing himself up for his daily sortie to meet his cronies at the Grand or to spend a few hours with his mistress. Pauline might be writing letters in the morning room or musing over what gown to wear at the evening concert. On the tennis court Alan and Paul are practising, while Beverley idly watches them as he plays with the household cats. It may not be a very exciting life, but on £2,000 a year it is a lazily pleasurable existence – even if the Pet Hog can be a beast when drunk. The servants are not yet discontented; radical thinking has hardly touched them. They count their blessings, accepting the station in life to which God has called them.

But all this was about to change.

The Great War, as it was to be known for twenty years or so, was a few weeks old when Beverley celebrated his sixteenth birthday. To say that the advent of war was to have a profound effect on his life is not as arid a cliché as might first appear: he was provided by it with opportunities which he could not otherwise have had. Had it not been for the war, he might have gone into law as his father wished. John often said that his son had the necessary qualities to make a successful barrister – and, besides, the law was a proper profession for a gentleman.

In Britain, the war was welcomed with a great deal of patriotic fervour and political rhetoric. The royal family's unruly relative, Kaiser Wilhelm, with his talk of 'a place in the sun' for Germany, needed to be soundly thrashed and stood in the corner until he learned how to behave in polite society. But it is still something of a mystery that the war should have been so popular with the mass of people, not only in the British Isles but in other European countries as well, though of course nobody anywhere had any clear idea of what modern warfare might mean. Britain had a strong navy, but she had no regular army of any size and when Lord Kitchener called for 100,000 volunteers, his appeal produced a phenomenal response: young men flocked to the recruiting stations and by the end of September some three-quarters of a million men had enlisted. Most people believed that the war would be over by Christmas and, as Lord Stockton later put it: 'Our major anxiety was by hook or by crook not to miss it.' Young men who associated with each other socially or at work joined up in groups. Battalions were identified by secondary titles like 'Church Lads', '1st Football' and 'North East Railway'. The clerks of Cunard in Liverpool formed their own platoon and the rallying cry was 'Those who join together will serve together.' Poets reflected the national feeling, Rupert Brooke thanking God 'who has matched us with His hour'.

John Nichols's reaction was typical. He knew what he would do to the Hun if he had the chance; a pity he was too old to fight, but there were other ways to help. There must be something a brilliant ex-solicitor could do, but what that might be he was not sure. He wrote endlessly to old friends and contacts or, to be exact, he frequently dictated the letters to Pauline who wrote them in her elegantly formed style. Too often he was incapable of holding a pen between his shaking fingers, an after-effect of drinking the previous night and before topping up the alcohol in his system sufficiently to control the morning's withdrawal symptoms. Unfortunately, all the approaches proved futile; if he had found a job, it might have halted his accelerating slide into alcoholism. Beverley always spoke contemptuously of this effort to help the war, refusing to give John even credit for trying.

Alan, caught up in the initial frenzy, joined the Gordon Highlanders, hoping against hope that the epilepsy from which he suffered would somehow leave him. John was inordinately proud when Alan came home for his first leave in Torquay, but a few weeks later Alan had an epileptic fit on the parade ground. After his discharge, he tried again, changing his name and once more suppressing his medical history, but his stay in another regiment was equally short-lived and he returned home, heartbroken. Beverley alleged that his father was so paranoid about the war that he could not accept the facts of Alan's illness and called him a 'putrid funk'. This goes against all logic, and if he used these words at all it was more likely to have been with reference to Paul, who by now was working in India as Secretary to the Bishop of Bombay, and was to be ordained in 1916.

Beverley's own attitude to the war was ambivalent from the start. Despite his patriotic feelings, he regarded the whole business with suspicion and refused to be caught up in the general hysteria. This might have been the result of his study of history, in which he now specialized, or an instinctive reaction, but, whatever the reason, he found himself paying lip-service to the 'cause' while remaining at heart a detached and sceptical onlooker. At Marlborough there was now an even greater emphasis on fitness and he was forced to join the Officer Training Corps. The endless routine of march, counter-march, slope arms (with dummy rifles), stand to attention and stand easy he described as 'beastly'. Otherwise, life was not too bad. His history studies were not onerous and his life was more relaxed as a specialist.

More importantly, he was doing well with his music under the tuition of the young George Dyson who became eminent in his field and was later knighted. Dyson was quick to realize that Beverley was untypical of the often reluctant boys he had to teach. Beverley's technique, learned under Miss Herridge and Miss Rossiter, might be lacking, but he had that additional 'something' which could lead to fine musicianship. Dyson cut through the showing-off which Beverley had acquired in the drawing-rooms of Torquay and made him work at the piano as he had never done before. Dyson recognized his talent for improvisation and taught him to compose. For Beverley, it was a time of revelation and self-discovery: he saw that music could become his life.

He won first prize for composition at the annual Speech Day, and was dubbed the 'Schoolboy Chopin' by the headmaster. Quoted in the local press account of the occasion, this filtered through to a national newspaper. At home it was greeted with delight by Pauline but with some indifference by his father who placed no importance on the piano beyond its entertainment value in the drawing-room. In a badly judged moment, Beverley told them he wanted to make a career of music. His father dismissed the idea out of hand as a schoolboy whim. When Beverley persisted, and Pauline mentioned the opinions of Dyson in his support, John waved them aside. Who was Dyson? Just a twopenny music-teacher. The law was the career for Beverley, after Oxford and the Inns of Court, but the piano would always be a social asset, so his lessons could continue. When John called on Pauline to agree, she dumbly acquiesced. For this, Beverley never forgave him.

To a lesser degree, he did not forgive his mother either because she could have defied her husband but later claimed that it was not in her nature to do so. It might have been that she agreed with John, for a career in music was as precarious a prospect as going on the stage. She may have asked herself how many musicians actually made an adequate living, and the answer would have been 'Not many.' Beverley later admitted that he could not, after all, have been as ruthless and dedicated a musician as he had thought himself, otherwise he would have done something about it. He even commented that, if all this had happened after the change in the law some fifty years on, he believed he would have become a homosexual prostitute, if it could have furthered his goal. This ultimate degradation was unimportant, he contended, compared to the deliberate murder of a talent – the murderer, of course, being his father. In actual fact, he was offered the opportunity to concentrate on his music not many years afterwards by a wealthy would-be lover but he turned it down. Nevertheless, he clung to the dream of what might have been and blamed his father for its lack of fulfilment.

Meanwhile, the war went on and the prospect of its being over by Christmas or, for that matter, by any foreseeable Christmas, grew remote. The full horror of events on the Western Front hit the population when the casualty lists were published. By Christmas 1914 the casualties amounted to nearly 90,000, and by the middle of 1915 to over 380,000, with 75,000 dead. The pals who had joined together to fight had died together. The flower of British manhood was being wiped out. The lack of officers became so acute that the OTC certificates which guaranteed the rank of subaltern and had produced over 29,000 officers in the first seven months of the war were waived, and a public school or university background was sufficient to obtain a commission. Beverley saw sixth-form boys from Marlborough sent straight to France as second lieutenants. The school magazine told its own dreadful story as its pages were filled with accounts of the dead, the missing and those wounded in action. The survivors who visited the school were greeted as heroes, but the eager boys of a few months ago returned with the eyes of disillusioned old men.

Shakespeare's words, 'Close the wall up with our English dead,' took on a new and macabre reality as the generals flung more and more men to almost certain death, directing operations from safe positions as if they were playing soldiers on the nursery floor. As the supply of recruits dwindled drastically, massive advertising campaigns were launched to encourage men to volunteer. By September 1915, fifty-four million recruiting posters had been issued. To support this advertising, meetings were organized throughout the land, often with well-known stage stars, to exhort men to enlist. At a meeting in London, small children paraded with banners with slogans such as 'My dad's at the front – where's yours?' The propaganda machine also circulated blood-curdling stories of German atrocities which were intended to warn what would happen should England ever be invaded. Beverley remembered these tales being retold with some relish at the 'At Homes' which carried on as usual in Torquay. 'Mother always took these tales of Germans raping nuns wholesale with healthy scepticism.'

Eventually the government was forced by heavy British and French casualties to introduce conscription in 1916, although it was limited to single men and a pledge was given that no eighteen-year-olds would be sent to France. These new measures revealed the ill health suffered by the low paid in pre-war Britain: in some industrial areas, seventy per cent of men were found to be unfit for overseas service. This graphically illustrated the gulf that existed between the upper and middle classes and the labouring men and their families. A report pointed out that often the children of a working man had less to eat than those in the workhouse. The war hastened social change by the redistribution of wealth and, ironically, the population benefited overall. Women, for instance, took well-paid work in factories, and for many it was a new experience to have money to spend on clothes and decent food. Once established in this new role, women were not to be easily thwarted in the future. For the first time in middle-class homes, people spoke of 'a servant shortage' as ill-paid skivvies moved on to a better way of life.

The Nichols family, like many on an income derived from dividends, found their cash in hand eroded by heavy tax increases and rising prices. John tried to recover the situation by reinvesting capital but not always with much success. Pauline was used to affluence and her cook was used to having ample money to buy food. There must have been mutual bafflement about what to do to economize, and they both saved dignity by pretending that cutting the food bill was their contribution to the war effort. A similar explanation could be found for burning fewer fires in the bedrooms and no fires at all in the morning-room. Above all, though, an illusion of life as usual must be maintained: the 'At Homes' and the occasional reciprocal luncheon or dinner party continued as before. It is difficult to feel much sympathy for the declining financial position of the Nicholses who were, after all, still far better off than most of their fellow countrymen. What they were not to know was that the golden age of the middle class which they had experienced under Victoria and Edward VII was almost finished.

In addition, there was the problem of Alan. After his sad but valiant attempts to join the army, he tried to get work but his epilepsy always betrayed him. A friend got him into the touring company of the highly successful musical comedy *The Arcadians*. He seemed to have all the necessary qualifications: he was handsome and possessed a strong personality and a good singing voice. This venture also ended in bitter disappointment when he had an attack of epilepsy on stage and so it was back to Cleave Court and dependence on his father for everything.

Under the law of conscription, Beverley in due course attended a medical board, but was turned down because of his old leg injury and his propensity for nervous illness. He believed that was the end of the matter but it was not, for Colonel Wall, the Commander of the Officer Training Corps at Marlborough, with the full support of John Nichols, had been pulling strings and eventually Beverley was given the lowest medical grade which made him eligible for call-up to the Labour Corps, a body of men unsuitable for frontline combat but capable of carrying out duties behind the lines. Because of his grade, however, Beverley was excused overseas duty.

· 4 ·

Military manoeuvres

1917–1918

BEVERLEY left Marlborough in 1916 just before Christmas: he won the Junior Common Room prize for history in March 1916 but did not reach the top form – indeed, he spent five terms in the same form. He then entered for the Balliol-New College Scholarship examination offering Latin, French and history. The archives show that he was not among the Scholars or Exhibitioners but he was 'accepted for matriculation' at a college meeting held on 11 December 1916. This meant that his father had to bear the entire cost of his university education. In January 1917, Beverley arrived at Balliol for the Hilary Term. In a letter postmarked 1 February to cousin Cornie, who was convalescing in Westcliffe-on-Sea after an illness, he wrote:

In a way, I am enjoying myself immensely here only I cannot get over the feeling that everything is intensely unreal. You see Oxford, to begin with, is now a phantom Oxford. 300 people are all that are up here and the great huge old grey stone quadrangles remind one only too insistently by their emptiness of what has been. It is like what I imagine Versailles must be, or a deserted village. All my friends are either at Marlborough or fighting. I know no one I am really fond of – I feel in many ways like a ship without a rudder. But it is a pleasant sea to be lost on.

At present I am working at Greek – apart from that I have lectures – crowds of music. A piano is in my rooms and often people come up who play or sing or fiddle and we have splendid times. Then there are the remnants of Balliol concerts – there is magnificent choir music, and I have been introduced to nearly all the musical profession in Oxford. I have been playing a lot too – the Chopin B minor 2nd Scherzo – a wonderfully fine thing – also his Fantasie Impromptu – some Scriabin and the Carnaval. I do wish I could see you sometimes and talk re music – and we might play the Unfinished Symphony. It would sound well in these rooms. They look out onto the Cornmarket, full of cadets with white hats, and buses, and busy, unreal puppets whom I suppose have hearts. They – the rooms – are decorated in a nasty light wood but I have a Whistler and a Beardsley to adorn the walls, and a little yellow mimosa for the table, and always a small coalmine on the fire. And I have bought two paper Liberty lampshades – one with butterflies in blue and gold that take on a temporary existence in fire when one switches on the light. . . .

I had a splendid time as a temporary millionaire in town with Egerton Edwards whom I sent home [to Torquay] quite cheered up. I never get tired of London – Soho – the Café Royal, the people in the hotel – the streets, the shops, especially the jewellers, full of opals – and the bookshops which drive me mad. And then when one can really afford the best for a week it is perfectly delightful, although I know I should love London even à la Francis Thompson, with an Aeschylus in one pocket, a Blake in the other and a copper in neither. . . .

Everything is so unreal here that I leave an hour or two at night to creep into my brain and really live. Sometimes I spin all over England, sometimes I have long conversations with my friends, sometimes I have vast triumphs singing before a thousand souls – it is the only way to convince myself that I am alive. Even now

> 'Is all that we see or seem
> But a dream within a dream.'

Even now those lines take on a new significance.
But I am becoming riotous – so goodnight.

Ever your loving
Bev

When he failed his exams, he left Oxford vowing never to return, intending instead to go straight into law once his period of army service was over.

In his autobiography, Beverley ignores this whole Oxford period, in effect losing a year which he covers by saying he was in hospital with some unspecified illness. He goes on to be specific about dates:

August 1917.   Left Marlborough for Army. Sent to Cambridge to train for a commission.
November 1917. Posted to Thetford.
February 1918.   Posted to the War Office attached to the Secret Service.

This is completely inaccurate. Beverley often altered facts and stirred in a dash of fiction, usually to provide drama, as in *Father Figure*, but there appears to be no reason in this case. He justifies his version by saying that he had no records or diaries to refer to and relied on memory, yet the diaries were neatly stacked within two paces of his writing table. It might have been carelessness, but Beverley was rarely deliberately careless. By moving his entry into the army from March to August, he falls into a trap of his own making. He tells of his brief but intense friendship with the Master of Magdalene, Arthur C. Benson, but by August Benson had left, struck down by a mental condition which was to last for five years. In May, when Beverley actually went to Cambridge for Officer Training, Benson was still in command, and was to be a vital influence on his future.

Benson was the eldest surviving son of Queen Victoria's favourite cleric, Edward Benson, who had risen to be Archbishop of Canterbury. The Bensons were a strange family. Arthur's father had fallen in love with Minnie, his future wife, a second cousin, when she was only eleven, and he proposed marriage as she sat on his knee a year later. They married when she was eighteen. She was not in love with him and was completely ignorant of sexual matters. The honeymoon was a dreadful experience for her: he had no idea of love-making and the coupling amounted to rape. Afterwards, she suffered his attentions as a duty and bore him six children between 1860 and 1871, before refusing any further sexual intercourse. She was later to find love through her passionate devotion to a series of women friends. When Edward died, she took her friend Lucy Tait into her bed and from then on called herself 'Ben' at Lucy's suggestion. Of the children who survived to any age, Maggie had periods of insanity, Fred and Arthur were homosexually inclined, and Robert, who became a Catholic priest, was asexual. All of them were spiritually troubled and Arthur was given to moods of deep depression.

According to Beverley, Arthur picked him up in the porch of Magdalene and promptly took him to the Master's Lodge for tea. Beverley already knew of him as a celebrity: Benson had made a great deal of money writing novels, essays and verse and he was particularly popular with women readers in England and America. With Viscount Esher he had edited the letters of Queen Victoria at the request of Edward VII, for whom he had written the words to Elgar's music for the Coronation Ode. From this work, 'Land of Hope and Glory' still survives. None of his other writing is read today, posterity having accepted his own verdict which was 'twaddle'. Twaddle it might have been, but it earned him a great deal of money and it enabled him to accept a Fellowship at Magdalene without salary. He not only spent his own money on the College but also administered a vast sum given to him by one of his American admirers to extend and beautify it and to finance students who might not otherwise have afforded to go to Cambridge. In 1915 he was elected Master. He was given to sentimental attachments to young men but it is almost certain that he did not become involved with them physically. His brother Fred was different: he, too, was a successful author and his Mapp and Lucia novels with their stylish mockery of English society are still popular today. Fred had a close friendship with John Ellingham Brooks, a wealthy homosexual dilettante who had fled England after the Wilde affair. He spent much time with him in Italy and at one stage they shared the tenancy of the Villa Cercola on Capri with Somerset Maugham. Arthur rather disapproved of Fred and the *émigré* set of Capri which included Compton Mackenzie, Norman Douglas and a host of lesser lights, but indirectly, Beverley's friendship with Arthur Benson was to provide a link with this group, particularly with Mackenzie and Maugham.

Beverley described Benson as a father figure, as usual losing no opportunity to disparage his real father. It would be more accurate to describe Benson as a jovial uncle who had discovered a new, agreeable nephew. He was a witty chatterer but, when in the mood, he could switch from the trivial to the profound, bringing to debate the wisdom of the middle-aged scholar without losing the eagerness more appropriate to inexperienced youth. He found an admiring audience in Beverley, who responded with earnest comment enlivened with a feline humour that amused Arthur. He gave his protégé the freedom of the house and introduced him to his friends. Of these, the most important was Professor Dent who took an instant liking to Beverley and became another jovial uncle and a long-term friend. He encouraged Beverley's musical ambitions and handed him a key to his home so that he could practise the piano whenever he was free from his army duties. On the piano, he kept a statue of Paganini which displayed an enormous erection. As he was a wicked old man in a voyeuristic way, he enjoyed disconcerting new young friends and undergraduates by asking what they thought of it. Forewarned by Benson, Beverley replied that he could do better himself, which sent Dent into a fit of giggles.

Benson took a keen interest in Beverley's future and strongly advised him to go back to Oxford despite the initial failure. He also suggested that he might write a book. He never questioned whether he could write; he assumed, correctly in this case, that, as Beverley talked well, he could write well. The subject almost suggested itself. Arthur's brother Fred had enjoyed a success with a romanticized story of his school life at Marlborough called *David Blaize*; Beverley could provide a contemporary and more realistic version. Unknown to either of them, Alec Waugh was about to publish *The Loom of Youth* set at 'Fernhurst', a thinly disguised story of life at Sherborne School. When it came out in July 1917, it caused a minor sensation because the boys in it used bad language and there was even a gentle account of a love affair between the hero and his friend. There had been something similar in *David Blaize*, but it was all so noble and redolent of Jesus and his beloved disciple John that nobody bothered with the implications. The Sherborne authorities, however, were so incensed by

Waugh's account of 'Fernhurst' that they refused to accept his younger brother Evelyn at the school.

Beverley was greatly taken with the idea and Waugh's success spurred him on no less than Fred Benson's. He tossed the theme around in his mind and began preliminary work on the novel which he was to call *Prelude*. Waugh's viewpoint had been that of an athlete; his would be that of an aesthete.

His time spent with Benson, Dent and their circle was in sharp contrast to his army training. One was stimulating and formative, the other tedious and dull, relieved only by a battalion concert at the Guildhall which he opened with a 'pianoforte solo', as the programme puts it. If he found army life in Cambridge dull, it was nothing to his experience at an army camp at Thetford where he was posted when he received his commission. He wrote in despair to Benson who replied that he was planning something better for him.

In a few months, Beverley found himself transferred to 'Intelligence' at the War Office in Whitehall. London had become the centre of escapism: men on leave from the horrors of the trenches needed to forget, however briefly, in a frenzy of pleasure. The providers of this pleasure were the pubs, restaurants, hotels, cinemas, theatres and prostitutes and all did excellent business. Beverley plunged in and took what was on offer. His officer's pay was supplemented by generous cheques from his father, and he lived life to the full. His duties at the War Office were undemanding and after office hours he was free to do as he liked. He set out from the rooms he had taken in Bryanston Street ready for pleasure and, if possible, sexual adventure. In a fit of vanity he had bought himself a very expensive officer's greatcoat which he had seen in the window of a Hanover Square tailor. The coat just managed to comply with regulations, although the lining in scarlet silk gave it an unexpectedly jaunty air. At this time, he was inclined to be plump, which bothered him: 'Must lose weight,' he told his diary. With his rounded features, the outrageous overcoat made him look like a schoolboy playing a major-general in an end-of-term operetta. A touch of burnt cork on his upper lip would have completed the illusion.

His unit at the War Office had no real job for him to do until someone concocted the absurd plan that he should sally forth, overcoat and all, to places like the Café Royal to act as a sort of *agent provocateur* to lure pacifist activists into trying to entice him to their cause. It is difficult to believe that this was meant as anything more than a joke, but Beverley took it seriously. Sending him to the Café Royal was like giving a greedy child the freedom of the sweetshop. The Café bore little resemblance to the refined grandeur of the building we know today, which is the product of the rebuilding of Regent Street in the 1920s. It was then housed behind a stucco-faced edifice, part of Nash's original street. In the basement there was a billiard room, and on the ground floor were the Grill Room and Domino Room, with private salons upstairs. The Café had become an informal club for writers, theatre people and artists, and for anybody who wanted to see or be seen: even royalty patronized it. The Domino Room, with its glitter of mirror and gilt, was the hub of the place, its habitués seated on red plush at marble-topped tables, lingering over drinks, arguing, and discussing themselves and their contemporaries.

When Beverley strolled in, scarlet lining flashing, he was aware that his thin veneer of sophistication might deceive no one, but for once, and probably for the last time, he underestimated himself. He glanced round the crowded room and, taking a cigarette from his case, he asked the painter Augustus John for a light. The great man provided it, invited him to join his table and, in a flurry of introductions, Beverley met Osbert Sitwell and Jacob Epstein.

It was an astonishingly easy entry into a circle which might otherwise have been closed to him. Soon he was as much a fixture as the gilded decorations, chatting to personalities as diverse as Ramsay MacDonald, the future Labour Prime Minister, at that time regarded with suspicion for his pacifist views, and D.H. Lawrence, whom he found lacking in a sense of humour. It is a pity that he did not make notes of his conversations but he recalled at least one example of the Sitwell wit. One evening, a militant lady declaimed, 'No woman ever gained anything from domesticity.' Osbert stared at her beadily and asked, 'What about Nell Gwyn?' The Sitwells came to be among Beverley's closest friends, probably because he had the knack of admiring people he liked and because he made them laugh. Osbert was later to remark of him, not unkindly, that he was the original bright young thing. It was perhaps this ability to admire which prompted Augustus John to give him two of his paintings, although what subsequently became of them is not known.

Beverley attended several private meetings of pacifist sympathizers through his contact with Ramsay MacDonald but although their opinions attracted him he found them, as a group, dim and lacking in practical solutions. Anything he reported to his superiors is hardly likely to have come as much of a revelation. If his mission was a joke, it began to misfire, for the constant presence of this baby-faced officer in the Bohemian surroundings of the Café Royal attracted the attention of plain-clothes police, whose suspicions of him could only have been fuelled by his fairly obvious sex life.

One evening, he was sitting alone at the Café when a waiter approached him and handed him a note, inviting him to join a young man at another table for a drink. The note came as no surprise to Beverley for he and the young man had been eyeing each other for some little while, and the note resolved the question of who would make the first move. When Beverley crossed the room and sat down, he was astonished to see a likeness of himself, stark naked, drawn in pencil on the marble table top – a provocative invitation to further investigation which Beverley could not refuse. It began a passionate and stormy affair.

The young man was Alvaro Guevara, a Chilean known to his intimates simply as Chile. Although only a few years older than Beverley, he was already regarded as an artist of some distinction and his work had been seen at a number of exhibitions, including a one-man show at the Chenil Gallery in the King's Road early in 1917. His portrait of Edith Sitwell, now in the National Portrait Gallery, was painted in 1916. Chile, a bisexual, later settled down, married Meraud Guinness, the painter, in 1929 and had a family. For a time during the Second World War he was Honorary Chilean Consul in London and afterwards Cultural Attaché in Berne. He was not exactly good-looking but he had an impressive physique and was an exceptional boxer. He was a type which fascinated Beverley, many of whose subsequent relationships were with men of similar physique but, fortunately, not always of similar temperament, for Chile was hot-tempered as well as hot-blooded. During the period that Beverley stayed with him at his studio, there were prodigious drinking bouts, violent sex and violent rows. It was a relationship which could not last, but when the affair ended the friendship continued. While they were together, Chile painted a full-length portrait of Beverley in uniform, but this no longer exists. Beverley told two stories about it: in one version, the picture 'just vanished', in the other, his father burned it in a drunken rage. Ronald Firbank described the portrait as 'charged with exquisite menace' which may be why it angered John Nichols – if that story is true.

Beverley's way of life, once the police had begun to take an interest, was bound to result in a crisis. It came shortly after they searched his rooms in Bryanston Street while he was away. They were apparently looking for evidence that he took drugs, presumably because others in the Café Royal set did so, passing round cocaine quite openly. Such evidence would have added dramatically to the dossier they were compiling about him. They cross-examined his landlady about who his visitors were and whether they stayed the night. In his autobiography, Beverley comments that it was at the Café Royal that Oscar Wilde played some of the ludicrous and tragic scenes which littered his path to destruction; he himself tiptoed along a similar path and might have suffered a similar fate if a case could have been made against him. In the event, there was no hard evidence, only his association with 'undesirable people' who held pacifist beliefs or led unconventional lives. When the matter was passed to the army authorities through the usual channels, there was considerable embarrassment. After much huffing and finger-wagging, during which Beverley was lectured severely for his *naïveté* and lack of discretion, it was decided to send him away from London immediately. On 2 February 1918 he found himself back in Cambridge as an instructor to the Officer Cadet Battalion.

There was now no Arthur Benson to play the jovial uncle for he was in an Ascot nursing-home fighting his melancholia, but Professor Dent was ready to take Beverley in tow. The reception he received from Lieutenant-Colonel H.A. Craddock, the Commanding Officer of the Battalion, and from the men who were to be his colleagues was, however, not propitious. Some word of his activities in London seemed to have filtered through and on his first night there was hostility in the air. At dinner, a captain said, apropos of nothing, 'Talking of buggery.'

The major opposite grinned. 'What about it?'

'I never understood why, if a chap wants to go in for buggery, he doesn't bugger a woman?'

Much laughter greeted this, but Beverley wisely kept quiet and got on with his meal. It was obvious that he would have to put up with covert and overt forms of persecution and so it proved over the next few weeks. What his detractors could not have known was that this baby-faced nineteen-year-old was tough, despite his slightly effeminate manner. It was an aspect of his character which was to come to his rescue in the years ahead and considerably surprise his enemies.

Colonel Craddock began his anti-Nichols campaign by complaining that Beverley wore slacks and not the usual puttees. He knew, of course, that this was a special dispensation because of Beverley's leg problem. Having begun on this topic, to which he was to return regularly, he then ordered him to instruct C Company in drill and bayonet practice. The drill was easy but Beverley had no stomach for the ritual of the bayonet which required the use of vivid imagination to stir the men into believing that sacks stuffed with straw were human. The bloodthirsty cry was, 'Stick it in, twist, out, in again,' accompanied by suitable exhortations to boot 'him' in the balls as they twisted the steel in the guts and ripped open the belly. Beverley was just about to grit his teeth and try to demonstrate to the fifty men watching him when his sergeant, a small, wiry man whose ribbons told the story of his gallantry, sprang to attention.

'Permission to speak, sir!'

'Yes, sergeant.'

'Shall I take over, sir? Your leg, sir. Might be a bit awkward, sir.'

'Very good, sergeant.'

'Sir!'

As he saluted, Sergeant Lewis Cohen winked, and Beverley watched with admiration as his saviour gave a performance of blood-chilling conviction touched, he noticed, with Chaplinesque comedy.

Into this scene marched a furious Colonel Craddock, upbraiding Beverley for disobeying his orders. 'Why are you not demonstrating?' he demanded.

Beverley, well aware of the rapt attention of the audience, replied firmly, 'Because, sir, I have not yet been instructed in the use of it myself.'

Nonplussed, Colonel Craddock blustered for a moment or two and marched away. Sergeant Lewis Cohen gave Beverley another wink.

The atmosphere in the mess grew daily more oppressive: every opportunity was taken to make his life unbearable. Although he was miserable, Beverley maintained an outward air of calm which provoked even greater retaliation. Matters were not helped when, as Orderly Officer of the day, he arrived in the cadets' mess to ask the routine question, 'Any complaints?' One of the cadets pointed out that the soup was uneatable. Beverley tasted it and, instead of replying in the time-honoured fashion that it was perfectly edible, he agreed that it was 'foul'. His fellow officers saw this as the breaking of an important unwritten code. It is possible that everyone would eventually have tired of baiting Beverley, but before this happened, Colonel Craddock arranged for him to attend an instructors' course at Berkhampstead, and on 27 February he went off, relieved to get away.

The atmosphere at Berkhampstead was completely different as, apart from the usual routine parades and drills, it was more like being back at school again. The men were bound by a common desire to pass the end of course exams and the sessions were for the most part absorbing, the most interesting being on the techniques of public speaking.

He made two close friends on the course. One was Harold Sloman MC, later to have a distinguished career in education at Rugby, St Paul's and Tonbridge, and to be an adviser to the government in the 1939–45 War and to the British Council at the end of it. In addition to being a brilliant Balliol scholar, he was an all-round athlete and a keen musician with a flair for composition. He had installed his wife Mary at the King's Arms and Beverley spent many evenings with them, making music. The other friend was Nevil Beechman MC, who was later to become the National Liberal Member of Parliament for St Ives, Cornwall. He was to be particularly important to Beverley when they met at Balliol after the war.

On Friday 15 March, Beverley gave a lecture on 'Organization'. It was a great success and his instructor told him he was very good, fluent and confident, if a little 'clerical' in tone. This cheered him up enormously. At the end of March, he passed the course and was posted back to Cambridge. On Easter Monday, before they dispersed, there was a celebration dinner at the King's Arms. Everyone got rather drunk on champagne and rather smutty toasts were made in doggerel verse. The one to Beverley went:

He's the Labour Corps' real joy,
He's the darling of the WAAC's.
They think his smile so very coy

And they all avow
You want it – don't you dearie?
Well what about right now?

Back at Cambridge, there was a noticeable change in the atmosphere. Colonel Craddock had hoped that Beverley would fail and be posted elsewhere, but he had not only passed but received a glowing report: 'Cheerful, good bearing and example, displays a sound military knowledge, a fluent lecturer, but must avoid being verbose.' Colonel Craddock conceded defeat for the time being, informed Beverley that he had been promoted to First Lieutenant, and invited him to play at the forthcoming battalion concert at the Guildhall. Beverley played Chopin's 'Study on Black Keys' and composed two songs for the occasion which were sung by Cadet Jackson. He also, as pianist, accompanied everyone else that evening. It was typical of Beverley that he should plunge so enthusiastically into this activity as a result of Craddock's small gesture of reconciliation. The *Cambridge Chronicle*, reporting the concert in the manner of the time, said:

> The musical portion of the programme was of a far higher order than has been attained at recent concerts, rendered possible by the presence of Lieutenant Nichols who is a brilliant accompanist and contributed in no small measure to the unqualified success of the programme. Cadet Jackson gave a sympathetic rendering of two songs, 'Come Not When I Am Dead' and 'Ask Nothing More', two delicately written songs composed by Lieutenant Nichols who accompanied them, and a tremendous burst of applause at the conclusion showed how much the audience appreciated them.

It is interesting that the local reporter used the word 'delicate' in describing Beverley's compositions, for this was a quality inherent in the songs he was to write for Dame Nellie Melba, Dame Clara Butt, Mary Ellis and others.

Colonel Craddock might not have been quite the odious creature that Beverley described in *The Unforgiving Minute*, but merely a rather puzzled regular soldier who felt uncomfortable about having someone of this type in his team. Although he established a truce, he still criticized whenever he could, and as part of his campaign to get rid of the cuckoo in the nest, he sent Beverley on another course, 'The Use of the Revolver', knowing how much Beverley loathed firearms. Once again he reckoned without the Nichols toughness, for Beverley came out with top marks – in the simulated trench attack, for example, he scored 45 hits out of a possible 50. In July, Craddock sent him away again, this time to Crowborough to the Eastern Command School of Instruction in Anti-Gas Measures, where once more Beverley was a success, his report carrying the comment 'Distinguished'.

One almost feels sorry for the Colonel, whose frustration was not eased by Beverley's popularity with the cadets and with Mrs Craddock and the Craddock children. She found him quite delightful and liked inviting him to tea. It is surprising that, with his talent for comedy, Beverley did not use this situation in his autobiography.

Craddock suffered further annoyance when Beverley was taken up by Dr Arthur Shipley, Master of Christ's and Vice-Chancellor of the University, with power over the entire military establishment. Beverley, exploring the grounds of Christ's College, came to the mulberry tree in whose shade Milton was said to have composed some of his early verse. As he gazed at it, remembering the words bewailing the death of a friend by drowning in 'Lycidas', he heard a voice behind him: 'Are you by any chance a Miltonian?' He turned and saw a short, plump man of about sixty in a well-worn scholar's gown who exuded benignity. They fell into deep conversation, but it was not until Dr Shipley invited him into the Master's Lodge for tea that Beverley realized who he was. An affinity quickly became apparent, and he had another jovial uncle, even more powerful than Arthur Benson had been. Once again, he confided his hopes and ambitions and spoke of *Prelude*, which was well into its early chapters. Dr Shipley was intrigued and invited him to come to dinner and read *Prelude* to him after. He became a close friend, and introduced Beverley to his wide circle of academic colleagues.

This period at Cambridge lasted until the end of September when Dr Shipley provided him with a unique opportunity to broaden his experience. Until then, it was a time of frantic activity. Apart from his military duties, he worked hard at his music and his writing and led a full social life. One of his new friends was Cyril Roothman, Fellow and Musical Director of St John's College, who was completing his opera, *The Two Sisters* (today, along with his other compositions, mostly forgotten). Beverley was so inspired when Roothman played a section of this work that he wrote part of *Prelude* with the structure of the music running through his mind. This relationship between his prose style and music is constant in his writings, the key to the rhythm of his style, which rarely jars unless he planned to do so for effect.

On a brief leave in Torquay, Beverley comments that everything at home was very much as usual, very pleasant, quiet and comforting, the drawing-room sweet-smelling and pretty with flowers. His father took him round the town to show him off. 'I wore my pale grey.' There were visits to friends where he was asked to play the piano, always the obligatory 'Keep the Home Fires Burning' of which people never seemed to tire. Paul was also at home with his intimate friend, Lord St Audries. After hearing Paul preach 'very well', there was a lunch party at Cleave Court with Egie as a guest, and there were visits to the cinema with his mother. One of the films was a sentimental epic called *Mother Love* which she found hilarious.

Beverley spent part of a leave at Marlborough to work on the novel, and wrote a long account of it for future reference. In it, he is at first surprised by his lack of sentimental reaction but this soon changes and he is overwhelmed by the recollections of the past. He watches a cricket match, strolls past the bathing pool, along the terrace, past the 'bum bush', attends morning service in chapel and meets the new occupants of his old study, even offering to buy the furniture so that he can recreate the room at Cleave Court. Most of all, he is drawn back into the comradeship of the boys themselves, who welcome him as if he had never gone away. He feels torrents of love for the place, despite a realization that the educational side of it 'is all wrong'. Does it really matter, when all is said and done? The main thing is that public schools provide 'a sheltered and idyllic time for a few of the adorable boys there are in the world. Let it be a time of joy, sunny cricket, spiritual and physical licence, because it is there they discover that they have a soul and, what is more, a body.' There are, he muses, thousands of beastly details, missed opportunities and tragedies, but it is the place which has in it all the days when he was really young, and it fills him with sheer burning love. He ends his account: 'It's all over now, but what if it had never been?'

In London, still on leave, he enjoyed non-stop meetings with friends in the setting of the Savile or the Bachelors' Club, the Ritz, the Carlton or the Café Royal. There were romantic interludes, trips to the Turkish Baths for casual encounters. Once, he remarks regretfully, he spent an 'uneventful night' at the Russell Square Baths. He went to see Guevara at his new studio at 117, Fulham Road: 'He had clap and looked deadly.' There was a 'delightfully Bohemian' party at the Sickerts, and dinner with the Sitwells at Swan Walk, a house filled with Victorian bits and pieces which contrasted oddly with examples of modern art. A young artist, Harly Trott, whom Beverley secretly thought rather common, did two large pencil studies of him in the nude, which still exist. They portray Beverley's physical beauty at that time, and this is confirmed by contemporary photographs.

Back in Cambridge, Colonel Craddock still planned to get rid of him. At the beginning of July, a fellow officer warned Beverley that the Commanding Officer had written a report complaining that he was too young to be an instructor, had not had the advantage of serving at the Front and was an aesthete who did not play games. Beverley at once rushed out to buy a book on cricket so that he could improve his small talk on the subject. He also wrote a frantic letter to Peter, the son of Viscount Churchill, who had befriended him during his brief career in Intelligence, begging him to use his influence to get him away from Cambridge into a job in London. At the end of July, Craddock called him into his office for a talk. There was a problem, he told Beverley. People were saying he was a sod because he behaved like one, and he added, somewhat curiously, 'Sodomy is more prevalent than you may imagine, dear boy.' Beverley should take a keener interest in games, be less conceited, and stop speaking so familiarly of Dr Shipley. This last comment revealed the real reason for Craddock's hostility: Beverley was accepted in social circles of the University which were closed to the Colonel. He ended by saying it would be best if he left Cambridge.

Beverley did not know what to do. Peter had not replied to his letter and he dreaded the prospect of spending the rest of the war stuck somewhere as soul-destroying as Thetford. He explained his fears to Dr Shipley after dinner one evening, and was flabbergasted when his friend said without preamble, 'You must come to America with me as my aide-de-camp.'

Dr Shipley and leading members of the educational world had been invited to tour America to investigate means of closer co-operation between the institutes of learning in the two countries. The other members of the Commission were Sir Henry Miers, Vice-Chancellor of the University of Manchester, Dr John Joly, Professor of Geology at Dublin, Sir Henry Jones of Glasgow, an expert on, among other subjects, early Byzantine mosaics, the Reverend Edward Walker of Queen's College, Oxford and, representing the female educationalists, Caroline Spurgeon of Bedford College and Rose Sidgwick of Birmingham.

Beverley was overjoyed by his friend's offer. Dr Shipley wrote immediately to the Foreign Office requesting that Lieutenant Nichols be released from his military duties to act as 'Secretary to the Commission'. With extraordinary speed, the reply came back: the Foreign Office agreed. Beverley was ecstatic. He appeared at a garden party hosted by Shipley and, slightly drunk, sang songs from *The Merry Widow* for the guests to dance to. They rewarded him with three cheers and an American woman promptly asked him to marry her! 'I was inconceivably brilliant,' he wrote in his diary.

· 5 ·

The American way

1918

THE trip to America was scheduled to start on 28 September 1918, but before then Beverley was to pass through moods of deep gloom because, somewhere in the complicated system of officialdom, there was opposition to his going, although he never discovered its source. In the mean time, he carried out his normal duties and his busy social life, trying also to get as much of *Prelude* completed as he could. As if this were not enough, he decided for some unknown reason to learn Spanish, and attacked it with his usual energy. Within a few weeks, on a leave in London, he was practising phrases with a Spanish friend whom André Gide had brought to supper. He noted that Gide's French was 'charmingly naïve'.

Colonel Craddock had to give his formal permission for the American tour – either to say no and have the pleasure of angering Beverley, or say yes and have the pleasure of losing him. After a struggle, he opted for the latter course. Then it was ordered that all payment and allowances would cease while Lieutenant Nichols was on secondment, and he must pay his own fare and expenses. This plunged Beverley into despair until Ian Hay at the Ministry of Information stepped in and decreed otherwise.

As the War Office itself still refused to confirm the secondment, Beverley was given leave to go to London on 9 September, his twentieth birthday, to sort things out. Here he joined Humphrey Hitchcock who had taken a suite at the Savoy Hotel for both of them. Humphrey had entered his life a month previously in Cambridge and what had begun as a casual encounter had developed rapidly into a heavy romantic relationship. From what Beverley said, the infatuation was mainly on Humphrey's side, but not for the first time and certainly not for the last he accepted the position of being adored and all that went with it – gifts, being treated to lunches and dinners and theatres. (When roles were reversed and Beverley became infatuated with someone, he could, in his turn, spend lavishly on the object of his affections. After one such episode, he ruefully counted the cost and remarked, 'No more Huberts!')

After dinner at the Savoy Humphrey took him to see the successful musical comedy *The Lilac Domino* at the Empire Theatre in Leicester Square. Beverley described the next day as one of laughter. Ian Hay was away from the Ministry of Information and Beverley went to the War Office where chaos reigned because all his papers had been mislaid. He left them to it and met Humphrey for an 'amusing' tea at the Trocadero, a popular meeting-place for the homosexual fraternity, then went to choose a ring for his birthday present. After dinner at the Café Royal with Robert Nichols, the soldier poet, and C.R.W. Nevinson, the artist, they went to see Charles B. Cochran's production, *As You Were*, at the London Pavilion, a sensational success partly owing to the complaints of the critics that the star, Alice Delysia, wore dresses which were too revealing, but mainly because it had a tuneful score by Herman Darewski and witty lyrics and book by Arthur Wimpress. Several of the songs became hits, sung and whistled all round the country, and were taken up by the troops in France. Beverley was enchanted by Delysia and for years afterwards one of his party-pieces was his impression of the lady singing 'If I Could Care For You', which he performed with a great deal of 'camp' innuendo. He was even more enchanted by the Cochran style, and as he sat dazzled by *As You Were* he resolved to work for Cochran – a dream he was to fulfil in ten years' time.

He spent the next few days being passed like a parcel from one official to another at the War Office and the Ministry of Information where no one appeared capable of making decisions. Humphrey returned to Cambridge leaving him alone at the Savoy waiting in vain for telephone calls. Then a letter arrived telling him that, in spite of Ian Hay's assurance, all pay would definitely be stopped while he was in America, if in fact he went at all. He reported back to Cambridge with only ten days to go to the sailing date, still uncertain as to the outcome. In a bitter mood, he collected the expensive new clothes he had ordered for the trip, but was cheered up by their effect, particularly by a dress uniform in blue which was tailored to his own design. Arthur Shipley, outraged by the nonsensical muddle, took him back to London where, after another day of to-ing and fro-ing, the muddle was sorted out, the question of expenses solved and the necessary papers cleared.

The last days in Cambridge were spent in a rush of farewells culminating in afternoon tea with the Craddocks, with the Colonel being charming under the watchful gaze of Mrs Craddock who, with the children, was sad to see Beverley go. She was fearful for his safety on a sea-journey at the mercy of the enemy; what the Colonel thought about the possibility of his troublesome lieutenant being torpedoed may be left to the imagination. Finally, there was a sad parting with Humphrey who broke down and wept. The next day, as Beverley was driven away in a cab, he saw the captain who had made the remark about buggery staring malevolently from a window and, with a big grin, he gave him a two-fingered 'Fuck you!' gesture.

In Liverpool, he joined the rest of the group at the Adelphi Hotel who were in a state of consternation because none of the boat tickets had arrived. The next day, after a morning of extraordinary complications with telegrams and telephone calls, a courier arrived with the tickets at the very last minute.

The group, finally settled aboard the ship, ate their first meal and were astonished by the complete lack of austerity. There was white bread instead of the grey wartime loaves they were used to, and real butter and white lump sugar. It was a hint of the plenty waiting for them in America. It was also one of the last meals any of them ate for a few days, for they were all horribly seasick and Dr Joly, who believed with religious fervour that only the worst could happen, predicted that if they did not die of seasickness they would all perish at the hands of a German submarine. He was so convinced of his fate that he refused to take his clothes off, on the basis that a fully clothed body stood less chance of shock in cold seawater than a naked one. The other members of the party were free of such eccentricity, unless the Revd Edward Walker's habit of putting his boots outside hotel bedrooms for cleaning, and steadfastly refusing to accept that this familiar English service was unknown in America, counted as such. His boots were always fortunately traced to the maids, who had borne them off under the impression that they had been thrown away. Apart from finding the clerical boots, Beverley often had to find Sir Henry Jones's false tooth. This appendage screwed into the gum and when he did not need it to aid mastication Sir Henry was apt to take it out and forget where he had put it.

Beverley had little to do on the voyage except listen to his distinguished charges discussing their favourite topics. It confirmed his belief that the art of listening can get one a long way in unfamiliar circles, even if the conversation is above one's head. People, he decided, will ascribe great intelligence to you if you have the appearance of appreciation and nod in the right places. He found this maxim hard to follow when Dr Jones and Dr Joly both talked to him at the same time, one about Byzantine mosaics and the other about the canals on Mars, but he 'listened like mad'. The other passengers were a dull lot except for his friend, the young poet Robert Nichols – no relation – who was a few years older than himself. He had served in the Royal Artillery from 1914 to 1916 when he was invalided from the Somme suffering the effects of shell shock. He was considered one of the best of the war poets, a friend of Rupert Brooke and Siegfried Sassoon. He, too, was travelling under the auspices of the Ministry of Information, but was to be disappointed in America for, to him, the place was frightening, the people unreceptive and he did not get the 'platform' he anticipated. It was a lesson Beverley did not forget: henceforth part of his career strategy was to choose the right 'platform'.

On Wednesday 8 October 1918 the ship docked in New York. During the slow approach, Beverley and Robert stood on deck with their fellow passengers, awe-struck by the sight of the skyscrapers and the sun glittering on a million windows. They were small skyscrapers by comparison with the monsters of today, but to the British newcomers they were a wonder of their modern world. In a moment of emotion, Robert saluted the Statue of Liberty in military style but he misjudged the time it would take the boat to sail past and he was forced to lower his arm with an attack of cramp. For Beverley, not so demonstrative, it was nevertheless love at first sight with New York and with nearly all things American.

When the press came aboard, they saw a group of eminent greybeards with a tall, handsome, boyish officer and they sensed a story. Who was he? Beverley replied as best he could, but his interrogators had written the answers before they had asked the questions. The *New York Times* gave him his own headline: 'Canadian Aviator Arrives'. If this came as a surprise, more was to follow on the tour. In Houston, a glamorous head-and-shoulders picture appeared in the *Post* with the caption, 'Lieut. Beverley St Clair' which must have been a flight of fancy on the part of the reporter, but then Beverley did look rather like a leading man in a screen romance. In New Orleans, the local paper enthused: 'A young English soldier, blue-eyed, blond and big! Shivers of excitement were noticed among the girls when he appeared.' Everywhere he went, Beverley was treated as a hero and anything he said in protest was dismissed as modesty. With the scent of victory in the air, the Americans were in a mood for heroes and Beverley suited the mood. His flair for acting or, as he described it, 'posing', came to the fore, and shows in the photographs taken on the tour. In England, he had seemed effete, but in America he looked the part he was expected to play – strong, authoritative, every inch a war veteran.

The first day in New York passed in a whirl of delight, as anyone who has thrilled to New York for the first time will understand. After a reception at Columbia University, the party was dined at the Century Association, a club formed to encourage literature and the arts. Even the unrationed menus of the Cunard Line had not prepared him for the lavish display of food, which was to become a recurring feature of the tour. Then a new friend took him walking in the early hours. Everywhere was surging with people: Broadway and 42nd Street were bright with electric signs, in vivid contrast to the drabness of blacked-out London. After a look at the magnificent new Grand Central Station, they went to the top of the Biltmore Hotel to look down at the city 'dizzily shining below'. It was a marvellous, a never-to-be-forgotten day.

More marvellous days followed: a motor tour of the sights; visits to museums; a trip on the elevated railway; lunch at the New York Yacht Club; a parade on Fifth Avenue where Theda Bara, the film star, was selling

Victory Bonds; dinner at the Ritz Carlton ('most swagger'); a Liberty Loan parade in Madison Square ('most marvellous sight, millions of people waving flags, President Wilson marching'); lunch at the University Club; another night walk along Broadway ('one of the most marvellous sights in the world'); and dinner with 200 guests at the Aldine Club where he made his first important after-dinner speech. All this, and meeting with New York's academic and social sets, was heady stuff for a boy just turned twenty. J. Pierpont Morgan, the financier, and his wife were particularly nice to him, as was E. Root, the editor of *Life* magazine.

On Tuesday 15 October, the party was in Washington in the White House to meet President Wilson. In *Twenty-Five* Beverley was to comment on the lack of formality and, sixty years later, on the absence of even the most nominal security which now would be unthinkable. Wilson was, he wrote in his diary, quietly spoken, rather cold, despite his impeccable courtesy, and looked terribly tired. He talked of the latest German peace moves and his reluctance to accept them at face value. 'A man asked me what I should call an overt act. I said I didn't know but I would recognize it when I saw it. In the same way I feel I shall recognize a real act of peace when I see it.' As Beverley studied this man, he was overcome with awe at the feeling that he was in the presence of someone on whom peace or continuing war would probably entirely depend. This mood lasted until the evening, when he was on his own for a change, met a couple of sailors and took them to his room. Next day, it was back to the busy round of meetings, sightseeing and formal meals. Then the party left for its tour of educational centres, travelling by rail in luxurious accommodation that was the pride of the system: nothing was too good for this group of distinguished scholars. For a detour into Canada, they had the use of the Duke of Devonshire's private car. If a film had been made of the trip, there would have been a sequence or two of speeding trains with names super-imposed: Baltimore, Philadelphia, Boston, Montreal, Toronto, Detroit, Chicago, Minneapolis, St Louis, New Orleans, Houston and finally back to New York.

Beverley's duties were hardly onerous, consisting mainly of writing letters of thanks to their hosts, but he had very little time to himself. In Boston, he escaped long enough to meet a sailor called Paradise with whom he spent as much time as possible during the three days they were there. In Baltimore, he visited the grave of Edgar Allan Poe and was distressed to see the marble tomb covered with weeds, sordid and unkempt. In Philadelphia, Dr Shipley took him to meet Tait Mackenzie, the sculptor, who was working a figure of a male athlete, using as his model a baseball player posed *à la Grec*. They also visited the Widnes mansion, a vast place with footmen marching in parties like guardsmen, where Beverley was entranced by a dazzling collection which included Rembrandt, Corot, El Greco, Manet and Benvenuto Cellini. Widnes Junior, as he showed them round, kept referring to the importance of the collection but never once to the beauty of it. This, a puzzled Beverley decided, was the American preoccupation with size; it was a form of boasting which in fact missed the point. During a stay at the large Pryne estate near Princeton, he was amused by Mrs Pryne who, speaking of the war, complained that they were feeling the pinch. 'This part of the garden really needs lots of attention and we can't get more than eighteen men.'

On 7 November the newspapers run by Randolph Hearst announced in headlines five inches tall 'WAR OVER' and gave a graphic account of the signing of the armistice on the 'field of battle'. When Beverley's party got off the train at Chicago, the city was in the throes of hysterical and drunken celebration. Then the 'news' was officially denied and a dreadful gloom descended. The next evening, after the day's usual routine, Beverley's own gloom was partially relieved when a young university professor picked him up at a formal dinner and took him home for the night. At 2 a.m. on 11 November, Chicago went mad again when the war really ended. Sirens woke the city and the streets rapidly filled with people waving flags; bands played; cars with strings of tin cans tied to their bumpers hooted; revolvers were fired into the air and everyone yelled and shrieked. The group had a few hours' respite at the North Western University in the morning, but back at their hotel the celebrations went on and on, and the drink flowed unceasingly. Edward Walker observed tartly that it was 'terrible' and a good case for Prohibition. No one agreed with him, least of all Beverley who made the most of every opportunity that offered – and for him, in his British uniform, there were plenty of offers.

In the chaotic mêlée of celebrations that evening he met an artist, Purcell Jones, who whisked him off to see an exhibition of his work at the Reinhardt Gallery, and then to dinner at the Ryerson house, the home of the millionaire family. Here he met Emily Borie Ryerson, another chance encounter which was to pay dividends, for she had a wide circle of important friends including Madame Nellie Melba. In *The Unforgiving Minute* Beverley gives a completely different account of their meeting: it was, he says, in a Chicago hotel, in a lift which stuck between floors. 'What are you doing in our crazy city?' she asked and he confessed to her that, far from being a war veteran as everyone assumed, he had not taken part in action and was weighed down with guilt and shame. If that conversation did take place, it was not in the lift of a Chicago hotel, and why he concocted the tale is unclear, unless it was to side-step his association with Jones. Mrs Ryerson took an instant liking to him. After dinner they went to a dance at the Casino where he was introduced to 'at least a hundred people'. They then went on to meet Laurette Taylor, the star of *Happiness*; the curtain was just down and she was in her dressing-room with her husband, Hartley Manners, author of her stage success, *Peg o' My Heart*. Both were delighted to meet the 'war hero' and they all went for supper at the College Inn, where Beverley ate his first avocado pear and watched skaters on the ice-rink in the middle of the restaurant. The next day, the group left for Madison, and Beverley promised to call Purcell Jones who would be back in his New York home in December. By happy coincidence, Mrs Ryerson would also be in New York at that time.

In the old area of New Orleans which Beverley visited with Dr Shipley, a rumour spread that he was the Prince of Wales and, despite denials, he was besieged by people who wanted to shake his hand or take photographs. Shaking hands he found an exhausting business. In Minneapolis, at a vast evening reception, he stood in line while several thousand people filed past. His older companions bore it all stoically, but just after midnight, Beverley's knee gave way and he had to be helped to his room. While they were in Houston he caught the flu virus which caused a large number of deaths across America, and was overwhelmed by the kindness shown to him, though he rather wished that his anxious hostess and the nurse engaged to look after him would leave him in peace.

The tour ended when the train arrived in New York at five o'clock on a December afternoon. Beverley was round at Purcell Jones's home within half an hour. Although there were still a few official engagements with Dr Shipley, he was free to do as he liked, and that evening, Jones and he dined with Mrs Ryerson at the new Avignon restaurant which was filled with women in 'marvellous dresses wearing pearls the size of grapes'. With the contacts he had already made through Dr Shipley and with those he was about to make through Jones and Mrs Ryerson, Beverley spent the next two weeks in a bewildering round of social occasions. Not for the first time was he pleased with his investment in well-tailored uniform clothes and expensive accessories: he cut a dashing figure and he knew it. War heroes were the darlings of the hour and he let people believe what they wanted to about his 'exploits'. Sunday 8 December was 'Britain's Day', and Fifth Avenue was hung with Union Jacks. He spent the day dashing from one social gathering to another, ending up with Lady Colbrook and Lady Fitzclarence at an entertainment for British sailors, who responded to the hospitality by dancing the hornpipe 'delightfully'.

So it went on day after day: lunches and dinners at the Bankers' Club, the Century, Del Monicos, Sherreys, the Baltimore and Ritz Carlton, visits to the Metropolitan Opera where someone gave him the use of a box – 'I know almost everyone.' There was a private concert at the Waldorf with Caruso singing, and tea with Cathleen Nesbitt, the English actress and close friend of Rupert Brooke. Beverley took tea, it would seem, with all the wealthiest ladies in New York. He comments: 'She was wearing her £200,000 necklace,' or 'Terrible snobs but I like them.' There were visits to the J. Pierpont Morgans where Jack Morgan gave him a single hair from a lock of

Keats' hair. 'If I give any more of these away, there won't be a lock left,' said Jack. In the midst of all this activity, Beverley, at the instigation of Dr Shipley, wrote an article on Anglo-American relations entitled 'Hands Across The Sea' for *Outlook*, an influential magazine. A few days later, the editor invited him to call, and handed him the article in proof and a cheque for forty dollars. Beverley headed this entry in his diary in block capitals, 'MY FIRST LITERARY SUCCESS!'

The day before he left for England with Dr Shipley, he dashed round saying his goodbyes and taking flowers to the ladies. When he arrived on board the *Caronia*, he found a pile of cables and letters and, to his surprise, a stack of farewell presents. In *The Unforgiving Minute*, Beverley confessed that at that moment he was tempted to desert from the army and stay in New York, but Dr Shipley brought him down to earth with a brief lecture on the consequences of desertion.

It had been a triumphant progress for Beverley and, although it might be easy to dismiss it as all froth with little substance, it had given him that most valuable of assets – confidence in his own ability. He had not only seen a great deal but had also met Americans in every sphere of society, and slept with a few of them. It had been a unique education for a twenty-year-old blessed with good looks, a sense of humour and charm, and there was little doubt in his mind that in the future the triumphal progress would continue.

If anything was calculated to dampen his euphoria, it was the voyage home. They should have been on the *Carmania* but it had been laid up with engine trouble and Cunard had transferred them to the *Caronia*. Dr Shipley and Beverley shared a splendid suite, but as the rest of the mission had left some days earlier they found themselves isolated among an uninteresting bunch of passengers consisting mainly of a large party of YWCA ladies who wore blue caps and 'shrieked from morn to night'. Beverley made the mistake of accompanying the Sunday service on the first day at sea, and from then on was plagued with requests to 'play something', as if he were the ship's entertainer. The Nichols charm wore rather thin and he took refuge in his cabin with the excuse that he had work to do. This was more or less true, for there were letters to write and it was also an opportunity to polish the manuscript of *Prelude* which he had finished on one of the many train journeys across the States. But he could not escape for long, and on Christmas Eve he played carols for the YWCA ladies who sang with gusto. On Christmas Day, he gave an after-dinner recital in front of an audience stupefied after a long day of Cunard-style feasting. After a gigantic breakfast, which included grilled mutton chops, and a six-course lunch, the passengers settled down to serious eating with a traditional English Christmas dinner, starting with oysters and moving through soup, fish, and roast turkey to mince pies and Christmas pudding. This culinary marathon, which matched the lavish menus of the whole trip, was in stark contrast with the comparative austerity waiting for them in England.

Beverley eventually surrendered to the demands of the ladies and played the piano for them each afternoon and evening. After a concert on the 27th, a Nonconformist bishop lectured the audience on sin, the emphasis being on adultery and strong drink, with appropriate quotations from the Good Book. An over-rouged lady, not of the YWCA sorority, endeared herself to Beverley by drinking neat whisky steadily during the bishop's tirade and commenting in a stage whisper, when he referred to the stoning of the woman taken in adultery: 'They still stone fallen women but now the stones come from Tiffany's.'

The celebrations continued unabated until the ship docked in Liverpool.

· 6 ·

Oxford,
failures and successes

1919—1920

A FTER the hectic months in America, Beverley at first enjoyed the
relaxed tempo of life at Cleave Court and being the centre of
attention among the Torquay set. He still dithered over the
question of whether to go back to Oxford, obtain a degree and then take up
law, or whether to start studying law as soon as he was demobilized. His
father was prepared to finance a period at University and this was eventually
agreed on. It is worth emphasizing that there was no discord between father
and son at this time, contrary to accounts Beverley was to give later. He was
also to say that he had to fight to get to Oxford, but this was quite untrue:
any unwillingness was on his part, but everyone he had consulted, from
Arthur Benson to Arthur Shipley and the Dean of Balliol, F.R. Urquhart,
urged him to take the opportunity. Now, with the support of his father, the
matter was settled. Apart from a trip to Cambridge to report to Colonel
Craddock, and a few days in London to see Alice Delysia and friends at the
Café Royal, he stayed in Torquay.

Suddenly, in a typical change of mood, the people and the place seemed
to him dull and boring. 'It is like chloroform to the mind,' he said; 'the very
air makes one think mediocrely.' The small talk of the women was all to do
with shortages and the difficulty of getting servants. At Cleave Court, the
indoor staff had been reduced to two, an elderly husband and wife who were
less than competent. Pauline was now forced to cope with some of the
housework herself. The small 'select' fraternity that revolved round Egie,
once the height of sophistication to the schoolboy, now appeared for what
they were – suburban poseurs with nothing worthwhile to say but intent on
saying it. 'I feel mentally like a pink worm fed on pink nougat,' he said, after
an evening with them.

As he often did, Beverley escaped to stay with his well-to-do Uncle
George and Aunt Blanche in Bristol. Though he libelled them in *Father
Figure* his diaries suggest that he was as fond of them as they were of him;
indeed, they treated him as a surrogate son. Blanche was an educated
woman who shared her husband's passion for music, and they both

encouraged their nephew's musical aspirations.

By the middle of January, Beverley was established at Balliol in the first of a series of rooms he was to occupy while he was there. Within three days he had hired a baby grand piano for five guineas a term, installed new furniture, carpets, curtains and covers from Liberty's of London, and hung his pictures – the presents from the Augustus Johns, perhaps? His wild happiness at the simple fact of being in Oxford was slightly dulled when he received a letter instructing him to report to Colonel Craddock for duty. He dropped this in the fire, praying that nothing would stop the process of demobilization, and on 24 January, he was officially a civilian again.

Oxford was a strange place in 1919. During the war, it had barely functioned as a centre of learning and most of its clubs and institutions had withered or died. Now, instead of being populated by teenagers fresh from school as it had been before the war, it was packed with men bloodied by conflict for whom the halcyon days of school were on the other side of memory. Broadly, they divided into two categories: games players and aesthetes, although there were many sub-divisions within these groupings. Beverley knew from experience that it was easy to attract a coterie, especially those with homosexual inclinations, but what he wanted was respect and popularity from all factions in the University, to make a name for himself which would echo beyond the confines of Oxford. In his autobiography sixty years later, he rationalized this as an escape route from the horror of his home life: he needed to make money, and to make money he needed a name. But the true explanation, explicit in his diary of the time, is simply a driving ambition to succeed in whatever he did and to establish a public figure called 'Beverley Nichols'. He was convinced of what he called his 'innate brilliance', hardly an uncommon conviction among young men. What set him apart was that at Oxford he did precisely what he intended to do, with the combined skills of modern practitioners in public relations and in marketing.

First of all, he provided open house to all comers in the civilized atmosphere of his refurbished rooms in the First Court at Balliol. He was an amiable and considerate host and he attracted the attention he wanted. Second, from this circle, he instigated the Psittakoi Society, dedicated to the discussion of a wide range of topics but with an emphasis on the arts. It held its first formal meeting on 18 February. Third, he asked for, and got, the editorship of *The Isis* (as it was then called), a virtually defunct weekly magazine. This arrangement was confirmed in a letter from the Holywell Press on 8 March. Fourth, he started a new magazine called the *Oxford Outlook* which came out on 15 May, and had a Liberal flavour, though it was not wholly political. It provided a platform for a diversity of views, although the editors prudently distanced themselves from an article attacking the government for its hostile view of the 'democratically' elected

Dáil Eireann in Dublin. The magazine contained contributions from Professor Gilbert Murray, Dr Arthur Shipley, Lord Charnwood whose son, John Benson, was at Balliol, Sir William Osler, Vera Brittain, Philip Guedalla and Siegfried Sassoon. Beverley was particularly pleased when John Masefield, to whom he was distantly related, responded to his approach by writing two sonnets 'On Growing Old'. Finally, Beverley became an active member of the Liberal Party and initiated the New Oxford Liberal Club.

Of course, he did not do all this alone, but it is a tribute to his persuasive charm and ability that he found ready support. His chief collaborator was Nevil Beechman whom he had met at Berkhampstead. At first he was not sure whether Nevil would share his enthusiasm but he proved to be a shrewd choice. He was a brilliant scholar who, after becoming a barrister, had a notable political career, ultimately becoming a member of the government in 1945. Beverley described him as very much the Grand Signior.

As a result of all this activity in such a short time, it was impossible for anyone in Oxford not to know who Beverley Nichols was. Needless to say, he had his critics who found his penchant for self-publicity too much to take, and who disliked his ready charm and his outré taste in dress (which was, incidentally, a costly item in the Nichols family budget). It is very probable that they also detected and abhorred his homosexuality. Some of them were to get their revenge, albeit temporarily, the following year.

In addition to these activities, Beverley was leading a life which, for most people, would have been more than enough to fill their days. After discovering, to his own disappointment and that of another friend and confidant, Paul Springman, that there was no adequate provision for the study of modern languages, Beverley opted for the short course, devised for ex-officers, in modern history. The Dean, Francis Fortescue Urquhart, otherwise known as 'Sligger', told him he was capable of obtaining his degree in four terms, if he worked hard. Not surprisingly, he did not manage this because of all his other activities; in the end, he just managed to get a BA after two years. Sligger had become a friend, albeit not as close as Benson, Shipley or Dent at Cambridge, while Beverley was in the army, and they had met from time to time in London or Oxford for lunch or dinner. He was one of those who persuaded him to return to Oxford, and now lent his powerful support to Beverley's various ventures, at the same time lecturing him on the poor quality of the work he produced for his 'Collecers', a slang term for a 'collection' which was an informal examination written in the calm of one's own room, as opposed to regular exams held in the frightening formality of the Examination Schools.

Apart from his erratic attempts to study history, Beverley made a rule to practise the piano every day and also to compose the occasional song or

Chopinesque piece. As a result of his work on the *Isis* and the *Oxford Outlook*, he was able to send off articles to New York and London with some success: the *New York Evening Post*, for example, paid him twenty-five dollars for his views on 'Education'. Interlaced with his social round was an active romantic life. Humphrey was still very much in evidence, popping up to Oxford frequently or entertaining Beverley in London at weekends, and there were others, not always fully identified in his diary. Who, for example was 'B' who was 'distressingly Nancy' and had a room in Trinity decorated like that of 'a 4th-rate prostitute'? Whoever he was, he became an intimate friend for a few weeks. Beverley hired a punt for late-night trysts on the river, and this ploy was apparently successful. He noted, however, in his entry for 1 June that after dinner with 'C' at the Golden Cross and a 'glorious hour' at the Mitre, an unnamed third man tagged along and joined them on the river: 'It was consequently a failure.' Another failure was Clive Burt, a popular man who had been a star at Eton. He was so self-conscious because of Beverley's blatant interest in him that he blushed deeply whenever they met, but he did not succumb.

As for the social round itself, dozens of names are mentioned in his diary, again not always in full. Sacheverell Sitwell ('Sacky' for short) crops up frequently, sometimes joined by Osbert, together with Bob Boothby, Raymond Massey, Leslie Hore-Belisha, George Anthony Mostyn (the artist), Siegfried Sassoon and Victor (Teeny) Cazalet.

Hovering in the background to his Oxford life was the unresolved question of the publication of *Prelude*. He was very proud of it and required little encouragement to read excerpts to anyone who would listen. He was encouraged by their praise but so far no publisher had made an offer for it. The general reaction was that there had been too many novels of school life recently. Beverley was sure it would be accepted eventually, and, after further revisions made during an enforced rest in a nursing-home recovering from jaundice, he sent it off to another publisher and waited hopefully. After a long delay, they made an offer, but it was so derisory that he refused. It says much for his confidence that he did so; most budding authors would have leapt at the chance to see their work in print, however poor the remuneration, but he believed that he could do better. So the manuscript began another series of journeys back and forth.

By the end of 1919, Beverley had achieved nearly all his Oxford goals, but he had one major ambition left: to be President of the Oxford Union where he had already made his mark as a brilliant speaker. His secret was preparation: he spent hours writing and polishing his speeches, then he learned them by heart until he could give an impression of spontaneity. He also rehearsed the answers to those questions he could anticipate, spicing them with epigrams. His lists of these do not stand the test of the passing years and lie dead on the paper, but, given his talent for timing, he could set his audience roaring with laughter. Bob Boothby, later Lord Boothby, described him in the political context as one of only two undergraduates to command public attention. The other was Hore-Belisha, but Boothby maintained that Beverley was the better of the two. One of the undergraduate magazines, of which there were many published in 1919, said of Beverley:

> Jocular levity,
> Seasoned with brevity,
> Wisdom that's rare,
> Hark to our Beverley,
> Talking so cleverly,
> Young and so fair!

Despite his success, Beverley's moods fluctuated between happiness and depression; sometimes, even when surrounded by friends, he felt a desperate loneliness. Following the visit of a boy to his rooms, he wrote enigmatically, 'How long will these people come and break their hearts before me?' and he confesses his terror of growing old. All was well while he was young and could wield power, but what would happen when his looks faded? His answer was to establish his fame as rapidly as possible, in the hope that it would give him security; thank heaven, he said, for his insatiable ambition. To fend off gloom, he plunged into pleasure and work with equal intensity, but his 'work' was centred on the *Isis* and the *Oxford Outlook*, piano practice and composition, with the minimum time spent on modern history.

Just before the end of term, his Uncle George and Aunt Blanche visited Oxford. Beverley went out of his way to make their visit memorable, taking them round the town, on the river and to a Union debate where he was speaking. He was very pleased that a lunch served in his rooms, at which Nevil Beechman and Neville Barclay were the other guests, was a great success. There was a genuine affection between them all, particularly between Beverley and George with whom he had so much in common. Blanche, with her knowledge and love of the arts, was a lively contributor to the relationship.

After taking his exam, in which he did badly, he spent several hectic days in London with 'the ever-faithful' Humphrey. He noted the stars lunching at the Criterion Restaurant: George Robey was very amusing and Jack Buchanan looked as if he 'doped'. There were nights at the theatre and the ballet, full of amusing people: Ronald Firbank, whom he knew slightly, drunk – 'too awful' – several musical shows, the wonderful Moiseiwitsch at the Queen's Hall; and so on. 'Poor Humphrey', he commented, 'will be ruined!' Following a short stay with Arthur Shipley in Cambridge and a day in London at Liberal headquarters to discuss his plans for the new Club in Oxford, he went down to Torquay. The Pet Hog was drunk, not a propitious omen for the summer. He tried to catch up on work for his degree, for his bad end-of-term results had shamed him into action. His diary tells little of the day-to-day routine, but he wrote with significant brevity on 17 July: 'Pet Hog not drunk.' It was a miserable summer for him, relieved only by 'shallow' periods of happiness, such as a tour of Devon with Arthur Shipley and the family celebration of his twenty-first birthday.

To the ordinary holidaymaker, there were few signs of change in the Queen of Resorts in that first summer of peace but in the large houses a chill reality was dawning. People who had been securely affluent before the war considered themselves hard pressed by the effects of inflation and taxation, but it was to be several years before they abandoned their homes and before the charming Italianate villas became flats or guest houses. In the mean time, they hoped the golden age of the middle class would return, now that the war was over. They were not to know that the style of life they had enjoyed was doomed in the form they had known it. When they moved on, it would be to homes which were easier to run and not so wholly dependent on servants.

The Nicholses at Cleave Court were typical of thousands of similar families in those post-war years: somehow, they made do in the battle to keep up appearances. The social round went on, but there was no general return to the formal dinner and luncheon parties of the old days, and even the afternoon 'At Homes' were a pale imitation of their Edwardian glory. The ladies accepted falling standards and tried not to catch the eye of the parlourmaid who was the same girl whom they, too, had hired especially for such occasions.

John tried to convince Pauline that they should sell Cleave Court but she stubbornly refused. It was only to be a matter of time before, like Madame Ranevskaya in *The Cherry Orchard*, she would be forced to leave, and it was a measure of her strength and of John's weakness that he could not persuade her. He knew only too well, as he paid the household bills, financed Beverley at Oxford and maintained Alan, now condemned by his epilepsy to almost certain unemployment, that it could not last, and sought escape from reality in a haze of alcohol. All Beverley could see was his mother's struggle to maintain not only the façade of normality in the dying social order of Torquay but also the pretence that his father was not a drunkard but a sick man. Her greatest fear was that his addiction might become public knowledge and she went to farcical lengths to preserve secrecy, even burying empty bottles in the garden so that the dustmen should not know. Sometimes John would appear at the 'At Homes', bubbling with *bonhomie*, impeccably groomed, a flower in his buttonhole and his eyeglass firmly in place, to flirt delicately with the ladies. At other times, Pauline prayed that he would not bump about too noisily in the bedroom above, or, worse still, lurch downstairs in search of more liquor. The guests, who must have had some inkling of the situation, joined in the pretence that poor Mr Nichols was unwell again.

His father's behaviour only served to accentuate the boredom and frustration Beverley felt in Torquay compared with the excitement of his recent past and with his future at Oxford. Apart from John's regular outbursts of temper about the financial problems of Cleave Court, for which he blamed his wife entirely, he began to show signs of growing eccentricity. He took to ostentatious displays of activity in the garden, clipping hedges or mowing the lawns. Having done enough to make his point, he then left little notes all over the house reading, 'Your bloody garden is killing me.' He would ferret out old family portraits from the local junk shops which he brought home, announcing that they were pictures of his noble ancestors. His language became cruder, as did his clowning. He would appear with his flies unbuttoned, a tuft of shirt sticking out to simulate a penis, pretending he was unaware of it, or he would tell bawdy little schoolboy jokes which entailed miming a penis with his forefinger. Beverley interpreted this as deliberately designed to humiliate his mother, forgetting that she was more likely to be bored than humiliated.

The climax to John's drinking came on Friday 12 September. Beverley had been playing tennis with the Evans family and had stayed to supper. He arrived home just as a cab drove up with Alan and his father, who was barely capable of moving without assistance. At first Pauline thought he was genuinely ill but it was the usual problem, and Alan had rescued him from a brawl outside the Queen's Hotel. Once inside the house, Alan gave vent to his fury, Beverley supplying a verbal descant. Alan was soon threatening to horsewhip his father and tried to smash into him with his fists, but Pauline prevented this by pulling Alan off him. Momentarily sobered by his son's fury, John escaped up the stairs and locked himself in his bedroom. Pauline tried to calm her sons, then went upstairs and begged John to let her in. They could hear him weeping and crying out, 'I'm a failure.' His drunken hysteria went on into the early hours and only stopped when Beverley threatened to blow in the door with his service revolver and silence him.

After a fitful night, Beverley was woken by shouts from Alan's room. He rushed to him and found him tearing his hair, fighting against an attack of epilepsy. He called his mother, and between them they gradually calmed him down by pouring water and eau-de-cologne over him. Just as he was settling into an exhausted sleep, 'that bestial cur comes in more or less sober and asks to be forgiven. Forgiven! Christ!' Alan swore at him and Beverley shouted him out of the room. Later that day, 'to show his real penitence, he went out, got a bottle of brandy – 30/- (and mother denies herself a new blouse) and locked himself in the coach house. He is now dead to the world.'

These events marked the point at which Beverley's dislike of his father turned to hatred. He poured his feelings out on to the pages of his diary in a passionate frenzy. He longed to kill the man who treated his mother so badly, the mother

> who has sacrificed her life for him and us, who has worked like a slave that we may be happy and keep on in this house, who has in her all the love of Beauty and Colour that she gave to me. I've thought time and again how best I should like to kill him. I want to see him starving, broken and afraid. I would give ten years of my life if tonight I could spit on his corpse. I cannot live in this house with that cur. I shrink into myself, I get clogged up with the stupidity of it, sickened by the smell of spirits, stinted by the constant poverty and maddened by the slow murder of mother. When I get away, I suppose it will be all right again. I shall be 'brilliant'. I shall live in a fool's paradise. I shall receive homage for possibly a few years more. I don't see the end. I can't. I can only hope. I must succeed. I must make good. I must triumph or fail utterly. I must live gloriously or die shamefully, but whatever I do, it will be done in scarlet and written in gold.

There are no fine shadings in his attitude, only black or white. His mother is the saint; he himself, like her, is a victim; his father is a swine, a cad and a bully. He saw his father's desire to be rid of Cleave Court as an attack on Pauline, and failed to realize that a stronger man would have taken the necessary action despite his wife's protestations. He blames the 'poverty' entirely on his father's drinking when the Nicholses were in fact suffering financially for more fundamental reasons. And their 'poverty', as he insisted on describing it, bore no relationship to poverty in the true sense. With a strange logic of his own, he cursed his father for spending thirty shillings on that bottle of brandy when in his opinion his mother needed a new blouse, and yet he accepted his father's money to pay his own extravagant tailor's bills. He could not have known that his mother had her own small fortune and would die with it intact. Beverley was to change his mind about many things but on the question of his father he stuck rigidly to this point of view.

On 15 September he left Torquay to spend a night with George and Blanche followed by another night with Shipley in Cambridge where he was given an antique plate for his birthday. On Thursday, he spent the day in London buying a 'ripping' but very expensive grey satin evening cloak, leaving the latest version of *Prelude* with Chatto and Windus, and having 'a camp lunch' with a friend at which 'I got very drunk'.

Back in Oxford, he began his usual hectic routine, trying to study as well as pushing on the decorating of the new Liberal Club, and rushing about entertaining and being entertained as people arrived for the new term. One morning, he ran into David Maxwell Fyfe who told him that he was starting a Tory paper, the *Oxford Review*, and that the Conservatives would be financing the Carlton Club which he had started with Charles Petre. Beverley did not care for Maxwell Fyfe's air of confidence which was clearly intended to needle him in his Liberal role. This was the same Maxwell Fyfe who was to become a leading figure in the Tory party and finally to become Lord Kilmuir. He was short and thick-set, some might say ugly, with a brilliant mind, ambitious and pugnacious. He was to become wholly concerned with political advancement. A strong puritan ethic governed all he did and his stubbornness attracted much criticism in later life when he became Home Secretary. His name remains associated with his refusal to show clemency in two notorious murder cases. One involved nineteen-year-old Derek Bentley who was actually in police custody when murder was committed by his friend, Christopher Craig, resisting arrest: it was argued that Bentley had murder in mind and so he was hanged. The other case concerned Timothy Evans, subsequently shown to be innocent, who was also hanged on dubious evidence. In addition, Maxwell Fyfe instigated a homosexual witch hunt, of which more later. It is not difficult to imagine his attitude to someone like Beverley in the Oxford of 1919, not only as a political opponent but also as the antithesis of himself and all he represented. His opposition was made manifest in the *Oxford Review*, of which he was the first editor, and in the campaign he and his Carlton Club cronies later conducted against Beverley's first attempt to become President of the Union.

A strike on the railways in October caused general chaos and people talked gloomily of revolution. Beverley did not think there was much chance of that, but he was worried about its effect on the economy and more immediately that the decoration of the Liberal Club was held up because the wallpaper was strike-bound in Scotland. He was discussing this with friends over lunch at the Randolph Hotel when a fracas broke out: the management had ordered three army privates to leave on the grounds that only officers were allowed in the hotel lounge. Beverley, disgusted with this example of class distinction, invited the Tommies to join his table, which they did.

He expected to be trapped in Oxford by the strike one weekend when he had planned to be in London, but Humphrey drove up to collect him and took him back to town where he had booked a 'ripping' suite of rooms at Jermyn Court which had that essential ingredient to Beverley's happiness, a piano. In a crowded Saturday they saw Alice Delysia yet again, then went to the ballet where they collected 'Eric, Alan, Colin, Duggie', whoever they might have been, and several other friends, and went back to the rooms for a party. The next day, Beverley was thrilled to see that the *Sunday Times* had printed his article on 'Anti-British Propaganda in America' – the first English national newspaper to publish him. When Humphrey drove him back to Oxford, Beverley was even more thrilled to find a letter from Chatto and Windus saying that they were to publish *Prelude*. When he told Sligger, the Dean 'merely coughed' and made no comment.

Later in the term the Liberal Club finally opened with great success. Beverley, now Secretary of the Union, began planning to gain the Presidency. As ever, his mood swung from confidence to doubt: he asked himself whether he was liked and then assured himself that he was. He became suspicious of his closest ally, Nevil Beechman, and imagined that he was part of a plot to prevent him speaking at a meeting on Saturday 15 December, at which the principal guest was to be Henry Asquith, ex-Prime Minister and doyen of the Liberal party. Whether such a plot did or did not exist, he set out to lobby everyone concerned and, as a result, gained the star spot at the meeting. At the reception which preceded it, Beverley – dressed in style and complete with his new satin cloak – presented Mrs Asquith with a bouquet and escorted her to the meeting. The speakers included Gilbert Murray, John Masefield, Nevil Beechman, Asquith and finally Beverley himself. Mrs Asquith told him that she had never heard a better speech.

He was very taken with Margot Asquith and more so when she invited him to lunch at her home, The Wharf, where he was one of three guests, the others being her daughter Elizabeth, who was married to Prince Antoine Bibesco, and Lady Bonham-Carter. He received highly flattering attentions from the Asquiths, who were keen to recruit him to their cause against the Lloyd George Liberals: Beverley, as a leading figure in Oxford Liberalism, was just the type of young enthusiast they needed to assist Asquith's return to active politics from the shadows in which circumstances had placed him. At the end of February 1920 the ex-Prime Minister was to win the seat at Paisley and to return to the House of Commons; the night the result was announced there was a great celebration at the University Liberal Club. In a biography of Margot Asquith, it is said that Henry 'Chips' Channon introduced Beverley to her but this is incorrect. He did not meet 'Chips' Channon socially until the following May and then took an instant dislike to the brash, ambitious young American with social pretensions who told him in all seriousness that he was out to capture an heiress who must be of good blood, after which he intended to become a Tory Member of Parliament and achieve a knighthood. (Young Channon married the daughter of the wealthy Earl of Iveagh, and the rest duly followed.) Beverley never understood the secret of Channon's success but finally attributed it to his mastery of the game of snobbery, coupled with his ruthless determination to climb the social ladder. It is probable that Beverley's dislike was based on a recognition of traits which were not dissimilar to his own and his awareness that, as a young man about town, Channon was something of a rival.

Before going home for a quiet Christmas in 1919, Beverley was elected Junior Librarian to the Union in succession to Jack Russell. He was sure that Russell, Maxwell Fyfe and others of the Tory group were potential enemies and should not be underestimated when he made his bid for the Presidency the following term. One way or another, he felt that he was riding high in the Oxford community, but he was brought down to earth by a warning lecture from Sligger on the quality of his academic work.

After Christmas, despite the warning, his main preoccupation was his campaign for the Presidency. Russell had at first refused nomination but had then accepted, so it became a battle between the two of them. Beverley did not really believe that Russell, whom he regarded as a colourless candidate, could possibly defeat him, but he took no chances. In order not to appear so exclusively associated with the Liberals, he attended Labour party meetings and was seen as often as possible in the Tory Carlton Club although he hated almost everyone in it. In other words, he tried to convey the impression that in the matter of the Presidency he was above sectarian politics. There was no doubt that, when it came to the important Union debates, Beverley was the better man.

Two weeks before the election, the national press began reviewing *Prelude*. The *Morning Post* said of it: '. . . a sure mastery of English – the best of all latter-day school stories'. *The Times* was even more effusive: 'The most remarkable study of a boy since Compton Mackenzie's *Sinister Street*, indeed one of the most remarkable studies of a boy that can ever have been written.' It was heady stuff and for the publicity-conscious candidate the reviews could not have been better timed, for everyone in Oxford was now talking about him and, more to the point, buying the book. On top of the world, he consolidated his position by going hither and thither to be seen, and exuding a mixture of confidence and modesty, overlaid with the ever-present charm. However, he had a nagging feeling that, despite all the signs to the contrary, he might still lose.

The final battle between Russell and Beverley came on 24 February in a Union debate on 'The Peace Treaty'. Beverley put his argument with great skill, contending that the treaty spelled economic disaster for Europe. To his disappointment, it was not a full house and although he won in terms of applause, he knew that this was owing as much to the friends he had coerced into attending as to the merits of his case. Until the results of the poll, which took place two days later, he was in a state of misery, unable to do anything but hope. On St David's Day, 1 March, the figures were announced: Nichols had lost by sixty-eight votes.

He was mentally and physically shattered by his failure. Nearly two months of intense effort had been wasted while Russell, who had not made any real effort at all, had triumphed. At this distance of time, it is not clear exactly what happened; possibly his supporters were so convinced that he would win that many did not bother to vote, a situation not unique in the business of elections. Possibly it was a backlash against the publicity he had received for *Prelude* and against the golden-boy image he had cultivated. He was certainly not helped by a last-minute campaign by the Carlton Club Tories who placarded their walls with pro-Russell notices, or by a rumour that, even if he were to win, Beverley would not be in Oxford to take up the Presidency. This rumour was really his own fault because he had jokingly referred to the possibility of his being sent down because of his neglect of academic work. His dismay turned to fury when Russell remarked to him, 'You've made it so very clear from your public utterances that you are going down, that you've put me in a very difficult position.' In other words, Russell, who had at first declined to stand, now appeared to blame Beverley's rumoured departure for forcing him to accept nomination. It is difficult to believe that anyone, including Russell, would actually baulk at the opportunity to be President, and it was, at the least, a graceless comment to the defeated candidate. In a melodramatic entry in his diary, Beverley swore to make Russell and his future wife and children suffer until they wished they'd never been born. He never achieved this over-heated ambition but he did pillory a thinly disguised Russell in the Oxford novel he was to write the following year.

The lesson that Beverley failed to learn from this whole episode was when to keep his mouth shut. For the rest of his life, he would say or write things which afterwards he had cause to regret. There had been a basis of truth in the comments he had made about leaving Oxford, but two days later, Sligger told him he could stay on at Balliol for the rest of the year – which, as Beverley wrote gloomily in his diary, was some consolation. Sligger was a kind-hearted man who tried to avoid sending students down. In the case of Raymond Massey, for example, it was suggested that he leave of his own accord, but the Master, A.L. Smith, let him continue to row in the eight, having advised him that there was no point in his taking his exams. Something similar seems to have happened to Beverley. It may be deduced that he was reprieved so that he could run for the Presidency and that, when he lost, Sligger relented and reprieved him again.

His tutor at this time was the Revd Kenneth Bell who knew that Beverley could produce good results when he worked hard but, despite a determined effort to catch up, Beverley ended the term with poor marks. He hoped that he could make up for lost time during the vacation but he found it increasingly difficult to absorb the intricacies of modern history and this, combined with a deep sense of loss of status following his defeat, thrust him into a sort of melancholia which was not helped by the worsening problems of Cleave Court. There had been two or three bright interludes before he left for the holiday, when he forgot everything in a brief splurge of sex, but the effect of this was temporary. He had also met, at a dinner party, Sir Sidney Greville, an elderly man with a fondness for younger men. He was comptroller to Edward, Prince of Wales and lived in St James's Palace. Before they parted, Greville invited Beverley to stay with him and, as he noted in his diary, this was an opportunity he could not miss.

It is indicative of Beverley's character that the success of *Prelude* could not drive away his melancholia, even though the first edition had attracted excellent reviews and sold out within three weeks. It was over and done with, and the only thing that mattered was the next success, whatever that might be. In many ways this was a sensible attitude, but he did not seem able to enjoy his success. He must surely have been delighted by his mother's pleasure in the book, which was dedicated to her, and by his father's inordinate pride as he paraded him around the town, although he was to say later that he resented this.

Despite a tendency towards sentimentality, *Prelude* remains surprisingly fresh in its account of public school life. Paul, the main character, is a portrait of the author as he would like to have been, with a mother not unlike Pauline who encourages the boy's artistic flair and eccentricities that others do not understand. Significantly, there is no father in the story, he having conveniently died before it begins. There is, however, an uncle who declares that the boy is too effeminate and needs the discipline of a public school to make a man of him. The sequences at school follow Beverley's own experiences closely, except that Paul is a brilliant scholar, which Beverley was not, and wins an Exhibition in modern history at Oxford, which Beverley had failed to do. There is a deeply felt account of a romantic friendship with another boy which could offend no one, and a detailed sequence which describes Beverley's own beliefs about Christianity, his revolt against the manifestation of it in formal religion, both Catholic and Protestant, and sums up his conclusions with a paradox from Bishop Blougram's *Apology*: 'With me, faith means perpetual unbelief.' He challenges the author of *The Loom of Youth* who must, he suggests, have loathed his school (Sherborne) whereas the boys of 'Martinsell', despite all its faults, learn to love it. He develops this idea into a debate on the public school system which is based on a discussion that took place on his visit to Marlborough to research the book and to refresh his memory. The book criticizes the attitudes to education taken by masters and boys, but declares that the school gives the handful of boys who are able to do so the chance to educate themselves, to pierce right through to the heart of everything, be it politics, art or anything that matters in life and say, 'This is truth.' The book ends suddenly with Paul's last letter written from somewhere at the battlefront in France. It is sadly romantic and yet joyful, concluding with a eulogy to 'Martinsell'. Abruptly, the story concludes with Paul's obituary in *The Times*, followed by the quotation, 'Greater love hath no man than this, that a man lay down his life for his friend.'

Beverley said years afterwards that it was only too easy to 'send the book up' and one would not argue with that, but what it displayed was his gift for conveying emotion and his talent for observation. In the mood of 1920, with memories of the war still so fresh, it is hardly likely that his readers put the book down without being deeply moved by the final *coup de théâtre*. *Prelude* captures Beverley's real feelings about Marlborough, with all their inconsistencies. In his autobiography, *The Unforgiving Minute*, he concedes that he must have loved the place although, looking back down the years, he remembers it with more hate than love. On a minor point of accuracy, he says that he wrote *Prelude* when he was a schoolboy, although he actually began it when he was in the army, and most of it was written when he was nineteen.

As usual, Beverley was relieved to get away from Cleave Court after the vacation: 'Life', as he put it in his diary, 'starts once more.' It started on a high note, for Sir Sidney Greville had confirmed his invitation and Beverley went to stay with him at St James's Palace. There was nothing particularly regal about the place, which came as something of a surprise – apart from the sounds of the guard changing and the occasional burst of military music, he might have been in an attractive, old-fashioned house almost anywhere. The real pleasure came when he went out with Sidney, for then everyone bowed and scraped. Beverley enjoyed the reflected glory of what he called 'ridiculous obeisance' as they swept round the West End, finishing up at Alice Delysia's latest show. The next evening, after dinner at the Inner Temple, he met a friend, unidentified in his diary, and they went to Drury Lane to see Pavlova, afterwards calling on Ivor Novello in his flat over the Strand Theatre. This was an important meeting, for it took Beverley straight into the heart of a glittering theatrical set and provided the springboard for his own entry into the theatre as a writer and composer.

Novello's story has been told many times, but most comprehensively in Sandy Wilson's biography. He was one of the most successful British show-business personalities of his time and he remained a star until his sudden death in 1951 at the age of fifty-eight. Although best remembered as the composer of 'Keep the Home Fires Burning' and for a string of musical romances like *The Dancing Years* and *Glamorous Night*, he was also a successful playwright, contributor to revues and the idol of the hundreds of thousands who packed the theatres to see him perform. They also packed the cinemas, for he starred in more than twenty films. He was a man of outstanding physical beauty, with a mellifluous voice tinged with a Welsh accent. Noel Coward, when unknown, envied him and vowed to be as big, if not bigger, than he. Novello's contribution to the theatre might have been recognized with a knighthood, as Coward's was, if he had lived longer, and if a ridiculous prison sentence for a very minor petrol offence had been forgiven, as Coward's minor offence against currency regulations eventually was.

Novello was enchanted with the young author of *Prelude* and took him off to a party at Ned Lathom's house in Cumberland Place. Beverley needed little encouragement to sit at the grand piano in the huge, long, gold room and to play and sing his own compositions. Like many amateur performers, he knew no fear, and his competence, coupled with his charm, carried him through: 'I was a brilliant success and played and sang marvellously.' The next day, by way of contrast, he dined at the Savoy with the future Archbishop of Canterbury, William Temple. His life did not lack variety.

Ned, fifth Earl of Lathom, was one of the reasons why the '20s could be called gay in both the old and the more recent senses of the word. He had inherited a vast fortune which he seemed intent on spending as quickly as possible. His London home was a dream of decadent luxury and his country house in Lancashire – not the family mansion which he did not care for, but Blyth, the dower house – was rebuilt to his taste at enormous expense. His extravagance was legendary. When guests arrived at his houses, the rooms were heady with perfume which footmen dripped into heated spoons so that the aroma burned itself into the air. Everywhere flowers were banked in calculated confusion, and orchids massed in front of long mirrors. The richest foods were served and the best wines treated as if they were no more than bottles of lemonade. Lathom thought nothing of sending a footman in a specially chartered train from Blyth to collect a box of his favourite sweets, or of dictating long letters which he then had sent as telegrams. One of his favourite scents was 'Suivez Moi, Jeune Homme' and it summed up his attitude to life. The young men who followed him were amply rewarded with money or with lavish presents from Cartier. He was mad about the theatre and spent a fortune on staging masques in which his wide circle of friends eagerly participated, dressed in costumes of extravagant fantasy. Beverley was later to appear in several of these entertainments. Lathom also invested in the professional theatre and in theatre people with mindless generosity, often with results that were disastrous for his dwindling bank balance. He was witty, kind and completely foolish, and the unscrupulous took full advantage of him.

From Lathom's point of view, Beverley's qualifications for joining his set were obvious: he was pretty, gay and talented. Later on, Beverley, Collie Knox, Noel Coward and Ivor Novello, all of whom had reason to be grateful to Lathom, were among the small number who rallied round when he was eventually penniless, but most of the young men who had followed him kept well away. He died of consumption in distressing circumstances in 1930. In his autobiography, *All I Could Never Be*, Beverley carefully distanced himself from Lathom, perhaps out of prudence, but he paid a graceful tribute to him, as well he might. Lathom used his considerable influence to help his career and, indeed, he may well have been the mysterious millionaire who, several years later, offered to keep him so that he could concentrate on musical composition. Beverley did not wish to be quite so obviously a kept boy and declined, a decision he later regretted. But in April 1920, the exotic world of Lathom added yet another dimension to the young Nichols's already broad knowledge of life.

Back in Oxford, Beverley ordered a new dinner suit, another suit in white, a pair of very pale grey flannels with a mauvish jacket and waistcoat, and made a resolution to work hard. He would get up early, exercise before breakfast, make up his mind what needed to be done, and then do it. 'Do try, Bev!' he wrote in his diary. He did try, but his tutors, Professor Henry Davis and the Revd Kenneth Bell, did not think he tried hard enough. When he read an essay to Professor Lewis Namier on the French Revolution, that gentleman pointed out that it had been cribbed from Hilaire Belloc, and delivered a brilliant oration on the subject which made Beverley realize how superficial his own work had been.

Although he made strenuous efforts to study, he was preoccupied once again with the elections for the Presidency of the Union. This time, he took nothing for granted, and instead of rushing about dispensing *bonhomie* to all he trod very carefully, intent on creating an impression of reliability and maturity. This new approach entailed mixing with all factions, however boring those factions might be to him, and it also meant suppressing his normal exuberance in favour of quiet, scholarly charm. He went out of his way to be pleasant to people like his hated enemy Russell and Maxwell Fyfe, entertaining them to lunch or dinner or at a series of tea-parties in his rooms. At the Tory Carlton Club, he tried to overcome what he believed was an underlying hostility to him: he had, of course, many friends and, he hoped, supporters in the Tory group, men like Bob Boothby whom he much admired, but it did not follow that they would actually vote for him. He penetrated the Labour faction, giving them the impression that he was really a socialist at heart.

He also took a hard look at his Liberal allegiance. Up until that time the Club, which he had helped to found, was pro-Asquith and anti-Lloyd George, but he had gradually tired of the Asquith followers, however much he still liked Asquith and his redoubtable wife. He knew that he could be an Asquith candidate if he should choose to take up politics seriously, but he saw that the battle between the two wings of the Liberal party was increasingly irrelevant in the national context, and his instinct took him towards Lloyd George who, with his Coalition Liberals, appeared to have a more sensible approach to the country's problems. Matters were brought to a head when the New Reform Club was inaugurated in Oxford at the instigation of Lloyd George. Beverley had signed a manifesto deploring this, but he now reneged, sympathizing with the Coalition Liberals but maintaining his ties with the old Liberal faction at the same time, and remarking that keeping in with all the political groupings in Oxford was 'enough to kill one'.

On top of this tactical social round, Beverley had his real social life with the aesthetic set. His intimate friends were named only Teddy, Desmond and Dick in his diary, and perhaps because of his new image, he found the chitter-chatter of what he called 'the bitches' suddenly tiresome. To complicate polling week, Mrs Evans and her daughter Rose, neighbours in Torquay, arrived on holiday and assumed that Beverley would entertain them. He did his best but it was a great strain on the anxious candidate. And then the day before polling he met Norrie, a friend of an old chum, Ernest Roberts. According to Beverley's description, Norrie was all that a man should be, very masculine, very natural, chivalrous, kind and 'rippingly good looking'. Over lunch at the Clarendon, the air was electric with mutual sexuality, but Norrie was in Oxford only for the day and Beverley had to spend the afternoon 'vote-cadging'. That evening he took Norrie to the Mitre for dinner before seeing him on to his train. When he eventually returned to his rooms, a passionate letter from Norrie was waiting for him. He vowed to keep it always but then decided it would be prudent to destroy it.

His brother Paul came for polling day with Ernest Roberts, but Beverley was hardly aware of them. He remembered walking endlessly round the streets trying, without appearing too obvious about it, to stir up last-minute support. Finally, he went back to his rooms, dreading the result and attempting to keep his equilibrium by playing the piano. Suddenly, Paul dashed in with the news: Beverley had won an overwhelming victory and was President of the Union.

That night Beverley wrote in his diary that life was good and, with a typical Nichols touch, added that at last he could wear suede shoes. The following day, telegrams of congratulation poured into his rooms and his celebrations reached a climax at a concert in the evening at which Irene Scharrer played Chopin, releasing all the emotion pent up inside him in a kind of spiritual orgasm.

Before the business of the Union got under way and took up all his attention, an episode with Norrie serves to illustrate a problem characteristic of his personal relationships throughout his adult life. Ernest and Norrie collected Beverley in their car for a weekend in Cambridge with a boy called Eddy, whom Beverley had met briefly in Professor Dent's home. Although on the car journey Norrie fondled Beverley and made it clear that he could not wait to get him into bed, he promptly switched his attention to Eddy once they arrived in Cambridge. That night Beverley slept alone or, to be more accurate, lay awake in a state of frustrated fury and tears while Eddy and Norrie shared the adjacent bedroom.

Somehow, Beverley managed to conceal his feelings the next morning and took Norrie off to see Shipley. Norrie behaved as if nothing had happened and gave Beverley the impression that he was the only person who mattered to him. In the afternoon, Ernest, Norrie and Beverley drove to London and after dinner at the Café Royal, Norrie saw Beverley off on the last train to Oxford, Beverley by now even more infatuated and the matter of Eddy forgiven. On the train, he drafted a long love-letter which he completed and posted the next day. The reply he received showed a complete indifference to his intensity of feeling and Beverley wrote a bitter note in response. This produced a letter of 'utter contrition', as well as one from Ernest Roberts expressing sympathy and inviting him to join them for a few days in London, followed by a weekend on a friend's houseboat moored at Henley. When Beverley arrived at West Kensington, where the two men shared a flat, there was an atmosphere of constraint until Beverley went into his bedroom to unpack. Norrie followed him in and all reserve then broke down. This happy state of affairs lasted for two days, but Beverley was under no illusion, knowing that his own affections were invariably short lived. There will be, he told himself, 'rocks ahead'. It is just as well that he adopted this attitude, for who should arrive to accompany them to Henley but the detestable Eddy, with his 'bad complexion and a Cockney accent'. Instantly, Norrie was all over him and Beverley was forgotten. The weekend, not surprisingly, was a complete disaster. Once again, he tried to put a brave face on it and when they were joined by a boy called 'Steegy', he made a bid for the newcomer – only to be outflanked by Norrie who finished up with both Eddy and Steegy.

Beverley collected his things from Mornington Avenue Mansions on the Monday, resolving never to enter the flat again and never to have anything more to do with this ménage. He had been humiliated beyond endurance by people whom he now saw as inferior to himself and he did not understand how he had allowed himself to be so cheap. His problem was largely of his own making: he was searching for a companion to fit his preconceived ideas of what a perfect mate should be, someone who would be both slave and master, and adapt to his volatile changes of mood. It took him many years to discover that such a creature did not exist and that he would have to make compromises.

During the long summer vacation, Beverley lost no time in seeking opportunities to advance himself. In August, articles appeared in the *Saturday Review*, in the *Daily News* and *Outlook*, which brought him a total of £10. Each of these articles dealt with *A Man of the World's Dictionary*, published in 1822, which he said he had found in an old bookshop. The cynicism of the definitions greatly amused Beverley. With a nudge in the direction of Coalition Governments, he quoted the definition of 'coalition':

'A combination of marauders to plunder a neighbour but which is most frequently broken by division of the spoil.' He points out that modern epigrammists are not as modern as they might think: 'Youth is the age of a man till he is twenty and of a woman till she is fifty.' Democracy is a 'system of government which can be sustained only by virtue. It is rarely durable.' Truth he defined as 'the last refuge of the liar and the knave.' The Virtuous Man is 'a name given to him who has the art of concealing his vices'. Beverley asked if the author would alter any of his definitions if he were alive today.

He picked up another fee for an article in the *Westminster Gazette* on the subject of politics in Oxford, and there were further payments for items in the *Express*, but the most successful from a publicity point of view was a letter in the *Morning Post* for which he was paid £4. This was in reply to a letter written by a 'Bewildered Parent' bewailing the attitudes of modern youth, and displaying narrow-minded prejudice about almost everything, from the undue familiarity of children who had forgotten the rule that they should be seen and not heard, to 'hasty marriages'. It boomed pompously that, the way things were going, the young might take over, and demanded: 'Will our next Soviet be a Soviet of Youth?' This was a source of rich pickings for Beverley, who replied as President of the Oxford Union Society when, as several correspondents peevishly pointed out, he was technically only President-Elect. He based his reply on the Bewildered Parent's assertion that 'the wisdom and experience hitherto associated with Age are quietly but effectively being put on the shelf.' Was this surprising, Beverley asked, when there was a monument to this wisdom which stretched through France, decorated with the bones of British soldiers and the crosses of their graves? As for a Soviet of Youth, why not? At Oxford, preparations were already under way for students to have a voice in the government of their colleges. Self-determination was the order of the day. What sort of world had wisdom and experience produced? 'Why not let Youth have its try? We have tried everything else and every time it has failed. Youth has ceased knocking at the door, already the citadel is being stormed. Youth has scaled the heights and is waving its banner in the sky.'

It was calculated to provoke, and it did. Letters flooded in from infuriated parents together with a long, well-argued piece from the President of the Oxford Carlton Club who advised the Bewildered Parent not to take Mr Nichols too seriously. 'Despite his eloquence, he has failed to make good his claim to speak in the name of youth.' In the body of his letter, Beverley had compared the spirit of Kipling unfavourably with the passion of Sassoon, which aroused as much controversy as his support for a Soviet of the young. The anger of some of the respondents with references to 'swollen heads' and 'know-alls' was to be expected but the neatest reply came in the form of a sonnet which ended:

Self-advertising, though done ne'er so cleverly,
Is not good form at Oxford, my dear Beverley.

Good form or not, the publicity was exactly what Beverley had hoped for and he was delighted when the debate spilled over into other newspapers, with headlines like 'Youth on the Rampage'. In the *Saturday Review*, an unnamed writer attacked Beverley as a defender of upstarts, 'who has no claim to attention beyond the fact that he has published a public school novel of negligible interest'. Yet another piece in the same magazine purported to come from a fellow pupil from Marlborough who claimed to know Beverley well, 'but the least said, the better'. He attacked Beverley for *Prelude* and its 'gross bad taste' in picturing his housemaster as a ludicrous man who thought of nothing but games. What this had to do with the Bewildered Parent was by no means clear, but it added fuel to the debate on Nichols. The *Saturday Review* gave Beverley space to reply. The gentleman from Marlborough was given short shrift: with his tongue firmly in his cheek, Beverley commented that 'nowadays fiction is becoming more and more biography, with the result that biography is today the only province of literature where we can be quite certain that we are soaring in the realms of pure imagination. *Prelude* has no more to do with facts than has the letter of your correspondent.' He then dealt with the other article and referred readers to his original letter in the *Morning Post* rather than to the falsifications of his argument which had appeared since. 'I am not fighting those who are old in years but those who are old in spirit. As it was in the war, so has it been in the peace.' The Treaty of Versailles, he continued, was saturated with the spirit of a man (Clemenceau) who was living in the world of 1870 which did not consider the ideals of the League of Nations worthy of attention. It was an argument to which Beverley was to return in the years that followed. He prophesied that the revengeful terms of the Peace Treaty were such that Germany would be forced by economic pressure to fight again. This was to lead to the accusation that he was pro-German, by those who could not see what lay ahead. The lesson was eventually learned the hard way: after the Second World War Germany's place in the economic structure of Europe was supported, not destroyed.

All this fuss over his letter to the *Morning Post* was very gratifying, particularly when reports of it appeared in the American press. To add a final touch, *Punch* made fun of him in two of its articles. It was a sure indication of growing fame.

During this long vacation, Beverley worked hard to catch up with his studies which had been so badly neglected and, between times, began work on a new novel. He had discussed the theme of this with Raymond Savage (of the literary agents Curtis Brown) who was keen on the idea. The book was to be set in America and had as a working title *The Democrats*. Savage suggested that, once it was published in Britain and the USA, Beverley should let them arrange a lecture tour for him, broadly following the route he had taken in 1918. He could not get to grips with *The Democrats* and he eventually abandoned it, but he still hoped for a lecture tour as soon as possible.

Back in Oxford for the Michaelmas Term, Beverley divided his time between study and his duties as President of the Union. It was one of the happiest times of his life and it was generally agreed that he was a brilliant President. (After Beverley had left Oxford, a successor President was described by the *Isis* as at last having the ability to restore the popularity and position of Union debate it had achieved under Mr Beverley Nichols and which it had lost after his departure.) He was particularly gratified when Winston Churchill accepted his invitation to speak against a motion in favour of the immediate dissolution of the Coalition Government. Needless to say, Winston carried the day and the motion was defeated. Beverley also persuaded a popular personality of the time to speak, a scoundrel called Horatio Bottomley who eventually went to prison for swindling the public with his Victory Bond scheme.

At the end of term, Beverley left Oxford for good and the *Isis*, the paper he had restored to its pre-war importance, wrote a long valedictory. It listed his successes and said of his Presidency: 'He is one of the most popular and, at the same time, one of the most polished speakers the Union has ever had.' Referring to his ambition to compose, it commented: 'Oxford doesn't give people like him much time,' and it ended:

And what of Beverley at home, the domestic Beverley? I'm afraid there is nothing sensational to narrate. He is just extraordinarily good company. He has the secret of eternal youth. It is true that he is addicted to the prevailing vice of wearing suede shoes, but that, no doubt, will pass away when he has grown up. He has nothing in him of that most poisonous of creatures, the Varsity snob. He chooses his friends for no other reason than he likes them. And you will find that whether they agree or not with his various enthusiasms (and some of them are a little wild), they will stick to him throughout his life. And so, Beverley, you can depart with the blessing of 'The Isis' and its readers and go on your way rejoicing.

· 7 ·

Future indefinite

1920–1921

BEVERLEY's version of his departure from Oxford and the immediate aftermath goes like this:

> My career at Oxford was exceptional but in the middle of it, after only eighteen months, when I was on the crest of a wave, father abruptly withdrew all financial support. As a result, the degree I obtained was an MA designed for ex-officers which carried no academic distinction. If he had given me notice, I might have been able to raise money. I don't know why he behaved as he did; to try and find an answer, one would have to understand the labyrinth of the alcoholic's mind. He simply said, 'Enough is enough.' I was faced with a stack of unpaid bills from wine merchants, florists and tailors. All I had were my scanty earnings from *Prelude* and these were swallowed up by keeping him in whisky and helping out with the housekeeping.

This story is pure nonsense. By the time he wrote it, his obsessive hatred of his father made anything which could be twisted against him into 'truth'. First, Beverley obtained a BA, not an MA, and his assertion that it was of no academic distinction would have been challenged by his contemporaries. Second, John Nichols did not withdraw support on the spur of an alcoholic moment. The plan agreed with his son was that he should obtain a degree after his seven terms at University and then study for his Bar exams. All the arrangements had been made and Beverley had signed his bond at the Inner Temple on 18 September 1919. His father had committed himself to several years of providing support until Beverley started to earn enough to keep himself. If his father had killed this prospect by refusing to fulfil his promise, why did Beverley not say so? It would have made a more convincing story. It is more likely that he decided to abandon law and put forward an alternative plan that he should continue at Oxford. In his exasperation and disappointment that his hopes for his son were thwarted, John may well have cried, 'Enough is enough.' Beverley had no income of his own apart from an army gratuity which had soon disappeared and a few pounds here and there for his writing; everything was paid for by John Nichols, who had also spent a small fortune educating the two older sons. The story of Beverley paying for his father's whisky and helping out with the household bills does not bear examination. The Nicholses were short of money, but not as short as all that: indeed, by dropping out of law, Beverley relieved them of a considerable financial burden. It is also difficult to see what the extra years at Oxford might have achieved. His academic record was not good and if he had studied for a better degree, what career lay at the end of it? Beverley offers no clues.

He paints a miserable picture of the first few months after leaving Oxford. He went back to Cleave Court because he had no alternative, he tells us, apart from offers from people which depended on his going to bed with them. Having refused opportunities which had sexual conditions, he said that he was forced to write his novel about Oxford, a process he claimed he loathed because he had no urge to do it. Before this, he tried desperately to get a job, even to the extent of advertising his services in *The Times*, but without success. His friend Sir Arthur Shipley wrote to Henry Asquith on his behalf, apparently without Beverley's knowledge. Asquith pointed out in reply that he would be glad to help in any way he could but commented that it was perhaps just as well if life had a few curves and zigzags to start with. As for offering employment, he could only quote Abraham Lincoln: 'There are more horses than oats.'

Beverley never mentioned the unrealized American novel in his autobiography. He also omitted his foray into politics. After his flirtation with the Lloyd George Liberals, he had switched back to the Asquith fold, and early in the year spoke at public meetings in his favour. The press reported his speeches made at Bethnal Green and Torquay, and there were others elsewhere. Asked at Bethnal Green what he thought of the industrial policies of the Conservative and Labour parties, he replied that the Liberals were opposed to the Conservatives' blind faith in capitalism at one extreme and to Labour's doctrine of State control and nationalization at the other. Liberals believed in judging each case on its merits, and not sticking to doctrines for their own sakes. If a case were made for nationalizing a particular industry, it would have to ensure the betterment of the workers, make the industry more financially sound and benefit the community as a whole. He went on to condemn the General Election of 1918 as disreputable and disgusting: the government had promised a land fit for heroes, a paradise within a matter of months, but when Asquith had pointed out what nonsense this was and warned of extremely hard times ahead, the electorate had refused to listen. Amid the hysteria generated by government supporters, the Liberals had kept their heads and told the truth, but had lost parliamentary seats for their pains.

A Torquay newspaper, commenting on his impressive performance as a speaker, said that Mr Nichols might be the candidate the local Liberals were seeking. There is no direct evidence that Beverley sought a career in politics but he was very close to Henry Asquith and his Liberal entourage. Two of his contemporaries, Hore-Belisha and Boothby, thought at the time that he had the necessary abilities for Parliament but, many years afterwards, Lord Boothby said that Beverley was too gentle for politics and could not have stood that rough life. This may well be true, and could explain why, at a later stage in his career when he was a famous personality, Beverley declined to stand as a Conservative candidate.

Apart from appearing on Liberal platforms, he was quickly establishing himself as a feature writer in the press. Newspapers were looking for new names and in his capacities as ex-President of the Union and a proven writer, Beverley was an obvious candidate. In 1921, he wrote for the *Sunday Times*, the *Daily Express*, the *Daily Mail*, the *Daily News* and the *Daily Mirror*. In America his writing appeared in the *Weekly Review*, *Outlook* and the *New York Evening Post*. His subjects were as diverse as the papers themselves, ranging from 'The Emancipation of English Women' to 'Have You Got Telephone Ear?' a witty article on the maladies produced by modern inventions. An exercise in irony warned of the increasing return to Victorianism after the wild licence which had followed the war; it cited the erection of barriers by the Serpentine so that Londoners should not be led astray by the spectacle of shivering, semi-nude bathers, and he pointed to the film star 'Fatty' Arbuckle who overnight became the object of hysterical vituperation when falsely accused of causing the death of a girl by a particularly revolting form of rape. Do we really want the sham of Victorian virtue, the article asked, warning that Hell knows no fury like that of a reformed sinner. Readers of the *Daily Mail* were instructed light-heartedly on how to speak in public, how to make their own old-fashioned pot-pourri and how to compose a popular song. Often, however, there was a serious slant to the work. In the *Daily News* he hit on a device which enabled him to make serious points in the guise of humour. He created an awful child called Crystabel who, with perfect reasonableness, asked an increasingly impatient parent awkward questions about everything from Sinn Fein to the problems of post-war Britain. He later developed this satirical approach in the full-length *For Adults Only*.

In addition to this steady output for the press and his political activities, Beverley was also hard at work on the Oxford novel, *Patchwork*, which he completed in four months. It was a sequel to *Prelude* whose hero, Paul Trevelyan, was resurrected as Ray Sheldon. The story was simply a retelling of Beverley's own experience as recorded in his diaries, with a strong dash of imagination. He forestalled any repetition of the criticism he had received for basing his characters on real people in *Prelude* by stating boldly that not only had he used real people but he had also received their approval for doing so; what was more, they had read what he had to say about them and had raised no objections. It is difficult, however, to believe that his old antagonist Russell approved of his counterpart in the novel, Panton, for, as he had sworn to do, Beverley avenged himself by painting a portrait of a mature student (Russell was nearly thirty) who was a fool and the antithesis of everything an Oxford undergraduate should be.

The main difference between *Patchwork* and his own life was that the fictional story ends after Sheldon loses the election for President of the Union to Panton. His mother, Lady Sheldon (another idealized portrait of Pauline Nichols) is taken ill and Sheldon rushes to her sickbed at her villa in Cannes, but arrives too late. He spends the night kneeling at her bedside, the room heavy with the scent of roses and the sickly aroma of anaesthetic. Her death affects him so deeply that he cannot face student life which he now sees as shutting out the harsh brutality of the real world. Instead of returning to Oxford, he plunges into writing, and two years later he is in New York, having become a successful playwright. Someone asks him why he likes New York and he replies that it is true to modern life, whereas Oxford is a dream world, a patchwork of colour and emotion. But while he is praising modernity with an almost fanatical fervour, the grief he has buried within himself suddenly surfaces. Sheldon feels desperately lonely, and inexplicably, he longs for the Oxford he has just disparaged, the city that belonged to youth, to enthusiasm, to impulse and to laughter.

As he had done in *Prelude*, Beverley gave the new book a bitter-sweet emotional ending. He was to comment fifty years later that the death of Lady Sheldon was what he wanted for his own mother, to relieve her of the suffering of her life at Cleave Court, but neither Mrs Trevelyan in the earlier book nor Lady Sheldon bore much resemblance to Pauline Nichols as she really was. Both fictional counterparts were what he would have liked her to be. Pauline loved Beverley but she loved her other sons as much and, to Beverley's constant anger, she loved her husband. Perhaps he wanted her to be like Ivor Novello's mother who devoted her whole life to her son and accepted his homosexuality because it meant that no other woman would ever replace her in his affections.

Patchwork was reviewed in every leading publication. His friend Leslie Hore-Belisha said in the *Observer*: 'At last! Here is not only a novel which will live but one which has been lived.' Alec Waugh in the Labour newspaper, the *Daily Herald*, was critical: Nichols had little gift for the presentation and interpretation of character and his book was a study of only one person, the author. His strength lay in the description of speeches for the Union which suggested his future should be in politics or at the Bar where success comes through the spoken, not the written, word. But Waugh called him 'one of the most important figures of the younger generation'. The *Saturday Review* said the book was a surprising advance on 'the jejune and wholly derivative *Prelude*. He has produced a novel wholly delightful, which at once takes a distinguished place in the gallery of University fiction.' The *Spectator* was cross about what it saw as the motives behind the book: 'He wishes to amuse himself and his reader. He wishes to gain reputation. He wishes to have written books.' The *Sunday Times*'s criticism ended: 'It would be unjust to ignore the force and energy of the narrative and the extraordinary insight into some phases of youth in the present day.' The wittiest and most perceptive article came from the *Morning Post* which described the author as being here, there and everywhere: 'He is everything, anything, something and nothing in the same twinkle of time. He is a good window-dresser both on and off the stage. He is so replete with pretty, surreptitious scintillations as to resemble a Persian kitten being stroked by seven old maids on a frosty night.' It also remarked on Beverley's assertions about real people in the story: 'The debagged person has been allowed to see the manuscript and raised no objection. Others who act as their own publicity agents, take note of this ingenious innovation. If any objection were to be raised to *Patchwork*, it would come from those whose careers and characters have been libellously left out.'

On balance, the book's reception in Oxford was good, with a rave review from the *Oxford Chronicle*. If *Patchwork* had been published today and caused a similar stir, young Mr Nichols would have been on endless chat shows and heard in interviews, but even without the benefits of television and radio he was not far short of becoming a household name. The *Bystander* described him as 'the author of the moment with the book of the moment.'

The present-day reader going through *Patchwork* might be surprised that in some reviews there was criticism of the sexual content, which now seems mild, to say the least. It centres on a sequence when Ray impulsively leaps on a bus going to the East End. The rhythm of the bus seems to have an almost sexual stimulation. (The *Daily Express* got into a proper tizzy of moral indignation at this: had Mr Nichols ever travelled on a bus, it demanded – the writer apparently being unaware that the pulsating motion of the engine gave most lusty young men an erection.) Ray surveys his fellow passengers: there is a fat policeman, a pasty-faced clerk and a prostitute, her face aflame with artifice and with hair of tinsel gold. He imagines himself in bed with her. What is life, he asks himself, if it is not a vast form of prostitution of the brain or the heart or the body? When she gets off the bus, he follows and then stops her. She assumes her professional smile, he invites her to have dinner with him. While they eat, she talks about her life, assuming that they will go back to her room afterwards, but he does not want her services. He gives her a few pound notes and escapes into the street, hoping she will not feel humiliated or angry. He is surprised by the feeling of excitement at what he realizes was a very ordinary encounter. If such an incident was so exciting, he wonders, what would it be like to preside over Bacchanalian orgies, playing a thousand parts in a thousand different costumes? Though this said quite a lot about Beverley, it hardly qualified for censure. The readers, not to mention the *Daily Express*, would have swooned with shock if he had told the true story, for his real pick-up had been a young male prostitute, a sad and pathetic person. Whatever Beverley's initial intentions might have been, all sexual desire left him as he got to know the young man over a meal in a café, and he felt profoundly sorry for him. There were other coded references to sex in *Patchwork* but these were so obscure that only his closest friends would have been able to interpret them. It infuriated Beverley that he could not write honestly about his sexual tastes. He did produce a homosexual romance a few years later, but so crafted as to avoid public awareness of what it was really about.

The advance for *Patchwork* had been in the region of £100, which gave him plenty of pocket money. Many friends were ready to welcome him with open arms – some quite literally; if all else failed, there was always the faithful Humphrey. For a time he stayed again with Sir Sidney Greville at St James's Palace but this soon palled, particularly as his host hid him from sight whenever Queen Mary dropped in. Beverley wanted very much to be presented and asked why he was not. Sir Sidney did not tell him that his having a pretty young man about the place might create the wrong impression; he simply smiled, put his hands on his shoulders, and said, 'My dear Beverley, don't you ever look in the glass?' While he was there, Beverley noted the constant flow of telephone calls from the Prince of Wales who, it seemed, did nothing without consulting his comptroller. When should he wear a dinner jacket as opposed to tails? Could he be seen in an open car without a hat? The longest discussions concerned the placing of guests at luncheons and dinners. The Prince liked to seat important guests like ambassadors as far away from himself as possible and give the places of honour to his friends; Sir Sidney constantly dreaded the possibility of a diplomatic incident.

Beverley also stayed for a few weeks with his brother Paul who was by then curate at St Peter's, Eaton Square and had a flat in Pimlico which Beverley thought 'a hateful little slum'. It was while he was there that he received an invitation to the Duchess of Marlborough's home in Carlton House Terrace, for dancing. Having committed the social gaffe of arriving too early, he suffered the humiliation of waiting while the guests who had been invited to dinner finished the meal. Those who, like himself, were to appear later for the dance eventually drifted in. He was not able to explain why this incident remained indelibly fixed in his memory, but it was probably because he was angry with himself for not knowing the social rules. It was not a mistake he would repeat.

During the summer of 1921, Beverley joined the family in rooms at

Portsmouth which they had taken while Cleave Court was let, to supplement John Nichols's income. The mention of this in *The Unforgiving Minute* puts his father in a poor light as Beverley describes his mother dragging a basket of logs across the floor to hide a burn mark in the carpet, a memento of one of the occasions when father had fallen into the fireplace. Beverley needed peace to complete a novel which he had begun the previous December. In a letter accompanying his Christmas present to Cousin Cornie he had written: 'It is to be called *Self* and I hope it will be rather more worthy than the last.' When he finished it, he sent it off to Chatto and Windus and waited hopefully for a favourable reaction. In the mean time, one of his songs, 'Eve', appeared in the André Charlot revue *A to Z* at the Prince of Wales Theatre. The show starred Jack Buchanan and Gertrude Lawrence and featured the Trix Sisters who performed his number; other contributors were Ivor Novello and Irving Berlin. It was a small but vital step towards Beverley's ambitions in the theatre.

· 8 ·

Greek tangle

1921–1922

WHILE he was waiting for Chatto and Windus to deliver their verdict on *Self*, Beverley received a letter from them, dated 4 October 1921, containing a startling proposition. Would he care to go to Athens under the special protection of the Greek royal family? He would be given access to secret archives to enable him to write a book containing sensational information that would restore the prestige of King Constantine and persuade the British government to recognize him. As publishers, they regarded this as an adventure and he must also see it as such. The advance would be £50, with all expenses paid by the Greek government. The proposal must be treated in the strictest confidence.

Beverley was staggered by the letter; whatever the outcome might be, it was a wonderful opportunity to see Greece at no cost to himself and to enter the highest circles in Greek society. He accepted by the next post. In due course, he went to a briefing in London, the main point of which was to emphasize the secrecy and delicacy of the assignment. Naturally, he could give limited information to his family but no one else must know where he was going or why. He was warned that the British Legation in Athens did not have formal diplomatic contact with the royal family and he could therefore expect no help from them. The drama of the situation appealed very much to his sense of theatre and he entered fully into the conspiracy, though, despite the clandestine nature of the affair, he travelled under his own name. As it transpired, any pseudonym would not have succeeded, for no sooner had he settled into the boat train at Victoria Station than a young man said to him, 'You're Beverley Nichols!' Momentarily thinking that this was an indication of his fame, he admitted that he was, but the young man continued, 'I was at Oxford with you.' Beverley could not remember ever having set eyes on him, but 'His name was Lamb and he was a lamb and very charming, so we agreed to eat together.'

The intricacies of Balkan politics from 1912 onwards – the background to Beverley's assignment – are so complicated as to defy succinct explanation, but at the time of the Great War Venizelos, the leader of the Greek government who was alleged to be in the pay of the French, wanted to join the Allies. His motive was to drive back the Turks and to restore the Hellenic Empire. King Constantine wanted Greece to remain neutral, and forced Venizelos out of office, but the leader formed a rebel government in Crete and declared war on Germany and Serbia, later moving to Salonika which the British and French took with his backing. Constantine, stubbornly continuing to support a policy of neutrality, was forced to abdicate in 1917, but he was returned to power in 1920. Venizelos failed to gain Anatolia at the Peace Conference after the Great War and declared war on Turkey. (This led to his defeat in elections and he finally fled to France in 1935 after an unsuccessful uprising against the Greek government.) The opportunist manoeuvrings of Britain and France during the Great War did not reflect much credit on either country, their crude anti-royalist propaganda making exaggerated use of the fact that Constantine's Queen was the sister of the Kaiser.

Beverley did not know exactly what he faced but was happily absorbed in the pleasures of the journey, though Mr Lamb was a rather loquacious and exhausting companion, and Beverley sometimes wished he were alone. His wish was granted when Lamb was hauled off the train by the Italian authorities and Beverley never saw him again. All went well until the train entered Yugoslavia, when it travelled more and more slowly, and acquired broken-down carriages which were packed with white-faced people peering mournfully out of filthy windows. In Zagreb there was a long delay, so he alighted with the other passengers. The station was full of soldiers in ragged uniforms, looking half starved and hopeless. In the sidings were derelict cattle-trucks crudely converted into homes with the help of old packing-cases, from which dirty children and unkempt women peered at the strangers. The train eventually arrived in Belgrade late at night, more than a day behind schedule, and next morning the first-class passengers discovered, to their horror, that the restaurant car had vanished overnight together with the broken-down carriages; all that was left were the first-class sleeping compartments and the engine. The sleeping-car attendant, the only official left behind, offered no explanation but declared, with complete indifference, that they would have to find their own food.

The furious passengers split into groups and set off. Beverley joined forces with a lone English girl and a Greek couple. They walked into Belgrade, assuming that the capital of Yugoslavia would be a Balkan version of Paris with cafés and food shops in abundance, but the streets were silent and desolate, the shops empty of goods. Everywhere, poorly dressed soldiers slouched against buildings, though their officers, Beverley noted, were well fed and smart, like characters out of an operetta. After combing the bitterly cold streets, the travellers found a café and breakfasted on bread, rancid butter and warmed-up coffee. Near the station, there was an open-air market of sorts, and they bought bread, some apples and a crude kind of chocolate which, with a drink of water, was to form Saturday's lunch. Beverley jotted down his impressions of the local people: women who might have sat for Leonardo da Vinci, and 'such men!' as Michelangelo would have been proud to paint. When they finally returned to the station, there was a fuss over luggage when an official threatened to confiscate it unless the passengers paid a fee which worked out at the equivalent of £1 per item.

The train set off again and lumbered into Nisch late that night. The passengers, cold and hungry, found a café, dirty beyond description, with a display of cold boiled fish and a confection of toffee mixed with stewed apple. There was no food at all at their next stop but the following day they managed to buy some bread, olives and tea. Beverley noted in his diary that the tea probably prevented the semi-hysterical English girl from committing suicide. Somewhere along the journey, another broken-down carriage had been added, packed with soldiers who sang mournful songs. Beverley wrote that he did not think he would forget that sound for the rest of his life.

At last the train crossed the border into Greece and stopped in the early morning at Ghev-Gelli. It was like stepping into spring: the sun was bright, the skies blue and the passengers cheered up and ate their first proper meal for days. Back in the train, Beverley was formally welcomed to Greece by a young officer who handed him sealed letters and announced that he was henceforth under the protection of the government. The officer was so beautiful that Beverley found it difficult to speak. As the train started, a platoon of smart soldiers presented arms while the officer saluted: what the other passengers made of this, Beverley does not record. In Salonika the performance was repeated, but this time he was welcomed by the Chief of Police. The combination of his reception, the excitement of seeing the countryside, and absorbing the atmosphere of Greece was overwhelming. Late on Wednesday he arrived in Athens, his journey having taken eight days.

He was in the middle of dinner at the Grande Bretagne hotel, which he described as a smaller version of the Ritz, when a bouncy Englishman, Stuart Hay, arrived. It appeared that he was the architect of the entire scheme, a go-between who would introduce Beverley to the royal family and to everyone else he needed to know. He dragged Beverley off to meet a former government minister and then to a café where Hay chattered enthusiastically about his plans to exonerate Constantine, while Beverley tried to keep awake.

For the next few days, Beverley was paraded from one social gathering to another as if he were a prize exhibit. None of this, delightful as it was, had anything to do with his job, and he began to suspect Hay's motives and weary of his exuberance. Eventually, he was introduced to a Greek author who he found, to his surprise, had been engaged to write the book; all Beverley had to do was to translate his work into English. Beverley, extremely angry, nevertheless listened patiently while the author described his plans for it: it sounded like a romantic history combined with a political treatise, and at its heart was to be the sensational exposure of Compton Mackenzie as the villain of the saga. Beverley was completely taken aback. He knew Compton Mackenzie as the author of *Carnival*, *Sinister Street* and other novels, but he did not know that he had been Military Controller of Athens in 1916 or that he had been Director of the Aegean Intelligence Service until he was invalided out of the army. Mackenzie, it was said, had supported the rebel Venizelos against the King and was responsible for the defamation of Constantine. Beverley asked for documentary evidence, but the Greek author evasively explained that many papers had been destroyed by the rebels. It was not an auspicious beginning.

Madame Condostavlos, the Queen's lady-in-waiting, whom he met next, had no doubt about Mackenzie's role, and spoke of two assassination attempts which he had masterminded. In the first, Mackenzie had told a member of the royal guard that the King had been bewitched by his German Queen and could no longer think for himself: he could only be released from the spell by a magic powder mixed into his wine. The soldier took the powder straight to a Court official, who discovered it to be arsenic. In the second attempt, she said, Mackenzie had arranged for the royal palace at Tatoy to be burned down while the King and Queen were in residence.

Beverley listened to these stories in amazement, but when he enquired further he found that, in some respects, both were true. There had been a poison attempt, and the palace at Tatoy had been destroyed by arson. In both cases the perpetrators were suspected to be associates of Compton Mackenzie – but then all his associates were pro-Venizelists which, Beverley decided, proved nothing. He refused to believe that Mackenzie was involved and, consequently, knew the sensational revelation at the heart of the proposed book was nonsense. Nevertheless, he was being paid to write, so he began an account, as seen from the royalist point of view, of the events which started in 1914, but he appears to have refused to work with the Greek author whose opus he was supposed to translate. He continued to try to find hard evidence to support the allegations against Compton Mackenzie, but instead uncovered information in police and government files which showed Mackenzie's associates to be very unpleasant characters indeed.

Shortly after his arrival, Beverley was invited to the Palace by the Queen for a private meeting. He was conducted along a formal avenue of palm trees into the Queen's own walled garden, and for a moment thought he was back in a Devonshire garden on a bright summer's day. There were roses everywhere and, in the lush grass in the shade of the trees, grew great drifts of late violets. In the midst stood Queen Sophia. From the stories he had read in the British newspapers, Beverley had expected to meet the monstrous, avidly anti-British female who had conspired against the Allies and prayed for Germany to win the war. Instead, he found a woman of patent sincerity who convinced him that the lurid stories about her were untrue. She spoke of her mother, the Princess Royal, Queen Victoria's eldest daughter, who was hated in Germany because she was so pro-British: 'Nobody will ever know, nobody will ever guess the things she endured and the things she achieved. I often try to think of what she would have done in my position.' She described her terrible dilemma in 1914, for she loved both England and Germany, and spoke longingly of her childhood in England where she was brought up by her grandmother, Queen Victoria. She told Beverley that her greatest wish was to return to England and that her greatest dream was that her daughters should marry Englishmen. Beverley was entranced by her and concluded that she was much wronged by Allied propaganda.

In a letter to his parents, whom he always addressed as 'My Dearest People', he wrote on 23 January:

> I don't think you need worry about indiscretion in letters or, indeed, in people knowing more or less what I am up to. It is hopeless to try to conceal the fact that I am in Greece, and as everybody out here knows I am going to write a book about it, they will probably learn the same in England soon.
>
> A very interesting function on Saturday at the Palace in the afternoon. The King was there and was charming to me. He struck me as transparently honest, but exceedingly harassed by his continual non-recognition. Also the Queen who was as delightful as ever, and she is going to ask me to play the piano to her. I danced with two of her daughters, the Princesses Olga and Irene (who are rather the Princess Mary type, only without the stodginess) and also had a long talk to Prince Andrew's wife who is a sister of Louis Mountbatten . . . Chatto and Windus wrote charmingly about *Self* . . . I miss the cats exceedingly . . .

To keep his name in front of the public while he was away, he wrote a series of articles for the *Daily News* under the punning title 'From an Attic Window'. Other articles appeared in the *Sunday Times*, the *Daily Mail*, *American Outlook* and the *Baltimore Sun*. His social life was, as always, hectic: everyone, it seemed, wanted to entertain him. As the weeks passed by, he tired of it, for the activities became as predictable as the social life of Torquay to which Athens sometimes bore an uncanny resemblance. Whenever he could, he escaped to the rough sexual pleasures of the waterfront and the back streets, but he had to be exceedingly careful.

The early section of his diary is full of impressions of Greece, often along the lines of 'Socrates and Plato are gone but their spirit lives on.' Much of it is no better and no worse than the record of any tourist, but through it all blazes a love of Greece, as if he had been converted to a new religion. Not all his experiences were happy, however. He was particularly saddened by a visit to the house of Skouloudis, a man of eighty-three who had been Prime Minister and who was a fervent royalist. (He had given Beverley access to confidential files, but the only interesting information was that Tsar Nicholas had protested on several occasions at the way the Allies were treating neutral Greece.) During an uprising, Venizelist supporters had smashed Skouloudis's vast collection of art treasures, and Skouloudis had left everything as it was, a memorial to stupidity. Beverley was escorted through room after room of broken porcelain, wrecked bronzes and statues and pictures slashed with knives: this a Velasquez and that a Van Dyck.

At the end of January, Beverley left the Grande Bretagne and moved to the smaller Hotel Splendid in a quieter location. It cost a third of the price he had been paying and, as his expenses were fixed, he was able to pocket the difference. He later moved into an apartment with two British Embassy staff which reduced his costs even further. In this way, he had built up his bank balance quite usefully by the time he left Greece at the end of May.

By March, he had abandoned the book. He had done his best but there was no story. He blamed Stuart Hay who, he decided, had misled everyone – the Greek government, the royal family, Chatto and Windus and, last but not least, Beverley himself. It had been nothing but hot air from a man who revelled in his own self-importance and in his contacts with the upper echelons of the Greek hierarchy. Beverley suspected that in normal times Hay would not have been able to ingratiate himself with the Court, but that, with the British Embassy staff and families forbidden to have any contact with the royal family, Hay provided a link with England.

Beverley destroyed what he had written and began work on a novel partly based on his research, with characters who were thinly disguised versions of people he had met, including Stuart Hay whom he drew as a pompous but kindly little man with delusions of grandeur. He completed the book within two months and called it *The Athenians*. He wrote in his diary:

I know now with a confidence I have never fully experienced in the past that my writing will one day be read by all the world. And Chatto and Windus know that too. These first novels are nothing at all except signs of precocity. With regard to the book itself, I am still a little in the dark. I have written what seems to me to be a good detective story of a curious nature and I have managed to get one fairly sensational incident. What effect it will have I don't know. It is so completely different to anything I have ever read or done before.

Towards the end of his stay in Athens, his friendship with the royal family grew stronger. He was invited to family occasions as well as to formal ones, and they made it clear that they liked him. He was particularly struck by the beauty of the royal women: apart from the Queen and her children, there were Princess Helen of Romania, the Grand-Duchess of Hesse and the astonishing Queen Marie of Romania, a grand-daughter of Queen Victoria, 'with the remains of great beauty, fair hair and grey eyes'. He also got on well with the royal men, particularly with Prince Philip of Hesse who took him off for a day in the country. He had several private meetings with King Constantine and accepted his version of the unhappy events of the previous years. The King was particularly vehement about the débâcle of the Dardanelles and the subsequent failure of the Allies at Gallipoli. He had been blamed for not allowing the Greek army to help. 'It is the Greek dream to capture Constantinople from the Turks but we know the territory well enough to know what can and cannot be done.' He had begged the Allies not to attempt the impossible. 'We have studied the position for years, but our expertise was ignored.' He also pointed out that, if he had been pro-German as alleged, he could have attacked the Allied forces during the terrible autumn of 1915 when they crossed into Greece, beaten and exhausted. Instead, he had warned the Kaiser that if his German forces pursued them, he himself would declare war on Germany.

Beverley admired the family's lack of ostentation, their cheerful acceptance of reduced financial circumstances, and the pride that forbade them to accept help from the wealthy American wife of the King's youngest brother, Prince Christopher. Above all, he admired the strong bond between the various branches of the family which, he believed, stemmed from the grandmother of Europe, Queen Victoria.

His experience also taught him something which was to stand him in good stead in the future: if Royalty accepted him, he was not to be intimidated by lesser fry, however highly they might think of themselves. This new confidence was put to the test when Stuart Hay called on him a few days before Beverley left, in a blazing temper, blaming Beverley for the failure of the original project, and accusing him of going around Athens 'sneering' at him and of caricaturing him in *The Athenians*. Beverley replied that if he cared to read the manuscript and suggest revisions, he would make them. Hay declared that he had 'not the faintest desire to read it' and stormed out. Beverley wrote in his diary: 'I, as author, have the whip hand. I have not the faintest intention of being brow-beaten by anybody.'

Later, at the Palace, he told Madame Condostavlos the story and she was highly amused by it. 'She said that Hay had been exceedingly rude to her too and the reason for his conduct was jealousy. As she said (and I suppose it is true) I had been an almost dangerous success with the royal family. Whenever they were doing anything they always suggested that I should be asked. He [Hay] knew that he would never be asked on such occasions and hence a sort of petty anger which turned against myself. The climax appeared to be when I went off with Prince Philip.'

The diary continues with a description of his departure from Athens:

But the most extraordinary thing of the past week has been the sudden arrival in Athens of Mrs Ryerson. I at once went to the Grande Bretagne and found her there. She is travelling with her brother, and Mrs George Keppel and her brother, Sir Archibald Tomlinson. I dined with them all and found them quite delightful. It resulted from this that, after I have visited Rome, I am to go on to Venice where Mrs R. has taken rooms for a week or so.

I said goodbye to the King and Queen on Sunday morning and was entrusted with a great many letters to take to England including one to Princess Victoria. I was also given photographs galore, which speak for themselves.

Monday morning was spent in wild rushing round Athens saying goodbye and then at 1 o'clock I found myself on board the 'Aventino' sitting in Mrs R.'s salon with her and Mrs Keppel, watching Athens fade slowly away in the distance.

It was like a great veil suddenly torn from my eyes. It was the opening of a door which has long been shut. I found myself talking and laughing and enjoying life with a fullness that I had almost forgotten. To speak again to intelligent people, to discuss again the things I love, to be able to say things by suggestion, to colour my conversation as I desired, to stretch out my hands for ideas, to play with facts – in a word, to talk – I cannot express the relief I found in it all.

And then, in a typical Nichols volte-face, he wrote:

Now that I have left Greece I realize how all the time I loathed and detested the place. It was barren and desolate and beastly. There was not a soul there I cared for except the Queen and one or two of the royal family.

It is a pity he did not record his impressions of his meeting with Mrs George Keppel who had been the mistress of Edward VII, but he was more interested in Philip Mueller, the American playwright, another member of the party. 'A most charming man. He knows a great many of my friends, and to talk to him was like renewing acquaintance with them.' He had kept in contact with Mrs Ryerson since their farewell in New York over two years before, and while he was at Oxford, her son had called on him, accompanied by her brother John. The son he found rather dull, but he became a close friend of John and paid several visits to his cottage, Thatch Roof in the village of Glatton in Huntingdonshire, which he shared with a musician friend. If, at this time, Beverley had been told that Thatch Roof would one day be the means of creating his biggest success, *Down the Garden Path*, he might have thought the possibility absurd.

After a brief stay in Rome, Beverley went on to join the party in Venice where he made another new friend, Mrs Sybil Colefax as she was then. She was one of the leading hostesses of her day and through her friendship he was to meet a formidable array of personalities, from Lord Berners to Bernard Shaw.

Beverley eventually arrived back in England in the middle of June and, after leaving a copy of *The Athenians* with Chatto and Windus, he went on to Torquay. Much as he loved seeing the family again, he was conscious of a gulf growing between himself and them. They listened with interest to the story of his adventures but, as so often happens in these circumstances, they could not respond to his enthusiasm because it was all so unreal to them. For his part, he found the atmosphere depressing. John Nichols still wanted to sell the house and move on but Beverley supported his mother in her determination to stay. As soon as he decently could, Beverley returned to London, but before he left, he received a long letter from Queen Sophia, dated 24 June, thanking him for a letter he had written her from Venice. She wrote: '. . . I think it is we who have to thank you for all the touching trouble and interest you took in our difficult and sad cause.' She wished him success with *The Athenians* which he had dedicated to her.

Beverley could not believe it when Chatto and Windus turned down *The Athenians* out of hand. There is no record of any explanation for their rejection. In *The Unforgiving Minute*, Beverley said that he had destroyed the typescript but had given the original manuscript to Dorothy Hart as a Christmas present, having had it bound in white leather by Aspreys:

> Very peculiar things happen to writers after their death. Some quickly vanish into the waters of Lethe; others refuse to sink and are washed back to shore by the shifting tides of public taste and resuscitated by literary beachcombers. In case I should come into the latter category, *The Athenians* might be an interesting piece of literary driftwood. Eighty thousand words, bound in white leather . . . It ought to be worth a fiver, if only for the binding.

The hand-written manuscript was in fact found in a cupboard at his home after his death. Some of the early chapters are missing but it is otherwise intact. Reading it, one can easily see why Chatto and Windus rejected it. It tells a Buchanesque story of a young Englishman who is caught up in a plot to kill King Constantine but who, at the climax, foils the scheme. As with many of Beverley's books, it mixes fact with fiction, and it is the factual side which must have alarmed Chatto and Windus: apart from the characters so obviously based on living people (Stuart Hay for one) there are sensational accusations which would have provided cause for several libel actions. Compton Mackenzie's henchman, Charles Tucker, is named as the man directly responsible for the attempt to poison the King. The fire at the Tatoy Palace is described in detail as being a scheme engineered by the Allied Secret Police which was under the direction of Mackenzie and a Captain de Roquefeuil. Other names given include that of George Melas, who is described as a spy for Mackenzie against the King, though Constantine had shown him special favour and had paid for the education of his son. (The King had told Beverley how deeply hurt he had been by the treachery of someone he regarded as a friend.) Beverley even provided a footnote to explain that Melas was 'the author of a scurrilous book entitled *Ex-King Constantine and the War*, published in 1918 by Messrs Hodder and Stoughton'.

In short, *The Athenians* was the type of book which no publisher in his right mind would print. There was a glaring inconsistency in Beverley's logic: if the evidence against Mackenzie and others was insufficient to justify the book he was commissioned to write, how could he justify its use in a work of semi-fiction? Could he have been as naïve as he appeared to be? Aside from the contentious material in the book, there is a long account of the hero's meeting with the Queen in her garden which Beverley rewrote, with some other sequences, for inclusion in his biography, *Twenty-Five*. He was not to return to sensationalism until he wrote *A Case of Human Bondage* and *Father Figure* many decades later. In each of these, as well as in *The Athenians*, the central figure is a woman who has been wronged: Queen Sophia, Syrie Maugham and his own mother.

There was a sequel to Beverley's Greek adventure: among the mass of flowers at his funeral in 1983, a simple royal tribute echoed back to the strange events of 1922.

· 9 ·

London to Lilydale

1922–1924

WHILE Beverley was in Greece, *Self*, dedicated to his father, was published on 18 May 1922. It was an ambitious work by comparison with his earlier novels and he hoped it would signify an advance in his literary career. A pastiche of Thackeray's *Vanity Fair* and Mrs Gaskell's *Cranford*, it satirized the social life of England in 1918. It also included literary elements from other authors, not the least of whom were Oscar Wilde and Ouïda. Unfortunately, there were inconsistencies in the otherwise clever mélange of styles, whenever Beverley lost his satiric intent and lapsed into sentiment. If he had been in England, his publishers might have pointed these out to him, or he might have seen them for himself at an early proof stage, but once he had handed over the manuscript he saw nothing of the book until it was on sale in the shops.

Today, the underlying joke seems glaringly obvious but at the time the critics, missing the point, took *Self* seriously. The *Daily Telegraph* said: '"Self" brings the fulfilment of earlier promise. It is a finely wrought piece of work which definitely places Mr Nichols among the little band of men and women who must be read.' The *Manchester Guardian* described it as a novel of absorbing interest on which the author was to be congratulated. The public agreed and Beverley had to accept tht he had scored a success for the wrong reasons.

Friends ribbed him about the book's more overblown passages, and he agreed that they were awful, apparently deciding that if his friends could not see the joke, the fault lay with himself rather than with them. The initial favourable reaction from the reading public was no fluke, for the book continued to be in demand for over sixteen years, finally appearing in a cheap edition under the Penguin banner in 1938. Beverley wrote a light-hearted foreword for this edition which began: 'One of the reasons why this novel is reissued, in such an alarmingly cheap edition, is in order that the intelligent reader may amuse himself by spotting the numbers of authors from whom its ideas are gently but firmly stolen.' He suggested that they consider it a parlour game for not less than twelve players and, as the book cost only sixpence, that each player should have no fewer than three copies each. Perhaps the public took his advice, for Penguin had to reprint immediately. *Self* only vanished from the shops with the outbreak of war.

Some of the misunderstanding of the book's intention may be attributed to its heroine Nancy, a re-interpretation of Thackeray's Becky Sharp as a 'modern girl'. Like her counterpart, Nancy was ruthless in her determination to survive and used sex to do so. The essential difference was that, while Becky accepted sex as an inevitable means to an end, Nancy thoroughly enjoyed it. In 1973, Beverley was to explain that, as far as her sexuality was concerned, he was actually writing about himself, but he allowed his own emotions to overcome satiric objectivity with a seriousness which he did not intend. Nancy should have had more in common with Lorelei of *Gentlemen Prefer Blondes*. The choice of her name was a joke, reflecting the term 'nancy boy'.

One sequence was based on the incident at the Café Royal when he was picked up by Alvaro 'Chile' Guevara. In *Self*, Nancy goes to the Café Racine to find a man for the night. She knows from the admiring glances that she can have any man in the room.

> And then suddenly she saw him. He was sitting alone at a table on the far side of the room, watching her intently. He appeared to be about twenty-five and there was an expression on his face which made the colour flood her cheeks. He was not particularly good looking but he was exceptionally attractive, to Nancy at any rate. His whole poise indicated colossal strength. As he leaned forward she could see the muscles of his great arms swell out distinctly.

A female habituée of the Café tells her his name is Bill, and he is a boxer, like Chile. The two of them go back to his room. Thereafter Nancy's other men never quite satisfy her and at the end she returns to him. '. . . over her nakedness came his arms, powerful and protecting. In a world of dust this was the one thing that was real, the one thing that might help her to forget.'

This last sentence sums up Beverley's entire attitude to sex. And from what he said, despite all his efforts, he never found any man to match Alvaro Guevara.

When he wrote *The Unforgiving Minute* in 1977, fifty-five years after the publication of *Self*, he had the opportunity to explain how the point of the book had been missed, but instead he denigrated it, describing it as the worst novel ever written. 'The characters were wooden, the story was hackneyed, the dialogue was trite and it contained not a grain of humour. The whole thing was so ghastly and I hated it so much that I finished it not in ten weeks but in five . . .' Explaining that the first edition sold out, he continued:

For one of the very few occasions in my life, I showed a glimmer of artistic integrity. I informed Chatto and Windus that if they insisted on reprinting *Self* they must also let me write a foreword stating that in my opinion it was muck, and that I was ashamed of it and that anybody who bought it would be justified in asking for his money back. To my surprise, they agreed . . .

This foreword never appeared. Why Beverley should have written such a farrago of nonsense and untruths about *Self* when four years earlier he had spoken of it with some affection is beyond comprehension.

If *Self* was not the literary breakthrough he had expected, he was somewhat consoled by the reviews of *Patchwork* when it was published in America. They were more than kind, but the *Literary Review* – correctly as it transpired – doubted 'whether the bulk of American readers will be intensely interested in a work which presupposes an all-consuming interest in and first hand knowledge of Oxford'.

Beverley's urgent priority was now to make a living and to find somewhere to live. He had previously worked for a short time as a cub reporter on the *Sunday Dispatch*, a paper published by Lord Northcliffe's empire, where he had been paid for each inch of copy printed after editing. A story about Gladys Cooper brought him one guinea and a piece of nonsense about an elephant made fifteen shillings. It was an uncertain way to earn money but he went back to Fleet Street, nevertheless. He was now recognized as a writer and had three published books to prove it, so he had no difficulty in getting work. One of his chores was to turn out short stories for the *Daily News* under the heading 'Little Tales'. Most of them had a twist in the last few lines and were gently ironic, sometimes having an underlying bitterness. One of them told the story of a lady on a bus who noted with approval that the male passengers respectfully took off their hats as they were passing the Cenotaph in Whitehall, the memorial to the dead of the Great War. She was filled with outrage when the burly young chap in front of her ignored the Cenotaph, and in a fury accused him of disrespect. To her amazement, as they passed the Savoy Hotel, he snatched the pipe out of his mouth and the cap off his head with military precision – and the conductor said that the man, who had been blind and deaf since Ypres, travelled every day on the bus and usually calculated the time it passed the Cenotaph to the precise second. On that day, heavy traffic had delayed them. The conductor turned to the woman, told her sternly that she ought to have got off at Trafalgar Square and charged her another twopence. (The modern reader may be astonished to learn that in those days London buses ran reliably on time and that the cost of the fare was so small that it has no equivalent in present currency.) The *Daily News* published thirty of Beverley's stories in a booklet and followed it with a sequel of thirty more.

John Nichols and Pauline Shalders in 1890 at the time of their engagement

'The laughing child'—Beverley photographed in Suffolk, aged three

Beverley at home in the garden, aged sixteen—very smart in white!

Beverley at Oxford in 1917

Beverley in 1918 in his army greatcoat

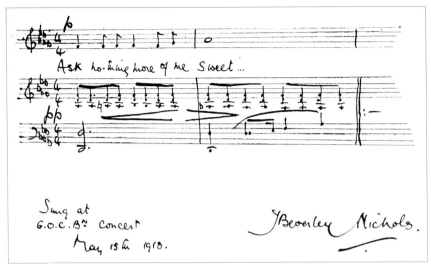

Manuscript fragment of 'Ask Nothing More', which he composed in 1918

The Nichols men with billiard cues, circa 1920: left to right, Paul, John, Beverley and Alan

To dear Beverley from Nellie Melba

Dame Nellie Melba, whose memoirs Beverley ghost wrote; he was her trusted confidant

Syrie, Liza and Somerset Maugham at the Villa Eliza in 1925 on the terrible weekend when matters came to a head

King Constantine; Beverley became a
friend of the Greek royal family in 1922

Publicity photograph to promote
Twenty-Five in 1926

Beverley at the piano—a gifted musician and composer

Beverley with the British ambassador to the United States at the White House in 1928

Beverley in New York, 1929; the photograph may be Cecil Beaton's

A portrait of Beverley taken circa 1930

The garden path—Thatch Cottage garden in high summer

Gardening at Glatton; in fact, Beverley usually left chores like weeding to others

The dining hall at Thatch Cottage

The sitting room at Thatch Cottage

The cottage at Glatton in the 1930s

Arthur Diamond at Glatton

Beverley with his jet-black half Siamese
cats, Rose and Cavalier

Sheet music title page, 1930

On the Elstree set of *Glamour* in 1931—one of Beverley's rare screen appearances

Sheet music for a hit song from *Floodlight*,
Beverley's 1937 revue

Dame Edith Evans as the Melba character in *Evensong* on Broadway in 1933

Frances Day, star of *Floodlight*, and Beverley in a
publicity photograph for *Revue*, Beverley's subsequent backstage novel

Beverley on 'live' television from London Studios, November 1938

In the Hampstead garden, late 1930s

The garden at Beverley's Hampstead house before work done to his design

Cyril Butcher at the house in Hampstead

Passage to India, 1943

The 'secret' door at Merry Hall where the selected few signed their names

The music room at Merry Hall; the 'secret' door is behind screen at right

Beverley at the party to welcome Oldfield's regale lilies

Reginald Arthur Gaskin ready to party at Merry Hall

Broadway stars Alfred Lunt and Lynn Fontanne sign the 'secret' door at Merry Hall in 1952; Beverley is between them and Gaskin to the right

At a Merry Hall party—Beverley (seated center) with Hermione Gingold (seated left) and Bob Boothby (seated right); others are unidentified

Beverley in the Merry Hall greenhouse with Oldfield the gardener

Beverley, Gaskin and Oldfield in the gardens at Merry Hall

Beverley at Merry Hall

Typical of publicity for Beverley's books in the 1950s

Publicity for Beverley's column in *Woman's Own*, which he began in 1946 and continued until 1967

Rebecca West and Beverley in the south of France

Noel Coward's dedication reads: 'For Beverley with our love—Noel.' When asked by Beverley if he minded cats, Coward replied: 'My dear Beverley, I adore all animals to such an extent that I cannot see a water-bison without bursting into tears.'

Cecil Beaton, Gladys Cooper and Beverley at a celebrity lunch at the Savoy Hotel in London

In *Father Figure* Beverley captioned the top picture of his mother as follows: 'My mother as an old lady. She had been ravaged by suffering and hid her face from the camera.' But the picture below it, which was taken at the same time, shows that her face was unravaged and in the first picture she was merely cuddling the cat.

Side entrance of Sudbrook Cottage, where Beverley lived from 1958 until his death in 1983

Open garden day at Sudbrook Cottage; Gaskin takes money for charity while Beverley looks on

Beverley at Sudbrook Cottage, 1970

Some light pruning at Sudbrook Cottage, 1981

In addition to this, he worked on a wide range of news stories.

The most important event for Beverley in 1922 had an unlikely origin – the trial of Bywaters and Thompson, which he was assigned to cover for his newspaper. The case itself did not at first appear to be anything extraordinary. Edith Thompson, aged twenty-eight, bored with her humdrum marriage to Percy Thompson, took as her lover Freddy Bywaters, a twenty-year-old employee with the P & O line. He rented a room at the Thompsons' house in Ilford, but this arrangement did not last long as the two men quarrelled and Freddy left. In between his sea-trips, he met Edith furtively and while they were apart they wrote passionate letters to each other. His were sent to the firm of wholesale milliners in Aldersgate Street where she was employed as book-keeper and manageress. On 3 October, they met in a café near her office before she joined her husband to see a Ben Travers farce in the West End. Later, when the Thompsons returned to Ilford around midnight, Freddy was waiting in the street for them. There was a quick exchange of words, then Freddy stabbed Percy in the neck and ran off. By the time a doctor had arrived, Percy was dead. Witnesses had heard Edith cry out, 'Don't, oh don't!' and met her running for help. To a police sergeant, she said, 'They will blame me for this,' but she did not mention Bywaters. The police however, tipped off by someone who knew of the love affair, were quickly on Freddy's track. When they searched his cabin, they found all Edith's letters and, as a result, both were charged with a series of offences which added up to an equal charge of murder.

As soon as Beverley saw Edith in the dock, he was struck by her beauty, for she had pretty hair, lovely eyes and a long, slender neck. Freddy Bywaters was tall, broad-shouldered, square-jawed and good-looking. The trial moved on for five days: there was no doubt about his guilt, but hers seemed questionable until carefully selected extracts from her letters were read out. They revealed her as a woman living in a dream world, driven by sexual longings mingled with explicit erotic desires culled from romantic novels. But what really condemned her were her elaborate fantasies on ways of killing her husband. She spun tales of her attempts to poison him, and of her experiments with broken glass in his food, and would beg Freddy to find alternatives, enclosing cuttings of murder cases and novels dealing with murder.

For reasons not clear, the defence did not exhibit the letters in their entirety, seeming content with the extracts chosen by the prosecution. These seemed to be an effort to convince her young lover that she would do anything to keep him while, in reality, doing nothing risky herself whatsoever. Against the advice of her lawyer, Edith insisted on giving evidence, but this proved a fatal mistake. She appeared vain and obstinate and, under the eyes of a hostile judge, her confidence deserted her. In his summing up, Mr Justice Shearman was correct in law, but indulged in his personal views on adultery. He ignored the failure of the post-mortem to find any trace of poison, and did not remind the jury of Edith Thompson's capacity for make-believe. The verdict was inevitable.

When Beverley heard it, he rushed from the court and was physically sick. He had become so emotionally involved with the woman and her sexual dream world – a dream world not unlike his own – that he could not bear it. And her lover, young and over-sexed, was the type that attracted him. But worse was to come: Beverley was ordered to do a deal with Edith's parents, the Graydons, for the rights to her life story. Against competition from other newspapers, he succeeded. Every day, until the murderers were hanged, he met the family, listened to stories of their daughter, and was drawn into their grief and incomprehension. He felt their misery deeply, but the journalist in him was never far away; when Mr Graydon cried out in pain: 'That this should happen to people like us!' Beverley knew he had the line which would make the story echo round the world. Later, Frank Vosper used *People Like Us* as the title of a play based on the trial.

Beverley lived with the Thompson-Bywaters case for six weeks, and between the verdict and the hanging he had the additional job of persuading celebrities to give their views in articles which he ghosted for them. His editor, Bernard Falk, was pleased, but thought what was missing was a woman's comment. Beverley made what he thought was a fatuous suggestion: 'What about Melba?' His editor was delighted. 'You've got it! "We Women and Edith Thompson," by Dame Nellie Melba.'

Melba was staying at the Empress Club in Dover Street, an exclusively female domain. Beverley telephoned her secretary but was fobbed off. He then sent a telegram, but still heard nothing. In desperation, he went to the club, evaded the commissionaire while he was handing a lady out of a taxi, and made for the stairs while the receptionist was looking the other way. Once on the first floor, he had no idea what to do next, but then, in the distance, he heard Melba's voice singing the 'Addio' from *La Bohème*. He followed the sound until he was standing outside the door to her room, and when she had finished he knocked, and was commanded to enter. Melba took one hard look and said, 'Who the devil are you?' and Beverley replied that he was a friend of Mrs Ryerson, the American artist Purcell Jones and Mrs George Keppel. The rest was easy. They developed an immediate rapport and, like Mrs Ryerson, Nellie Melba adopted him as a surrogate son.

For the next few months, she enjoyed taking him with her to social functions and to visit friends, but most of all she enjoyed talking about her life; she was in her sixties and there was a lot to talk about. Listening to this flow of fact and gossip, Beverley could see rich possibilities for a book, but she was offended at the idea that one as young as she should contemplate a biography: there would be time for that, she said, when she got old. Wisely, he did not press her. She left England to return to Australia, and he did not know when he would see her again.

By 1923, Beverley was installed in a two-roomed flat at 54, Bryanston Street, but his ambition was to find a small house to rent as soon as he had enough money. His already extensive circle of acquaintances was growing rapidly, with Ned Lathom playing an important role in introducing him to new people. It was at Lathom's house that he first heard Noel Coward play while Gertrude Lawrence sang his songs for a forthcoming André Charlot revue. He never forgot her singing 'Parisian Pierrot', holding a large pierrot doll in pale yellow satin with a face like a Picasso harlequin and green gloves on its drooping hands – the type of doll often found lolling on sofas in the '20s. The show, *London Calling*, opened at the Duke of York's Theatre in September 1923. Beverley longed to be another Coward and, having seen his own song performed in *A to Z*, he was convinced that he could write words and music as prolifically and effectively. At his flat he composed romantic ballads and sharp little songs on a piano he had hired from Whiteley's of Bayswater, but the realization of his theatrical ambitions had to wait for another four years. He was also beginning to get a glimmer of an idea for his next novel, but his journalism and social life gave him no time for concentrated effort.

Busy as Beverley undoubtedly was, his career at this point was in the doldrums. He was growing increasingly discontented with the newspaper world and was ready for a change. So when Melba cabled and asked him to go to Australia to assist with her farewell opera season, he accepted. He did not know what it entailed, but he hoped she would change her mind about the biography. By the end of 1923, he was on his way. Before he left for Australia, he sub-let his flat to a Mr Lionel Fielder at a profit of £30 a quarter over the rent he paid his landlord, and he asked his father to deal with this while he was away.

The tedium of the long voyage was brightened by Seymour Hicks, knighted in 1935, and his wife Ellaline Terriss who, with their theatrical company, were travelling to Australia to present a season of plays and musicals. In conjunction with Charles Frohman, the American impresario, Hicks had built the Aldwych, the Globe and the Queen's theatres in London. His wife had been a star of the Gaiety Theatre at the height of its fame in Edwardian times and when the couple joined forces they made a formidable team. They played the leading roles in the original production of J.M. Barrie's *Quality Street*, but were prevented by other commitments from appearing in *Peter Pan*, which Barrie had written with them in mind. Ellaline Terriss's famous father William Terriss had acted with Sir Henry Irving and Ellen Terry, and was at the height of his powers when he was stabbed to death at the royal entrance to the Adelphi Theatre by a madman who mistook him for someone else.

Beverley was fascinated by them. The importance of the friendship between him and the Hicks family cannot be overestimated; he already knew the young crowd – Ivor Novello, Gertrude Lawrence and Noel Coward – but this new friendship introduced him to the theatrical aristocracy of the day and was to provide him with copy in the years that followed. The most important aspect of their meeting was the start of his enduring friendship with the Hicks's daughter Betty, a beautiful and intelligent eighteen-year-old with a capacity for laughter which Beverley shared. Their friendship lasted until the day of his death.

When the ship arrived in Melbourne, Beverley's new employer was waiting. She knew who Hicks and Terriss were – there were very few people who did not – and she greeted them graciously, the Queen of Song meeting two of the crowned heads of the Theatre. She was not so gracious to Betty and did her best to break up her friendship with Beverley. At a dinner she gave for them, she made Betty feel gauche and unhappy. She also contrived to block any meetings between the couple and when Beverley stayed the night at the Hickses' home Melba created such a storm that he did not do it again. She wanted him with her all the time and she made sure he was. Although he afterwards complained that he was never let off the lead, and, as a consequence, saw very little of Australia or anyone outside the Melba circle, he enjoyed it at the time. It was pleasant to bask in the aura of the legendary Melba. Their relationship naturally created speculation and it did not please him when anonymous letters assumed he was a 'Pommie gigolo'.

Melba's house, Coombe Cottage, in the prettily named Lilydale, near Coldstream, was then in the country, not engulfed by the creeping suburbs of Melbourne. She lived in considerable affluence, looked after by her English butler and a retinue of servants. The house, a large rambling place in the colonial style, was filled with antique furniture and paintings, many by Australian artists. She ran the house and garden like a sergeant-major, and this supervision extended to the local town: once, when she expected visitors, she got up early in the morning and took her niece along to help her clean the littered main street through which her guests would drive. She was an early riser, and guests would find on their morning tea-tray a flower which she had picked herself, together with a note asking what they would like to do that day. She was fond of the ceremonial of afternoon tea, and dinner was also a formal occasion, although she reluctantly accepted the fashion for dinner jackets which was gradually replacing white tie and tails. Seymour Hicks, appearing at her dinner-party in white tie, murmured, 'I appear to be overdressed.' She always tried to serve some delicacy shipped in from Europe, and was delighted to sing for her guests if they wanted her to, which, of course, they invariably did. At one of her parties the guests were so reluctant to leave that finally, at three in the morning, she ordered her butler to round them up into the ballroom where, with the lights out and only a single candle burning in a silver candlestick, she sat at the grand piano and sang 'Home Sweet Home'. They took the hint. Afterwards, when they had all gone, she beckoned the band into the kitchen where, in her white satin gown and with a diamond tiara in her hair, she cooked them bacon and eggs.

She never employed a manager and negotiated her own contracts with a shrewdness which the toughest agent might well envy, for she was fully aware of her worth and allowed nothing to escape her attention. She could be cantankerous, suspicious, irrationally jealous and given to dramatic changes of mood but, to balance this, she was also a loyal friend and generous with her affection and her money.

It is unlikely that Beverley contributed much to the organization of her opera season in 1924 apart from listening sympathetically to her private explosions of anger against some minor inefficiency, or her tart criticisms of the other artistes. She knew she could trust him to treat anything she said as confidential, and she told him much about her private life. She told him, for instance, the details of her love affair with the Duke of Orleans which had created a scandal in the 1890s and nearly finished her career. The couple were wildly indiscreet, much to the indignation of European society which was not in the least bothered by what they did as long as it was done in private. Matters came to a head when her estranged husband, Charles Armstrong, sued for divorce, citing the Duke as co-respondent. The press, as usual, had a field day but, quite unexpectedly, Armstrong dropped the case, finally obtaining a divorce in Texas in 1900 on the grounds of desertion. The Duke remained the only man Melba really cared about: she had known from the start that there could never be a marriage and was prepared to be his mistress. Their contempt for social mores and the resulting scandal, however, ended the affair.

Beverley never made use of the information she gave him about this affair, or about her other lovers, although he was frequently tempted to write a book about her. As time went by, public interest in Melba waned until it was revived by John Hetherington's comprehensive biography published in 1967. Ten years after this a television series was mooted and Beverley was at last prepared to tell the story, but nothing came of the project. Before his death, he hinted at the startling nature of what he could reveal about Melba, but whatever his stories were they died with him. Who knows what she confided to him at Coombe Cottage as they sat drinking into the early hours?

After Beverley had ghosted Melba's book for singers entitled *The Melba Method*, he persuaded her to let him ghost her 'memoirs', which sounded less final to her than 'autobiography'. They would appear under her name but he would receive half the advance and the proceeds of the serial rights, if any. At first, all went well. Melba rambled on over familiar ground: her discovery by Lady de Grey, the powerful force behind Covent Garden policy, her acceptance into the highest echelons of Victorian society, her appearance before the Queen at Windsor, and so on. He took copious notes and wrote them up, trying to recapture her style of speaking. But to his consternation, she became her own censor, eliminated any abrasive edge he reproduced and refused to allow him to record any criticism of a fellow singer. Tetrazzini, whom she loathed and accused of faking top notes and of looking common, suddenly became a charming, delicious artiste. Caruso's trick of playing jokes on her on stage to put her off her stride was forgotten and so, too, were his garlic-laden breath and his habit of softly breaking wind so that she was enveloped in a noxious stink at quite the wrong moments. She enveloped reality in a heavy mist of golden good-heartedness which distorted the book Beverley had hoped to write. She was also occasionally carried away with attacks of 'creativity' during which she invented shamelessly. When the book was ready to go to the printers, Jean de Reszke died. This distressed her deeply and brought on a final surge of inventiveness: de Reszke, who had not sung for twenty years, sat up on his deathbed, according to her, and sang the great arias with which he was associated. The recital went on for three days before he sank back exhausted, and died. The facts were more mundane: in a delirium, he sang a snatch or two from *Tristan und Isolde*, but his last three days were spent in a semi-coma.

Beverley was disappointed with the book but it was hers, not his, and he had been over-optimistic in expecting it to be anything other than it was. The lady who had once been snubbed by Queen Victoria for social indiscretion was now firmly protective of her public persona and had no intention of tarnishing the image she had created over the years.

With the book out of the way, Beverley became bored and frustrated, having been for nearly a year at the beck and call of his employer. He was grateful to Melba for the material benefits of her patronage and, above all, for giving him the opportunity to live in a world dominated by music; she had encouraged him to compose and she had sung his songs. But enough was enough: he had his own career to consider.

· 10 ·

Twenty-Five

1924–1927

BEFORE he left Australia to spend a holiday in New York, Beverley conceived the idea of his autobiography, to be called *Twenty-Five*, and the opening lines had a Wildean flourish: twenty-five, he said, was the latest age at which anyone should write his autobiography. It was an audacious approach, characteristically impertinent, and it was to pay off handsomely. He came to life again in the dynamic atmosphere of New York, throwing off the inhibitions of the Melba months with typical freneticism, and before he left again for Europe he had sold the serial rights of Melba's book, *Melodies and Memories*, and discussed *Twenty-Five* with his American publisher, George Doran of Doubleday, Doran.

In England he found that Cleave Court had been sold. His mother had finally come to terms with reality, but it was terrible for her to leave the home she loved. Their new home was at 4, Cambridge Square, Bayswater, the vicarage of St Michael's Church, Paddington where Paul was now the incumbent. It was a sensible arrangement: the furniture from Cleave Court filled its many rooms and Pauline acted as Paul's hostess and helpmate. There was no niche for John, who made a life of his own around the local bars.

Bayswater was still clinging to its past glory, but deterioration was setting in rapidly as the grand terraces became flats and rooming-houses, and the brothel area near Paddington Station grew even seedier. It was becoming a district where eccentric old women and tired old men attempted to retain some semblance of dignity in furnished rooms, with a gas ring to cook on and a shared bathroom on the first floor. But errand boys still whistled popular tunes as they cycled round delivering orders, a muffin man still rang his bell in the afternoon and a potato seller pushed a cart with a glass tank of peeled potatoes floating in water. Occasionally, maids in uniform scurried to post letters and the sight of a policeman on his beat was commonplace – it was safe to walk the streets at night. Westbourne Grove could no longer be compared to Bond Street but Whiteley's still prospered: the orchestra played in the balcony while the displays in the magnificent food hall rivalled those of Harrods. There were plenty of local cinemas, such as the Roxy or the Blue Hall, to provide relaxation for Pauline. Hyde Park was only a short distance away, and in Oxford Street she could wander round the big shops. Altogether, it was a livelier place to be than Torquay, but she missed having her own garden, and the fresh air. London air was heavy with pollution and in Bayswater the sharp, gaseous smell of coal-fired trains drifted over from Paddington station.

The Nicholses were comfortably off, though care had to be taken over the housekeeping and there were also John's drinking bouts to be paid for. Pauline made do with a cook, a parlour-maid and a cleaning lady who came in to do the heavy work. By the standards of the women Beverley mixed with, Pauline was dowdy but, by her own, she was well dressed: she could sit over afternoon tea at Whiteley's or Selfridge's, secure in the knowledge that her clothes were good and that she was a lady. John did not let his appearance deteriorate either and when he sallied forth, eyeglass and button hole firmly in place, he still looked the prosperous gentleman.

Beverley returned temporarily to his rooms at 54, Bryanston Street but, with money in the bank, he decided it was time to rent a house. If his mother hoped to persuade him to join them in Cambridge Square, only a short distance from Bryanston Street, she was disappointed. He started his search well away from Bayswater; however much he loved her, he did not want his mother on the doorstep. He eventually found a small house in Hasker Street, not far from Harrods, and took it on a short lease. Melba, back in England, gave him several items including a set of Queen Anne chairs, a small Empire desk, a Marie Antoinette couch, a Louis Seize ormolu clock mounted with cupids and two gouaches by Guardi. These gave the house an air of elegance well beyond his pocket. Melba later demanded, following a slight tiff, that all her gifts be returned. In the mean time, Beverley settled down to write *Twenty-Five*. He was also working with Northcliffe newspapers as a theatre critic and general factotum, and soon realized that he could not run the house with the sole help of a daily woman. He decided to find a manservant who could act as cook, housekeeper and valet.

In *Down the Kitchen Sink*, he told the charming story of the man he employed, Reginald Arthur Gaskin. It was his mother, he said, who had discovered him while she was visiting Alan who had been taken to a nursing-home in Norfolk. Gaskin, only twenty-one, apparently ran this establishment almost single-handed, scrubbing floors, changing beds and doing the cooking. This paragon eventually appeared on Beverley's doorstep in his ill-fitting suit, pink-cheeked and bright-eyed, the epitome of the country boy. The truth was not so romantic: Gaskin was found through a domestic employment agency. He had all the necessary accomplishments but, almost as important, he was a homosexual. A contemporary remarked of him, 'Gay? He invented it!' Whether, as with many of Beverley's male friendships, there was an initial sexual attraction is not clear, but the two men got on well from the start. Gaskin made an important contribution when he introduced a kitten into the house. Beverley had always been fond of cats; in his schoolboy diaries, he had written of a new 'Mookit' with eyes like stars, of the panic when one of the household cats went missing and of the joy when it was found. But it was Gaskin who took responsibility for the cats which were to feature in Beverley's books. Among his other skills, Gaskin was an excellent chef and Beverley was soon entertaining a growing circle of friends to dinner-parties at his little house. Those in the know looked forward to Gaskin's delectable cooking and he was often approached with seductive financial offers to leave Beverley, but he always declined, with tact and dignity. Noel Coward once asked if there was the slightest chance of persuading Gaskin to change his allegiance, knowing full well what the answer would be.

Beverley's home rapidly became a centre for the bright young things of the day but their behaviour did not always meet with Gaskin's approval. He found Tallulah Bankhead particularly trying. After one party, she seated herself on the red carpet outside the front door and insisted on being pulled up and down the street by a contingent of whooping young men whom she flayed with an imaginary whip and urged on with language strong enough to embarrass the entire neighbourhood. Gaskin glowered at this spectacle and later remarked icily to Beverley, 'I believe she was *born* a lady?' Telling this story years later, Beverley added, 'The custom of putting a red carpet down on the pavement so that one's dinner guests could get out of their cars on to a soft surface was not unusual. Today, people would think it a mad thing to do – besides, the carpet would be stolen within minutes.'

Among his new friends were Somerset Maugham and his wife Syrie. Their marriage was under considerable strain and Beverley experienced some of the unpleasantness at first hand. After their divorce, his sympathy lay with Syrie but he was not prepared to lose the patronage of one of England's most acclaimed authors, so he trod a delicate tightrope between the two protagonists and managed to remain friends with both. This meant accepting Gerald Haxton, Maugham's American lover, whom he disliked intensely. Another new friend was Barbara Back, the wife of Ivor Back, a prominent surgeon. She was bright, charming and pretty, and enjoyed the company of gay men who, in response, confided their problems to her. Beverley liked her enormously, but years later he was appalled to discover that she not only betrayed confidences but also fabricated stories about people to amuse her friends. She found particular pleasure in telling Maugham her titbits and Beverley was distressed by the salty tales she invented about his own love life. Another of this circle was Rebecca West with whom he developed a close affinity. She, too, was appalled by Barbara Back's behaviour when she found out about it many years later, and in letters to Beverley made no secret of her disgust with her old and once trusted friend.

Beverley completed *Twenty-Five* in 1925, and dedicated it to George and Blanche, his uncle and aunt. It included an interview with Maugham, which was something of a coup, for he rarely gave them. In the interview, Maugham said, with what may have been deliberate irony, that he could not understand why there were so few tales told about him. It was a neat portrait which concealed more than it revealed, and the same might be said of the sketches of Noel Coward, Michael Arlen, Winston Churchill and Elinor Glyn (who told Beverley in all seriousness that he had been a horse in a previous existence). He described his visits to America, Australia and Greece – in the Greek section, as has already been mentioned, he re-used material from *The Athenians*. As well as his interview with the Queen, he included one with King Constantine, and, with the careful use of the word 'alleged', he also told the story of Compton Mackenzie's activities against the King, managing to make it all appear faintly absurd. Mackenzie, in his book *My Life and Times, Octave Six*, published in 1967, dismissed Beverley's story as a piece of 'juvenile silliness' – which was not the same thing, however, as a denial. It is quite clear from Mackenzie's writings that he regarded Constantine at the time as an obstacle to his work on behalf of the Allies.

Twenty-Five was not autobiographical in the conventional sense. Alec Waugh pointed this out in his review, saying that the autobiographical element was very clearly dependent on the effect others had on the author rather than anything the author said about himself. This, he added, was something new, subtle and indirect. It would today be easy to underestimate *Twenty-Five*, but at the time, nothing quite like it had been seen before, and it spawned a host of imitators, none of whom captured its originality, humour or beguiling audacity. It soon shot into the best-seller list, helped on its way by an article in the *Sunday Times* by Maugham himself, who wrote his piece without payment as a birthday present to Beverley. It was not a critique in the accepted sense and in it Maugham poked gentle fun at professional book-reviewers, some of whom he had been 'privileged' to meet from time to time, who had impressed him with their flashing eyes, wanton hair and looks of eager determination, and had awed him with their universal knowledge and confidence in themselves. At a dinner given for such a group by Osbert Sitwell, he had listened, forlorn and strange, while they discussed James Elroy Flecker. In order to show an intelligent interest, he had asked the least formidable of them if he did not find it very exhausting to read books for reviews. With a smile the reviewer replied that he seldom came across a book whose heart he could not tear out in an hour.

For such a drastic operation, Maugham admitted he had no facility – he must read to the end. He confessed that the first chapter he had read in *Twenty-Five* was the one about himself, and he was much excited to discover that, to Beverley, he was romantic, saturnine and bleak, whereas he thought of himself as a very quiet, retiring person.

Noel Coward reviewed the book for the *Daily Mail* with wit and perception. Naturally, he said, he was pleased to find that he emerged from it a 'darling', but rather dampened to find that nearly everyone else was a darling too. There were, he was happy to note, several refreshing lapses when Mr Nicols discarded his sympathetic conception of humanity and administered a few sharp and well-deserved slaps, but these were too few. England demanded more vituperation from her young writers. (The notable slaps were administered to Rudolph Valentino for his lack of humour and overweening vanity, to the censorship of the theatre and, of course, to the British government's treatment of the Greek royal family.) Coward praised Beverley's account of the Bywaters and Thompson trial as one of the most moving things he had ever read. P.G. Wodehouse in the *Weekly Dispatch* remarked on the excellence of the writing; the *Morning Post* described the book as first-rate entertainment and *The Times* praised it as entertaining and lively. The applause rolled on, from the *Church of England Newspaper* to the *Architects' Journal*, and several magazines nominated it as the 'Book of the Week'.

In more than sixty reviews, only three were critical. The *Star*, a London evening paper, accused him of bad taste and *Gentlewomen* mocked it and declared that it had lacked a sub-editor to consign chunks of it to the waste-paper basket. The reviewer warned that if Beverley was like this at twenty-five he would become a very boring old gentleman indeed. The Baroness Clifton, in a long diatribe in the *Sunday Express*, begged to be saved from very dainty young men with hides of brass and a profound lack of taste.

Beverley was again the man of the moment: photographs and articles about him appeared in the press, one under the heading, 'Men Girls Admire'. His opinions were quoted and articles by him were in demand: typical of these was one entitled 'The Madness of the Modern Girl'..He was also commissioned to write a series of portraits similar to those in *Twenty-Five* for the glossy magazine *Sketch*, under the general title, 'Woad: Celebrities in Undress'. His first portrait was typically impudent, its subject being himself. The series was subsequently published in book form as *Are They The Same At Home?* which he dedicated to 'My dear enemy, the Baroness Clifton, in the knowledge that one of us should know better and that one of us does.'

Twenty-Five continued its success in America, Canada, New Zealand, South Africa and Australia. In the overseas press there was frequently a note of asperity from anonymous reviewers. One complained of his habit of calling people by their first names as if he actually knew them, selecting Noel Coward and Robert Nichols as examples, unaware that both were his friends. Another described it as a 'literary curiosity', yet another as 'naïve but showing promise.' A review which appeared in an Indian newspaper sounded a warning. It remarked on Beverley's sympathy for his subjects, a refreshing change because the young were usually intolerant, and wondered how, if Mr Nichols lived to a ripe and literary old age, his last impressions would compare with his first. There was no hint of bitterness in his book, and bitterness was something we all had to guard against as we grew older. Beverley probably did no more than glance at this in 1926 and very likely forgot it. Decades later, it was his bitterness which attracted the attention of reviewers, bitterness that reached its climax in *Father Figure*.

Beverley had been a popular figure on the social scene before *Twenty-Five* but after its success no London hostess of any consequence could ignore him. There is no modern equivalent of the hostesses of those days, for the circumstances which bred them have vanished, together with the structure of society as it was then. Four leading hostesses occupied centre stage in Beverley's social life. There was Lady Sybil Colefax who assembled the pick of the brains at Argyll House in the King's Road, Chelsea: George Bernard Shaw, Max Beerbohm, Diaghilev, William Walton, Artur Rubinstein, Rachmaninoff, Duff Cooper and Virginia Woolf. When her husband died leaving her very little money, Sybil Colefax sold the house and started a decorating business with the brilliant young designer John Fowler. Her lunches and dinners continued in a small house in Westminster, with the larger gatherings at the Dorchester. When she grew too old and her income diminished, her friends tactfully contributed to the cost and this she accepted gracefully without anyone's being in the least embarrassed. Next door in the King's Road, at 213, was Syrie Maugham, something of a rival, who captured an equally splendid list of intellectual lions. Lady Cunard held court in her house in Grosvenor Square, a Dresden china-like figure whom Beverley compared to E.F. Benson's immortal Lucia. She collected ambassadors, cabinet ministers and eminent artists, and at her house Beverley met Pavlova, Lady Diana Cooper, Sir Thomas Beecham and his old acquaintance, Winston Churchill. Last but not least of the hostesses was the Hon Mrs Ronald Greville, a down-to-earth Scotswoman whose vast fortune came from her father John McEwen, the brewer. She specialized, if that is the right word, in royalty. Her friend Queen Mary would drop in quite informally for afternoon tea at her large house in Charles Street, off Berkeley Square, where teas were magnificent affairs in the grand tradition. Her country house, Polesden Lacey, built in 1824, she lent to the then Duke and Duchess of York for their honeymoon. Beverley was once there when the Duchess was the guest of honour. Guests used to get up very late on Sunday mornings but Beverley, unable to lie in bed, went down to the drawing-room and tinkered on the piano. Perhaps influenced by the presence of the royal visitor, he was extemporizing on the theme of the National Anthem, and playing it in the style of a Bach fugue, when he glanced up to see the Duchess watching him. As he rose to his feet, she asked what it was he was playing, since it sounded faintly familiar. 'Just something of my own,' he replied lamely.

One of Beverley's accomplishments was the ease with which he charmed elderly ladies. He genuinely liked them, treated them with respect, listened to them, and never forgot small courtesies like buying flowers for them. He treated obscure ladies just as well as ladies of wealth or influence and there are stories of lonely women whose lives were brightened by his attention and the inevitable bunch of flowers. The ladies could adore him without any of the messy complications of emotional involvement: if any hints of this arose, he coped with the situation with such tact that there was no distress and, if anything, greater adoration than before. The only time that he found himself in an intolerable situation, which he did not handle very well, was with an elderly widow who was insanely impassioned, convinced that a man half her age was equally in love with her. She lavished presents on him to an embarrassing degree and refused to accept any gentle rebuff he offered. Beverley thought of returning the presents but he was afraid of hurting her feelings; he tried to avoid her, but she would hover in wait for him with more gifts. She also bombarded him with invitations to visit her country house, and eventually he agreed to go.

It was an unwise decision, for, instead of being one of several guests, he found himself alone with her, and spent a dreadful evening fending off her increasingly coquettish advances in a room she had turned into a Nichols shrine, decorated with his photographs. At last, he escaped to bed but woke up in the middle of the night to find her, stark naked, in bed with him. This might have been funny if it had not been so sad. He ordered her out of the room and, after an hysterical scene, she left in tears. He dressed, crept out of the house and drove away. Even this did not end her infatuation, and he was in despair when a friend, reminding him that she was an ardent spiritualist, suggested that Beverley write to her saying that, at a seance, he had been commanded not to see or contact her again if tragedy was to be avoided. Incredibly, this worked, and she left him alone from then on. Beverley deleted the whole incident from his autobiography, *The Unforgiving Minute*, probably because it reflected very little credit upon himself.

What with his journalistic work, constant appearances at social functions and an active sex life, his days and nights were fully occupied, but there was still an underlying dissatisfaction which could only be assuaged by setting himself new goals. He began writing his first play, composing for a revue, and started a novel which he finally completed during a working holiday in Norway. For this novel he chose the old theme of an innocent young man drawn into a world of immorality and vice. If *Self* was his version of *Vanity Fair*, the new book owed more than a little to Oscar Wilde's *The Picture of Dorian Gray* and Michael Arlen's *The Green Hat*, but he had his own experience to draw upon and *Crazy Pavements*, as he called the book, was more autobiographical than his readers could know.

His hero, Brian Elme, an aspiring author, is forced by the spectre of the dole queue to write a society gossip page for a women's magazine. With the help of Debrett and a vivid imagination, he concocts snippets of gossip, managing not to sail too close to libel. Elme is a twenty-year-old of startling purity and modesty, unaware of his own beauty and potent sex-appeal. He lives a blameless life with Walter, an ex-naval officer a few years older than himself, who adores him in a healthy, hero-worshipping way: Beverley went to some lengths to stress the idealistic and sexless nature of the relationship. The plot darkens when Brian is sent to the home of Lady Julia Cressey to apologize for a fiction he has written about her romantic involvement with the degenerate Lord William Motley. Brian, who has adored Julia from afar, is stunned by her and she by him. Her astonishment at his obvious innocence turns to a passionate desire to add him to her list of lovers, and before he realizes what is happening, she has introduced him into her corrupt social set. Brian accepts the role of gigolo without a qualm but, despite his modern rake's progress, retains a fragment of decency. In a happy ending, he is reunited with Walter, having, by some miracle, reverted to his old innocence. This framework gave Beverley ample opportunity to satirize Fleet Street, the public's voracious appetite for gossip, and the Mayfair society of the time with its cast of people who, if not always as young as they tried to be, were certainly startlingly bright.

Crazy Pavements received mixed reviews when it came out in February 1927. Some critics refused to accept the characters and the plot as anything other than preposterous nonsense; others, rather more worldly wise, saw the book as a cruel but valid satire on a section of society. Oliver Baldwin, the Socialist son of the Tory politician Stanley Baldwin, made a fierce attack on the wealthy who appeared oblivious of the poverty around them. Some attacked Beverley for the theme which, they maintained, was as old-fashioned as much of the wit; most admitted that Beverley's sense of humour was irresistible, however repulsive the characters.

The most analytical review, written by Arthur Waugh, the father of Alec and Evelyn, appeared in the *Daily Telegraph*. Nichols, he said, was one of the few young writers worth watching, but he had created a dilemma for himself. He was likely to irritate both the serious older readers and the irresponsible young ones – the former because of his cheerful laughter at offences they would denounce as disgusting, and the latter because of his frequent floods of sentimentality. This neatly summed up a problem which Beverley never satisfactorily resolved: his apparent cynicism about the modern world could change almost in mid-sentence into a passionate plea for moral values, justice for the underprivileged, or whatever happened to touch him deeply at the time. This habit could make critics cringe but probably reassured those of his readers who were as much beguiled by his public charm and vivid sincerity as they were by his actual writing. Waugh did not take him to task too harshly over the sentimental outbursts in *Crazy Pavements*: they might not ring true to some but then, he pointed out, one man's sentiment was invariably another man's nausea. He added that the sentiment was at least as prettily executed as the satire, and the combination was daintily mixed with a variety of flavours and dressed with bite.

All in all, *Crazy Pavements* was a resounding popular success, though for different reasons to different readers, and it went on to further success abroad, collecting serviceable reviews wherever it appeared. Sales were helped by speculation about the identities of the real life counterparts of the characters and by rumours of legal action. It was generally believed that Lord William was based on Ned Lathom but Beverley issued a strong denial of this and emphasized that all the characters were fictitious.

Discussing the book in 1982, Beverley confessed that it had caused him problems, first because the set-pieces in it were based on personal experience and he had had some difficulty in disguising what was essentially reportage; and second because it was really a homosexual story doctored for general consumption. 'Today I could write it as it actually was, but, in those days, it was out of the question. Of course Brian and Walter were lovers, and Lady Julia was based on one of those predatory young queens who collect conquests like scalp-hunters collect scalps.' He refused to name the real-life counterparts of his characters: 'They knew who they were and they were furious with me.' The dreadful Lord William was partly based on Ned Lathom, whom he adored, but mostly on another socialite whom he had detested. He was still amused by those critics who had refused to believe that the incidents could happen in real life, 'poor, blinkered darlings!'

The novel reads today as freshly as when it was written, even allowing for the validity of Arthur Waugh's critical observations. It is strange that it has not had the continuing life enjoyed by Evelyn Waugh's first two novels which followed it, especially *Vile Bodies* (1930) which has points of direct similarity. Beverley did not know how to react to this at the time. Coincidence may have played its part, but he remained suspicious that Waugh had used his book as a crib and never quite gave him the benefit of the doubt. Champions of Waugh would very likely maintain that *Vile Bodies* was by far the better book and so deserved to survive. Nevertheless, Waugh may have been encouraged by the success of *Crazy Pavements* to write something similar which would prove more to the public taste than *Decline and Fall* (1928) which had disappointing sales until the success of *Vile Bodies*.

· II ·

London opening,
New York closing

1927–1929

O N 20 April 1927 an intimate revue, *Picnic*, opened the newly built
Arts Theatre Club in the West End. It was credited to Herbert
Farjeon with music by Beverley Nichols and Harold Scott, and
additional lyrics by Beverley Nichols and Eleanor Farjeon.

The intimate revue has no professional equivalent today. An enfeebled
imitation of it still exists among amateurs but it died out in the professional
theatre in the early 1960s. To convey its appeal to anyone who has never
seen it is difficult. In form it was a medley of sketches, solo 'turns' and
musical numbers. This could also describe much of the light entertainment
seen on television today, but there the resemblance ends. Revue had wit,
topicality, charm and pace all governed by style and elegance; above all, it
had a belief that its audience had brains. At its best it provided an evening of
sheer enchantment and laughter. It often attracted writers, composers,
choreographers and designers of great skill and ingenuity, and it produced
stars who enthralled audiences on both sides of the Atlantic. The roll-call of
names associated with it would require a *Who's Who* of its own; many of
them are now forgotten but among those who still stir a magic memory are
Noel Coward, Jack Buchanan, Gertrude Lawrence, Jessie Matthews,
Elisabeth Welch, Joyce Grenfell, Cyril Ritchard, Henry Kendall and
Hermione Gingold.

Beverley's participation in *Picnic* was an important step in his theatrical
ambitions. He was involved in half the fourteen items which made up the
programme, including the intriguingly named 'Libido Baby'. Of all the
material the only item to survive from this particular revue is the song by
Farjeon and Scott, 'I've Danced with a Man' which went on, 'who danced
with a girl who danced with the Prince of Wales'. The press was as much
concerned with discussing the Arts Theatre building as it was in reviewing
the opening show. Apart from praising the facilities the point was made
that, as a 'members only' theatre, it escaped the censorship controls of the
Lord Chamberlain. Today, in an age when almost anything goes, it may
seem extraordinary that this rigorous control actually existed. The Lord

Chamberlain's Office was highly sensitive to the use of bad language and references to sex, even banning the innocuous '*Victoria Regina*' by Laurence Housman because it portrayed the royal family. In its review, the *Morning Post* remarked regretfully that the Arts was not taking any risk with its first show. Subsequently it took a great many risks, not only in presenting plays which might not be approved by the Lord Chamberlain but also in providing a platform for writers whose work could be categorized as experimental and non-commercial. Unknown actors and directors were also given opportunities: among the directors, perhaps the best known is Sir Peter Hall.

Most of the press was favourable to *Picnic* but a sour note was struck here and there. Beverley's successor as theatre critic at the *Weekly Dispatch* said that one of his songs brought the house down when a large lump of the new plaster fell while it was being sung, and that this was quite the funniest incident in the show. He went on to praise Beverley for the boyish zest with which he had written the music, saying, 'I did the same thing years ago but I was never brave enough to let the public hear it.' Apart from this specific mention, only the *Daily Mirror* singled out a Nichols item, 'The Toreador', for special praise; elsewhere if he was named at all it was merely as a collaborator. When the show was revived to celebrate the first year of the Arts, most of his material was dropped: the new title *Many Happy Returns* was not a happy one as far as Beverley was concerned. Nevertheless, when it transferred to the Duke of York's Theatre for a reasonable run, he was at least represented in the West End. If *Picnic* was not a success for him, it was not an entirely wasted effort for it led to a major opportunity under the Cochran banner three years later. It also led to a commission to write for *White Birds*, a spectacular entertainment lavishly financed by a wealthy young man with more money than sense. The show proved to be a failure on a scale rarely seen since. Billy Milton, who appeared in it for a few performances, did not believe Beverley's contribution was used. In the course of conversation with him in 1989, he confessed his intense personal dislike of Beverley: 'He was vain and unscrupulous.'

Following the success of *Crazy Pavements*, Beverley's publishers brought out a compilation of his essays about famous people, most of which had appeared in the *Sketch*. Predictably, it received mixed reviews but sold well. The style was similar to that of *Twenty-Five*, impudent both in its title (*Are They The Same At Home?*) and in its content, but very much to the public taste. Many of the sixty personalities are still remembered today but for the student of the period there is an interest even in those who are half forgotten, for Beverley's portraits revealed details unlikely to be found in more scholarly sources. He could pin his subjects down with the delicacy and swift cruelty of a lepidopterist, but the cruelty was not always immediately apparent. His portrait of himself revealed very little but was calculated to confirm the worst fears of his critics: he dismissed religious faith, mocked politics and praised flippancy which he defined as a brave gesture by one who has seen through life. He said he rejoiced in being a poser and challenged his readers to deny that each of them was one as well. This being so, he asked why the English so often adopted a pose of stupidity. He admitted to a bitter knowledge of his own vices but claimed to have created a character to strut upon life's stage, a performer brilliantly lighted, a creature of dreams. Noel Coward, reviewing the book for the *Daily Mail*, briskly dismissed the self-portrait as inaccurate and described Beverley as a romantic idealist. Coward was somewhere near the truth, but romantic idealists rarely make money and the creature Beverley had created most certainly did. Away from the glare of the publicity he so assiduously sought, he longed to be accepted as a serious author and composer, but the tinkle of cash registers and the thrill of applause were too seductive for him to ignore.

Throughout 1927 he performed whenever required. Apart from the books, he kept up a steady output of short stories and articles for newspapers and magazines. In *Hearsts* he could be found discussing 'The Trouble With Women' and in *Good Housekeeping* advising women how to keep house with the aid of a good manservant, while in *Nash's Magazine* he gave a glance at what was involved in the preparation of a novel. On radio he was featured in a series called 'Writers Of Today'; the publicity in the *Radio Times* described him as 'of the moment and in the swim'. At a public debate, this time in aid of hospital funds, he presented an ironic lecture arguing that amusement was a bore: George Grossmith, the actor and co-author of *The Dairy Of A Nobody*, argued against him and, judging by the laughter, won easily. That this event was widely reported in the national and provincial press says something for the news value of Grossmith and Nichols, although it should be added that Grossmith got 'top billing'. At the New Theatre on 6 May, Marie Tempest organized a *London Pride* matinée in aid of the Save The Children Fund. It included a pageant of great lovers in history portrayed by a mixture of society figures and actresses: Gladys Cooper as Helen of Troy, Tallulah Bankhead as Cleopatra, Prince Nicholas Galitzine as Abelard, Stephen Tennant as Prince Charming and Lady Ravensdale as the Empress Josephine. Beverley portrayed Lord Byron. One newspaper complained that he looked too effete to represent the virile Lord Byron.

In the autumn, he went to America for a lecture tour, arriving a few weeks after the publication of *Crazy Pavements* by Doran. In a carefully orchestrated publicity campaign, it was implied that his visit had been delayed because of threats of legal action by a 'certain peer' over the portrayal of himself in the book. This was a dead story in England but new to America, and its revival helped to boost sales and arouse curiosity in the

young author who could write beguilingly of 'nymphomaniacs, homosexuals, sadists and drug addicts', as one paper bluntly put it. It was also
announced in *Variety* and the New York papers that *The Stag*, a new play by
Beverley Nichols, was to be produced during the 1927/1928 season, but
nothing came of this. It eventually surfaced in London in 1929.

He thoroughly enjoyed the lecture tour, which was more like a triumphal
progress as he was fêted by women's clubs in town after town – in a sense a
natural progression from entertaining ladies in the drawing-rooms of
Torquay. Occasionally, if there was a well-tuned piano available, he played
some of his own compositions. He boasted that, on this and subsequent
visits to the States, he rarely stayed in hotels because of the rivalry between
local hostesses to have him as a guest. The trip gave him the opportunity to
interview personalities for another book to be called *The Star-Spangled
Manner*, and it says something for his reputation and persistence that he
persuaded President Calvin Coolidge to see him. Coolidge was an introvert
given to laconic comments, and Beverley found the interview hard going,
getting only a non-committal 'Oh' to his opening patter. The President,
who was known for an apparent lack of interest in anything outside politics
and was regarded as a Philistine when it came to the arts, was eventually
stirred to life when Beverley suggested that most Americans, including Mr
President himself, failed to appreciate that the younger generation in
Europe, overshadowed by the possibility of future war, was often filled
with feelings of utter futility. This, Beverley contended, now in full
debating spate, was illustrated in every phase of European art. Coolidge
replied that he had visited an exhibition of modern European art in
Pittsburgh and seen the signs of neurosis: if a nation's psychology was
diseased, so was its art. But if the people were rediscovering happiness, that
story was told in the pictures too, and 'I thought I observed as much
evidence of recovery as of sickness.' This admission by a man as taciturn as
Coolidge gave Beverley the twist which he needed to make the interview
unexpected.

Beverley's technique was always to attempt to find some aspects of his
subject's character which belied the commonly held view. As an interviewing technique it might not have been new but Beverley made it appear so
and provided his readers with the thrill of surprise. A good example was his
piece about Gloria Swanson, beloved of the gossip columnists, which
showed her to be a woman with 'a keener, more masculine intelligence than
that of many men'. 'Beverley took me seriously at a time when most people
did not. I was grateful to him for that. His article was and still is the best
ever written about me because it was and is me. He called it "Swanson on
Skyscrapers". I liked that. My autobiography will be called "Swanson on
Swanson", a kind of tribute to him.' Gloria Swanson said this in her Fifth
Avenue apartment in 1979, more than fifty years after their first meeting.

They remained friends and it was not unusual for him to be roused from sleep because Swanson was in the mood for a long telephone conversation. As he said, 'She never really believed in the time difference between London and New York.'

Another of Beverley's interviewees was Otto Kahn, financier, millionaire and patron of the arts. Kahn may be remembered for many things but in England his enduring memorial was his endowment of St Dunstan's home for soldiers blinded in the First World War. Kahn could deal with the most complicated financial matters with persuasion and tact, but when it came to his passion for bridge, according to Beverley, all restraint left him and his temper could be awesome. It was therefore with some trepidation that Beverley accepted an invitation to join Kahn and a party of friends on an American train tour, first to Miami and then to Los Angeles, during which the main recreation would be bridge. Beverley's game was not up to the Kahn standard and he took a week's crash course with a lady who, in deference to his nationality, named his mythical opponents Sir Thomas and Lady Jones. This led to a flow of dialogue which distracted him from serious study. 'My!' she would cry, pointing to the empty air. 'Look what Sir Thomas is doing with his ten of diamonds!' or, 'Goodness! Just watch what her ladyship is doing!' as she moved the wrong card from the hand laid out in front of the invisible Lady Jones. 'What a wicked lady!' – this accompanied by a playful slap at thin air. It is not clear what beneficial effect all this had on Beverley's game but it apparently proved a fatal experience for his instructress who committed suicide shortly afterwards.

Kahn was a thoughtful and generous host, making certain that his guests lacked nothing. To Beverley's consternation, this included the provision of lady companions wherever the party stopped overnight at an hotel. In accordance with the Anita Loos injunction, the ladies ordered in advance were blond, either natural or out of the bottle. Beverley never discovered whether any of the gentlemen availed themselves of the opportunities on offer as he was always busy avoiding the advances of the blonde he had, as it were, drawn for the night. The guests endured the procedure, entering into the spirit of the game at the inevitable warm-up dinner parties, until they reached New Orleans where, just before the arrival of that night's contingent, they made their excuses and disappeared. Beverley, deserted in the hotel lobby, found the sight of eight blondes bursting through the swing doors too much, and he fled to the men's room until the danger had passed. After this, the provision of blondes was stopped, much to the relief of Kahn's guests.

Beverley's close encounter with this 1920s version of the 'hostess' industry linked neatly to his meeting with Anita Loos whose *Gentlemen Prefer Blondes* was a best-selling novel. The astonishing fact emerged that in the States as well as in Europe only a small percentage of readers appeared to understand that Lorelei, the heroine, was a whore with social ambitions. Miss Loos, at first stunned by this, had become resigned to an avalanche of fan mail which spoke of Lorelei as a clean-living girl who just enjoyed a nice time, but was surprised to find that this misunderstanding extended even to Hollywood. She thought it important that the film's leading lady should have some inkling of the character's morals, though one actress interviewed for the part denied that Lorelei could behave in an immoral fashion, and the producers of the film were also blind to the truth.

While he was in Hollywood, Beverley was given a screen test at the instigation of Jesse Lasky of Famous Players-Lasky-Paramount to whom he was introduced by Kahn who had a financial interest in the group. According to Beverley, Lasky took one look at him and asked if he would like to be a leading man. The test was said to be a great success, but Frank Tuttle who directed it advised Beverley to stick to writing. Tuttle, who is best remembered for his direction of *This Gun For Hire* which made Alan Ladd an international star, knew when someone had screen magic and when he had not, and in Beverley's case the magic so potent in real life failed to transfer to the screen. His later venture into films proved Tuttle correct.

In Hollywood, Beverley also met Charles Chaplin on several occasions but the complexity of the man seems to have baffled him. Chaplin discoursed gloomily on his theory that cancer was the result of a subconscious desire for death. Rather more cheerfully, he responded to Beverley's comment that his films, however disjointed the story or disconnected the incidents, appeared to have a uniform colour and unity of thought, by saying that he always had a melody running through his head: 'It would be too much to say that I set everything to that melody, because one cannot set such a diversity of action to music. But at least it means that I achieve a unity of mood and of rhythm.' This was precisely how Beverley described the method he employed when writing. He summed Chaplin up as the moodiest of creatures, 'stepping quickly from the shadow into the blazing sunlight and then back into the shadow again', and he called the piece on Chaplin that he wrote for *The Star-Spangled Manner*, rather predictably, 'Pagliacci'.

In the book Beverley interspersed his interviews with impressions of America; these have staled with time but one curious chapter still intrigues. He paid a number of visits to Black Harlem which both fascinated and repelled him with its theatres, dance-halls, nightclubs and homosexual bars. It was a culture entirely alien to him and it was clearly the sexuality of the blacks which made such a deep impression. He concluded his book with a sermon on the economic faults of Britain and Europe, stressing what might be learned from America in terms of production and marketing (he called it advertisement) and advocating the benefits of some form of economic unity in Europe. He also criticized the States for its self-absorption and lack of interest in events across the Atlantic, because such isolationism lulled America into a sense of false security. 'Soon the Atlantic may itself be hushed by a whirr of wings', he wrote, in reference to bombers.

While *The Star-Spangled Manner* contained sharp entertainment larded with common sense, it was also decorated with the verbal sugar-icing which Beverley seemed unable to avoid. This, however, did not prevent it from being a success on both sides of the Atlantic.

By 1928 Beverley could feel considerable satisfaction with his public success and his secure finances, but happiness in his personal relationships still eluded him. He ricocheted from one brief encounter to another, always hopeful but always disappointed that beyond the sex act there seemed to be nothing. In an astonishingly frank conversation with the young Cecil Beaton, he boasted of his sexual activity and implied that he had slept with, among other well-known men, Oliver Messel, Somerset Maugham and Noel Coward, adding that if he were to be castrated there would be nothing left to live for. Beaton, at twenty-four, was surprisingly innocent and was understandably startled by these revelations. Reading between the lines, it sounds as if Beverley was either intent on getting Beaton into bed or was trying to persuade him to admit to his own sexual preferences. Whatever the motive, it seems a risky thing to have done, even if he felt certain that Beaton was homosexual. Such a supposition would presumably have been based on Beaton's effete manner which was sufficiently distinctive for Noel Coward to lecture him about it.

Beaton was already a celebrity in London but Beverley advised him to go to America. In a letter to him written from his recently acquired cottage in Glatton, he promised to help by way of introductions to Mrs Cornelius Vanderbilt ('a *very* good friend of mine'), to Carl Van Vechten, Otto Kahn and 'all sorts of millionaires'. He went on: 'You are far too intelligent for it to be necessary for me to try to persuade you how infinitely important it is for you to go to New York and succeed, as you will.' In the same letter he formally guaranteed a commission for ten new photographs at £100 'for which I hold myself responsible as editor of the *American Sketch*'.

This letter is interesting because it alludes to two events in his life which were significant but not in the way he may have seen them at the time. The first was his purchase of Thatch Cottage in Glatton, a tiny village near Peterborough. For reasons best known to himself, he always described this as having happened in 1929, a year later, and, in his autobiography, *All I Could Never Be*, he told a typically Nichols story about its purchase. He was returning to England from America on the *Mauretania* when he read an item in an old copy of the *New York Times* about the death of John Borie. At once Beverley remembered the idyllic Tudor cottage Borie had lived in when he was in England and which he had visited with Borie's sister, Emily Ryerson. On an impulse, he sent a cable to Mrs Ryerson who was in Timbuctoo at the time, making a fairly low offer for the cottage, shrewdly believing that, for friendship's sake, she would accept. He proved to be correct. When he eventually visited his new house, however, he was sadly disappointed. It had not been occupied for some while and there were signs of neglect everywhere. The garden, which he remembered glowing with flowers, was kept just short of being a wilderness by the occasional attentions of a local odd-job man. The only consolation was the low price he had paid for it and the fact that the contents were included. Borie had furnished it with decent country stuff and everything from pots and pans to linen was of good quality. Otherwise, Beverley was faced with major expenditure both inside and out.

His plans for this work were delayed indefinitely when the second event occurred, which he hoped would be of great significance for his career. He was dining at the Savoy Restaurant with George Doran, his American publisher, when Doran offered him the job of editor of the *American Sketch*. Envious of the success of the *New Yorker*, he wanted to beat it on its own terms, and believed that the *Sketch*, a low-circulation 'society' periodical, could be transformed into a money-making magazine along similar lines. He offered Beverley a contract on generous terms which included the transportation of his furniture to New York along with Gaskin; indeed, the thought of a little piece of England complete with manservant set down in Manhattan had irresistible publicity value. Such was his salesmanship and confidence in Beverley's abilities that the answer could only be 'yes'. In a state of brandy-induced euphoria they clinched the deal. Years later, Beverley expressed his astonishment that anyone could have believed that his brand of Oxford-cum-Fleet Street humour, with its British irony and understatement, could be any match for the machinegun-fire of American wit as epitomized by the *New Yorker*. He came to regard this venture as a disastrous failure but it was not quite the failure he made it out to be.

He arrived in New York in September, and found an apartment on the top floor of a house in East 46th Street not far from Doran's office in Madison Avenue. As soon as his furniture arrived he sold it all at a good profit; it was mostly French and not evocative of the British background George Doran wanted. In its place he bought solid Victorian mahogany and, with Gaskin installed, he was ready to astonish the readers, present and future, of the *American Sketch*. Doran's publicity machine had been hard at work and the papers were full of stories of Nichols's smartness and wit. At a cocktail party for the press he worked hard, throwing off epigrams and being brittle about American women in a manner which evoked bright young people and Mayfair sophistication, in accordinace with the brief supplied to him by the publicists. He afterwards said he was amazed that the press did not demand his immediate deportation for his performance of outrageous decadence.

All he knew about the *American Sketch* before he left England was that it was said to resemble English society magazines; what was unexpected was its dull format and even duller content which consisted mainly of snapshots of dreary people doing dreary things. Even more unexpected was the advertising which was devoted almost entirely to dogs and dog-breeding. Beverley now discovered he had no staff apart from a secretary and a managing editor who was so imbued with the spirit of the old magazine that he had nothing to contribute to the new version except gloomy prognostications. Even worse, a major problem was the fact that Beverley knew nothing of the practicalities of editing a magazine. At Oxford, with the *Isis* and the *Oxford Outlook*, the mechanics were looked after by the printer who was used to holding the hands of undergraduate editors with no professional knowledge, but in New York there was no such person. As far as George Doran was concerned, he had bought Beverley at great cost and felt it was up to him to get on with it. Badly needing an assistant, Beverley managed to persuade Doran to let him hire Ray Harris, whom he had met and liked instantly on his lecture tour. Harris, a budding writer, knew little more than Beverley but this pair of amateurs were allowed to fumble their way through the process of producing what was, in effect, a new monthly magazine.

In the circumstances it was surprising that the new *American Sketch* looked as good as it did when it appeared in December 1928: not nearly as bad as Beverley said it was. Reading it more than sixty years later, one finds it amusing, often witty, frequently ironic and neatly bitchy. It covers the New York scene with an emphasis on Broadway theatre, has gossipy pieces about London and Paris and a feature on the crisis in Hollywood caused by the arrival of talking pictures. There is a column on the popularity of beige in fashion, a rather dull article on tennis and a feature on dogs, presumably left over from the old magazine. The illustrations tend towards the sombre. Among the contributors are Ethel Barrymore on 'Herself' and Rebecca West on legs (of the show-girl variety). The dog advertisements are bunched towards the back – 105 display pieces, to be exact, enlivened somewhat by a full-page advertisement about horses.

Beverley's editorship lasted for four months. He had made a decision early on not to use photographs and Cecil Beaton, who had arrived in New York in November, was understandably angry when he found that Beverley had reneged on his promise. As it transpired, Beaton had little need of Beverley's help; his anger did not last, and his photograph of

Beverley set against the background of New York at night appeared in the London *Sketch* the following April. In the years to come the two men remained friends and, as they grew older, their letters to each other became increasingly affectionate. Those written by Beaton after his stroke in 1974, when he had lost the use of his right hand and had taught himself to use his left, are indicative of his attitude in old age: a mixture of bravery and despairing sadness. Beverley's letters to him are in similar vein. Each man expressed admiration for the work the other was still doing, and they seemed to find mutual satisfaction in their continued survival and success when so many of their contemporaries were dead and forgotten.

Although each issue of the *American Sketch* improved and circulation edged upwards, it was not enough, and the *New Yorker* remained unaffected by its would-be rival. In February, Doran told Beverley that following reorganization of the company the title was to be sold and he was no longer required. As a consolation, he offered him a deal for future books to replace his contract. In a semi-formal letter to Ray Harris to assure him that there would be a place for him in the new set-up, Beverley said: 'I don't think it has really been a waste of time. I myself feel like someone restored to life after a six-month sentence.' He had hated almost every moment of the office-bound chore and the relief of redundancy was enormous. He sailed with Gaskin for England as soon as affairs in New York were settled, having no wish to hang around in a city which he had come to conquer and in which he had failed. Ironically, the March issue of the *American Sketch* was unexpectedly successful, although the increased sales may have been stimulated by the abrupt departure of its editor. The new owners sent him a long cable, which he received in mid-Atlantic, offering generous terms if he would resume work, but as far as he was concerned that chapter in his life was finished. He threw the cable into the sea.

Beverley regretted leaving New York partly because he had begun an affair with a young man called Warren, but before he had left he had promised to arrange for him to come to England as soon as possible. He had also made substantial profits in the Wall Street boom. When he had first arrived to work on the *American Sketch* he had been astonished at the ease with which people were making money; even his secretary had made a small fortune and the office boy proudly boasted of his capital of $15,000 in shares. Beverley promptly joined the game, bought into Montgomery Ward and Internal Combustion stock, and in a few weeks made $12,000 profit. So his departure was not all gloom. There was a round of farewell parties, friends gave him a champagne send-off in his cabin, and his bruised pride was assuaged by the knowledge that, after several attempts, he was to have his play *The Stag* produced in the West End. As a postscript to this period in New York, Ray Harris wrote in an article that Beverley, tired and distressed, wanted to live down his reputation for 'lightness and smartness', and in a prophetic aside, commented that this unwelcome reputation would be revived, however serious Beverley's future work might be.

· 1 2 ·

Theatrical occasions

1929–1930

ARRIVING in London in the middle of March, Beverley was plunged into the rehearsals of *The Stag*. The week before the opening night, John Nichols ended a bout of hard drinking. It was arranged that he should spend a few days at the cottage at Glatton to 'recuperate', so that he would be able to take Pauline to the first night on Tuesday 2 April. Beverley was confident that the married couple he had engaged to look after the house and garden would be capable of keeping the old man in order.

In *Father Figure*, he tells the following story. On Saturday 31 March (this must in fact have been 30th) he drove up to Glatton to spend the night and to bring John back to London. He arrived to find the house was in darkness, and on the hall table a note from the couple saying Mr Nichols's behaviour had become so monstrous that they had left. He found John lying on the floor of the sitting-room dead drunk; his fly-buttons were undone, he had been sick, and the room stank. Beverley was filled with wild fury that this monster had defiled the home that he had 'built so painfully and tried to make so beautiful'. Then he saw the broken china figure of a shepherdess which he had discovered in a blocked-up alcove 'some months before', clutched in John's hand. This was the trigger; Beverley decided again to kill the man who had made everyone's life such a misery. He forced a double dose of his father's sleeping-pills into his mouth, knowing that they were lethal when mixed with alcohol. To make doubly certain, he dragged John, a deadweight of seventeen stone, through the French windows into the bitterly cold night and manhandled him into the entangled branches of an old rosebush. Snow had begun to fall heavily and this, he hoped, would obliterate any signs. Surely, he reasoned, the combination of sleeping-pills, alcohol and bitter cold would finish the old man off? Then, as he had done on the occasion of the first murder attempt, he went to the piano, but this time he set the incident to music in a frenzy of composition. 'It all came out as a sort of furious and disjointed étude.' The first draft was completed in the early hours of Sunday morning. 'And then – there was a crash and a splintering of wood, and he fell into the room covered with snow, with blood streaming down his face. Rasputin! That was the instant literary analogy.' Could the monster ever be killed?

The murder attempt having failed, Beverley concentrated his efforts for the next thirty-six hours on getting John into shape for the first night of the play. By Monday morning John was trembling violently but was almost back to normal.

It is a lurid tale but if the third murder attempt actually took place, it could not have been at the end of March 1929. As we have seen, he completed the purchase of the cottage in 1928 but before work could begin on it he left England to take over the editorship of the *American Sketch*. Yet in *Father Figure* he writes as if work on the cottage had been completed, and refers to the house and the garden as if he had been living there for years, whereas he had then hardly set foot in the place. There are other obvious mistakes in the narrative: the Saturday date is incorrect, twenty-four hours becomes thirty-six hours, and he gives Monday as the opening night of *The Stag* when it was Tuesday. The dating of the murder attempt becomes completely impossible if we accept Beverley's statement elsewhere that he bought Thatch Roof in 1929 and did not live in it for nearly a year. This is an example of the confusion which is prevalent in his autobiographical work.

The Stag opened at the Globe Theatre, Shaftesbury Avenue on 2 April 1929. The cast, all stalwarts of the West End theatre, was headed by Adrienne Allen and Reginald Owen and the play was directed by Beverley's old friend from Oxford days, the distinguished Raymond Massey. Beverley expected it to establish him as a new and controversial playwright with something worth saying, and up to a point he succeeded, for he took themes that were unexpected. He argued that the law against abortion was cruel to the women who, for good reason, wished to have one, and cruel to the unborn child destined to come into the world unwanted by its mother. He also treated with scorn those who indulged in blood sports, and showed the same group to be cruel in their treatment of someone they mistook for a fool but who was a man of kindliness and common sense. The problem with the play, partly dictated by the censorship of the time, was that his themes were implied rather than clearly stated, and the points, although made with dramatic skill, were obscured rather than helped by an overlay of comedy sometimes dangerously near to farce. He afterwards said he had made the typical beginner's mistake of trying to cram too many elements into his first play which he had written in a mood of angry sincerity, thus losing the objectivity of a cooler approach.

His verdict on himself was harsh, for the play showed and still shows considerable merit. Perhaps its main fault is that it does not clearly signal how the audience should react to its subject matter. It is also easy to see how word of mouth might deter prospective theatregoers. 'What is it about?' 'Well, it's about this unmarried woman who wants an abortion and it's also about stag-hunting.' It sounds an uneasy mixture and in 1929, when unmarried mothers were treated by society as near-criminals and abortion was a squalid backstreet affair subject to heavy legal penalties, it might not have appeared all that beguiling as a theatrical entertainment. Those who spoke out against blood sports were regarded in many quarters as cranks who were somehow unpatriotic. In passing, it is of interest to note that Beverley's attitude was a revolt against the hunting and shooting tradition of the Nichols family.

The Stag was an honourable failure, well received by the press but shunned by the public, and after six weeks at the Globe Theatre it came off. However, it enjoyed productions around the repertory theatres and in 1934 it appeared as the second half of a double bill at the Malvern Festival Theatre, preceded by the first performance outside London of Bernard Shaw's *Village Wooing*. Both authors attended the first night, Beverley making a curtain speech thanking everyone and saying how honoured he was to be in the company of Bernard Shaw, both on stage and in the audience. His speech was reported at length in a local paper punctuated by 'laughter' in brackets and ending with 'laughter and prolonged applause' in brackets. The *Birmingham Post*, reviewing both plays with the seriousness to be expected of a major provincial newspaper, commented that, despite the verdict of the West End, *The Stag* had qualities of permanence – a judgement sadly not borne out by time.

Beverley had little leisure to mourn the demise of *The Stag*. As usual, he was in demand as a journalist, as well as facing the task of getting Thatch Cottage put in order and replanning the garden. In this he was helped by the practical advice of his father which he acknowledged in later books. He did not always take his advice, and made the mistakes common to all first-time gardeners who believe what catalogues tell them and are convinced that scattering flower-seeds will produce a result as colourful as the picture on the packet.

He also continued to buy and sell shares and make profits – although, as history has recorded, an investor had to be particularly stupid to make a loss in that boom period. He was in Paris with C.B. Cochran when the first signs of the Wall Street crash came, but he was so preoccupied with a commission from Cochran to write his *1930 Revue* for the London Pavilion that he did not realize what was happening until he had sustained substantial losses. The effect of the crash left him with a caution in money matters and a horror of poverty for the rest of his life, although it is characteristic of his temperament that caution often gave way to extravagance, which was followed in turn by stringent economies.

Cochran's choice of Beverley to write the book and lyrics for his *1930 Revue* was, on the face of it, an unlikely one. True, he had contributed to several shows but he had not made a strong impression. Why was Cochran prepared to take a chance on this comparatively inexperienced author? The answer was simple: he had the gift of seeing talent which others, with the same evidence under their noses, often missed. But he was shrewd enough not to lay the entire burden of the show on Beverley's shoulders and, although he accepted some of his compositions, he placed the musical side of the show in the hands of Ivor Novello. He also bolstered the team with contributions from other established writers, not least of whom were his old friends Rodgers and Hart, whose 'With A Song In My Heart' became the hit of the show.

The press announcement that Beverley Nichols and Ivor Novello were to write *Cochran's 1930 Revue* caused a suitable stir. In Vivian Ellis it aroused a momentary anger because Cochran had previously called him to his office to congratulate him on his contribution to *Mr Cinders* and had spoken of his working on the next revue, after which there had been total silence. It was, to say the least, impolite of Cochran to raise Ellis's expectations and then ignore him but such behaviour was, and still is, a common feature of show-business. Writers are expected to grin and bear such disappointment without complaint.

The collaboration between Beverley and Novello began happily enough. Cochran accepted Beverley's first contribution, a jazzy number called 'The Little Things You Do' which he dashed off immediately after Cochran had commissioned him. He was also pleased with everything else Beverley wrote or suggested. For the rise of the curtain he wrote a short film sequence making fun of the 'talkies', which gave way to a big production number, 'Chasing the Talkies Away'. For the first half finale, always a make-or-break point in revue, Beverley wrote a sequence set in Heaven, a new idea for revue, combining dance and song with sharp comments from historical characters such as Lola Montez, Byron, the Empress Josephine and Lord Nelson. He worked intensively and quickly but Novello did not keep up with him and, with the show about to go into rehearsal, Beverley commented in his diary on 23 January: 'The revue position grows more hectic every minute. What will happen eventually I don't know, but anyway I seem to have done all right. Ivor, however, has done nothing at all.'

In fact, Novello had supplied some music but did not seem able to get to grips with the show and some of his work was disappointing. Faced with a crisis, Cochran, in effect, sacked Novello, apparently without rancour on either side, and called in Vivian Ellis to rescue the show. Ellis, still somewhat upset, negotiated a financial deal which was probably better than he would have got in the first place, and set to work, offering straight away a song called 'The Wind In The Willows' in which another manager had shown interest but had vacillated over too long. This became another of the show's big successes.

Until this time, Ellis had never met Beverley and only knew of him as the *enfant terrible* of *Twenty-Five* and *Crazy Pavements*. Beverley sat unmoved in Cochran's office while Ellis played some of his work, but when he heard 'The Wind In The Willows' his reaction of delighted admiration broke down any barriers that might have existed. The two men went on to work well together and a lifelong friendship developed, which extended to Ellis's sister Hermione. As a memento of his affection, Beverley left them a charming portrait of Pavlova by Laura Knight in his will.

Since the show was already in rehearsal when Ellis joined it, there was a great deal of work to be done and the next few weeks were unnerving and hectic. At last, on 22 February, Beverley was able to note in his diary that, apart from one number, the show was complete. This was optimistic, for after the opening in Manchester more work was considered necessary by Cochran, always a perfectionist.

It is not easy to evoke the Cochran magic for those who have never seen his productions, which included Noel Coward's *Cavalcade, Private Lives, Bitter Sweet* and *This Year Of Grace*. Cochran's skills have been described as a combination of those of Diaghilev and Ziegfeld with a touch of Barnum, which gives some idea of them, but cannot describe his particular taste and style. The best talents were attracted to work for him, and the line-up for his *1930 Revue* reads like a *Who's Who* of the theatre of the day. In addition to work by Nichols, Ellis, Novello and Rodgers and Hart, there were ballets composed by Lord Berners and Henri Sauguet, with ballet choreography by Georges Balanchine and Serge Lifar, and tap and other dances staged by Ralph Reader; sets and costumes were designed by Doris Zinkeisen, Oliver Messel, Worth and Rex Whistler; the company was led by Douglas Byng, Maisie Gay, Serge Lifar, Ada May, Roy Royston and Leslie Hutchinson, better known as Hutch; the dancers included ex-members of the Diaghilev Ballet Company; and among the supporting players were Barry Fitzgerald and Richard Murdoch. There were also, of course, the famous Cochran Young Ladies, sixteen of them. This is not a comprehensive list but it gives an idea of the scale of the enterprise, the cost of which could not even be contemplated today. The fact that this array of disparate talents could be drawn together by Cochran to provide an evening of near perfection gives some idea of his magic.

But before the triumph in London, there was a terrible opening night in Manchester: as the show over-ran by forty minutes, the audience's initial enthusiasm drained away. Reviews in the local newspapers were bad, the main criticism being the lack of good tunes! Everyone was devastated except Cochran, who restored morale by his confidence and sheer charm. He boosted Beverley and Vivian Ellis by visiting each of them in his hotel room and reading a press release he was about to issue, saying that his belief in his principal authors was such that he had asked them to prepare his revue for 1931. Then, with his indefatigable stage director Frank Collins, he set about cutting and speeding up the show for London.

Beverley managed to escape to Glatton for a weekend rest and wrote in his diary on 14 March:

> Have arrived here in a state of exhaustion, battered, older but on the whole triumphant. I believe the revue will be brilliant in London but in Manchester, quite frankly, it was not, at least my very tired and muddled brain tells me it wasn't. However, the main, shining, beautiful fact is that the libraries [ticket agents] have taken £36,000 worth of seats which is a record.
>
> I have learned so much. To think that I, at the age of 31, should know so little about the stage. I have been a fool to neglect it, but perhaps it was just as well, I know so much more now. I believe I could write a revue in 6 weeks.
>
> I have so many memories, appalling notices, hours spent in a dark bedroom trying to write bright dialogue, Cochran being urbane, efficient and amazingly kind, of Vivian Ellis (such a charming, gifted person). Eating too little, drinking too much. But it was worth it.

He was back at the cottage after the opening at the London Pavilion and again his diary tells the story:

> Thank the Lord it is a success. I have various memories – of a long line of chorus girls in smoke grey and black dresses singing 'The Little Things You Do' too enchantingly – of the opening number, the film, being greeted with a roar of 'ah' – of the numbers really holding the audience – of the delighted Cocky – of supper at Lady Cunard's afterwards, everybody being a little weary and wondering whether they ought to patronize or gush, and myself not caring two hoots what they did – of some wonderfully good and wonderfully bad notices the next day – of Cocky at lunch asking me to write the next revue. So really what more could I want?

What more indeed? For both Beverley and Vivian Ellis it was the fulfilment of a dream. There is not much more to add except that Beverley began work on the 1931 revue the following September, and despite his brave words about writing a revue in six weeks, discovered to his horror that all inspiration had deserted him. After frantic attempts to please Cochran, he finally asked to be released. It was a blow to his pride but at least he was honest enough to admit his failure in time for Cochran to make other arrangements. Perhaps 1931 was jinxed, for the talents of his replacements, including Noel Coward, failed to satisfy the public and the show lasted for only thirty-seven performances. *Cochran's 1930 Revue* had run for 245 performances: it might have run longer but for the illness of one of the stars and that old enemy of the theatre, a heat-wave.

There is a bizarre footnote to the show. Shortly after Beverley's death, a record of Rodgers and Hart's work was compiled from old discs and it included 'The Little Things You Do', which was described as one of the famous team's lesser-known songs. Beverley, who, as Vivian Ellis attested, enjoyed a joke against himself, must have laughed with wry pleasure in whatever heaven he happened to be. But, as his agent remarked, 'He'll be very worried about the royalties.'

While all the excitement was gathering over the *1930 Revue*, work was progressing at Glatton. The renovation of the cottage was at last completed and the garden was beginning to take shape with the aid of a small team of local men and advice from John Nichols. By the end of January, the rock garden which Beverley hated because it was little more than a vast mound of earth with stones stuck on it, like cherries on a cake, had been removed. Roses had been planted in the front of the house and along the orchard path to grow over three rustic arches he had had erected. All seemed well except that he was disappointed in the sparse display of winter flowers. 'There should be seas of snowdrops, banks of Christmas roses and waves of aconites; next time I shall know.' Then he learned that the plot of land next to his garage was for sale and that there were plans to build a bungalow and develop a small pig farm. This so appalled him that he made the owner an offer which he would have been insane to refuse and, at a stroke, nearly doubled the size of the garden. (It is probably unkind to wonder whether the story of the pig farm was entirely for Beverley's benefit.) This purchase made him ambitious to buy even more land. Beyond the garden was a field with a pond which was used by the Co-op Dairy to graze cows. In his mind's eye, he saw the pond enlarged so that it became a small lake for swimming, complete with punt. His ambitions were similar (though on a much smaller scale) to those of his grandfather Alfred with his grandiose garden at Elmleigh.

Around this time Pauline's health began to deteriorate. The precise cause is not known but her sporadic symptoms were a high temperature, unexplained exhaustion and an ugly facial flushing. She could only obtain relief by complete rest and sometimes by the drawing off of blood. Beverley noted in his diary that she was not allowed to go to the first night of the revue because the excitement might worsen her condition. In after years he put the blame for her illness firmly on the shoulders of his father, recalling how John would tease her when her face went bright red and ask if she had been at the bottle again. He cited another example of his father's 'cruelty': she found John, wearing only a vest, lying dead drunk in the front hall of the vicarage at Cambridge Square on the day 'the Bishop was expected for tea'. The young maid was too frightened and shocked to help and Pauline, unwell as she was, had to revive John and haul him upstairs to his bedroom. This incident appeared in *Father Figure* but Paul Nichols dismissed it as one of his brother's flights of fantasy.

It was also around this time that Warren, the young New Yorker, arrived in England to live with Beverley. It proved to be far from the stable and idealistic relationship that Beverley longed for. Warren was only interested in the bright lights, found Glatton a bore, and was sexually promiscuous. A friend remembered visiting Beverley's London house late one morning to find that Beverley had gone out. Warren was still in bed and suggested the friend might care to jump in for a 'quick fuck'. Beverley soon heard of Warren's behaviour around the town and noted in his diary, that while he was away in Manchester his young lover was 'apparently not unconsoled by my absence'. Later, at a cocktail party thrown by Warren at the London house, Beverley met some of his newly acquired boyfriends and wrote wryly in his diary that Warren had 'good taste'.

Beverley had also acquired another new friend, Arthur Diamond, a young man in the wine trade. Diamond was the sort of person who is flattered at being befriended by a celebrity, is kind-hearted, and is taken advantage of. This at least was Diamond's own view of the friendship when he spoke of it over fifty years afterwards: 'Don't expect me to say nice things about Beverley. He was selfish, a dreadful snob and could be quite inconsiderate.' Diamond, as a member of the Nichols set, was close to Beverley for many years but eventually the relationship soured badly. He gave as an example of Beverley's snobbery the times he drove him to functions pretending, at Beverley's request, to be his chauffeur: 'He even made me wear a cap.' On one occasion, when they arrived at a party and Beverley left him to wait in the car, the hostess had seen them arrive from her window. 'Who is that in the car?' she asked. 'Only my chauffeur,' he replied. 'Don't be ridiculous, it's Arthur. Go and tell him to come in at once.' Diamond's opinion is in complete contrast to that of many of Beverley's other friends who always emphasized what a generous and charming person Beverley was.

Once *Cochran's 1930 Revue* had settled in for a run, Beverley took Warren on a two-week trip to the Continent. They had intended to spend time in North Africa but hated it so much that after one night in Tunis they caught the first available boat back. They spent a few days in Naples with Baroness d'Erlanger and a final four days with Gerald (Lord) Berners. With all the enthusiasm of a horticultural convert, Beverley listed the flowers and plants he saw on the trip and visited gardens wherever they went. Warren did not share this enthusiasm, and Beverley later complained in his diary about a violent quarrel on the second day out ('. . . the first of many') following an ill-considered visit to a male brothel in Marseilles. 'The whole trouble, in fact, about this trip was that Warren, dear and delightful as he is, is really not a fit mental companion to me. I don't mind ignorance, but apathy is a little wearing. And actually he is apathetic – physically and mentally. It exhausts him to walk and he appears incapable of remembering anything whatever.'

A few weeks later, in his entry about a day at Glatton with John Gielgud and some other friends, Beverley complains that Warren was 'as usual outraged at the suggestion he should breathe fresh air'. It is difficult from the various entries and, indeed, from two first-hand accounts of him to get any clear idea of the unfortunate Warren. It is equally difficult to understand why Beverley had such high hopes of the relationship. Warren returned to New York at the end of May, and Beverley wrote in his diary:

> I can't realize that he has gone and am therefore unable to gauge the hurt his going causes me. I feel at the moment great tenderness towards somebody who is, au fond, very sweet and lovable and devoted. There were many shortcomings on both sides but when I think of all that he had to learn and endure, of the things which must have bored him and of the trying times through which we passed, I marvel that it went so well. Yes – our friendship was like an English spring, stormy but full of blossom. I have a lump in my throat when I think that perhaps we may have parted for good.

This mood changed abruptly over the next few hours and he wrote a vitriolic letter to Warren pouring out his fury over his behaviour. 'I think it was as well to get it off my chest. One letter can't ruin a friendship. And everything I said was true.' But Warren, who had written a letter drenched with tears and sentiment before receiving Beverley's missive, cabled back saying he was heartbroken. Beverley wrote in his diary: 'I should hardly have been human if I had not been moved by it. Enough of that. I have made up my mind that I must go through life alone.' In another entry he declared, referring to Glatton: 'More than ever I relish this lovely place. If only I had somebody to share it with who really loved it. Thank God for this garden. Without it I should perish'.

The Warren episode is of minor importance in itself but, taken together with other examples of the abrupt changes of mood which occurred throughout Beverley's life, it indicates what some might see as a deeply troubled spirit, or others might see as something not far short of schizophrenia.

The garden at Glatton had begun to repay the time and money spent on it and a steady stream of guests was invited to tour it while Beverley rejoiced over every new bloom. His thorough conversion to gardening is indicated by the detailed record in his diary; some entries are little more than lists, but a typical example heralds the whimsical prose he was later to employ in his books, either to enchant or to sicken, depending on the reader's taste.

The lupins are at their best. The wistaria and lilac are over. There is a bunch of Gloire de Dijon roses on my dressing-table. About six other roses in the garden. The laburnums are at their crowning hour. A new, lovely flower like a yellow delphinium is out in the herbaceous [border]. One red-hot poker, to my fury, has had the effrontery to blossom. It appears to have no sense of fitness. I would like to smack it on its head and tell it to go back to bed, but what can one do? I used foul language at it but it only stared back entirely unmoved. The yellow irises are out – so lovely.

It was the same rose, the Gloire de Dijon, that he later maintained he was unable to grow because it, or he, was cursed by the evil emanating from his father, following the first catastrophic incident in his childhood.

Beverley, having given up the idea of a permanent companion, was by happy chance presented by Lady Cunard with a dog, the result of an unscheduled meeting between her poodle and a black chow that lived at the nearby Chinese embassy. The animal was a strange creature with an odd bark which gave it its name, Whoops. Beverley later wrote:

Whoops has really been the biggest thing in my life during the past months. The idea of me having a dog! But I do love him and he loves me. He has a sweet character like a dear little boy and yet he is a very doggy dog. Is this a sign of senile decay on my part or what?

Despite Whoops, however, he sank into a sort of melancholia which a few weeks in the south of France did little to relieve. Apart from writing for the newspapers, he had no major project in prospect and he complained of feeling dull and on the verge of a nervous breakdown. He was brought abruptly back to reality by a letter from Lloyds Bank informing him that his overdraft had soared to £2,200. In addition, he paid out £400 in life insurance and £300 in income tax. After the shock of losses during the previous year's market crash, he had believed his finances were better controlled. The letter from Lloyds disabused him.

There is no doubt that Beverley was frightened. He had £6,000 in gilt-edged securities, but he was determined not to touch a penny of this. He therefore took stock of his situation. There was his home in London run by Gaskin, and Thatch Cottage in Glatton with a live-in staff of housekeeper and gardener. Something must go. He decided to give up the London house in Ovington Street and get rid of Gaskin – a drastic step, for he had come to depend on him. Once he had decided, he convinced Gaskin that his future lay in New York and found him a new master. Within a month or so, he had completed the retrenchment, the London house was disposed of, and Gaskin had sailed to America. This marks the point in Beverley's career when he determined to write as much as possible to earn money, even if it meant producing work which was opportunistic and not always what he would have chosen to do.

In the mean time, out of the blue came a commission to write a play for Marie Tempest and Henry Ainley, two of the brightest stars of the English theatre, for production at the Theatre Royal, Haymarket. After four weeks of intensive work at the cottage, Beverley produced the first draft of what was to become *Daughters of Gentlemen*. The saga of this play went on for nearly a year, involving many rewrites at the request of Miss Tempest, who finally accepted it, then changed her mind, and the project sank without trace.

While waiting for the first reaction to *Daughters of Gentlemen*, Beverley unearthed a play he had written several years before and revised it. It had originally been called *Onward Christian Soldiers* but the Lord Chamberlain had refused to let him use this title because it might give offence. For a time he called it *The White Flag*, but finally settled on *Avalanche*. A London management expressed serious interest in it and asked John Gielgud to read for the leading role. 'He read it terribly. Never was there anything so unexpected. But I know he can do it and I have been deputed to bring about a psychological change, which I hope to accomplish by a supper at the Savoy.' The psychological change was not accomplished and, to his astonishment, Maurice Browne, the producer, asked to hear Beverley himself read the part, then said he was satisfied that Beverley could play it. Beverley agreed on two conditions: that there was a try-out away from London and that he could choose the director. Maurice Browne was unable to accept these conditions and Beverley assumed that was the end of the matter. He was particularly disappointed because the play dealt with pacifism, a subject about which he felt very strongly. He described himself as 'an idealistic pacifist' and he believed there were many who shared his views, so many that, if they were organized, they could prevent another war.

He next put together a volume of essays and short stories with the working title *Women and Children First* which he delivered to his publisher on 6 November. All this time he was, of course, still writing for the press and composing individual items for cabaret and revue; these included a song entitled 'Dancing in the Dark' and a number for Sophie Tucker, the American entertainer, called 'A String of Pearls'. In November he was able to record that he had reduced his overdraft by £1,000 and 'felt well and quite content'. In December, one of his songs, 'Keep Tap Tap Tapping', was featured in *Caviare* at the Little Theatre.

Although he spent most of his time at the cottage, Beverley soon found the lack of a London base a nuisance and decided to rent a bed-sitting room. George Shanks, whom he had first met at Oxford, offered him rooms in the basement of his magnificent house at 10, Great Stanhope Street off Park Lane, with the occasional use of the drawing-room, a concession which delighted Beverley who put it to good use when several articles about him were illustrated with photographs of his 'London house', showing Beverley posed at work at a corner table in the grand drawing-room. Another photograph showed him, in silk dressing-gown in the Noel Coward style, posed between two impressive sets of armour. His own rooms, however, in what had once been the servants' quarters were relatively small and simply furnished. He wrote of his new home: 'It is situated in the most exclusive of neighbourhoods and the net cost with service is 4 guineas a week, thereby I save £4 on Gaskin and a good £1 a week on taxis – making £250 to the good and greater comfort. How Pepysian that sounds.' He was, of course, also saving the running costs of a London house and felt so good about the improvement in his financial state that he hired a valet, one Teddy Croft. He also decided to create a wood on his additional piece of land at Glatton, although very taken aback by the expense. Planting began in December.

· 13 ·

Setbacks and triumph

1931–1932

ARLY in 1931 Beverley began work on what he described as the
'drunk novel' with the central character based on his father. This
proved emotionally so draining that he put it aside and did not take
it up again until many years later when it emerged in dramatized form as
Shadow of the Vine. There was another reason for postponing work on it, for
on 23 February 1931 Dame Nellie Melba died. Although their relationship
had broken down at one stage, there had been a reconciliation – indeed, she
had visited Glatton when she was in England to give her final public
performance at the Hippodrome Theatre, Brighton, on 5 October 1929, in
aid of charity. Beverley's lasting memory of her was singing for him at the
cottage. He had already begun work on a novel based on her and realized it
must be completed quickly while she was still fresh in the public mind. As
usual he was busy with further revisions to *Daughters of Gentlemen*, with his
weekly piece for the *Daily Mail* and with material for John Murray
Anderson's revue *Fanfare* due to open at the Prince Edward Theatre in the
summer, but he made time to escape to an hotel in the south of France to
write the first draft of the Melba book which he called *Evensong*.

Before this, his volume of essays, short stories and other writings came
out with the revised title *Women and Children Last*. He claimed the critical
reception was 'terrible' but on the whole the reaction was not too hostile
and he should have been pleased by a sentence from the *Manchester Guardian*:
'More almost than any other writer he has the knack of getting into close
contact with his readers, each one of whom must feel that his pages are
written directly at or for him – or still more for her.' The book was
reasonably successful both in Britain and America, bearing in mind that
much of its content had already been seen in magazines and newspapers.

His diary continued to illustrate his obsession with money and fear of
poverty. In it, he listed his basic outgoings – apart from run-of-the-mill
items they included a £4 per week allowance to his brother Alan. In his
diary he also chided himself for his personal conduct which he called 'rash
and foolish', and vowed to stop it, but only a week later he wrote: 'My

personal follies continue unabated. Nothing seems to alter them. I shall just let things rip' – which is what he did. Sex was easy to come by but the shallowness of each experience left him dissatisfied. On 28 March he wrote: 'On the whole I am coming to the conclusion that the best thing I know in life is myself, a disagreeable angle from which to view the world. But I have yet to meet anybody with my ideas of honour or friendship or continuing instinctive courage. Which is the first pat I have ever given myself on the back.'

Part of the trouble was his refusal to confide his real feelings to anyone. Perhaps he did not feel secure enough with the friends who constituted his social circle. His brother Paul, who spent weekends at the cottage with his boyfriend, was to comment years later that they were never as intimate as brothers, particularly homosexual brothers, could be. 'Beverley bottled his feelings up and we never talked.' Predictably, during his working visit to France to write *Evensong* Beverley became infatuated with someone who, as before, quickly disappointed him.

Although he was unhappy with the *Daily Mail* which he did not believe treated him with proper respect, Beverley noted on 27 May that he had signed a new contract, for one article a week at the rate of £18 per article, and that he needed to earn another £22 a week to survive. As an economy measure, he dismissed his valet, Teddy Croft, which saved a weekly wage of £2 10s plus insurance. 'Never again do I saddle myself with a manservant. I am sorry because I was fond of him.'

On 11 June *Glamour*, a film directed by Seymour Hicks, opened at the London Pavilion starring Beverley as the romantic leading man. In the previous December Hicks had asked him to do a screen test for the part. After the Hollywood test several years before, Beverley was dubious, but as the offer followed so soon after Maurice Browne's assurance that he could act, he agreed to the test. He wrote:

Quite exhausted yesterday by a film test at Elstree. This was so gruesome that I do not think it is ever likely to fade from my memory. I remember driving out with Seymour, being made up, being put off till after lunch and then sitting in a chair in a great barn of a place with about forty workmen gaping in the background and having to say, 'I wonder where Seymour is?' and get up and call him, and then pull his tie and have a cigarette – God, it was awful. I am sure I was terrible. Anyway, I shan't do it.

He wasn't terrible and he signed the contract.

Seymour Hicks's film went in front of the cameras at British International Pictures' studio at Elstree, the English equivalent of Hollywood. To be strictly accurate, it was, and what is left of it still is, located at

Borehamwood, some distance from Elstree. The script by Hicks, as the critics were quick to point out, owed more than a little to a play by David Garrick, and the plot concerned a great actor, played by Hicks, who falls madly for a young lady half his age who is flattered by his attentions but is really in love with the handsome Hon. Richard Wells. The great actor is upset by this until he discovers that the Hon. Richard is really his illegitimate son whereupon, in a noble gesture of self-sacrifice, he relinquishes the young lady who falls happily into the Hon. Richard's arms. The title of the piece, *Glamour*, suggests a sophisticated romantic comedy calling for understated playing, but from the start things went badly wrong. Hicks, who had been an internationally acclaimed stage star for years, dominated the film but did not modify his performance for the camera, so that what might have seemed delicate comedy on stage appeared as outrageous overacting on screen. As Beverley put it, 'Nothing quite so like Henry Irving has been seen before or since, even in the days of Irving himself.' Hicks's wife Ellaline Terriss played the Hon. Richard's mother (charmingly) and the Hon. Richard was, of course, Beverley. If Hicks was overacting, the problem with Beverley was to get him to do any acting at all, for although he had been giving performances ever since his childhood in the drawing-rooms of Torquay the discipline of the studio terrified him. His chum Betty, the Hickses' daughter, also in the film, recalled his terror: 'Looking back it was really very funny because he simply froze in front of the camera and couldn't remember what to do and kept missing his mark so he was often in the wrong place.'

Beverley did not think it funny at the time, though looking back, he found it hilarious in a ghastly sort of way. 'My body seemed like lead and my mind refused to function and the endless re-takes just made it worse.' One of his worst moments was when he had to enter with a Pekinese clutched in his arms, deposit it playfully on a sofa, kneel, chuck his mother under the chin and remark to Hicks, 'Isn't she a little peach?' He was never quite sure whether this line referred to the dog or his mother, and the more they did it the more the line, tried in countless different ways, lost all meaning. As for the chuck under the chin, it came dangerously near to dislocating Miss Terriss's jaw. After two days of trying to get the scene right, the Pekinese expressed its view of the proceedings by being violently sick over Beverley.

Glamour opened with suitable razzamatazz in June at the London Pavilion, which was unexpectedly free following the demise of *Cochran's 1931 Revue*. The press without exception thought it dreadful. The trade newspaper, the *Daily Film Renter*, summed up the reaction: 'In the crudity of its material and characterization, *Glamour* recalls the days one hoped had gone for ever, when the British film deserved all that was said of it by its deprecators.' It was noticed by some that Mr Nichols constantly made entrances with the apparent intention of saying or doing something, but did nothing, though he made an exit as if he had; this was because most of the footage in which he appeared, including the 'Isn't she a little peach?' sequence, ended up on the cutting-room floor. Betty Hicks never knew what became of the film and attempts to trace a copy of it have failed – a pity, because it could have become one of those disasters beloved by film buffs for its sheer awfulness. It ended any hopes Beverley might have had of a film career; his only consolation was that he had not come out of it as badly as some of the others and the salary over six weeks had helped to finance more improvements at Glatton.

The following week, on Thursday 18 June, he wrote triumphantly in his diary: '6 p.m. I have just finished *Evensong* – I can hardly realize it. I feel a sense of lightness and exhilaration. I am not sure about all of the book but I know it contains some of the best writing I have ever done. Now for the next thing!'

Chronologically, the next thing was the first production of *Avalanche* at the Lyceum Theatre, Edinburgh by the Masque Players on 20 July, directed by Esmé Percy. The company had intended to present a different play as part of their season but at the last minute had been prevented from doing so, and Percy had remembered Beverley's play. With no prospect of a London production, Beverley had been only too pleased to see how his plea for pacifism would be received by an audience. The *Edinburgh Evening News* reported: 'The reception was all the author and actors could desire. At times the play was brilliantly entertaining and the action was not unfrequently held up by outbursts of spontaneous laughter and applause.' The *Daily Record* commented: 'Edinburgh audiences have hardly a reputation for enthusiasm yet the play was received with continual applause.' All the papers praised the leading performance by Alan Webb.

After its week in Edinburgh the company moved on to the Theatre Royal, Glasgow, where the *Glasgow Bulletin* described the play as 'an incredible mixture of brilliance and faulty mechanics'. In a snowbound chalet in Switzerland, the host announces that America and Britain have gone to war and his house-party believes him. Then follows a lengthy argument on war, with each member of the conveniently assorted party revealed in his true colours. The host, a playwright, confesses his pacifism and puts his case for it, which almost causes a war inside the chalet, and then has another confession to make: the story was a hoax to see how a cross-section of people would react, and the purpose was to help him with a play he proposes to write! But, unknown to him, one of his guests, a patriotic young man, has set out in the treacherous weather to fight for his country. Next day he is found dead in the snow – his sacrifice has been useless. The *Bulletin's* critic commented: 'This would be enough to strain the credulity of the lowest-browed audience ever assembled in a theatre. I enjoyed the play immensely by the simple process of forgetting the action and luxuriating in the play of words at which Mr Nichols has few equals.' The *Scottish Observer*, writing in similar vein, ended: '*Avalanche* is quite the most interesting play that has graced Glasgow for some time.'

Before the opening in Edinburgh, James Agate, the feared and revered critic of the *Sunday Times*, had telephoned Beverley and asked if arrangements could be made for him to see the play. He had also asked if a room could be booked for him at a 'discreet' hotel. Translated, 'discreet' meant an hotel that would not object to Agate spending the night with one or two male prostitutes. Beverley heard nothing more until he opened the *Sunday Times* and, to his astonishment, found that though Agate had said nothing about reviewing the play 'out of town', his entire column was devoted to *Avalanche*. As he read it Beverley became apoplectic with anger. On the credit side, Agate admitted that the audience responded to the wit in the writing and during the serious moments appeared to be deeply moved; the rest of the review was an attack on the playwright and his work so venomous that it must rank as a minor masterpiece of its type. For Beverley, the unkindest cut of all was the accusation that nothing in the play suggested that the author had been impelled by overwhelming emotion; Agate suggested that Beverley had chosen the theme because, looking around for one, he had deemed it as good as any other. Whatever else might be said about Beverley, his horror of war and his pacifist convictions were genuine and well known.

In his autobiography *The Unforgiving Minute*, Beverley states that, as a result of Agate's review, 'the backers took flight, the cast was dismissed and the play was killed, as far as the English-speaking world was concerned.' This was not entirely true. *Avalanche* was produced at the Arts Theatre in London the following year on 27 January. Esmé Percy again directed but with a new cast headed by Maurice Evans. John Nichols, who disagreed profoundly with his son's pacifist views, refused to be seen in the audience at the Arts Theatre in case his presence might be construed as support.

Avalanche was reviewed at length by all the national newspapers and leading magazines (even by the *New York Times*) and was treated as an important dramatic event. The consensus of opinion was not dissimilar to that of the Scottish critics: the hoax device, it was felt, broke the back of what promised to be a brilliant anti-war play which was both witty and moving. But a reading of the manuscript and of more than thirty reviews of the play makes it impossible to see how it could have achieved a commercial run.

In Beverley's life-story there are often sequels, and there was a surprising one to the Agate episode. Beverley was so touched by a review in *Country Life* which took Agate to task for his attack upon the play that he telephoned and asked for the address of their critic, George Warrington, so that he could write and thank him. After considerable prevarication, it was admitted that there was no Mr Warrington and that this was a pseudonym used by none other than James Agate! Trembling with anger, Beverley made an appointment to see the editor of the *Sunday Times* who admitted that Agate had broken his exclusive contract with the paper. But, as he had been paid a year in advance and had probably spent the money, there would be nothing but embarrassment . . . what did Mr Nichols suggest should be done? Beverley toyed with the idea of exposing Agate's duplicity, but in the end contented himself with writing a note to Agate threatening to expose his private life to the police. 'I should of course have done no such thing but I wanted to make him squirm.' When his anti-war book *Cry Havoc!* came out, he sent Agate a copy, suggesting that the review had better be a good one. In response, Agate acknowledged Beverley's passionate sincerity, thus withdrawing the accusation that he had made in the *Sunday Times*. But, before this, Agate had given the dramatized version of *Evensong* a good review in his guise as George Warrington, leaving the *Sunday Times* review to be done by somebody else.

Careful examination of this story suggests that only part of it has been told. What possible proof could Beverley have had of Agate's sex life which would have led to criminal proceedings without endangering his own safety? Agate was no fool, and he must have known as much about Beverley's sexual preferences as Beverley knew about his. To the question of why he did not expose Agate's duplicity, he gave his own answer: 'I am not a vindictive man.' If Agate had submitted to the rather feeble attempt at blackmail, it was far more likely to have been for fear that Beverley might disclose his activities as George Warrington, because in fact he wrote under this name and also under the pseudonym 'Richard Prentis' for *John O'London's Weekly*, and did not include the fees he received in his tax returns. Which would have been the worse fate – being accused of a fondness for male prostitutes or of swindling the Inland Revenue?

A week before the London opening of *Avalanche*, the press in Britain and overseas began reviewing *Evensong*. Beverley had anticipated that comparisons would be made between his fictional character and Melba, but was unprepared for the vituperative comment in Australia. He was accused of 'appalling ingratitude' and his action in writing the book was considered 'contemptible' and 'shocking and indefensible'. In a long leading article, the *Melbourne Argus* said, among other things: 'It is no offence to slander the dead; unhappily, there seems to be a danger that it will also cease to be an offence against good taste. It is not pleasant to have those who are honoured and loved delivered into the hands of exploiters for the entertainment of the mean of spirit and the unsavoury of mind.' In an interview for the *Australian Herald*, Beverley countered by saying that Melba had read some of the novel in manuscript and had been 'greatly amused' by it. Amid all the outcry, an Australian friend of Melba, Norman Lindsay, had this to say: 'The Australian press made a joke of Dame Nellie Melba all her lifetime. She told me she hated Australia because of its treatment, such as the silly stories of her being a drunk. Australia always deprecates great artists when they are living . . .' However, his was a lone voice.

While the Australian press was whipping itself into a frenzy, cooler heads were assessing the merits of *Evensong*. Everybody sensibly dismissed Beverley's protest that no resemblance to Melba was intended, some listing the similarities between the great diva and his Irela. The reviews, on balance, praised the author for his wit, cleverness and the pathos which he brought to his ageing prima donna, a figure of pity as much as of ridicule. The *Observer* declared: 'Mr Beverley Nichols has taken a bold stride forward into the company of considerable novelists,' and the American critics said much the same. But it was the public's reaction which mattered and its verdict was quite clear: within a week of publication, *Evensong* was a best-seller.

As soon as he read the novel, Edward Knoblock proposed to Beverley that they should adapt it for the stage. Knoblock, an American dramatist and screenwriter, had a reputation for successfully adapting novels for the theatre, his most recent successes having been *Grand Hotel* by Vicki Baum and *The Good Companions* by J.B. Priestley. Eddie, as Beverley called him, was not given to idle suggestions; moreover, he had sound connections in the theatre, so Beverley embarked on the collaboration with high hopes of a production at the end of it. He moved into Knoblock's house at 20, Clifton Terrace, Brighton and by the end of two weeks the work was complete, only ten lines needing to be adjusted when the play went into rehearsal. In structuring the play, Knoblock insisted on having a complete scenario before a line was written. Beverley later said that one of the faults of his own plays was that he began without a clear idea of how they would end, which accounted for their inherent weakness. Knoblock thought they had produced between them a tightly written play: 'Audiences are now quicker, they need less explanation, the soliloquy has disappeared because it is no longer necessary.'

The play was sent to four managements. Three rejected it, one of them complaining that it was a vehicle for one person, and that without Irela it wouldn't be a very good play. ('Neither would *Hamlet*!' Beverley retorted.) The fourth manager was Sir Barry Jackson, who had been knighted in 1925 for his services to the theatre. His crowning achievement was the founding of the distinguished Birmingham Repertory Company which produced actors of the calibre of Sir Ralph Richardson, Lord Olivier, Sir Cedric Hardwicke and Gwen Ffrangcon-Davies. Later he was to institute the Shaw festivals at Malvern and restore the post-war fortunes of the Shakespeare Memorial Theatre at Stratford-upon-Avon in three seasons which established the reputations of Paul Scofield and Peter Brook. When he read *Evensong*, he had no doubt about its potential success, and engaged Athole Stewart to direct it. A brilliant cast was assembled which included Violet Vanbrugh, Wilfred Lawson, Frederick Leister, Henry Wilcoxon and Joan Harben; however, it was the unexpected casting of Edith Evans as Irela which caused some surprise. Up to this time, she had enjoyed success in a series of roles for which the critics had praised her brilliance, but she had not made the popular impact on the general public that might have been expected. She accepted Irela, convinced of its importance to her career, and said, in a press interview:

> It is in another category altogether from anything else I have done before. Something broad and intense and at the same time eternally human and tragic. There's a fine satirical swing to it, too, a fine realism. It's a part I have been feeling towards for a long time, a real woman who isn't me. She's a great woman, too, you understand, selfish and domineering and full of petty little faults, but great, driven by her genius. She has the world at her feet. For it, I've changed my whole technique. My method of speaking is different, my method of moving my hands is different. Even my figure is entirely different. Some people think all we have to do is go on the stage and open our mouths. It makes me so angry, I could bash somebody!

The play opened in Edinburgh to an indifferent reaction and moved to the Queen's Theatre in London on 30 June. By the first interval, the audience had begun cheering and applauding and, at the final curtain, it was ecstatic. The tumultuous reception roared on for six minutes and was only halted while the audience waited for Beverley to appear. Despite repeated shouts of 'Author!', he refused to join Knoblock on stage, thus creating an awkward hiatus. The *Sunday Times* castigated him for spoiling Edith Evans's triumph, while the *Daily Mail* complimented him on following the practice of Bernard Shaw and Somerset Maugham, both of whom also refused to take curtain calls on their first nights. The last thing Beverley had intended was to spoil anyone's triumph, least of all his own; he had always taken curtain calls before and relished the personal applause. He had no rational explanation for his behaviour on this occasion; it was as if his body and mind had been paralysed by a conjunction of fear and joy.

For Edith Evans it was a triumph. One critic said she had contrived to exhaust the lexicon of praise, another that he would add her performance to his gallery of theatrical memories which included Bernhardt, Duse, Rejane and Mrs Patrick Campbell. Opinions about the play itself were divided into those which, like the *Daily Telegraph*, held that it was not a patch on the 'brilliant' novel and found the piece insubstantial, and those which praised it for its wit and honesty and the cleverness of the adaptation. James Agate, this time on the side of the angels, wrote, in his guise as George Warrington, a long essay congratulating everyone concerned and gave the entertainment what he called the critic's highest accolade: 'There was no moment at the Queen's Theatre when I wished I was somewhere else.' Beverley was not too bothered by the critics, for the play was a solid box-office success, and when a heat-wave destroyed business in other theatres the 'House Full' boards stayed up at the Queen's. Everyone wanted to see *Evensong*, including royalty, the ex-King of Greece, King Alfonso of Spain, the Princess Royal and the Earl of Harewood among them. Prince George, later Duke of Kent, also saw it, with a party: Beverley knew him socially as a visitor to 10, Great Stanhope Street and as a friend of Noel Coward.

In November Sir Barry Jackson sent out a national tour of *Evensong* with a new cast headed by Violet Farebrother as Irela. It is interesting that a Sheffield critic, describing the play as 'one of the great theatrical successes of our time', praised Miss Farebrother almost as much as the London critics had praised Edith Evans. Without in any sense detracting from Miss Evans's magnificence, the provincial reviewers suggested that there was more substance to the play than some of the London critics had given it credit for. However, when *Evensong* opened at the Selwyn Theatre in New York in February 1933, the press reacted much as their London counterparts had done, and although a standing ovation for Edith Evans on the first night led all concerned to believe they had a hit, their hopes were dashed by the mixed reviews and the production closed quickly, an honourable failure.

This was not the end of the *Evensong* story: it enjoyed a second life as staple repertory fare and also went on to be performed by amateurs with ambitious leading ladies, thus proving the old adage that amateurs know no fear. It reappeared in 1934, completely refashioned as a film vehicle for Evelyn Laye with a supporting cast that included Emlyn Williams, Alice Delysia and Conchita Supervia. Beverley was not involved with this and attended the gala première unaware of many changes that had been made. He sat bewildered as an almost completely different story unfolded on the screen, and just to prove to himself that he had not been dreaming, he kept the souvenir programme which helpfully contained a synopsis of the new plot. 'I know how Noel [Coward] felt when, some years later, he saw what Hollywood had done to *Bitter Sweet*. Of course, Miss Laye was enchanting, but far too young.' Many years later, a television version of the play starred Mary Ellis.

· 14 ·

Pathways

1932–1933

Bﾠack in 1931, Beverley had given an interview to the *Newcastle Journal*. The writer described his trepidation at the thought of meeting the author of *Twenty-Five* who, a colleague had warned him, had the vanity of a ballet-dancer and the affectation of Little Lord Fauntleroy, and was relieved to find Mr Nichols to be the antithesis of this objectionable combination. He completed the usual string of questions by asking what Mr Nichols intended to do next. 'A book about gardening,' came the reply. This unexpected item of information apparently remained confined to the Newcastle area, probably because the rest of the press thought it a joke that this sophisticated man-about-town should get his hands dirty in a garden, let alone write about it. Beverley's reasoning, however, was practical to the point of being cold-blooded; he knew that such a book from him would have both surprise and curiosity value, and he believed it would sell. The British public loved gardens, particularly the thousands who were gardening for the first time in the rapidly expanding suburbs.

His approach was calculated, but the passion was that of a convert. It has already been said that he had bought what he believed to be a dream garden and found a nightmare. From the moment he faced up to the work to be done there, the idea of the book began to germinate. At first he planned a straightforward account of the restoration of the dream, but he dismissed this as being too dull. Instead, he reverted to the format he had found successful before, a mixture of fact and fiction in quasi-autobiographical style. He changed the name of the location from Glatton to Allways after Irving Berlin's hit song of 1925, 'Always'. It was an apt choice, for the song celebrated love and Beverley's love for Glatton and all it represented lasted until his death when, in accordance with his will, his ashes were scattered in the grounds of the local church.

Once he began writing what he finally called *Down the Garden Path*, he found it astonishingly easy. 'It was more like arranging a bunch of mixed flowers, here a story, here a winding paragraph, here a purple passage, and suddenly there was a book.' When it appeared in May 1932, it was greeted, as he had anticipated, with great surprise that such a subject should originate with the person Beverley Nichols was believed to be. Apart from the critics who reviewed their prejudices rather than the book, the reception was enthusiastic. Few of the reviewers, however, enthused as much as did their American counterparts. In its magazine, for example, the grand sounding Gardening Club of America declared *Down the Garden Path* to be one of the most delectable and diverting books on gardening ever published, and urged its readers to beg, buy, borrow or steal a copy – 'Get it at once!'

Of all the accolades Beverley received, two of his most treasured came from Vita Sackville-West and Constance Spry, who described him as a pioneer in innovation for his experiment and development of winter flowers (for which he had acknowledged a debt to another pioneer, A.W. Darnell). Another accolade which he treasured came from an army private during the war. In a letter awkwardly put together, the soldier told how he carried a paperback edition with him and how, during pauses in battle, he read and re-read it because it reminded him what the war was all about – to save old England. The simplicity of the sentiment was all the more moving when Beverley learned that the soldier had been killed.

The success of *Down the Garden Path* is publishing history. In 1983, Beverley wrote a new preface to an edition brought out to celebrate the fiftieth anniversary of the original publication. During all that time it had been in print, and its longevity is easy to understand, for unlike many popular books of the period it remains as fresh as if it had been published last week. It is not only that gardeners can identify with Beverley's successes and failures, it is also the clarity of style, the wit and the sheer fun which make it difficult to put down. Even the whimsy and sentimentality which often marred his work is acceptable in its context.

An important element in the book's success was the contribution made by Rex Whistler with whom, according to Arthur Diamond, Beverley had a brief affair. When it was agreed by the publishers that the charm of the book would be accentuated by illustrations and decorations rather in the manner of the eighteenth century, Beverley urged the choice of Whistler. The artist himself was not too sure: 'It's the Tudor cottage to end all Tudor cottages. Not me at all. I'm only good at stately homes with long avenues and lakes in the distance and balustrades and cherubs holding heraldic arms over the roof.' He picked up a watering can. 'What could I do with a thing like that?' Beverley thought for a moment. 'You could give it to a cherub and by his side you could draw another cherub with a spade.' This suggestion unlocked Whistler's invention and he quickly drew the picture which subsequently appeared as the heading to chapter one. For the end-papers to the book, he drew a plan of the gardens to stimulate and guide the imagination of the reader. This happy collaboration was to continue with the sequels to *Down the Garden Path.*

In his volume of reminiscences, *All I Could Never Be*, Beverley paid a graceful and heartfelt tribute to Whistler. The news of his death in action in July 1944, he said, brought a special bitterness to all who loved him. England might have gained a hero, another legend to rank alongside that of Rupert Brooke but 'God alone knows what has been lost.' Beverley took a deep pride in their association and in his part in bringing Whistler's work to the attention of thousands around the world.

Beverley's third publication in 1932 was *For Adults Only* in which he revived the scenario of the child asking awkward questions, usually at a time inconvenient for the unfortunate parent. The point was that the questions made sense, but the parent's answers did not, and so the child always came out on top. The book was lightly satirical, but in the hands of Tallulah Bankhead, who read bits of it at parties, it plumbed depths of bawdry unsuspected by its author. Its sales were healthy, it was reprinted several times, and a cheap edition was published in 1934. It can often be found on the shelves of second-hand book shops and is worth reading, not only for its gentle wit but also for its reflection of the social mores of the time.

During the summer of 1932, Beverley was approached by James Drawbell with a proposition to write a weekly piece for the *Sunday Chronicle*, but he refused. Originally a Manchester-based paper, the *Sunday Chronicle* had a long and honourable history in the radical tradition, expressing broad Socialist and Liberal views, but it was in decline in the 1920s when Drawbell was appointed editor. He rejuvenated it in style and content, placing it below *The Times* or the *Observer* but above the sensational press, and his efforts were rewarded by increased circulation as readers discovered it to be intelligent and innovative. Beverley's initial reluctance was to do partly with an instinctive feeling that the paper was not the correct platform for his views and partly with the possibility that the more powerful *Sunday Express* might propose a more attractive deal – even that one of the upmarket papers might approach him. But nothing of this kind materialized, and so, when Drawbell increased the financial inducement and offered him page 2 of the paper with complete freedom to write what he wished, Beverley capitulated.

Years later, he was to say that his instinct had been correct and that the *Sunday Chronicle* was not the platform he should have chosen. The trouble was that he did not think the proposition through thoroughly. First of all, he did not anticipate the strain of filling a page a week, however busy he might be on other work; secondly, although Drawbell was as good as his word on the matter of freedom and printed Beverley's opinions however much they conflicted with the stance of the paper, he persuaded him to write about 'names', the more aristocratic and upper-class the better. The combination of these factors resulted in a wild variation in the quality of Beverley's work: at its best it was a considered essay on a problem of the day; at its worst it was little more than a superior gossip column. The pressure of deadlines often exposed his weakness for sentimentality and sensationalism, and Drawbell's attention-getting headlines, although mild by today's standards, made Beverley increasingly wretched. A few examples illustrate the point: 'I Danced With A Queen', 'Why Oliver Baldwin Will Never Have A Son', 'The Attorney-General Confesses To Me', 'Is Lady Astor A Liar?'.

This last headline appeared over a perfectly serious article about Christian Science, which so pleased Lady Astor that she invited him to her home, Cliveden. (He afterwards said that it had the impersonal atmosphere of a luxury hotel which, indeed, is what it was eventually to become.) Lady Astor asked him why he wrote for 'that rag', adding that it was not a 'gentleman's paper', and Beverley never forgot her comment for, however snobbish it may have been, it crystallized his own feeling about the *Sunday Chronicle*. The solution, of course, was in his own hands, but the fear of poverty haunted him and he could not resist the increasing annual remuneration and the security it gave him. Years afterwards, when he began writing for *Woman's Own*, he had given up hoping for a better press platform, and as he dictated his weekly piece the thought of the useful cheque helped to quell the nagging self-contempt for the direction his career had taken. He continued with the *Sunday Chronicle* until 1947, but never mentioned it in his entry for *Who's Who*.

And yet, when his column began, it promised much. Drawbell shrewdly engaged Rebecca West, Beverley's friend of ten years, to write a profile of him, thus pleasing Beverley and giving 'Page 2' a certain cachet in advance. There was, too, the usual blast of advertising trumpets to herald 'the new weekly diary' as it was loosely described: 'Something new, something different, not gossip, not small talk, not society silliness, but real life, real people. A page devoted to one of the most discussed figures of today.' Taking second place in the advertisement and in smaller type was an announcement that the serialization of J.B. Priestley's new novel *Faraway* would also begin 'next Sunday'. It was claimed that 'Page 2' increased the weekly sales of the *Sunday Chronicle* by 100,000 copies; the rival newspapers took action and the battle for readers accelerated, an eventual consequence of which was the emergence of Godfrey Winn. This in itself would be of no interest but for the curious relationship which existed between the two men.

Photographs of Winn as the South of England Junior Tennis Champion show him to have been pretty rather than handsome. His mother had been an actress and he also had theatrical ambitions. It was while he was appearing in an amateur production that Edward Marsh, later Sir Edward, an influential patron of the arts, took an interest in him. The biographer and friend of Eddie Marsh, Christopher Hassall, believed him to be impotent, but he took a particular interest in attractive young men, many of whom, as in Winn's case, were homosexual. Eddie engineered the sixteen-year-old Winn's first professional acting engagement, and introduced him into the world of Ivor Novello and Ned Lathom. This led to Winn's meeting with Beverley, for whom he developed a combination of hero-worship and schoolboy crush. He next decided he wanted to be a famous writer, and his first novel was published while he was appearing in Noel Coward's *The Marquise* which starred Marie Tempest. Winn's book being fairly success-ful, he asked Miss Tempest whether he should continue with acting or devote himself to writing. She replied, somewhat ambiguously, 'Juveniles in the theatre are two a penny.'

One of Winn's social accomplishments was bridge which he played almost as well as he played tennis, and it was at a bridge evening that he met Somerset Maugham. Maugham was greatly taken with him and promptly invited him to spend a month at the Villa Mauresque. They were lovers for a time and remained friends until Maugham's death. Winn constantly referred to Maugham as his 'literary mentor' but the only influence Maugham appears to have had on his career was his advice to pursue journalism, having made it clear that he did not think highly of him as a novelist. Indeed, the friendship appears to have been more on Winn's side than Maugham's, for his 'mentor' drew a wicked portrait of him disguised as George Potter in *Strictly Personal* (1941). The section was deleted from the British edition for fear of a possible libel action.

Winn had already produced pieces for the press which were imitations of those written by Beverley. Unfortunately, he was influenced by Beverley's weakness for sentimental whimsy and his writing emerged as an unwitting caricature of his hero's style, without its saving grace of humour or irony. Beverley was at first amused by Winn's emulation of his work and by his fawning devotion, but he became increasingly irritated when Winn was seen to be his rival in the field of journalism. Winn's first major success was a column in the *Daily Mirror*, which was followed by the offer of a page in the *Sunday Express* on similar terms to those Beverley enjoyed at the *Sunday Chronicle*. The irony was that Beverley had always hoped to switch to the more powerful *Sunday Express* and the Beaverbrook publishing empire, and believed that this might have happened if the editor, John Gordon, had not been so avidly anti-homosexual. It is an indication of Winn's character that, when Gordon began causing trouble for him, probably as a prelude to sacking him, he appealed directly to Lord Beaverbrook and from then on enjoyed a special status which Gordon could do nothing to weaken. By 1938 Winn was able to claim that he was the most highly paid journalist in

Fleet Street. Although he was frequently mocked, nobody could deny the popularity of his work, about which Beaverbrook commented, 'He shakes hands with people's hearts.'

Although Beverley and Winn maintained an affability which extended to entertaining each other in their homes, there was an underlying hostility. Beverley could not abide Winn's constant boasting about the people he knew and the money he made, his growing egomania, or his pride in being able to entertain guests at comparatively little expense. This meanness seemed to annoy Beverley most of all. Winn had a theory that his guests needed only one or two drinks, after which their adrenalin and his own vivacity would make everything go with a swing. One of his parties coincided with an advertising campaign which featured a photograph of Beverley with the caption, 'If Beverley Nichols offered you a cigarette, it would be a de Reszke.' Noel Coward, gloomily sipping his watered martini and finding the cigarette-boxes empty, hissed, 'If Godfrey Winn were to offer you a cigarette, it would be a bloody miracle.'

The final break came years later when Beverley published his defence of Syrie Maugham, *A Case of Human Bondage*. Winn was outraged at what he considered to be a libel of the dead Maugham. He was not alone in that, but Beverley believed that Winn should have seen the justice of the case, since he had often spoken of Willie's dreadful treatment of Syrie. Indeed, Winn frequently told the most scurrilous stories about his so-called friends, including Maugham, which made Beverley suspect that Winn told equally scurrilous about him. Beverley's hatred was intensified when Winn made a thinly disguised attack upon him in his autobiography *The Infirm Glory*, not, of course, mentioning their earlier relationship.

A few months before the break between them, Winn had been a guest at Beverley's home, and wrote next day thanking him for his hospitality. He went on in fulsome style to praise Beverley's talent, which was, he said, so much greater than his own, and to describe their friendship as infinitely precious to him. The letter managed to be both patronizing and sentimental and Beverley's friend Cyril Butcher later described Winn as a 'sycophantic little beast'.

When Winn died of a heart attack while playing tennis, a friend remarked to Beverley, 'We could hear the champagne corks popping for miles around.' Beverley replied, 'Not champagne but a good stiff celebratory gin.' Afterwards he said, 'I detested him. He was the worst kind of hypocrite. I was not aware of it at the time but I believe he caused great harm to me behind the scenes.'

In the autumn of 1932, C.B. Cochran had preliminary discussions with Beverley about a new operetta to be composed by Vivian Ellis. In his diary, Beverley gives no indication of the subject of the work, but he was to write the libretto with Edward Knoblock, and supply the lyrics. Vivian Ellis had no recollection of the project when asked about it more than fifty years later, and it appears that Cochran did not intend to approach him until he had received an outline from Knoblock and Nichols. In December, Beverley took the surprising step of withdrawing from the project, apparently expecting to resume work on it at a later date, and it is intriguing to speculate how his career might have developed if he had not made that fateful decision. Cochran must have thought it extraordinary when Beverley explained that he thought it more important to write a book in support of the peace movement. The origins of this decision lay in the invitation of the Publicity Club (composed of members of the advertising industry) to Beverley to be guest speaker at a meeting to debate the proposition: 'Can advertising help in the abolition of war?'

It is impossible to find a single cause for the spontaneous and highly vocal surge of anti-war feeling that swept England at this time. Of course, no one wanted war, except the diehards who maintained that Germany would have to be thrashed again, but in 1932 Germany was not the obvious potential enemy. Indeed, it is not clear if there was an enemy as such – instead, there seems to have been a fear that a war might erupt almost anywhere and that Britain would be involved. There were those who wanted the country to rearm as an insurance against an aggressor and those who demanded total disarmament; those who feared that a war might be an attack upon socialism, and those who foresaw an attack upon capitalism. Hovering uncertainly in the background was the League of Nations, dedicated to peaceful solutions, but already proving itself a forum for pious hopes rather than action.

Beverley had always made it clear that he was a pacifist and his play *Avalanche* had expressed that belief, but his definition of it was by no means clear. He declared that he would never fight for purely nationalistic reasons but that he would join an international army set up by the League of Nations to put down aggression. The matter of his personal involvement was, as he admitted, academic, as he had never been medically fit for fighting service.

In preparing for his Publicity Club speech, Beverley followed the routine he had perfected at Oxford. Once he had written the speech (his draft shows many amendments and second thoughts) he learned it by heart and rehearsed it to the point when it would appear entirely spontaneous. Judging by the report in the trade newspaper, the *Advertisers' Weekly*, the meeting was a success. All agreed that an advertising campaign – paid for, incidentally, out of public funds – would succeed in propagating peace, and Beverley devised a slogan for the campaign: 'Peace at any price'. Those words would return to haunt him in the years to come.

There the matter might have ended, but he was invited to repeat his speech at the Albert Hall on 15 November at a disarmament rally organized by the League of Nations Union. He promptly began amending the speech, making it more dramatic and provocative. He knew that his fellow-speakers would include Sir Stafford Cripps, the Archbishop of York, and Viscount Cecil, who would also preside, and he guessed correctly that the proceedings would be gentlemanly and in a minor key. As the final speaker, he proposed to alter this. His new version began: 'As I have been sitting here listening to the eloquent speeches of these distinguished men, I have been asking myself the question: "Are these speeches doing any good?" Are there any words, however moving or profound, which are powerful enough to defeat the massed forces of ignorance against which we are fighting? And there were moments when I felt a little hopeless about it. For, at the risk of appearing presumptuous, I would suggest that this meeting, up to the present moment, has been a good deal too polite. I would also suggest that the resolution, drastic as it is, has been a good deal too polite.' (The resolution proposed by Viscount Cecil concerned world-wide disarmament, the banning of heavy weaponry, aircraft and submarines, and agreement to collective security with the minimum of arms.)

On the night, Beverley's opening words aroused the audience which murmured its agreement. Those present had not been unaware of Beverley's presence before that moment: with his sense of theatre, he was the only person on the platform to appear in full evening dress, looking rather as if he had come to conduct an orchestra instead of to speak at a peace rally. What he now did was to conduct the meeting, moving his audience one moment with his quiet sincerity and stirring it the next with his emotional fervour. Of the resolution he said: 'There are four words missing from it, the only words which can really bring it to life, and those four words are "Peace at any price". The condition of the world is too desperate for half-measures. Unless you are prepared to accept these four words, don't fool yourselves that you are for peace.'

There was more in this vein and the audience loved it, apart from one or two persistent hecklers who were particularly annoyed when Beverley pointed dramatically to the huge Union Jack hanging behind the platform and said: 'I am standing in front of a great and glorious flag but I am not ashamed to acknowledge my loyalty to a greater.' To shouts of 'The Red Flag', Beverley shouted back, 'The white flag of Peace and it is the only flag I would die for.'

In his diary on 3 December, Beverley wrote retrospectively:

This was without exception the most remarkable personal success I have ever had. The hall was packed. The meeting was a dead flop until I got up and, from word one, they roared with delight and practically stormed the platform when I sat down. The meeting was practically barred by the press but was shown on Movietone [the cinema newsreel]. Mine was the only speech recorded at any length. So I am going to do a book on Peace and I see great publicity in it, and, I hope, acclaim, to say nothing of money.

At the beginning of 1933, Beverley looked back on the previous twelve months and described them as 'the most successful year of my life'. He looked forward to the future with high hopes. His financial affairs were in order and he had been able to add £500 to his savings which, since his standard of living was very high, could be counted as an achievement. He was able to leave the rooms at Great Stanhope Street and move to a house in New Street, Westminster, where Gaskin, newly returned from his exile in New York, resumed his control. This did not extend to Thatch Cottage, however, which was looked after by a separate staff. Beverley now employed a full-time secretary to deal with chores and to whom he dictated his weekly column and shorter pieces for the press, but he continued to write most of his output in longhand.

In his diary, after summarizing the success of 1932, he wrote: 'Added to which, there is Cyril, which means more than anything.'

He had first seen Cyril Butcher on stage at an audition for *Evensong* and had been instantly attracted to him. He was tall, well built and good-looking. In photographs taken at the time, he bore an uncanny resemblance to the males of the Nichols clan which may suggest that Beverley's consistent attraction to men of that physical type had some psychological significance. Cyril was jolly and outgoing, with a keen sense of humour which ranged from the wittily sophisticated to the downright earthy. There was an immediate rapport between the two men and Beverley hoped that his search for the ideal companion had ended; so it proved, for their friendship lasted, for better and for worse, until Beverley's death.

Cyril had begun his theatre career in repertory. He was also an aspiring writer. But he soon discovered that being Beverley's companion was a full-time occupation and, while he enjoyed his new, sybaritic life, he hankered after success in the theatre or as an author. Beverley did not actively encourage or discourage him, but steered a careful course which assuaged Cyril's pride while keeping him on a fairly tight rein. For example, he suggested that Cyril might ghost-write for him from time to time. This was flattering but it was also a trap. One of Cyril's first successes in this capacity was the 1933 guide to Brighton for which Beverley received many compliments as official author. How much of the Nichols output was ghosted by Cyril Butcher will never be known. When asked about it, Cyril indicated that the percentage was too small to bother about but, he added with a grin, 'The last thing Beverley wanted was a sibling Godfrey Winn in the house.'

While Beverley described the Peace book in his diary as 'the next big thing', he had also begun the sequel to *Down the Garden Path* which he called *A Thatched Roof*. There was continuing activity at Glatton to improve the gardens, but his ignorance about gardening and his frequent refusal to take advice led to expensive mistakes. On one occasion, he decided to plant a grove of mimosa. The soil was heavy clay, the location unprotected from the winds which swept across the Midlands, and, as any gardener will know, the idea was madness. Undeterred by gloomy prognostications from his father and the resident gardener, he ordered twenty plants from a nursery in Cornwall. In preparation, he had a vast tent of muslin erected over the site. A bitterly cold spell soon after, followed by heavy snow, destroyed the mimosa, which had never stood a chance. In a similar vein, he spent a fortune creating a wood and was mystified by the death of many of the trees. His father told him it was due to lack of drainage and ordered the gardener to dig down to prove the point; it was found that the trees were waterlogged. John Nichols then organized a new system of drains which solved the problem and prevented further disasters.

In March, Sir Barry Jackson produced Beverley's new play, *When the Crash Comes*, at the Birmingham Repertory Theatre. It was, as Beverley put it, 'an attempt to switch on the bright lights of controversy'; it postulated a situation in which the Communist party had won an overwhelming victory at a general election and had set in train the process of revolution. The central situation concerned an aristocratic family forced to share its large London home with those in need of housing. The idea was a promising one but Beverley lacked the skill to handle it as Bernard Shaw or Sean O'Casey might have done. The play suggested that the class system was so deeply ingrained in the English psyche that people would adapt to the new circumstances while leaving the class system intact. At the end of the play, the Communist government collapsed and the status quo was on its way to being restored: whether Beverley saw this resolution as good or bad was not made clear. Although the dialogue sparkled with wit and there were one or two touching moments, the audience was left bewildered, sensing that a strong idea had been inadequately developed.

A few weeks later, *When the Crash Comes* appeared in a collected edition of Beverley's plays together with *The Stag* and *Avalanche*. He had written a long argumentative preface in the style of Bernard Shaw to explore the themes he had used in the plays, and it was not until the final proof lay on his desk that he could be persuaded that drastic cuts and amendments were required, if he were not to face the possibility of public outrage and even legal action. It was with resentful reluctance that he set about rewriting, amending and cutting. The first section to go was in the middle of his argument in favour of legal abortion. Today, it appears innocuous but, at the time, the plea for sexual freedom which, by implication, included homosexual acts, was considered too provocative. It read:

What do you think your body is for? Is it to be a life-long bore or is it to be an instrument of happiness?

The Creator of this world has given us bodies which, generally speaking, are an infernal nuisance. They wear out, things go wrong with the works, some of them are impossibly inefficient from the moment they are delivered from the factory of the womb. However, as a compensation for these defects in craftsmanship, the Creator has also included, in the set of parts which compose the human frame, various instruments which are capable of giving us the most exquisite pleasure. We did not create these instruments, we received them. They are part of the complete set. And why on earth should we not use them as we think fit? We received very definite instructions, from the Maker, as to how the apparatus was to be used. These directions are printed in every man's brain in the shape of instincts, which are universal. Why should we deny the only authentic directions we possess, and follow out the directions of a lot of bogus people who did not make the instrument, and are usually in possession of old and worn-out apparatus? And since this metaphor is in danger of becoming mixed, let me sum it up by asking why we should not do with our own bodies exactly as we please, provided that we do not thrust ourselves upon people who do not desire our attentions?'

The second section which was cut in its entirety was written as a postscript to the discussion of his anti-war play *Avalanche*. As Beverley made clear, he had been disgusted by Noel Coward's *Cavalcade*, not only for its sentiments but also because it had been embraced by many as a timely endorsement of old-style patriotism. It had caused such a sensation that it was even credited with influencing the result of a general election, a belief bolstered by the attendance of the entire royal family on election night, two weeks after *Cavalcade* opened at Drury Lane in October 1931. Beverley wrote:

Noel Coward, whose brain is so delicate that it is intoxicated by the slightest waves in the ether, has, in desperation, taken a header in the wrong direction. He ought to be a white-hot pacifist. But somebody waved a Union Jack in front of him, and he tripped up, and he wrote *Cavalcade*. That play is about the finest essay in betrayal since Judas Iscariot jingled his thirty pieces of silver in the moonlight a number of years ago. And the tragedy of it is heightened by the fact that it is Noel who has been betrayed, and not his public. His public, which is deservedly vast, adored the flags and the streamers, the blood red, ice-white and royal blue which, in varying patterns, he threw across the stage of Drury Lane. And he, I am quite sure, adored the thirty thousand pieces of silver which, as a result of this play, he was able to jingle in his pocket. But the play was a tragedy, none the less. And the tragedy was not on the stage. It was in the Royal Box. It was focused in the thin, nervous face of the young man who had created this glittering tissue of dramatic lies, as he turned to his adoring audience, and said, 'It's pretty exciting to be English nowadays.'

I have to hold on to the table very hard before I can forgive Noel for those words. If we go on saying to ourselves that it is pretty exciting to be English we shall very soon cease to have the privilege of saying to ourselves that it is pretty exciting to be alive. The statement is, to begin with, inaccurate. And even if it were accurate, it would be damnably mischievous. It may be pretty exciting to be English if you are sitting in the Royal Box with two thousand people adoring you, but it is assuredly a vast bore to be English, or anything else, if you are sitting on the Embankment with your toes protruding from your boots. People who have been on the dole for five years have no very exalted ideas of nationalism. There were two million of them, outside Drury Lane, at the moment when Noel Coward made his speech. And if they had been listening in they might have made some coarse, but illuminating comments upon this statement.

However, the cruelty of that sentence is comparatively unimportant. What is important is that it was a sentence which was hailed with hysterical delight by the whole middle class of England, whose members immediately clasped Noel Coward to their bosom, saying 'the boy's heart is in the right place after all.' The English middle class had so frequently expressed misgivings as to the precise location of this important organ, that their conversion was all the more significant.

Well – I have no time to express my hatred of this sort of flag-waving. Even if it were beautiful (which it is not) it would be suicidal, because unless we stop waving flags and get down to facts we are courting destruction.

Nigel, in *Avalanche*, expresses my views on the subject better than I could do here. And it is pretty certain that the average Englishman would argue with him along the same lines as I have suggested. For the tragedy of *Avalanche* is the tragedy of England – the tragedy that we have learned nothing from the war. We are still blinded by the same lies. We are still slaves to the same superstitions.

The preface was written after his success at the Albert Hall and while he was in demand as a speaker on pacifism as far afield as Berlin. Arthur Diamond said that audience acclaim went to Beverley's head and he believed he had a mission to change the world and a divine right to say what he thought without consideration of the consequences. This is reflected in his comments on *Cavalcade*.

Beverley called the collected edition of his plays *Failures*, and while it was widely reviewed there appears to have been some bewilderment among the critics as to why it was published at all. The *Belfast News Letter* concluded it was because 'Mr Beverley Nichols likes to do things that no one else would dream of doing.'

In the mean time, fired by his new-found sense of mission, Beverley had begun preparations for the Peace book. It was to prove a watershed in his career but its success led to a series of ill-judged statements which damaged his reputation. In old age, he remarked wryly, 'It might have been better if I had written that operetta for Cochran,' and then added sadly, 'but I believed I was doing something worth doing at the time.'

In *The Unforgiving Minute* (1978) he said of pacifism that it was more than a philosophy, 'it was a religion and a way of life, cutting through every barrier of class and political tradition, setting husband against wife and father against son.' He attributed the genesis of his own pacifism to his father's attitude during the First World War: 'Reclining in his armchair during four years of carnage, he gained a vicarious, sadistic satisfaction through the blood sacrifices of the world's youth. One of his bitterest disappointments was that none of his own sons was ever slaughtered.' The cruel accusation is consistent with the frightening portrait Beverley drew of his father.

Beverley also wrote of his pacifism:

> The most extraordinary aspect of it all and, from the contemporary angle, the most inexplicable, was the conviction that one could 'do anything about it'. What young man today, armed only with a pen, could be so deluded? Where have all the crusaders gone? To claim the accolade of 'crusader' may seem an empty boast but it was not, for many of us were prepared to lay down our lives in the cause of peace. How otherwise is the historian to interpret such a bizarre phenomenon as the 'Peace Army' which thousands of young men, including myself, pledged ourselves to join, with the object of marching out to the battlefields in the event of war and standing passively between the opposing armies, holding white flags, under the delusion that they might thereby compel the opposing armies to hold their fire? The idea, of course, was ridiculous and came to nothing, but the fact that it was ridiculous does not imply that it was contemptible.

In January he went to Geneva to observe the League of Nations at work discussing disarmament. It was a dispiriting experience. He was particularly interested in the Russian delegate Litvinoff, who had proposed total disarmament a few years before – a radical suggestion that had been turned down by the great powers. Litvinoff rose to speak, but what he had to say was incomprehensible and nobody paid much attention. Beverley discovered later that all the speeches had been circulated, read and discussed twenty-four hours before and so the meeting was a routine formality whose outcome was already agreed. The resolution stated that all members would have to justify any rearmament they undertook, and Beverley discussed this with a fellow journalist who represented a popular English newspaper. Yes, the journalist agreed, it was an encouraging decision – but his employer was against the League, so his story would read: 'Another staggering blow was dealt to the moribund League of Nations'.

Beverley left Geneva for Brussels, where arrangements had been made for him to interview several young men undergoing savage prison sentences for refusing to do military service. He arrived at the prison to find that permission had been withdrawn at the last minute. It was his first but not his last experience of this kind. His views were well known, and, despite assurances to the contrary, he now found his investigations blocked. For example, Beverley had studied the League of Nations' paper, published in 1921, which accused the armaments industry of using every stratagem to promote its own interests and to fight the possibility of disarmament. He went to great lengths to arrange a visit to the Schneider armaments factory at Le Creusot in France: Schneider was one of the largest manufacturers of war weapons in the world, and also had strong connections in international banking. It was probably naïve of Beverley to believe that Schneider would let him see what they were up to at Le Creusot, but he had the written assurance of the French War Office that he would be allowed to see anything there was to see. Instead, he was given a guided tour of a factory which manufactured parts for motor-cars, and when he asked about military production, his guide denied that they did any such thing. Back in England, it was only too easy to tour armaments factories where he found a child-like eagerness to boast of the killing powers of various weapons – though he was refused permission to visit Porton where the government's chemical warfare installation was sited. In addition to his exhausting and often frustrating programme of visits around Europe and Great Britain, he interviewed and recorded discussions between public figures, and read through a mass of material related to his theme. He began to believe that the vested interests and the economic power of the world-wide arms industry were unassailable; that there was no hope while governments paid lip service to disarmament but armed themselves to the teeth 'to ensure peace'.

By the time he sat down to write, he was in a cold fury. His research had shown him that waving a white banner and crying 'peace at any price' was a totally inadequate response to the world situation, and he now had doubts about the ease with which he could move thousands at public meetings to rise to their feet, cheering. Was this cheering of any significance at all? He now questioned the extreme pacifist attitude of complete non-resistance. His mind was in a turmoil, but one thing seemed clear to him: there was no point in writing a scholarly appeal to reaon. He must employ all the devices of popular journalism to present the facts as he and others saw them. It must be war on war. Once this thought crystallized, the title for the book leapt into his mind: *Cry Havoc!* In his reinterpretation of Shakespeare's line 'Cry havoc, and let slip the dogs of war,' the 'war' would be an attack on targets ranging from the world-wide armaments industry to the indoctrination of the young into accepting as noble and patriotic the slaughter of fellow-human beings. He would be the first militant peace campaigner.

The resulting book was a frontal assault, all intellectual guns blazing. Given that *Cry Havoc!* was very much a book of its time, how does it stand up today? It is generally easy to read although some sections are facetious and elsewhere it is too deliberately emotional, but one thing emerges with depressing clarity: despite the agony of the Second World War and the reappraisal which has gone on since, much remains fundamentally unchanged today. Take, for example, the chapter on chemical warfare: Beverley describes the stockpiling of this vile weapon in its various forms and points out that no attempt was being made at that time to stockpile gas masks, the bulk of those manufactured in England being exported. The instructions issued by the British Red Cross under the title 'First Aid in Chemical Warfare' stated that 'Any room with sound walls, roof and floor can be rendered gas-proof', and explained that windows should be puttied, the chimney blocked and the door sealed with strips of cloth. Beverley pointed out that this was not worth the paper it was printed on. Substitute today the words 'nuclear weapons' for 'chemical warfare' and the advice on making your own bolthole becomes startlingly familiar. The argument employed today in favour of nuclear warfare is precisely similar to that used to support the stockpiling of chemical weapons in the 1930s.

In his original draft, he had included a chapter on the problems of Germany and the failure of its squabbling political parties to unite against extremism. Events were moving so rapidly that he dropped the chapter and included instead a brief comment on the rise of Hitler, who in January had become Chancellor and by the end of March was dictator of the Reich. Rashly, Beverley suggested that, by the time *Cry Havoc!* was published, Hitler might be in exile or on the other hand might have repudiated the homicidal lunatics surrounding him and pulled himself and Germany together. With hindsight, this appears ludicrous but at that time the German people, let alone the rest of Europe, had not begun to see the full implications of what was happening. By the time that the book was on sale, all other political parties in Germany had been banned and Nazification was well on its way.

In one sense, *Cry Havoc!* was almost a decade too late. In another sense, it was timely because it presented facts and opinions which before had often been obscured by specialists lost in their own verbosity and by the hyperbole of the popular press. It became the basis for widespread debate at a time when debate was badly needed.

The reception by the critics in serious publications like the *Sunday Times* and the *Spectator* was thoughtfully favourable: elsewhere it was often treated as 'news' with headlines like 'Gassing of Babies'. All agreed it was a book that demanded serious attention, but perhaps the most surprising commendation of all came from the *Army, Navy and Air Force Gazette* which said, 'The book is an important one that officers of the Services should read and meditate upon. Mr Nichols is no fool and most of what he has to say is founded on fact and clear thinking.'

An astonishing furore followed its publication. Letters for and against it poured into the newspapers, and those published generated more letters. The *Daily Telegraph* commented that the very large correspondence they received came from people of every age and social class and from every part of the country. The debate rolled on, with other professional writers contributing articles, some in fierce opposition. One of the most vocal of Beverley's opponents was Major Francis Yeats-Brown, the well-known author of *Bengal Lancer* and supporter of Fascism, who advocated rearming on a massive scale so that the British Empire and the United States would become the guardians of peace. People like Beverley Nichols, he asserted, were a public danger. In 1934, he published a riposte to *Cry Havoc!* called *Dogs of War* which Beverley's father approved of, much to Beverley's disgust.

It goes without saying that *Cry Havoc!* was a best-seller. In America it sparked off an argument on arms manufacture which went on in the press for nearly a year; across the border in Canada, it was the subject of sermons and radio broadcasts. In Ontario, 5,000 copies of the book were circulated for study in schools with heavy cuts made to those sections which were considered to promote 'extreme socialism'.

According to Arthur Diamond, Beverley revelled in the controversy and the publicity, though he was aware that it brought him as much dislike as popularity. He admitted to Diamond that the whole business had got out of hand, but the acclaim from audiences and the massive post he received became a drug he could not resist and did nothing to avoid. He was so blinded by his sense of self-importance that he would not see that his crusade for peace was increasingly irrelevant, as the build-up of Hitler's new war machine became public knowledge. But the British government itself refused to accept the implications of this arms build-up until it was nearly too late.

During Armistice week in 1933, a short documentary made by Movietone was shown in cinemas around the country. It was called *Peace or War?* and consisted of a discussion between four women, the most effective of whom was Miss Madeleine Carroll, BA, better known as a stunningly beautiful film star. Beverley provided the introduction and epilogue, and was described by *Cinema Today* as 'rather good'. The *Sunday Express* deplored his mention of 'that depressingly juvenile work *Cry Havoc!* which, when last heard of, was, I believe, in its seventeenth edition and still going strong.' At a showing of this film Beverley encountered Noel Coward. 'I've come to hear what you've been up to,' said Coward. 'You won't like it,' Beverley observed. 'I'm quite sure I shan't,' came the reply. 'I've come to hiss.'

For the *Newcastle Journal* Beverley gave a long interview to Raymond Burns who asked penetrating questions about his pacifism. Once again he stated that he would fight in an international army, provided that the League of Nations was truly representative which meant that the USA and Japan were members – a slight change of stance since the publication of the book some months before. On the subject of Hitler he said, 'I am thoroughly opposed to Hitler and his methods. Hitler is backed by German munition makers who stand to gain enormously from the present rearmament drive. A break with these supporters would mean Hitler's collapse.' Beverley was not to know that Hitler's position was now unassailable; his remark was based on ignorance rather than *naïveté*, and his old arguments were rapidly becoming outdated in the changing scene. It took him nearly five years to accept that *Cry Havoc!* was, in many respects, a mistake. Both pride and stubbornness were involved, but it must be remembered that many thousands of others went on deluding themselves for as long.

In November *A Thatched Roof* was published, and it must have come as a relief to many of his readers that, far from there being a hint of the militant pacifist in it, it was a return to the cosy, sentimental Beverley of old. His publishers, Jonathan Cape, held a cocktail party for their author in their Bedford Square house, with an impressive array of guests: Somerset Maugham, Lady Diana Cooper, Osbert Sitwell, Raymond Massey, Michael Arlen, Gladys Cooper and the Dean of Windsor among them.

Beverley claimed, somewhat pedantically, that *A Thatched Roof* was not a sequel to *Down the Garden Path* but 'the other half of the same love'. Nevertheless, a sequel was what it was, not something he had intended to write until the astonishing success of the first book convinced him he was on to a winning streak which it would be madness to abandon. *A Thatched Roof* told of the transformation of a neglected Tudor building, originally three or probably four hovels for labourers and their families, into a delightful home with electric light and central heating. The work also included a new roof, the piercing of the thick walls to make new windows, combating damp and so forth. Anyone who has undertaken similar work while living in a property will know that it requires dedication, patience, a bank balance to cope with the unexpected, and the ability to withstand a nervous breakdown. Beverley sensibly chose to stay away, leaving the full horror of the operation to be borne by his domestic staff. It was not his intention, in any case, to startle his readers with chilling reality, but instead to paint a romantic picture of achievement. He was the designer, just as he had been with the garden where he was not a hard-working participant but more of a dabbler, leaving the heavy chores to others. As he loved messing about in the garden himself, he assumed his guests would enjoy it also. Few escaped and few objected: be it Noel Coward, Hugh Walpole or Rex Whistler, the visitor quickly learned it was advisable to purchase a pair of gloves in case he was pressed into a little light weeding.

Arthur Diamond remembered a weekend when he and Geoffrey Harmsworth, who had rooms in Beverley's London house, were persuaded to go with Beverley on a foray into a wood several miles away to collect leaf mould. They had just finished loading the car when the owner of the land appeared brandishing his stick and threatening them with the police for trespass and theft. They made a quick getaway and for the next few hours half expected the local bobby to arrive on his bicycle to arrest them. Beverley thoroughly enjoyed frightening himself with the thought of headlines in the press such as 'Dirt on Famous Author', and later used a version of this story, without mentioning the irate landowner.

An incidental pleasure resulted from the fictionalized account in *A Thatched Roof* of the discovery of a hand-written notebook of recipes and household hints dating from 1698, which Beverley found sealed up in a long-forgotten cupboard. He included examples in the narrative, among them an alarming remedy for the bite of a mad dog. He always intended that this slim volume should be published but it was not until 1968 that it appeared under the imprint of Cecil and Amelia Woolfe with the title *In an Eighteenth-Century Kitchen*. Beverley wrote the preface, Dr Dennis Rhodes the introduction, notes and glossary and Duncan Grant did the illustrations. Apart from several pages which Beverley retained, the original manuscript is in the Hammond Museum, North Salem, Westchester, New York, which houses a unique collection of English domestic artefacts.

A Thatched Roof was enthusiastically received by the press who described it as entirely enchanting and witty. The few dissident voices were helpless against the army of Nichols fans who rushed to buy it and relished vicariously the joys of a dream cottage. By now the real identity of Allways was well known and Glatton found itself something of an attraction to hikers, cyclists, coach-trippers and car owners. This provided a welcome boost to the economy of the village, whose shops began selling postcards of the cottage, even of Beverley himself in the punt on the pond, and of the statue of Antinous which formed one of the features of the garden. Beverley rather revelled in the attention of sightseers and in his unofficial position as village squire. He opened the annual garden fête, the proceeds of which went towards the cost of restoration work to St Nicholas's church, and conducted parties round his own garden and the cottage to raise money. Once he had begun this, however, it was difficult to stop and each year the attendance at the fête grew larger and the queue of fans eager to see his home grew longer.

Towards the end of 1933, it was announced that Beverley was to spend several weeks studying the conditions of the unemployed in Glasgow as part of his research for a new book. A Scottish newspaper observed acidly that he would need to spend several years if he hoped to begin to understand the full horror of unemployment. Beverley duly arrived in Glasgow wearing his oldest clothes and booked into a shilling-a-night hostel. Afterwards, describing it as a place of Hogarthian squalor, he said he did not know which was worst – the stink of unwashed humanity, the snores and cries in the night, or the bitter cold as he lay huddled under his dirty blankets. After paying for his bed, he had just over two shillings left for food each day out of a total of the twenty-three shillings which he allowed himself each week. He quickly learned the importance of a penny to the very poor, and above all he learned of the despair of men with nothing to do but huddle round the radiators of public libraries or trudge the streets. He was befriended by two brothers who took him to the two-room tenement home they shared with their mother, father and sister, all of them unemployed and without hope of work. The large families barely existed in this slum, with only a cold-water sink, a small range for cooking and heating, and one lavatory shared by eight families. He stuck it out for ten days before capitulating and booking into an hotel. Soaking in a hot bath, he knew he had only glimpsed what millions of his fellow countrymen had suffered for years. It angered him that he could find no answer to the problem. He did not believe the Socialists had an answer – not, at least, the Socialists he had met in the corridors of power, who, he considered, were merely full of theory. It needed a revolution, but of what kind he could not conceive.

He began work on the new book, but then abandoned it. He afterwards gave as his reason that J.B. Priestley had covered similar ground in *English Journey*, but the real reason was that he found it impossible to articulate his anger and despair in any way that would result in action.

· 15 ·

Matters religious and secular

1934–1936

IN 1934 there were signs that Beverley was slowing down the enormous output of the previous years. By normal standards his activity was still prodigious, and his social life exhausting as he dashed from engagement to engagement, from parties to dinners and first nights. He often said that he hated the social side of being a celebrity but Arthur Diamond remarked: 'He loved it.' A few items from Beverley's 1934 diary illustrate his social life.

20 February. Lunched today with Lady Mount Temple. The poor thing is in a great state of agitation and told me in a stage whisper that her husband had left her. 'He is a sadist,' she hissed. Next to me was Lady Lymington whose husband has just resigned from the Tory party. A nice woman, but unpardonably muddle-headed. She told me Lymington has founded a new political association called 'Mistery'. 'They want to wipe out the last hundred years altogether,' she remarked blandly. I asked her how they proposed to do it but received no adequate reply.

Dined with Catherine d'Erlanger. Catherine was in great form and dinner was typical. Either she or her son-in-law Johnny were at the telephone. Nobody was eating the same course at the same time. One never does at Catherine's.

Went to Noel's *Conversation Piece*. I have given up the facile criticisms I used to make of some of his work and gratefully accept his charm, his sturdy avoidance of anything 'shymaking' and his supremely brilliant direction. His performance was remarkable but left me with a sense of strain.

Back for a few minutes to Catherine's. How strange that great home in Piccadilly is! A night light burning in the hall, one of Catherine's economies. It had dripped wax all over an exquisite Louis XV table, spoiling the veneer. It will cost several guineas to repair the table, the price of about a thousand night lights.

21 February. Lunched with Mary Ridgely Carter at 41, Portman Square. Mary C. is a tiresome American who ought to have been cast as a housemaid and makes a very bad heiress. In love with me, apparently.

Dinner with Peter Spencer, now Lord Churchill. He ought to play a large part in any autobiography I may write. He dined with me at the Garrick. Arrived looking slimmer, paler and more distrait than ever. On the verge of a breakdown. I prescribed a course of rays and massage. Interesting part of the evening was Peter's revelation of the snobbery of his relations; after ignoring his existence for twenty years, they suddenly began asking him to dinner when his father died. He told me the late Lord Churchill had never lost an opportunity to put a spoke in Peter's wheels. Lord knows they were punctured enough without parental assistance.

23 February. Lunch at Claridge's with Mabel Corey, a rattling American who had collected the King of Greece, the Duke of Marlborough, Lord Elmleigh, Lady Birkenhead, Lady Alexander Haig and me. I sat next to Lady B. who told me she got £85 for saying she used Lyons Coffee Extract which she had never tasted.

5 March. Supper with Lady Colefax, Alfred Lunt, Lynn Fontanne, Victor Cazalet, H.G. Wells and Baroness Budberg (his lady love). I don't think H.G. Wells likes me. He said, 'You have made a profession of perpetual youth. Are you taking any measures to preserve it?' I replied, 'No. Only measurements.'

6 March. John Gielgud to lunch. Very gay and charming. Told me he had just bought a country home for £1,000.

7 March. Lunch with Barbara Back. Chiefly notable for the return of John Van Druten from America. Very acid about Willie Maugham's description of him as the 'coming young man'. John described Evelyn Waugh as a 'pancake stuffed with viper's blood'. I am tired out as usual.

13 March. I dined with Victor Cazalet at the House of Commons. After dinner, I went up to the Strangers' Gallery. I felt how easy it would be to dominate the mediocrities there, but what would be the use? It is a loathsome hell of a life. If anybody spoke as badly as that in the Peckham debating club, he would be howled down. [This entry is of particular interest because it was around this time that Beverley was again sounded out on the possibility of standing as a Conservative candidate for Parliament. What might have happened to him if he had? Would Winston Churchill, with whom he got on rather well, have given him a

junior cabinet post in the Ministry of Information in the wartime government, for example?]

14 March. Today I lunched at Claridge's with Alexander Korda, the Hungarian genius who has made such a great success with his film *The Private Life of Henry VIII*. He was full of a dinner which Roxy, the American film magnate, had given at the Savoy last night. Roxy wants to build a new super-cinema in London. 'We'll have the greatest ever,' he cried, 'with all the page boys trained at public schools and drilled by the finest generals in the British army. Why, we'll pay for them to be educated at universities if necessary. What's your best regiment? The Life Guards? We'll get them lined up outside the theatre. And we'll get some great English poet, who can act, to write a poem and recite it. Then he can say, 'Let there be light,' and the whole theatre will be illuminated.' Oh dear, oh dear!

17 March. I spent the weekend with Gerald Berners at Faringdon, motoring Peter Churchill up. Nobody there except Lady Birkenhead, Olga Lynn and Robert Heber-Percy, generally known as 'the mad boy' – why mad, I do not know, for he struck me as merely rude. The main interest of a dull weekend was the character of our host which is a fluffy mixture of a great many talents without any basis of work or application. You feel that everything in the house is done because it is 'amusing', the feather flowers, the big bowls of pink sweets under pink geraniums, the Nottingham lace curtains in the ultra-modern bathrooms, the paper shrines, the copies of surrealistic magazines, etc. In spite of these refinements, I was ungrateful enough to notice that the piano was atrociously out of tune, the food was loathsomely rich and that there were no Virginia cigarettes. Gerald is a curious creature, likeable but not lovable, because he puts a barrier between himself and you.

On his holiday trips to Germany and the south of France, Beverley could not let himself relax completely. He was constantly preoccupied with the 'next big thing' and material for his weekly 'Page 2'. The companionship of Cyril Butcher proved a blessing, but it was demanding: he wrote in his diary, 'Too many late nights with Cyril.' As for the 'next big thing', nothing came to mind. For a few weeks, there was excited talk of a new revue to be produced by Peter Spencer, the new Lord Churchill. Most of the finance was to be raised by Nicholas de Nolas who was also to design and probably direct the show. A meeting was held at Glatton to discuss plans:

Nicky arrived at 6.30 on Saturday [3 March] and instantly our peace was broken. N. is a brilliant stage designer with a truly Russian capacity for getting money out of people. But he has an idée fixe that, because he has done a series of designs, he has a revue and thinks all he has to do is to get various authors like myself and James Laver to sit down and write sketches and lyrics to his drawings. What will happen, Lord knows. I have done a song or two.

In the end, nothing developed as far as Beverley was concerned.

His publishers wanted a third 'Glatton' book, but the only major event in the garden had been the problem of the waterlogged trees and there was nothing more to be said about the cottage. Cyril Butcher suggested a book about the village itself but there was not much to say on the subject of village life which had not already been said by a host of other writers. Then Beverley hit on the notion of weaving a story around Miss Hazlitt, the character based on his governess, Miss Herridge. What eventually emerged was the tale of an elderly woman living in a tumbledown, damp-ridden cottage, eking out an existence on an income of £75 a year. When she loses all her savings in a share swindle, a few of her better-off neighbours rally round and set her up in a shop, but this is financially doomed from the start. In the end, she dies after several operations for cancer. The gloom of the theme is relieved by her refusal to see her life in anything other than the brightest terms because of her faith in an ever-loving God. What Miss Herridge thought about all this is not known, but the conclusion of the story was prophetic, for she was to die in an exactly similar manner many years later. In one of her last letters to Beverley, written following one of her operations, she wrote, 'I have to go a day at a time, for all my affairs are in God's hands and it is not for me to make plans or to be anxious at all.'

The story of Miss Hazlitt was at odds with the *joie de vivre* of the previous 'Glatton' books, but Beverley did not stop with her. He introduced a subsidiary theme of lonely women personified in a new character, Miss Bott, a middle-aged spinster, slightly masculine, usually cheerful, with an earthy sense of humour, desperately trying to make time pass. Loneliness and the knowledge that there is not one person who needs you must be Hell, Beverley surmised. He also paid tribute to the ladies of the village who kept up appearances in a world of rising prices and falling dividends: such ladies (and he used the term in its old-fashioned sense) were often laughed at for clinging to their standards, but he found that worse than unkind.

All this was so sombre that he introduced a lazy, tyrannical housekeeper and a wicked caricature of Lady Astor to provide some rather sour comedy. He mixed in a tale about a schoolboy who rediscovered the church stained glass long ago hidden from Cromwell's men, and the doings of an eccentric professor, based on his friend, A.M. Lowe. This strange mixture was laced with his own brand of wit and drenched unashamedly with sentimentality.

As if to preclude the possibility of yet another 'sequel', he ended with his vision of the demise of Allways, to which his ghost would return, drifting through the ruins and remembering the village as it had once been. If his ending echoed Goldsmith's *The Deserted Village*, it was none the worse for that.

All in all, *A Village in a Valley*, as he called it, published in 1934, was a strange book, deepy felt but self-indulgent. Rather more obvious than in the previous books was the almost total absence of real country people except as extras hovering in the background. It was extremely snobbish and class conscious, and more of the ring of hobnailed boots and less of the patter of patent-leather shoes might have added some reality. The critics were mostly kind, if somewhat nonplussed by the unexpectedly serious nature of the central story, but the public responded well. Thousands of his female readers must have wept, not only for the story but also for themselves, for Beverley had reflected the condition of women left alone after the slaughter of their menfolk in the war.

Of all the characters in the Glatton/Allways trilogy, the one who aroused the most interest among his readers and reviewers was the allegedly fictitious 'Mrs M.'. Beverley eventually surmised that she must be a projection of some of his own less attractive traits, but she was actually based on his mother, 'Ma Bird'. Pauline Nichols, like 'Mrs M.', could be imperious, stubborn and convinced she was always in the right. As one of her maids put it, 'She was difficult to please.' Beverley could not admit to the source of his characterization while his mother was alive, or indeed after she died, in view of his over-emphasis on her virtues.

In the foreword to the collected 'digest' of all three books, published in 1971 as *The Gift of a Garden*, Beverley had this to say about them:

At my time of life, the thought of all this literary outpouring provokes a feeling of profound fatigue. How did one keep it up? It wasn't as though one were doing nothing else; one wasn't a secluded *littérateur*, working to a regular schedule, attended by adoring slaves. One was a hard-working reporter, a conscientious critic, a dramatist *manqué* and frustrated composer, and one also had a private life which was not without its complications. Most important of all, one was a gardener, and gardens, like mistresses, cannot be neglected. They demand unremitting attention, endless flattery, and a constant outflow of cash.

Maybe that was the reason, that was the impelling, inescapable motive for it all. The short foreword to *Down the Garden Path* ends with the words … 'A garden is the only mistress who never fails, who never fades.' This phrase may not deserve inclusion in an anthology of immortal prose, but it was at least sincere. The garden was my mistress, and these books were written under the spell of her enchantment. In spite of their lapses into 'whimsy', the unforgivable sin of the modern era, they were written with dirty fingers, with mud under the nails.

It was inevitable that the huge success of the trilogy would spawn imitators, until this type of book became a cottage industry which still flourishes. When he was eighty-four, Beverley remarked, somewhat bitterly, that if he had collected a penny royalty from every copy sold by his multitude of imitators, he would be a wealthy man indeed.

One of the imitations out of the ordinary run was *Mon Repos*, a wickedly funny satire of *A Thatched Roof* published in 1934 with the author named as Nicholas Bevel. It caused such merriment in Beverley's circle that he sometimes implied, with a proper show of modesty, that he had written it himself. Indeed, the London *Evening Standard* suggested that this might be the case. In fact, it was written by Muriel Hine and it so nearly resembled the Nichols book that the publishers, John Lane, The Bodley Head, went to some lengths to establish that it did not infringe copyright. Unfortunately, the illustrations were a long way after Rex Whistler and it seems that an opportunity was lost to satirize his style also – if, indeed, that was possible.

The finality of the last chapter of *A Village in a Valley* marked the beginning of Beverley's disenchantment with the cottage in Glatton. The immediate reason was the rising cost of maintaining the house and garden to the high standard he had set, but the fact was that Beverley paid fewer and fewer visits to the place. Like a child grown tired of a toy, he wanted something new.

Although Beverley's income was substantial, he was haunted by the possibility of a drop in earnings and he was not saving as much as he had hoped. The obvious solution was to sell the cottage, but he could not bring himself to do so while it still had publicity value and while his readers believed, quite erroneously, that it was the centre of his life. Apart from the upkeep of the London house, in the charge of Gaskin, there was the salary paid to his full-time secretary, Barbara Dormer, a weekly allowance paid to his brother Alan – and of course, Cyril was not always in a position to contribute to the overall expenses. Among what might be described as peripheral earnings were lecture tours of America, fees for short stories and articles, the occasional wireless talk, and participation in documentary films and advertisements. Into this 'peripheral' category there came, in 1934, a lavishly produced publication from Hutchinson and Co, decorated with drawings and paintings by H.M. Brock, RI, entitled *A Book of Old Ballads*. Beverley provided the introduction and made the final selection of the contents. He did not regard it as sufficiently important to be listed with his other books, but it had a sort of 'suitable for an aunt' charm and is now something of a rarity.

Having abandoned the book on the state of the poor in Britain and facing the usual problem of 'the next big thing', he felt that he should again surprise his following. He settled on a book about Christianity, spurred on by the favourable response to a Sunday wireless talk in which, true to form, he had unpredictably adjured his listeners to 'go to church', an activity for which he was not well known. He had, however, paid several visits to the village church at Glatton where he found the atmosphere created by the familiar rites rather endearing, and he occasionally went with the family to hear his brother Paul preach. Having decided on the 'God book', he enlisted Paul to assist with the theology of it. As Cyril Butcher put it, 'There was no point in having a vicar in the family and doing the research yourself.'

He also renewed his association with C.B. Cochran to whom he offered a newly completed play about Franz Mesmer (1733–1815), the pioneer of hypnotism in the cure of emotionally induced physical ills. His methods had enraged colleagues in the medical profession who called him a quack. The plot concerned Mesmer and a young girl whom he cures temporarily of blindness and with whom he falls in love. In a large cast of historical figures, the best known was the young Mozart who was conveniently on hand to provide appropriate music (and who, compared with the later portrayal of him in *Amadeus*, was on his best behaviour). The play verged on melodrama: there was little of the Nichols wit in evidence, and far too much sentimentality. It ended happily with the blind girl, recovering her sight, all set for domestic bliss with Mesmer.

Today, it appears as a possible candidate for an Andrew Lloyd Webber musical and it might have worked better in 1935 as an operetta. Cochran was enthusiastic and treated it as a big-scale, lavish spectacle, but instead of casting a British actor to play the leading role, he gave it to the Austrian Oscar Homolka, who did not speak a word of English. Homolka, a star of the Berlin stage and of German cinema, promised to learn English in time for the production and spent six months studying on the Isle of Wight. The result was a commendable grasp of the language delivered with a heavy Viennese accent. This did not worry Beverley who had seen Homolka acting in Berlin and he was convinced he would be a triumph. He was frantically worried, however, when Cochran insisted on engaging Theodore Komisarjevsky to direct and design *Mesmer*, fearing that the combination of Homolka and Komisarjevsky might not be good for the play. In this, he was correct. The rest of the casting was particularly strong and Beverley could not have wished for a better leading lady than Peggy Ashcroft.

The play was to open at the Apollo Theatre, London, on 16 May 1935, following a week at the King's Theatre, Glasgow. When Beverley attended a final rehearsal, sitting in the front stalls, he was asked to move out of sight as he was making Homolka nervous. 'I retreated into the darkness and that's as much as I have dared to influence the production,' he remarked enigmatically to the Glasgow evening newspaper before the opening.

Komisarjevsky provided brilliant designs for the sets and costumes, and spent much of the final rehearsals concentrating on the lighting, leaving the actors to fend for themselves. On the opening night, it became increasingly obvious that Homolka's performance was at odds with those of the rest of the cast: it suggested power, but it was so restrained and static that instead of dominating the stage he appeared ordinary amid the glamour of the production and the performances around him. (One Glasgow newspaper commented that, by the third act, he was so ordinary he might just as well have been sitting in the stalls.) He contrasted particularly badly with the emotional brilliance of Peggy Ashcroft. The play itself suffered and Beverley knew early on in the evening that it was a resounding flop. He declined to take a curtain call, and was not surprised when Cochran decided to cancel the London opening, for there was simply nothing that could be done in time to save the production.

Three years later the Tavistock Little Theatre, a band of amateurs that still flourishes, gave their version of *Mesmer* in London. The event aroused considerable interest and critics from *The Times*, the *Daily Telegraph*, *Daily Mail* and *Daily Sketch* attended the first night. They all congratulated the company for tackling a piece so fraught with technical difficulties and for making such a good job of it, but there were mixed opinions of the play itself. In the *Daily Sketch*, Archie de Bear, well known in his day as a producer, praised it and said it deserved a West End run. The *Daily Telegraph* described it as an ordinary play about an extraordinary man but with enough in it to provide a good evening's entertainment. Beverley thought their reaction confirmed his conviction that, if Cochran had only listened to him on the subject of the director, the 1935 production might have stood a chance of success in the West End.

One of Beverley's many activities was broadcasting and in 1935 a slim volume appeared consisting of talks he, along with Compton Mackenzie, Marion Cran and V. Sackville-West, had given on gardening. The collection was called *How Does Your Garden Grow?* It said nothing particularly new and its main interest is that Beverley's name was given prominence, appearing in print twice the size of that accorded to the other distinguished contributors. It also appeared in an American edition advertised as a postscript to the Glatton/Allways trilogy.

After the débâcle of *Mesmer*, Beverley concentrated on the 'God book' which required rather more hard work than he had anticipated, despite Paul's assistance. He went to Cannes for a working holiday and in the somewhat unsympathetic atmosphere of his luxury hotel managed to complete the first half. Back in London he began the second half of what he now called *The Fool Hath Said*, but made little progress. For a time it seemed that he would abandon it but then, by a strange quirk of fate, he was invited by a friend to attend a weekend meeting of the Oxford Group. This had received a great deal of publicity, not all of it good, but it was supported by eminent churchmen and, in Beverley's mood of uncertainty, any fresh approach to Christianity could be of interest. The message of the group's founder, Frank Buchman, an American preacher, was startlingly simple: 'Put your life into God's hands, listen to what He has to say and all will be well.' It was exactly what Miss Herridge had been saying to Beverley for years. It was what Aimée Semple McPherson said to the thousands of her supporters who packed her temple in Los Angeles, but Beverley had found her highly resistible. What was so different about Buchman?

First, there was no hysteria, no vulgar display of personality which pushed Christ into a secondary role. Buchman was self-effacing to the point of invisibility, yet he radiated certainty and happiness. Second, he did not proclaim a new cult: his philosophy embraced all Christian denominations and he was supported by Catholics and Protestants alike. And it was classless, at a time when class barriers in society were still clearly delineated. Even more to the point was the conviction that Christ, in the Gospels, had an answer to every contemporary problem. Later, Beverley was to suffer disillusionment with the Oxford Group but for the moment he was enraptured by it and it gave him the structure and a point of view for the second half of *The Fool Hath Said.*

As soon as he had delivered the manuscript to his publishers in December, he took Cyril to Paris for a few days, where the nightlife and the Ritz Bar provided a refreshing antidote to religion. They decided to spend Christmas in the Austrian Alps, but the travel agency had difficulty in finding them accommodation. Eventually they were booked into the annexe of an hotel which, they were assured, was highly thought of, and it was only when they arrived that they realized that the hotel doubled as a sanatorium for consumptive patients, the annexe being normally used only by them. They stuck it out until Christmas Day, when the sight of patients trying to be jolly as they coughed their way through special diets proved too much. Next day they fled the annexe with its smell of disinfectant and sound of oxygen machines, and went to Vienna. Here they met a wealthy Hungarian and his boyfriend and were invited first to Budapest and then to the Hungarian's country estate. After a surfeit of tokay and *zigeuner*, Cyril returned to England and Beverley went to Bucharest.

He stayed at the Athenée Palace Hotel and on the spur of the moment wrote to Queen Marie, requesting an audience, reminding her that they had met at the Greek court, and adding that he was a friend of Ray Harris. (Harris, his assistant on the *American Sketch*, had been a pen-friend of the Queen for nearly twenty years.) In 1936, Queen Marie had been put under a form of house arrest by her son Carol, who had returned to Romania at the invitation of the government to resume the throne which he had renounced in 1925.

From his hotel, Beverley wrote to Harris in his most whimsical vein: 'You won't believe it, of course. The notepaper must be a fake. I'm not in Bucharest at all. I haven't just come from an audience with Queen Marie, we haven't been talking about you and yet, all these things are true!' After more of this, he went on,

> And then the sudden vision of her, slim, amazingly youthful, in a gown of coral silk with a fabulous rope of pearls, and an eager smile as though she had been lonely for a long time. She is a great woman of the most exceptional quality, fearless, loyal, lovely, brilliant, but entirely alone. I shall burst into tears if I go on but I want you to know she is deeply appreciative of your letters. Her position is one of the utmost difficulty. I can't write any more because I have to pack and catch a boat to Turkey. Why I am going there I really don't know but it may be fun. [He explained that he would not write fully, because] . . . in this parody of a country they have a habit of opening letters and hauling you up before a Chief of Police if you comment on the habits of Romanian lavatory attendants which, by the way, are most unimaginative.

It was surprising that Beverley was permitted to see the Dowager Queen and it can only be assumed that the officials concerned were unaware of his journalistic status. Following her death, he published a detailed account of their meeting which went some way to explain her son Carol's fear of her and illustrate the personality of the woman who had fought for the survival of Romania since 1893.

Bearing in mind his obsession with the Oxford Group, it was inevitable that they should have talked of Frank Buchman, whose meeting with Queen Marie during her visit to America in 1925 had been the subject of widespread press comment. She told Beverley that she did not like the man. 'He seemed to me a snob. He spoke of God as if He were the oldest title in the Almanach de Gotha.' Beverley had expressed some minor doubts about Buchmanism in *The Fool Hath Said* and it is possible that the Queen's verdict strengthened these, for it was only a few months later, in a complete reversal of opinion, that he broke with the Oxford Group.

Following a stay in Turkey, Beverley crossed to Egypt and from there flew to Palestine, where he did all the things that a visitor does in the Holy Land. It put him in the right frame of mind to return to England for the publication of *The Fool Hath Said* – a more appropriate frame of mind than if his trip abroad had ended where it began, in the Ritz Bar in Paris.

The Ritz was one of Beverley's favourite haunts, the place to see and be seen. Noel Coward wrote a play about it in 1926, eventually called *Semi-Monde*, of which Beverley tried to persuade Baron Wedel-Jahrlsberg to finance a production. The Baron, who was the Norwegian ambassador to

Paris at the time, was a wealthy patron of the arts, rather fond of Beverley, and took a keen interest in his sex life. He often adjured him to have what, in his heavy accent, came out as 'a good foking'. But he was not fond enough of Beverley to risk his money on *Ritz Bar* (as the play was then called) whose plot concerned the antics of the hotel's habitués and which took in its stride infidelity and homosexuality. It was refused a licence in England by the theatre censor, the Lord Chamberlain. Beverley's interest in the Ritz was coloured by the availability there of sex, if one had the money to pay for it, and in 1980 he wrote a poem about it which appeared in a volume of his poetry entitled *Twilight*. In describing the elderly ladies who gathered at the Ritz to collect their gigolos for the night, he also described his own sexual preferences:

> Now from the shadows creep the stallions
> Magnificently muscled and equipped,
> Dark suited, double breasted, heavy lipped,
> Shipped in battalions from the Argentine,
> From sunlit orchards in the Pyrenees,
> From slums in Rome, from naval stations in the Isles of Greece,
> Apollo's pupils who have come to know
> There is more profit in the role of Romeo
> Than any other arts of war or peace.
> Regard them, study their technique,
> So slim, so sleek, so straight of back,
> Apotheosis of the aphrodisiac . . .

This would definitely not have been the background from which to greet the public with a book on Christianity.

In constructing *The Fool Hath Said*, Beverley did not attempt to convince the atheist or the agnostic; he directed the book at practising churchgoers and the thousands who might not go to church at all except for weddings, christenings or funerals but who still thought of themselves as Christians. Casting himself in the role of a lapsed churchgoer, something of a sceptic, who was fumbling his way back to faith, he invited the complicity of his readers by assuming that they were on his side, ready to help him along like an audience applauding as he tumbled the anti-Christians from their perches.

The first half of the book presented the theological case for Christianity with the cobwebs blown off dusty scholarship and the arguments given the readability of 'Page 2'. It was theology for the masses. Opening the second half with a paean of praise for the Oxford Group, Beverley then applied Christian belief to the problems of sex, war and money. Finally, he addressed directly a 'certain woman' who had led a tortured life, who had, by her innate purity and magnificent courage, fought to keep her family together. If only this woman would turn to Christ, she would lose her fear of death for, through Him, death would become a friend. The woman was Pauline Nichols. By this time, Beverley openly hated John Nichols who he believed was driving his beloved mother to her death. It is worth repeating that his brother Paul, with whom his parents lived, did not take this view.

The chapter which, however, was closest to Beverley's concerns was headed 'Christ and Sex'. In it he argued that, as Christ was man as well as God, he suffered all the sexual desire of any human being. The fact that he conquered the temptations of the Devil in the wilderness did not prove that he was thereafter immune from temptation. Beverley also put forward what he acknowledged was an unorthodox proposition: that the attitude to sex adopted by Church and State was derived from St Paul, who incorporated a host of sexual complexes and phobias in his teaching in the name of Christ, but was against the spirit of what Christ actually said. He challenged his readers who found his proposition shocking to read what Christ himself had to say.

In 1936 it is more than likely that his readers were shocked by the association of Christ with lust because, at that time, sex was a taboo subject for millions of people. Sex outside marriage was considered shocking, let alone sex between people of the same gender. Beverley was treading on dangerous ground in challenging current sexual mores as well as criticizing St Paul in a book supporting the Christian faith. He had previously said publicly that he believed his own sexual instincts to be God-given and that what he did with them was his own business. Now, in contradiction, he said that his desires did not belong to him but were God's business, and advised his readers to deal with lust by turning to Christ and practising 'sublimation'.

Until he wrote the book, his usual way of dealing with lust was to succumb to it as quickly as was conveniently possible. This sudden conversion to purity was entirely genuine while he was in the throes of becoming a rededicated Christian, but the Beverley who returned to England after nearly three months was not quite the crusading Christian who had left it. His zeal was beginning to crumble and there was a genuine struggle within him. Arthur Diamond said that he became depressed and began drinking heavily; certainly he plunged into a heavy programme of work, which included a book based on his trip abroad, hoping that sheer exhaustion might save him from the arms of rough trade. It did not. It was with a sinking heart that he committed himself to a programme of Oxford Group meetings all over England as the principal speaker, beginning with a rally at the Albert Hall. He also allowed himself to be interviewed in the press about his support for the movement and, as a final touch, an Oxford Group book, *The Drums of Peace*, to which he had contributed, was published about this time. His mental state was one of confusion and guilt. He even tried confession as recommended by Buchman – not in public, as this would have brought the police to his door, but in private. Instead of help he received horrified disgust, and he realized with regret that Buchmanism was then only interested in 'respectable' sins, such as being nasty to one's maid.

While all this was going on, Gaskin went house-hunting. The lease on New Street was almost up and it was agreed that the next home should be in Hampstead where, in those days, the air was unpolluted and the regular dense yellow fogs of central London did not always reach. The house he found was Number One Ellerdale Close, a small new development designed by Clough Williams-Ellis in the Georgian manner. The house had four bedrooms, two bathrooms, a long, narrow sitting-room opening on to the garden, a small dining-room and a study. The kitchen area was luxurious by the standards of the time, and Gaskin soon had it equipped with the labour-saving devices he had grown used to in America. The interior of the house was '30s spartan and Beverley furnished it at great cost in the fashionable style. The result could not have been in sharper contrast with his previous homes or with Thatch Cottage. The only drawback was the garden which was long and triangular – 'a good cat run,' as Beverley described it.

Hovering in the background was the problem of Glatton. As well as its cost and its lack of privacy as a result of the books, there was a growing anti-Nichols feeling in the village. It is not difficult to imagine the impact on a tiny, isolated village of a personality like Beverley's and of the comings and goings of his visitors. As they arrived in their motors, bringing with them a strong whiff of exotic and undiluted 'Mayfair', it was all very novel, at first – but then the uninhibited behaviour of the guests began to shock: there was talk of nude bathing and 'goings-on'. Finally, rightly or wrongly, villagers identified with characters in the books and concluded that they had been made fun of. According to Arthur Diamond, the climax was reached when certain guests, whom he declined to name, began chatting up the local lads. When a friend gave Beverley a strong warning which carried the threat of police action, he drove to Glatton and closed up the cottage. In effect, he was finished with it, but with a stubbornness typical of his mother he refused to be seen to be defeated and did not put the property on the market until more than a year later.

Beverley was now in a wretched state. *The Fool Hath Said* was an enormous success; he had been applauded by leading churchmen for his clarion call to turn to Christ and held up as an example. But he knew he was sailing under false colours, and was overwhelmed by melancholy and self-pity, exacerbated by too much alcohol. Shortly after closing the cottage, he drove to a meeting of the Oxford Group to do his star turn. Following a dinner at which he drank too much, he rose to give his witness to the joy he had found in Christ and Buchmanism, but found it impossible to act out the role and broke down in uncontrollable tears. He left the meeting and managed to drive back to Hampstead.

At first, neither Cyril nor Gaskin realized he was in the throes of a nervous breakdown; they thought his incoherence was due to drink and, in an effort to sober him up, took him on a long walk round Hampstead Heath. Eventually, it dawned on them that the weeping and garbled self-pity might be symptoms of something more serious, and called a doctor who arranged for Beverley to go into a private nursing-home for complete rest and medication. In later reminiscences, Beverley described the nursing-home as a 'loony bin' and said he spent a month there believing he was going insane. This was not true. Newspapers reported that he was suffering from sleeplessness and exhaustion, and that his engagements were cancelled until further notice. This neatly disposed of the Oxford Group tour, and within hours Beverley was almost recovered. He spent a total of five nights in the nursing-home and emerged feeling better than he had done for months. He took life easily for a few weeks, and on Saturday 1 August left for the opening in Berlin of the Olympic Games, which he had been asked to cover for the *Sunday Chronicle*

While he was in Germany the press began to review *No Place Like Home*, described as a new type of travel book, which recorded his journey across Egypt to Palestine. It was extremely funny, wildly sentimental and often provocative, and at a time when foreign travel was for the well-to-do and most of the British took their annual holidays in genteel resorts like Eastbourne or in racier places like Blackpool or Margate, the book was pleasantly reassuring. Beverley did not intend to persuade the reader to rush abroad: Thomas Cook might not like it, but he confirmed to the armchair traveller that there was indeed no place like home. The real mystery of the Sphinx, Beverley confided, was why intelligent men of every age and race had found this utterly uninteresting piece of sculpture so mysterious. Why had so much time and labour had been expended on the Pyramids' banal design, which illustrated the foolishness and vulgarity of the Cheops dynasty? Some of the legendary holy places of Palestine uplifted the soul, but others depressed it. He praised the enterprise that had created Tel Aviv and regretted that its expansion was due to the anti-Jewish policy of Germany, but his reaction to a collective of farms run on the principles of communism was wholly unfavourable. After twenty years, the system had produced an equality of poverty due, he concluded, to the refusal to endorse any aspect of capitalist enterprise, let alone the spiritual values of Jewry.

James Agate found the combination of what he described as primness and spryness hard to take. Some of the writing was of the very highest order, he admitted, but as soon as emotion crept in, the style slithered down into pure treacle. Agate's was the harshest verdict, for other reviewers, in Britain and abroad, found the book to their liking in varying degrees. One American critic called it 'sharp in its condemnation of pretence and swift to notice what is lovely and charming.'

· 16 ·

Floodlights

1936–1937

BEVERLEY arrived in Germany in 1936 to find a country which had been prepared for the influx of visitors to the Olympic Games with meticulous attention to detail. Orders had gone out to tidy up the countryside: village properties were whitewashed, and all anti-Jewish signs removed. Farm-workers were forbidden to take food breaks at the roadside in case foreigners assumed they were wasting time. Convicts, political prisoners and concentration camp inmates were not to be used for farm work during July and August. In Berlin itself, a vast programme of renovation and redecoration had taken place; even the backs of those buildings that could be seen from trains were painted, and the main vistas were floodlit and decorated with flowers and flags. Everywhere the flags of nations competing in the Games could be seen, but dominating them all were huge banners bearing the crooked cross in red, black and white. In the shops, forbidden books suddenly reappeared, foreign newspapers were available and the German press was instructed to write objectively. The rabidly anti-Jewish *Der Stürmer* temporarily ceased publication and Berliners were told to show every consideration for foreigners, even if they appeared to be Jewish. The overall effect was stunning.

Looking back, it seems beyond belief that so many nations colluded in supporting one of the most spectacular political propaganda exercises ever mounted. Governments dubious about the Nazi regime hid behind the excuse of not interfering in the internal affairs of a friendly nation; the Olympic Committee bleated that politics must not be brought into sport. The Nazis, who were doing precisely that, preened themselves as they broke every rule that governed the Games, both overtly and covertly.

Beverley was deeply impressed with the 'New Germany', which was in sharp contrast to the demoralized country he had seen on previous visits. Any reservations were swept aside by his admiration. As all the hotels were full, he and a German friend, Peter Klaus, who had accompanied him to Berlin, stayed in rooms across the street from Goering's home. Within hours of arriving, Beverley had picked up a twenty-two-year-old German rent boy who might have been the prototype of the Aryan physical ideal, and 'Hans' (not his real name) was his companion for the rest of the visit. He showed Beverley the city nightlife which had been reinstated for the period of the Games. The Nazis, who had previously imprisoned habitués of the clubs and dance-halls, released a selection of them for the delectation of the visitors, and once again, every form of sex was for sale. These unfortunates played their roles with feverish gaiety under the supervision of the secret police; perhaps, as Beverley noted later, they hoped for a reprieve from the labour camps. Perhaps Hans himself was acting out a part, for he had also been in prison, his 'crime' exacerbated by one-time membership of the Communist party. When Beverley wanted relief from the crowded city, Hans took him to sunbathe at Wannsee. To Beverley's surprise, the section of the shore they used was almost deserted, while further along hundreds of Berliners were sunning themselves. Hans explained that this was the 'Jews only' area; the signboards might have been removed, but the Berliners knew.

In a volume of short stories published during the war, Beverley included a story about Hans. Briefly, it hinged on a muddle over tickets for the press box at the Games; Beverley found himself with two to spare and gave them to Hans, not appreciating at the time that the press box was situated directly behind the Führer's box. The police assumed that Hans's tickets were stolen and arrested him, though his companion, a female prostitute, managed to slip away in the crowd. The next day Hans was executed and a news item explained that, as a Communist, he was suspected of being party to an assassination attempt; 'So may all enemies of the Third Reich perish!'

It is difficult to believe that Beverley could have imagined that anyone, let alone a Communist male prostitute, could have got into the press box without proper identification: it was a standing joke among the press representatives that plainclothes police outnumbered the journalists in the enclosure. He was to retell the story, however, in two further books, not as fiction but as fact.

Before returning to England, Beverley went to Poland and was appalled by the conditions there, which contrasted sharply with those in the new Germany. In an article for the *Sunday Chronicle*, he unwisely said so, and received a vigorous protest from the Polish embassy in London, pointing out that Poland had suffered ten years of a deeper economic depression than other countries and listing achievements despite this. This rebuke had little effect on Beverley's thinking. As someone who had argued for years about the unfairness of the Versailles Treaty, he saw no reason why other countries could not follow Germany's example and out of despair find new purpose and confidence. If Britain, for example, with the resources of the Empire behind her, could not solve her problems and raise the spirit of her people, this must be a fault in the system. He began to compare Britain unfavourably with the regenerated Germany, and in a series of articles which he was later to regret, called for a fair deal for Germany which, he said, was a country from which there was much to learn. He praised the undisputed benefits the Nazis had brought. Comparing British youth unfavourably with the 'shining simplicity' of their German counterparts, he spoke of 'the essential decency of National Socialism' and declared: 'Hitler is not seeking war. He represents the soul of Germany. Pray God we do not cheat him as we cheated his country.'

With hindsight, Beverley's enthusiasm appears amazing but he was by no means unusual. Like many others, he was bamboozled by the great Nazi show of 1936 and believed that friendship with Germany could prevent war. Lloyd George, the British Prime Minister from 1916 to 1922, told Hitler on a visit to Germany: 'You have done great things for Germany. You have restored her honour. You have gained for her equal rights.' Nevertheless, Beverley was not completely unrealistic about the potential threat, and in November, when asked if he intended to speak at a peace rally at the Albert Hall, he made the following statement:

I have refused to take part in this meeting because I no longer believe in the doctrine of 'peace at any price' and I am not ashamed to state my change of view. Five years ago it seemed to me that if we gave a lead to Europe where disarmament was concerned all other countries might follow. We now know they merely laughed at us and went on arming secretly. I believed that the League of Nations was our best security for peace but the League has become a farce now that countries like Germany and Italy are no longer in it. I still believe to be a pacifist in peace time is an honourable creed. But to advocate a policy of non-resistance in war time simply does not make sense.

His recantation of extreme pacifism aroused little attention. As he put it himself, the public had seen him in a mood 'to blow up the War Office' and, while he was under the influence of the Oxford Group, 'to drag people to church by the scruff of the neck'. Passion spent was of little interest. He now concentrated his attention on persuading his readership that the way to avoid war was to strengthen friendship with Germany while, at the same time, rearming. Meanwhile, as a relief from such weighty matters, he turned once again to the theatre.

Ever since he had abandoned work on C.B. Cochran's 1931 revue for lack of ideas, his mind had become full of them. During 1936 he decided that he must try again, with or without Cochran, and promised himself that this time he would write the entire show and stipulate that no other author should be involved. Cochran was too wise to agree to such terms, but a business associate of Ivor Novello, an American, Richard D. Rose, was prepared to take on the Cochran role and to put up some of the money. An acquaintance, C. Dennis Freeman, who had staged a hit revue called *Spread It Abroad* at the Saville Theatre, was prepared to direct, and, encouraged by this, Beverley went to Paris and worked for two months. He was later joined by Freeman, and they agreed on the general structure of the show.

In a letter written to Ray Harris in October, Beverley said: 'I am now embarking (of all things) on a spectacular revue! The religious maniacs of the world simply drove me to it. I am doing all the music as well as the book and am having the time of my life. We shall need a chorus of Galli-Curcis and at least three John Barrymores and a stage that will hold the Statue of Liberty. I think it will be on in January.'

At first everything went very well. Beverley's initial work was impressive and Frances Day, a big West End name, was so taken with it that she disentangled herself from another commitment and agreed to star. She was joined by John Mills (who had been her leading man in the hugely successful Vivian Ellis musical *Jill Darling* in 1934), by the talented Hermione Baddeley and a vaudeville comic, Lyle Evans. Frederick Ashton was to choreograph the ballets and Buddy Bradley to stage the tap routines and modern dance numbers. René Hubert was brought over from Paris to design the sets and costumes. The young Benjamin Frankel was engaged to orchestrate and conduct, and the indefatigable Elsie April, who could turn any 'tum-te-tum' into a finished song, as she had done for Noel Coward and others, became Beverley's musical assistant. Beverley was musically more literate than Noel Coward, and presented her with a complete score. 'I'm afraid there's rather a lot,' he said apologetically. 'A lot!' she replied grimly. 'There's usually nothing at all.'

It was a formidable line-up, but because there was no big name on the management side financial backing proved difficult to find. Then, by chance, one of the investors, Lord Killanin, met his old chum, Alfred Shaughnessy, at a cocktail party and suggested he might care to help. Shaughnessy, many years later to be the principal writer and script editor of the enormously successful television series *Upstairs, Downstairs*, but then only twenty years old, was thoroughly stage-struck, and vastly intrigued by the idea. 'Beverley Nichols was something of a hero to me; in fact, his book *Cry Havoc!* had impressed me so much that it was partly responsible for my decision to give up a military career and to resign from Sandhurst.' Shaughnessy did not have any money of his own but he had quite a few friends who did and who might be persuaded to take a gamble for the sheer hell of it. A few days later, feeling a little like a budding Ziegfeld, he was invited to Beverley's Hampstead house for one of Gaskin's superlative dinners and to hear some of the music. Among the other guests were Eric Glass, who was Beverley's agent, Dennis Freeman, Lord Killanin and Frances Day. Beverley played his songs, Frances Day sang and Dennis

Freeman described the sketches and ballets. Shaughnessy found it all heady stuff and, when Frances Day sang 'I Will Pray', he was hooked: 'It was one of the loveliest waltz melodies I had ever heard.' Starry-eyed, he resolved to 'raise the backing if it killed me'. He did but, although it did not kill him, it provided a thorough blooding in the uncertain world of theatre. As the representative of a syndicate of backers, his name eventually appeared on the bills as co-producer with Richard D. Rose, and he had the odd experience of seeing buses with his name on the advertising go by the windows of the stockbrokers' offices where he sat at his desk as a junior clerk.

For the show's title Beverley came up with *Floodlight*, suggested by the floodlighting of buildings to celebrate the coronation of King George VI and Queen Elizabeth. Revue titles tended to be somewhat inane but this one had a little more point than most. The show went into production with everyone concerned quite convinced that they had the hit of Coronation year on their hands, but it soon became apparent that there was a major problem. Dennis Freeman was a cocaine addict, at one moment charged with fierce energy and the next lackadaisical and unwilling to make decisions. This first became noticeable to Beverley as he sat through endless auditions for the supporting company, while Freeman insisted on detailed discussions of the merits or demerits of men of every age, shape and size. This might have been amusing under other circumstances, but time was money. It then transpired that Freeman had promised so many boyfriends a place in the show that the male contingent increased by the day, and more girls had to be hired to balance the men. As the company expanded, so did the budget. Freeman showed no concern about finance, permitting the designer to do what he wanted without restraint and accepting Frances Day's plea for a large orchestra. The lack of control at the top resulted in an atmosphere of uncertainty and scenes of temperament at every level. John Mills appears to have remained remarkably stoical, but Hermione Baddeley was the reverse of stoical and complained about everything, including her billing. Though Freeman sometimes did not appear for rehearsals, it was too late to sack him, so everyone just hoped for the best. Beverley, rewriting to suit an ever-changing running order, was frantic but helpless, and at one point was not speaking to Freeman at all.

After one particularly dreadful rehearsal, Beverley took Shaughnessy off to the Garrick Club where they drowned their despair in champagne cocktails. 'Oh God, Freddy,' he moaned, 'will it ever open?' Shaughnessy, thinking hopefully of the old cliché about a first night triumph emerging from chaos, said it probably would. 'At least,' said Beverley, a little of his spirit returning, 'if it crashes in ruins I'll get a book out of it.'

As often happens in such circumstances, the sheer professionalism of the company somehow pulled the show together. The final rehearsals at the

Opera House, Blackpool, where *Floodlight* opened, lasted for nearly forty-eight hours with the cast snatching sleep and food when and where they could. With only minutes to go before the opening-night audience arrived, the stage was cleared and forty minutes later the curtain went up, and exhaustion was forgotten.

In his book of recollections, *Up In The Clouds, Gentlemen, Please* (1980), John Mills said that the show was memorable for the development of Frances Day into one of the most fascinating characters in the musical theatre. Of the show itself, he had little to say beyond the fact that both he and Miss Day thought it delightful. (In 1985, he also commented that he had liked and admired Beverley greatly, an opinion which echoed those of others who had known him professionally.) The provincial press was kind to the show, especially to Frances Day, and Beverley was complimented generously on the quality of his music. The *Manchester Guardian*, however, in a surprising display of ignorance, took 'orchestration by Benjamin Frankel' to mean that he was the composer. A few days later, after a furious protest from Beverley, a retraction and apology were published and the paper sent a cheque for £100 to an animal charity.

The two weeks at Blackpool were spent 'polishing' and *Floodlight* opened at the Saville Theatre in London on 23 June without any radical changes. The audience, packed with celebrities and willing the show to succeed, applauded the sets and costumes, loved the music, dance numbers and ballets, and cheered the stars. Now and again, but not often enough, they found something to make them laugh. The obvious fault of the long show (three hours plus the interval) was that the wit for which Beverley was noted was puzzlingly absent. Items began well, but instead of ending with a big laugh, they drooped. Here and there Beverley even resorted to schoolboy vulgarity and there was a particularly painful pun on the word 'oar'. Cochran would have had the scalpel out at Blackpool and used the work of other authors to bolster the comedy: indeed, Cochran or Charlot would have applied drastic surgery much sooner. Cuts were made next day and new material by other writers was rehearsed, but it was all too late.

Taken collectively, the critics disagreed with each other about almost everything. Some thought the music was 'unmemorable', 'thin', 'minor'; others that it was 'delightfully harmonious', 'too good for revue', 'first class'. The book and lyrics were either 'crude', 'stale' and 'inane' or 'charming', 'pleasant' and 'witty'. Nearly all hailed 'Little White Room' as a hit song (which it became) and 'The Port Always Goes To The Right' as a brilliant comedy number, and most gave Frances Day ecstatic notices. Several reviews were almost vitriolic, but on the whole the good outweighed the bad. Beverley set to with the press representative, W. Macqueen Pope, to promote the show; he and Frances Day gave countless interviews, and the extensive press coverage began to overcome any initial adverse impression. But in the end, despite good houses, the huge running costs of *Floodlight* killed it. As Beverley put it: 'If only things had not got out of hand. We did not need a cast of thirty and a twenty-two piece orchestra. Though I loved hearing my music, such a rich sound, with Ben conducting brilliantly, it was sheer financial madness.'

In a letter to Ray Harris he wrote:

> *Floodlight* is off. Not a spectacular flop but a failure all the same. If I begin to tell you half the disasters I should be up all night. Among them I might mention
>
> a) One of the chief backers' cheques for $10,000 was sent back by the bank on the eve of production leaving us with not a penny to nurse the show.
>
> b) A certain gentleman vital to the show decamped to Paris with money borrowed from me.
>
> As for temperament – oh dear – I could write another *Evensong* if only the beasts weren't still alive! My only regret is that I have wasted a year and now the music will be lost. I must now pull my horns in and get down to solid work.

Some of the songs were recorded and, from time to time, are still heard on radio, in particular 'Little White Room' and Frances Day's version of 'Artificial Flowers'. Enough of the music also survives in published and manuscript form to indicate that Beverley was a significant composer in the light tradition, but the opportunity to write for the musical theatre never came to him again, though he was to adapt an unstaged operetta for television in 1948.

Several months after it came off, *Floodlight* was resurrected in a radically altered version and went on tour with a company headed by Frances Day and a famous comedy man of the time, George Lacey. It proved a success; indeed, it became what it should have been in the first place. Alfred Shaughnessy's syndicate even recouped a little of its investment.

Speaking about the venture more than fifty years afterwards, Shaughnessy looked back on the nightmarish aspects of it with amused detachment, and still wondered how on earth C. Dennis Freeman had been given such a free hand. Beverley he recalled with some affection: 'He was perfectly charming and not in the slightest way camp, in fact I had no idea he was queer until someone pointed out his boyfriend [Cyril Butcher] who was in the show.' This comment confirmed the impression of others and belied hostile cartoons appearing in the press in the 1930s depicting Beverley as effeminate and limp-wristed. Cyril Butcher reported that Beverley was more good-humoured than angry about them: 'The poor dears are so bereft of ideas. Besides . . . I'll start worrying when they stop.'

After more than a year's prevarication, Beverley put the Glatton property on the market in September 1937. In his memoirs he placed this a year earlier probably because, tied in with his 'breakdown', it made a better story. In fact, he was prompted to sell by the loss of £3,000 on *Floodlight*, a hefty sum in those days. It was many years before he admitted that Freeman had embezzled the money which he had given him to help the show's cash-flow problems – Freeman being the person coyly referred to as 'a certain gentleman' in the letter to Ray Harris. Cyril Butcher believed that Beverley preferred to write off the loss rather than cause a scandal by going to the police.

Thatch Cottage was offered fully furnished with the surrounding land, except for the small wood which Beverley had created, which was not sold for several years because he hoped to see it come to maturity. But the trees had been planted too close together and strangled each other, so in the end he sold it. It is still there, but it is not the lasting memorial to his husbandry for which he had hoped. In several books he told the story of his 'last visit' to the cottage when, overcome with emotion, he had walked out, leaving it just as it was. This Marie Celeste departure was not entirely true: all personal items were removed, as well as several items of antique furniture. Afterwards, Beverley was dismayed to find that he had left other pieces whose value he had underestimated and which fetched high prices at auction. The sum he got for the property was the equivalent of £200,000 today so he did not do too badly. At the time, the newspapers were intrigued by the sale, and when a family from Blackpool, the Hollings-worths, bought the property, a ridiculous story that they intended turning it into a roadhouse with bars and restaurant circulated in the press.

Today the land has been carved up and two new houses stand on what was once part of the famous garden. Surprisingly, the statue of Antinous which often featured in the publicity is still there. The cottage itself has changed very little, and succeeding owners have preserved a section of wall in the sitting-room where guests including Winston Churchill, Rex Whistler and Vivian Ellis signed their names. On an external wall Rex Whistler once drew a portrait of a patriarchal figure referred to by everyone as 'God', but although this withstood the weather for many years it was eventually lost.

In 1983 Beverley looked back without sentiment. 'I made a small fortune out of the books, about three-quarters of a million pounds I suppose it would be today. I wonder where it all went?'

Beverley had declared to Ray Harris his intention to get down to solid work, his idea of which was to write three books in rapid succession, on top of his other commitments. The first was *News of England* which he hoped would attract the same attention and sales as *Cry Havoc!*. It was a controversial review of contemporary life, attacking everybody from the government, for its lack of resolution, to architects, for their destruction of towns and cities with feeble and derivative buildings. He castigated the gambling industry for creating false hopes and the Church for its ineptitude, bemoaned the increase of alcoholism and the general lack of self-discipline, deplored anti-Semitism and the lack of tolerance, buzzing from topic to topic without analysing any of them.

He was at his best when writing in anger about the life of the unemployed of South Wales. If unemployment was to remain a feature of British life, what steps were being taken, he asked, to give some purpose to men without work? He suggested heavy investment in sporting facilities might alleviate some of the despair and prevent physical deterioration, and forecast the arrival of the Age of Leisure, for which Britain was completely unprepared. *News of England* also gave him the chance to reiterate his retreat from extreme pacifism, and to admit that the most vociferous critic of *Cry Havoc!*, Francis Yeats-Brown, was, after all, correct. In a dedication he said, 'I am glad to have the opportunity of acknowledging it.' Although it was honest of Beverley to recant, it was a blow to thousands who had hailed him as a leader of the pacifist movement.

In his conclusion, Beverley suggested that the country needed a leader to reawaken the British spirit of enterprise, and if he had left aside the question of who that leader might be, he would have saved himself much trouble later. But having posed the question, he went on to answer it. Looking round the political figures of the day, he hit on the maverick leader of the British Union of Fascists, Sir Oswald Mosley, and declared him to be the man who could unite the nation and prevent war.

Whatever argument might have been advanced in favour of some form of National Socialism, its ugliest aspect was its anti-Semitism. Mosley assured Beverley that this would not be part of his programme if he came to power and, contrary to all the available evidence, Beverley believed him. He was, however, doubtful about Mosley's intention to further the creation of a Jewish state, which he felt to be impracticable. Where would it be? Palestine he thought was out of the question. Following the publication of his book, Beverley continued to urge Mosley to denounce anti-Semitism, but finally a letter of the utmost ambivalence and prevarication seems to have convinced him that Mosley was unprepared to do this, and that he could no longer indulge in the belief that Fascism eschewed anti-Semitism. It might have been expected that his disillusionment with the British Union of Fascists would have included Mosley himself, but Beverley stubbornly believed that Mosley had abilities which surmounted Fascism.

He also stubbornly committed his energies to building bridges with Germany by writing admiring articles and by working for the Anglo-German Fellowship, an organization of leading businessmen and others under the chairmanship of Lord Mount Temple. He believed quite genuinely that war was not inevitable, while maintaining that he was well aware of Hitler's ultimate plan as described in *Mein Kampf*. He even tackled Dr Goebbels on several occasions while visiting Germany, no doubt to the amusement of that gentleman. In speeches to the Hitler Youth which, somewhat surprisingly, he was permitted to give, Beverley preached peace and goodwill to all men; in London, he was involved in entertaining von Ribbentrop to a lunch at the Carlton Hotel, to give him the opportunity to explain Germany's views about her ex-colonies. Von Ribbentrop was arrogant and ill-mannered but the guests managed to find excuses for him.

In September 1938 the Anglo-German Fellowship arranged for a large group of leaders of the Hitler Youth to visit England on a goodwill mission. Beverley invited twelve of them to lunch in the museum-like atmosphere of the Garrick Club. It all went very well; the young men were charming, exquisitely well mannered, and Beverley was thrilled with them. After lunch, he took them on a tour of the club, though what they made of the theatrical ephemera and the paintings of famous English actors is not on record. When, however, they observed seven or eight old gentlemen fast asleep in the library armchairs, they were awe-struck by this glimpse of English life and, at a sign from the senior leader, sprang smartly to attention and bellowed 'Heil Hitler' as they gave the Nazi salute. The old gentlemen, rudely awakened, stared in disbelief at the invading force, probably thinking that the worst had happened while they were having their post-prandial doze. With considerable embarrassment, Beverley saw them off the premises. That night, Drury Lane Theatre was filled with the Hitler Youth watching Ivor Novello play the lead in *Henry V*. Afterwards, Novello told Beverley the boys were quite enchanting.

People like Beverley, and there were many of them, treated these demonstrations of Anglo-German goodwill with a seriousness that now seems pathetic. Asked why he spent so much time and energy on a cause which had little hope of success, Beverley replied, 'However mad it may seem, we hoped for a miracle.' Many believed they had one when Britain signed the Munich Pact with Hitler, but Beverley was sceptical and, although he still worked for the cause, he began to feel certain that war was not far off.

News of England was published on 1 April 1938, All Fools' Day. The critics treated the book with respect, with the exception of the *Daily Express* which mocked the praise he had accorded in it to British fashion and ballet. An analysis of thirty-five reviews shows that nine critics disapproved of the chapter on Mosley, thirteen did not mention it, and the remainder, while mentioning it, expressed no view one way or another. Evelyn Waugh in the *Spectator* considered that the book should succeed in stirring the sluggish conscience of readers, but Winston Churchill told Beverley, when they were guests of Mrs Ronnie Greville at Polesden Lacey: 'Nobody will take any notice of it. I can sympathize. Nobody takes any notice of me.' He was right: the book was a complete failure. Beverley's vast readership in Britain and abroad shunned it, probably because they were tired of his preaching at them, and it sank without trace.

He was on safe ground with his next, *Green Grows the City*, a re-run of *Down the Garden Path* set in Hampstead. As before, it was a mixture of fact and fiction, complete with London versions of the Allways characters who had previously delighted his readers. The gardening problem this time was to make something of a triangular piece of barren land. His resolution of the problem was simple, effective and cost a great deal of money – which the sales of the book more than made up for.

Revue came next and told the story of the production of *Floodlight*. It could have been sub-titled 'Nichols's Revenge'. If only the 'beasts' had been dead, he might have gone further but, even so, he managed to administer several claw marks on the living. The plot was similar to that of the 1933 film *42nd Street* which, in turn, was derived from a novel by Bradford Ropes. In Beverley's version the leading lady, Thelma Ganges, combined the less attractive aspects of Frances Day's character with those of several other leading ladies he had encountered, including Melba and Marie Tempest. Fay Pearl, the chorus girl who steps into the lead, was none other than Frances Day again, this time highlighting her charm, talent and incandescent beauty. To avoid legal action, he claimed, in a foreword to the book, that he had thought of Fay Pearl before meeting Miss Day; as for Thelma Ganges, he declared that any leading lady identifying herself with this monster was at liberty to do so. It was the technique he had employed when, with wide-eyed innocence, he denied that *Evensong* had anything to do with Melba.

Eric Glass, Beverley's agent, was more than happy to accept his own transformation into the enigmatic Mr Harris who finds a way to save the show. Thinly disguised portraits of Hermione Baddeley, Benjamin Frankel, Elsie April and Frederick Ashton, among others, peopled the plot. Oscar Homolka of *Mesmer* made a surprise appearance as the leading man who could barely speak English, and gave Beverley the opportunity for some feline teasing. He replaced himself in the story with a handsome, athletic Australian of vivid talent and, to prove it, printed his music of a song from the show, 'Dancing with the Daffodils', in the book. The only ugly note was the portrait of an elderly female alcoholic – apparently his father in drag. *Revue* appears to be the only novel ever written about that now defunct brand of entertainment, and, allowing for the inevitable coating of sentimentality, it is a fascinating, funny and instructive guide.

· 17 ·

A time of farewells

1938–1939

THE tense days of the Munich crisis in September 1938 passed in an atmosphere of profound gloom. The Munich Pact brought temporary relief, which gave way to deep apprehension. War, it seemed, was only a matter of months away, despite the sheet of paper Chamberlain had waved at cheering crowds.

Soon after Munich, Osbert Sitwell invited Beverley and Cyril to stay a few days at Renishaw, the Sitwell home in Derbyshire. It was to be the last time that Beverley stayed at a 'stately home' before the outbreak of war. Forty years later, he reflected that the war had ended the style of life led at great houses like Renishaw: no longer were there servants to maintain the luxurious life expected by the owners and their guests; no longer, for example, would it be possible to stagger to bed in the early hours to find a fire alight in the grate, jugs of scented hot water, toothbrushes already charged with toothpaste and fresh, monogrammed towels awaiting. In a letter to Ray Harris dated October 1940 he wrote: 'I knew those "stately homes" and although they weren't my cup of tea, I think they played a part in civilizing the world, and they had their moments of beauty. And now the shutters are drawn, the music is silenced and the lovely lawns are ploughed up to grow potatoes.'

Beverley and Osbert Sitwell had remained close since their initial meeting at the Café Royal some twenty years before. It was not a friendship which required constant proximity or regular contact to keep it alive; when they met it was as if the long lapse of time had not occurred. On this occasion, Cyril and Beverley found Osbert and his friend David Horner in pessimistic mood, quite convinced that the world was on the verge of annihilation. This made even the lightest topic of conversation difficult. When Beverley mentioned ballet, Osbert sighed and said that the next time they saw the curtain fall at Covent Garden would be the last, for soon the opera house would be a heap of rubble. During this litany of 'never more', it was decided that they should all visit South America before it was too late. Within a few days they had booked passages on the German luxury liner

Cordillera, which was due to call in at Dover just before Christmas on its way to Mexico. The choice of ship was particularly fortuitous for Beverley because he was able to pay for Cyril and himself from German royalties held in a blocked account in Berlin. He booked only as far as Panama, from where he and Cyril intended to 'explore' and to return eventually by ship from New York.

It is characteristic of Beverley that when, in *The Unforgiving Minute*, he comments on the state of his finances at this time, he says his account was deeply in the red; his only assets were the house in Hampstead and a portfolio of shares which never did well. He seems to have forgotten his nest-egg in gilt-edged securities, not to mention the proceeds of the sale of the Glatton house the year before. Within the year he was to buy another country house – a fact he does not mention in his autobiography – and now he was embarking on an expensive three-month holiday for two.

As the four friends boarded the *Cordillera*, it apparently did not occur to them that there was a touch of irony in making the trip on a ship owned by the country which they believed would shortly be bombing England to pieces. But during the cruise Osbert Sitwell and Beverley both became introspective about their writing careers. Beverley was, as usual, apprehensive about his future, longing for acknowledgement as a serious author but sensing, with the years slipping away, that this was ever less likely to be achieved. Osbert, on the other hand, envied him his creative ability as an imaginative writer, a quality he believed he lacked. The two men discussed possible subjects and Beverley suggested a biography of Edgar Allan Poe whose success, Gothic imagination and passion for the spiritually mysterious he thought might appeal to Osbert. It was a subject he himself had toyed with ever since the shock of seeing the neglected tomb of America's great writer in Baltimore back in 1918. Osbert was greatly taken with the idea but it came to nothing.

Among their fellow passengers on the *Cordillera* were nearly 300 Jews who looked forward to a new life in Mexico safe from Nazi persecution. Only forty or so were in first class and Beverley noted that the punctilious manner in which the crew served them barely disguised their underlying contempt. According to Beverley, Osbert was put out by their presence and made no secret of the fact. When he turned up at the swimming pool for the 'first class hour' and found it monopolized by the Jewish passengers, he turned to Beverley and quipped: 'When do you think it is Aryan hour?' Beverley incorporated this remark in a short story he wrote about the voyage in 1941, entitled 'Sea Change'. In the story, he put a riposte into the mouth of a pretty young Jewish girl: 'It would be better if you were to ask if there was an hour for gentlemen.'

One evening, Beverley was invited to drinks with the captain and found that he was the only guest. It transpired that the captain, who had little of the Nazi about him, was troubled by a cable he had received, advising him that the Mexican authorities had changed their immigration laws and only half the Jews would be allowed to land: the remainder would be returned to Germany as no other country was prepared to take them. Should he, he asked Beverley, tell them at once, or put off telling them until the last possible minute? Beverley suggested that a few more days of ignorance would do no harm; let them enjoy their 'freedom' while they could. The captain agreed.

Beverley later gave three differing versions of this story. In one the Jews, having decided among themselves who would go on to Mexico and who would be returned to Germany, watch the distressing scene while the unlucky ones are put ashore to await a ship. In another version, all 300 are refused entry to Mexico. In a third, the country is not Mexico but Guatemala. As so frequently happened with his writing, fact and fiction were so intertwined that it is often difficult to establish the correct version. Whether it was 300 or 150 Jews who returned to certain death in Germany, whether it was Guatemala or Mexico which refused them entry, the fact remains that this horrific situation was often repeated during the short period in which the Nazis permitted Jews to leave the Reich.

In 'Sea Change', the Sitwell character, quite unlike his real-life counter-part, is so shamed by the Jewish girl's riposte that he apologizes and gives her flowers. Gradually he falls in love with her and she with him. In a dramatic ending, he engineers her escape from the ship and they eventually marry in Venezuela, presumably living happily ever after. In fact, according to Beverley, Osbert was so upset by the news from Mexico and so ashamed of his remark that he atoned by holding champagne receptions for the Jewish passengers and parties for their children. It seemed not to occur to Beverley that there was something macabre about the picture his account conjures up – the wealthy English aristocrat lavishly entertaining doomed people to champagne. What the Jews thought about this can be imagined – assuming, of course, that his story is strictly accurate.

In Panama, Beverley and Cyril began a long and exhausting tour which included crossing to Cuba. They did not appear to enjoy much of it and they particularly hated Havana, geared as it was to the most debased desires of foreign tourists. In Vera Cruz they met Thornton Wilder who, like them, was on his way to Mexico City, and they agreed to share a suite on the train,

> at enormous expense . . . The long night journey from the fetid cesspool of Vera Cruz to the glittering miracle of Mexico City was one of the most unforgettable passages of my life. We were all exhausted but electrically awake, living with extraordinary intensity. I think we were living in terms of music. Cyril, gazing out of the window: 'Those mountains are pure Bach.' Wilder, as lightning flashes: 'But can't you hear Wagner in

the wings?' Beverley, as the clouds part and there is a glimpse of moonlight: 'But Chopin has the last word.'

Up to this time, Beverley had been dogged by a debilitating fever but in the high altitude of Mexico, he quickly recovered, and he and Cyril explored the country:

> As we wandered round Mexico there were times I felt very near to Heaven. I was able to forget the gathering clouds of war. In this unique terrain where savagery and sanctity went hand in hand there were monuments of beauty which, unlike their counterparts in Europe, were not lying in the shadow of destruction. Moreover, the air was so dry and crystalline that it was possible to see early Spanish baroque architecture in almost its original condition. I soaked myself in peace and sunshine and beauty.

He was not best pleased when he received a cable from his editor, James Drawbell, asking him to cover an important bullfight. He had never been to one, but he had once had a blazing row with Ernest Hemingway about the cruelty of the sport in the unlikely surroundings of the Ritz Bar in Paris, during which Hemingway had called him a 'cissy'. Beverley commented: 'Hemingway may have been a genius from time to time but I thought his overpowering masculinity was near to caricature. I believe he was a phoney, just like D.H. Lawrence.' Reluctantly he resumed his journalistic role and went to the bullfight. He saw nothing noble in the butchery of the bulls but what sickened him most was the death of a pearl-grey horse, which wore no protective padding. This was strictly against the rules but much to the delight of an audience eager for blood. 'Have you ever heard a horse scream?' Beverley asked his readers in the appalled article he wrote afterwards.

From Mexico, he and Cyril travelled to New York where Beverley booked a suite at the expensive St Regis Hotel on Fifth Avenue. A piano was installed in the sitting-room and he held a series of parties for his many New York friends. Recalling it many years later, he said: 'I shudder to think what it would cost today – it cost a fortune then. Cole Porter, Gloria Swanson, the Lunts, I forget – oh, everyone came! Usually, we ended up in Harlem. Imagine that today! All dressed in white tie and tails with diamond studs and cuff links! It would be more than your life's worth now, but then it was safe. The nightlife of New York was amazing in every sense. I suppose I thought it would be the last chance, and Cyril hadn't seen any of it.' It was suggested to Beverley that he stay on in America and he was tempted, but something compelled him to return to England despite, or because of, the certainty of war. He also received letters from his brother

Paul telling him of his mother's failing health and he knew that if he stayed in America he might not see her again. And so, after ten rumbustious days in New York, they sailed first class for England in early April.

Pauline Nichols was seventy-three when she died peacefully at the vicarage in Cambridge Square on 20 June 1939. John and Paul kept a vigil at her bedside, Paul administered the last rites, and when she died John broke down and wept. Beverley and Alan were summoned by telephone and, by the time they arrived, the undertakers were waiting to take the body down to Bristol for burial in the Nichols family grave. To the others, she looked a woman at peace, but to Beverley her face showed the torture of a bitterly unhappy life and he could barely conceal the hostility he felt for his father, whom he blamed entirely for her misery. It therefore was surprising that he suddenly suggested that John should go away with him for a holiday after the funeral. The old man, too preoccupied with grief to notice Beverley's hostility, accepted the offer gratefully and suggested Teignmouth, a small resort not far from Torquay.

The funeral, held at Long Ashton church, was very different from the Victorian grandeur of George Nichols's funeral in 1896. The simple ceremony was conducted by the vicar, the Revd Hugh Knapman. It was the first time John had visited Long Ashton since the unexplained departure of many years before, and also the first time he had come face to face with his brother George since the early 1900s, following an estrangement for which there is no explanation. What did he think of their respective situations, with George now a very wealthy man while he himself was poor by comparison? It might have been an occasion for reconciliation but there appears to have been nothing more than a polite exchange of words. After the funeral, Beverley announced a change of plan; instead of going direct to Teignmouth, they would first visit Plymouth, where he had already booked rooms at the Queen's Hotel. John had no option but to fall in with this arrangement.

In *Father Figure*, Beverley claims that Plymouth was his father's idea: 'Lots of pretty girls in Plymouth,' John had said with a leer. According to Beverley, he made a remarkable recovery as they travelled to Plymouth: 'His bowler hat was perched jauntily on the back of his head, the monocle was screwed in at a rakish angle and the voice no longer faltered. He suggested a man who had been lunching at a city banquet rather than one who had just attended the funeral of his wife.' Then he became talkative: George, he announced, had syphilis written all over him, and Blanche too. Well, their day would come and he would not be sorry to see it. At least he had kept himself clean. After this, he boasted of the sexual exploits of his youth and he described the women he had picked up, emphasizing in particular their heavy breasts.

By the time they reached the Queen's Hotel, Beverley wrote, he was full of rage and revulsion. A press photographer was waiting on the hotel steps and at once John resumed the role of bereaved husband and sniffed dramatically as he signed the register. 'The manager was all solicitude. My father was such a charming old gentleman, so distinguished, so obviously stricken.' Beverley hid his anger with a sympathetic smile, for in his breast-pocket he had the means of sweet revenge – a copy of his mother's will. Only a few weeks before her death, he and Paul had persuaded her to make a new will leaving her estate to be divided among her three sons, with nothing whatsoever for John. It was a document of 'three typed pages' and her signing it had been the 'only gesture of independence in forty years of married life'. (It was actually forty-nine years – forty years would mean that all the sons had been born out of wedlock: '*Father Figure*' is full of such discrepancies.) It had taken time and patience to persuade her, for she was scared that John might walk in, but Paul had reminded her that he was dead drunk in his own bedroom. Eventually she signed, on condition that it be kept secret. 'I have never kept anything from him, not till now. I have had no secrets, told him no lies.' 'More's the pity,' Beverley had responded.

Beverley's account claims that he let his father dream on about his future, but the next day after lunch, while they were drinking coffee, he handed John the solicitor's linen envelope containing a copy of the will. He left him to read it alone, and when he returned, John was still sitting in the chair where he had left him, 'staring straight ahead. His face was purple and the veins were swelling out of his forehead. When our eyes met, he gasped, "Is this bloody thing a fake?"

"No."

"In that case, I've only got £3,000 in the world to last for the rest of my life," and then his eyes searched the ceiling.' He was about to say what he had always said in times of difficulty with his sons, 'I'll tell your mother,' but Beverley cut in, 'There's nobody there. Nobody upstairs. Nobody left for you to hurt. Nobody to blackmail any more.'

This whole story bears no relation to the truth. Pauline's will was drawn up on 10 June 1936, and consists of a single page written firmly in her own hand. In it, she leaves all her property to her sons, 'subject to a life interest as to half the income thereupon to my husband John Nichols'. The only executor is 'my son Paul Randolph Shalders Nichols'. It is witnessed by Bridget Bunke, cook, of 4, Cambridge Square and Elizabeth Stokes, domestic servant, of the same address. It is also signed by Paul R.S. Nichols, executor, and R.H. Rummel, Commissioner. Her property included the marriage settlement made to her by her father. According to Paul, the provisions of the will were not kept secret from his father, who was perfectly happy with the contents and considered that, if his wife died first, the half share in the interest together with the income he received from his own capital was more than adequate for his needs. At the time the will was drawn, he was seventy-three and he knew that he was assured of a home with Paul for the remainder of his life.

Beverley's assertion that his father was drinking himself into unconsciousness up to the time of his wife's death was also untrue. John's drunkenness had gradually abated many years before, but the allegation gave Beverley the opportunity to provide his story with a dramatic twist. From the time of her death he said, 'My father never drank again. To the student of alcoholism this must sound incredible. Here was a man who, for over forty years, had lived in order to drink, and had drunk in order to live.' He had consulted various authorities about this phenomenon and they had agreed that it was unique in their experience: his sudden abandonment of alcohol was nothing less than a miracle. Beverley had his own explanation. 'My father was possessed. My father surrendered himself to the Devil and, having done so, selected my mother as the principal victim of the sadism that had been implanted within him. And when the victim was removed by death, he laid down his glass.'

Paul dismissed this story as nonsense and Arthur Diamond, who knew Mr and Mrs Nichols quite well, had this to say: 'After *Father Figure* came out, I told [Beverley] the book was all lies – he just laughed. I think he was insane by the time he wrote it.' Diamond was also involved in the Plymouth episode:

I had a phone call from Beverley. He said he was in Bristol visiting his relations there, Uncle George and Auntie Blanche; he was very fond of them, particularly Uncle George. Anyway, he was going on to Exeter. He did not say why but he could be very mysterious about what he was up to. Would I collect his car from Hampstead and pick him up from his hotel? When I got there, he said he wanted to take his father from the Queen's in Plymouth where he had left him after the funeral – actually he said he'd dumped him there – down to Teignmouth. We picked Mr Nichols up and Beverley made him sit in the back. It was an open car with two seats in the front and a sort of dicky seat at the back. I drove, and on the way it became cold and windy. I said, 'Mr Nichols must be freezing, it'll kill him,' and Beverley said, 'I want to.' I stopped the car and told Beverley to drive. I went in the back and Mr Nichols moved to the front. He was usually very jolly and chatty but he was very quiet. I suppose he was still stunned by his wife's death. Beverley didn't speak to him. I was starving by the time we got to Teignmouth and I thought we'd have a meal with Mr Nichols but Beverley said no. When we drove off he said, 'That's the last I expect to see of him.'

We drove back to Plymouth and I caught the train home. Beverley seemed the same as he always was. He didn't mention his mother. He gossiped about people; he could be very witty in a bitchy sort of way. I knew him for years and yet I didn't really know him. I don't think anyone got really close to him. He was always very nice to me but I knew he used me just as he used other people. Why did I let him? I honestly don't know. He had an amazing personality – so charming – I suppose I felt flattered. He was very unpredictable: he would suddenly decide to hate people, like he hated his father, for no particular reason as far as I could see. I don't know why he wanted to be left alone in Plymouth but I can guess. Sailors – he liked sailors and guardsmen, the rougher the better.

In *Father Figure* Beverley described a night in Plymouth when he cruised the dockland pubs, and dates this as the evening of his mother's funeral, after he had left his father at the Queen's Hotel.

At the bar, my arms stretched out for the friendly shoulders of the matelots who were taking my money. That night I was rich; that night I was gay; that night I was plunged in the pit of the ultimate despair. But even in the last degradation, when I woke up in a strange bedroom in a boarding house by the docks, I knew my mother would have understood. I looked up at the dirty ceiling and smiled. It was a smile without a trace of shame, a smile that said, 'Now, at last, you understand.' Dawn was breaking when I returned to the Queen's Hotel. I had passed a rough night in every sense of the word: my garments of mourning were stained and crumpled, my pockets were empty and I had a nasty bruise on my forehead but I felt purified and at peace.

This passage requires no interpretation. It confirms what others have said about him, namely that homosexual sex of the most violent kind was a necessity to him, and became more so as he grew older. A BBC producer remembers Beverley hobbling into his office one afternoon. 'I was practically ripped apart last night,' he said cheerfully. 'I've been sitting in a cold bath all morning to reduce the swelling.' Arthur Diamond said that some of the situations he got into were extremely dangerous: 'He paid for sex and goaded rough trade into violent assault. The stories he told of experiences abroad were blood-curdling. It was what he wanted and what he paid for.' In 1982 he boasted about the past: 'I had a series of bed-sitters in Chelsea, not in my own name, of course, where I could take people. If you knew how, you could always hire guardsmen for the night. I did it for years.' The damage he paid to have inflicted upon his body eventually proved irreparable.

Soon after his mother's funeral Beverley went to Lourdes. 'On the night before I set out, there was a party which went on till dawn. After the party I flew to Paris and picked up a car outside the Ritz.' He gave as a reason for the expedition that he was seeking a renewal of faith, hoping that the city of miracles would provide spiritual sustenance. The real explanation was that he was on a journalistic assignment for 'Page 2'.

Unlike many journalists he did not mock the commercialism of Lourdes, in spite of the more extreme examples of vulgarity, because the city had been 'built on faith'. After all, he said, wherever the crowds had gathered to listen to Jesus, no doubt the innkeepers and pedlars had done a roaring trade. In the piece he wrote for the *Sunday Chronicle* he described the throng of singing pilgrims processing to the Grotto carrying lighted tapers. 'At last when all the multitudes were gathered together, when all the nations were blended in a great mass that stretched to the far distance, there was silence. Never have I heard anything so beautiful as that silence. Nor is that a contradiction in terms, for true silence, the silence of the spirit, is not negative. So the nations prayed at the Grotto that night.'

A few weeks later, they were at each others' throats.

'From Lourdes, he wrote, 'I sped to Cannes, from the sublime to the second rate, from the pure radiance of Christianity to the neon glitter of café society. This confession might be cited as a damning proof of my superficiality.' Cannes was a 'lunatic asylum'. Rumour abounded that war had begun or was about to begin at any moment; the streets were jammed with laden cars queueing for petrol at any price as the wealthy deserted their playground. On the promenade, soldiers marched to man the Italian frontier.

When Beverley eventually reached the Carlton Hotel he found it practically empty of guests: the band had gone, the staff was decimated by the call-up, and the restaurant was on the verge of closing down. The place which had been a focal point of social life had the uncanny atmosphere of a sinking ship. In the cocktail bar, now almost empty, Charles, the barman, whom Beverley had known for many years, refused to accept payment: 'A last drink, Monsieur Beverley.' Out on the terrace he found Elsa Maxwell gazing out to sea, smoking a cigarette. She was delighted to see him. 'Come to the villa and dine,' she said. 'It may be the last time that I can ever ask you.'

Elsa Maxwell was a fat, unglamorous figure with an overwhelming personality, who by sheer audacity had created a role for herself in society as the party-giver of the '20s and '30s. These parties were legendary: both Noel Coward and Cole Porter wrote songs about her, and everyone who was anyone knew her. That night, in her villa up in the hills, her guests – only seven of them – sat on the terrace after dinner looking out over the lights of the bay. Suddenly the lights went out. It was probably part of an air-raid exercise, but it seemed like an omen. 'I wonder how long it will be before the lights go on again?' she asked. Many years later, Beverley remarked that it was then that the death-throes of the Mediterranean had begun. Though the lights did eventually go on again, the glory was tarnished, the scene merely vulgar.

Back in his hotel suite he wrote notes of the conversation at Elsa Maxwell's which read like a hymn to the past:

Do you remember Max Reinhardt's parties at Salzburg?
What will happen to that lovely city? Shall we have to bomb it?
Do you think they've moved all the pictures from the Louvre?
What is Noel Coward up to? Do you remember the first night of *The Vortex* at the tiny Everyman Theatre when we all stood up and cheered?
Where is Cecil Beaton? Will he photograph the war? Will he draw it?
Do you remember the Lido? And the parties at Constance Toulmin's palazzo on the Grand Canal?
Do you remember Mussolini and the audiences he used to give in Rome which always left us bewildered? Will he bring Italy into the war? Would that mean we had to bomb Venice?
Can any of us recall a single whisper of comment that has echoed from the Vatican during this ultimate crisis of Christendom? No, we can not. But when next we meet Evelyn Waugh we must ask him for an authoritative decision. Where is he? What is he up to? Something mischievous. Possibly something heroic. Even better, something funny.
Do you remember Budapest? And the little bars where one went to drink tokay at six o'clock? Do you remember Ludwig's fairy castles? Will they be bombed? Will we use gas?
Do you remember Le Touquet and Syrie Maugham's villa? And how we used to troop off to that little restaurant to join old Selfridge drinking champagne with his chères amies, the Dolly Sisters?
Suppose the Germans get the Channel ports? Can the French be trusted? What about Laval?

A few days later, when Beverley was once again on the terrace of the Carlton, he saw two other old friends, Eric Sawyer and Barry Dierks, who lived together in the Villa Trident along the coast at Miramar. The sight of them brought back a flood of memories of his friendship with Maxine Elliot, the undisputed Queen of the Riviera and one-time favourite of Edward VII. She had been an actress and even had a New York theatre named after her. When Beverley had first met her, she was in the throes of completing the Château Horizon which had been designed by Messrs Sawyer and Dierks, then virtually unknown young architects. The task she had set them was thought to be impossible: on a whim she had bought a narrow piece of rocky land between Cannes and Juan les Pins. Immediately behind the site was the coastal railway line and beyond that the main coastal road. The solution became something of an architectural legend: vast walls were built to blot out the sight and sound of the railway and a plateau of concrete and stone was constructed to project into the sea. The finished result was a house with a large terraced swimming pool floating, as it were, over the sea. Beverley, a regular guest, described life there as lazy, hedonistic, unreal and altogether delightful. But he never forgot an occasion by her swimming-pool when she rebuked one of her young footmen for forgetting to sprinkle sugar on a silver dish of strawberries for her pet monkey. The footman returned with the sugar and bent down. 'Mix it in well,' his mistress commanded, and he did so while the monkey tried to bite him. 'This', Beverley reflected, 'obviously was the stuff of which revolutions are made.'

He now asked Eric Sawyer and Barry Dierks if he could go to their villa and throw a coin in their pool for luck. Eric burst out laughing: 'You're a sentimental old ass.' But Barry said of course he must. So he drove to the Villa Trident and dropped a handful of change into the pool. 'Goodbye and good luck,' he said, wondering if he would ever see the Riviera again.

· 18 ·

Mission found
and completed

1939—1944

War was declared while Beverley was staying at the Ritz Hotel in Paris. He left for England, wondering what task the British government would find for him, just as Noel Coward arrived at the Ritz to set up a Bureau of Propaganda in collaboration with the French Ministry of Information.

In the early days of the war London seemed almost deserted. Most children had been evacuated, and many people had already left or were leaving. A wealthy American, in a hurry to depart, offered Beverley his large house complete with contents for the ludicrously low price of £500. He refused: what was the point in buying a property which would very likely be reduced to rubble by bombing? In the event, the house remained intact and would have proved an extremely valuable asset. He did not, however, regret refusing an opportunity to go to America on a special assignment for the government. Earlier in the year, while he was in New York, he had been tempted to stay, but had decided against it. Now in the first weeks of the war it was suggested he set up an organization in the States to rival the Oxford Group, funded secretly by government money: it appeared that Buchman was pro-German and an equivalent pro-British religious group would counterbalance any influence Buchman might have. Beverley found the idea too stupid to take seriously. He had already expressed deep contempt for his fellow countrymen who had scurried off to the safety of America, giving the most tenuous of reasons to cover their cowardice, and he did not intend to be tarred with the same brush. His decision was right for, as it turned out, Buchman was not pro-German.

During the first months of the war he received many letters from friends overseas commiserating with him on the turn of events. In a reply to Ray Harris, dated 18 September 1939, he wrote:

> In such a tragedy as this it would be indecent to claim any special pity, but you can imagine what this is meaning to me. For ten years I have been

obsessed with the idea of war, and the only really unselfish work I ever did in my life was in the cause of peace. Now all that is shattered and there is a temptation to think that it is shattered for ever.

The thing which strikes me about the present situation (I am writing this on the day Russia has marched into Poland) is that for almost the first time in the world's history great Powers have openly admitted their contempt of morality. Even Napoleon paid lip-service to decency, and lip-service is a far more important thing than most of us are inclined to admit. It is the abandonment of any pretence that is so horrifying. Things which come into the open are sometimes more menacing than things which are allowed to lurk in the dark. And today it is as though Hitler and Stalin were saying, 'All right, we are on the side of the Devil. So what?'

I don't know quite what I am going to do about it. I would like to say 'At all costs make peace.' I know that this is an unpopular idea, but at least, if we had not fought this war, the fate of Poland would have been infinitely preferable to her fate today, or to her condition even at the end of a victorious war. However, that is not a point that is worth labouring at the present time.

Ever since the sale of Thatch Cottage, Beverley had searched for a similar cottage in the south of England which would provide a retreat from London while being within easy reach of it. He hoped as well to create a garden in a kinder climate than he had experienced at Glatton. His search gradually narrowed to an area around Ashdown Forest, influenced by his friendship with Geoffrey and Dorothy Hart who lived at Wych Cross Place, a large estate between East Grinstead and Haywards Heath. They were noted for their collection of pictures and furniture, and Mrs Hart, who was always generous to Beverley, gave him a small painting of the Dutch School dated 1682, entitled *Skaters on a Frozen River*. In 1970, he sent this to Christie's for auction, and the money it fetched helped to relieve the financial pressure he was under at the time.

The house he found was Butcher's Barn, Danehill. The origin of the name was lost in the mists of time, but Beverley and Cyril found the coincidence irresistible. It had two living-rooms and three bedrooms, and there were several solid outhouses. Gaskin commandeered one of these for himself, and another became an unofficial bolt-hole for men from a Guards regiment stationed in the area. A bar was fixed up and kept stocked by Arthur Diamond through his connections in the liquor trade; he also managed to persuade Watneys to supply beer at no cost as a gesture of patriotic support for the boys in khaki. But the major attraction of the house was its comparative isolation – it could be reached only by a private road, and it stood in twelve acres of woodland and garden. This time, thought Beverley, there would be no prying neighbours to monitor his activities as there had been at Glatton. In a moment of remarkable optimism he planned to create his new garden and to write another *Down the Garden Path*; he also believed that this was one investment that could not possibly go wrong.

While Butcher's Barn was being made ready, Beverley stayed in York Cottage in the village so that he could supervise the alterations and redecorations, spending as much time at the house as he could. This all took place in the first months of the war, when shortage of labour and materials was not yet a problem, and life continued more or less normally – the 'phoney war'.

In later years Beverley was to regard the Butcher's Barn interlude as a sort of mental aberration during which he believed that, somehow, peace could still be reached with Hitler and that, whatever might happen in Europe, the British Isles would be spared the experience of war. He was by no means alone in his thinking: after the Dunkirk evacuation and the armistice between Germany and France in June 1940, the possibility of peace became likely. In July, Hitler, in his 'appeal to reason' speech, said that Britain had no alternative but to reach a peace agreement. This was rejected by Churchill and Hitler went ahead with his plans to invade in August – although the RAF had to be dealt with first.

Beverley's illusions were swept away by the Battle of Britain and the massive bombing raids which followed in September. Butcher's Barn was no longer a peaceful hiding-place and his plans for it looked increasingly futile, yet he continued blindly to spend money on the new garden. In the mean time his journalistic work continued: in December he made two trips with the RAF, the first with a patrol over the English Channel and the second over the North Sea. In a tiny act of defiance he had his tin hat painted with vine leaves. The Communist *Daily Worker* accused him of not taking the war seriously: 'Quite true,' he commented. 'There are some things too serious to be serious about.'

In February 1941 he wrote to Ray Harris, who was by this time working for *Life* magazine:

Some letters from America infuriate me with their 'why-don't-you-pop-over-here-and-forget-all-that-nonsense' attitude. Yours are very different, you do realize what we are going through. For nearly two years now I have felt utterly uncreative. Except for journalism, have written nothing. But am at last trying again. I have just returned from staying with Compton Mackenzie in the Hebrides, which is amusing after the Greek chapters in *Twenty-Five*! Actually he is charming and knows more about the Mediterranean than any man living. So, of course, he has been completely ignored by our propaganda people in this war – just as I myself and every journalist of importance. I wish I could take you, if only for a few hours, through London. It would alter your life. No more at present. We're still very much alive here. The sun is shining. I've just planted a new orchard and there are shrimps for tea – all under a sky not entirely devoid of things that go off with a bang.

Two points arise out of this letter. The first is that during his stay with Mackenzie he complained about the lack of a specific war job, despite his efforts to get one. 'Could it be', he asked Mackenzie, 'that I am thought of as a Fascist?' Mackenzie, who liked Beverley for taking his teasing reviews of the Glatton books in good part and had forgiven him for the attack in *Twenty-Five*, thought it unlikely, surmising that MI5 did not take him seriously. As for a war job, why not go to India and write a book about it? The government had doubts about the loyalty of India in the face of an attack from Japan who, in the previous December, had declared war on the USA and the Commonwealth.

The second point is the reference to 'trying again'. He had nearly completed a volume of short stories loosely based on various experiences in the years prior to the war. The working title was *Straws in the Wind* which he later changed to *Men Do Not Weep*. He said of them: 'I don't expect ever to rival Maugham but it is a good ideal to set oneself.' Indeed, the style was not unlike that of Maugham, in that the stories were written in the first person with real incidents interwoven with fiction. The book enjoyed a modest success; years later he hoped some of the stories might be adapted for radio or television, but nothing came of this.

The main interest of the book to many readers was probably the foreword in which he restated his position on pacifism. It was unfair to accuse pacifism of being partly responsible for the lack of preparedness in which Britain found itself. Many pacifists had argued for defensive measures, he said, and had been ignored. He castigated the pre-war government for assuring the public that all was well, and attacked the Foreign Office for its sycophantic support of France, reminding readers of an article he had written about French military strength in 1936: 'At the moment her support is so problematical that it may be ruled out altogether. France will let us down.' This assertion had been greeted with derision, so deep had been the conviction that the Maginot Line was as much Britain's insurance against Germany as it was for France: he himself had dubbed it the 'Imaginot Line'. This foreword was written with all the old Nichols fire, but, as so often, he strayed on to dangerous ground. Bearing in mind the fear of being thought Fascist that he had expressed to Mackenzie, it was reckless to say anything in Oswald Mosley's favour, but he did, pointing out that he had been thrown into prison without trial while leading Communists who were vocally pro-German had gone free.

In June 1941 he wrote to Ray Harris:

Have just finished correcting the final proof of *Men Do Not Weep* which is the amended and, I hope, superior title of my book. I simply don't understand what has happened to the US end of it. It was sent over weeks ago by Curtis Brown but no word has been heard. Not that it really matters. Sometimes I chafe when I think of what I might have been in America but the grim realities of these times (awful phrase) makes such fretting seem unworthy.

I'm doing what is known as 'carrying on'. This as far as I'm concerned means writing things I don't believe and talking to people I don't believe in and making speeches to troops in extraordinary circumstances – standing in wind-swept tents with the RAF, clambering on to platforms after concert parties in some great camp, or walking up and down a barrack hall answering questions. They seem to like me – in fact, that's putting it rather modestly, but the strain of pouring out moral encouragement is getting me down.

Six weeks later he wrote again to Harris telling him that he had left Butcher's Barn. 'I have shut it up, bolted the door, taken a last look at the woods and the garden I had hoped to make so lovely and have handed it over to a house agent to sell – at a staggering loss.'

The reason for this is not clear: it seems, like many of his decisions, to have been sudden and illogical. True, he was now on his own, Cyril and Gaskin having joined the Navy and the Army respectively; true, the isolation of the house and the problems of wartime travel made it inconvenient to get to; but probably the real reason was a discontent with himself, a malaise of the spirit, for which a change of scene seemed the only answer. The Hampstead house was temporarily out of action and he was not able to move in again until the end of the year. He now took rooms in St John's Wood but spent part of each week in Cambridge. In one sense, he was at his lowest ebb – his earnings had fallen dramatically and for the time being he was without his home; but in another sense he felt freer than he had for years. 'I was back to living out of a suitcase in lodgings and I rather enjoyed it. It was like starting all over again.' He was also enjoying the sexual adventures that circumstances provided. 'I had the time of my life. The blackout may have been a curse but to people like us it was a boon. The "trade" was there for the asking and I took full advantage of it.'

Ever since his visit to Compton Mackenzie he had been trying to arrange a trip to India, unaware that Mackenzie's suggestion had been made jokingly. The idea of a book on the Indian problem began to obsess him: he saw it as a means of proving his patriotism and it never occurred to him that there might be a point of view other than the official British line. At the height of war, a boat passage to India was not a matter of booking at Thomas Cook but of getting permission, provided that the purpose of the journey received the approval of government officials. Eventually Beverley was 'cleared' and allowed to go, ostensibly under the auspices of Allied Newspapers. Before he left early in 1943, he wrote this for the readers of the *Sunday Chronicle*:

> I am on my way to India, I am going because I believe that what is known as the Indian problem is urgent and delicate, that it has world-wide ramifications and that its importance will increase as months go by and, to speak frankly, because neither you, nor I, nor our American friends are sufficiently well informed about the subject. It is vitally important that we should know the facts. I want to discover at least some of them.

Before leaving England, Beverley was fully aware of the official attitude to India, which might be summed up as 'exasperation'. The Hindu-dominated Congress, which had been founded in 1885, preached self-rule and rebellion; by contrast the Muslim League, founded in 1906, was looked upon kindly, for its leader, Mohammed Ali Jinnah, believed that British rule was preferable to Hindu rule, though the ideal solution to the Indian problem was the creation of a separate Muslim state. British exasperation was exacerbated by the failure of Sir Stafford Cripps's mission in 1942 to rally India against the Japanese threat. He had offered an immediate form of self-government subject to the condition that any province could opt out in favour of an alternative form of government. The proposal, which would effectively have splintered India, was rejected by Indian leaders for various reasons. Cripps believed that Mahatma Gandhi exercised a malevolent influence on Congress in this decision, a point which had a bearing on subsequent events.

In August 1942 Congress passed the famous 'Quit India' resolution, asserting that if the British left, India would unite to fight the Japanese. True to form, Gandhi advocated passive resistance should the Japanese invade: he had once advised the Jews in Germany to use a similar tactic against the Nazis, assuring them it would be successful. Congress, while admiring Gandhi's idealism, took a more practical view, and gave notice to the British that, if they did not leave, a programme of civil disobedience would be implemented. The British government, its attention focused primarily on winning the war, saw the Congress resolution as subversive and imprisoned the leaders and workers of Congress. The Hindu public reacted with shock and anger, and widespread violent civil unrest met with an armed reaction from the British. The situation was eventually alleviated by Gandhi's famous fast which lasted for three weeks.

This was the background to Beverley's arrival in India, and although he claimed complete objectivity he was already heavily biased. His views were also influenced, some would argue distorted, by *Mother India*, written by an American, Katherine Mayo, and published in 1927. She saw British rule as beneficial, and felt that progress to modernization had been impeded by the Hindus' rigid interpretation of their religion, to the detriment of the people as a whole and to the financial advantage of the few. This view was backed by a catalogue of stomach-churning stories of child marriage (listing thirteen appalling cases of injuries inflicted on female children from seven years old upwards); of the social acceptance of venereal and other diseases and the overwhelming distrust of Western medicine; of Hindu Ayurvedic medicine which, she asserted, had as much claim to serious consideration as voodoo. In short, her book, with its anti-Hindu bias, was hardly recommended reading for a writer undertaking a fresh, objective survey of the Indian problem, but Beverley relied heavily on its contents for the work he ultimately produced.

Beverley's arrival in New Delhi as the guest of the Viceroy, Lord Linlithgow, created widespread speculation. What was the former crusader for peace and Christianity going to crusade about in India? In the atmosphere of distrust prevailing at the time, it was assumed that his welcome at the Viceroy's house implied he was on an official assignment, and his claim to be in India for Allied Newspapers was regarded with scepticism. Suspicions were confirmed when his first article in the *Sunday Chronicle* praised the imperial splendour in which the Viceroy lived. Beverley, personally attacked in the Indian Hindu press, was astonished that what he thought of as a mild piece of popular journalism should evoke such a bitter response. He had argued that the splendour of the Viceregal setting was fitting in the context of Indian history: 'An attempt at "White House" simplicity would be a piece of ludicrous affectation. The Hindus would laugh at it, the Muslims would despise it, the Princes would regard it as a form of lunacy.' It was the reference to the Princes that caused the bitterest response, for he soon discovered that, although the Princes ruled nearly two-fifths of India, most commentators preferred to ignore the fact. To nationalists they were an anachronism. Surely, Beverley argued, until the British came Indian history had been a record of unbridled despotism: the British had introduced the first steps towards democracy, a process now gathering momentum. Within days he had plunged into the minefield of Indian politics and every step he took confirmed that his attitude was biased against the Hindus.

Soon after his arrival, he journeyed to the North-West Frontier. It was here that a nail in his sandal pierced his heel – a trivial injury of which he took no notice, until infection set in. So began a six-month saga of illness which took him in and out of hospitals. His injury was serious and at one stage there was even talk of amputation to stop gangrene spreading. If nothing else, the experience provided Beverley with a first-hand knowledge of Indian hospitals and contact with the people, which he would not otherwise have had.

Eventually, from Government House at Darjeeling, he wrote to Ray Harris on 12 October 1943:

I have come up here for a final convalescence after the heat and horror of Calcutta. I am really quite well again but these last six months have been hell, and I was so very near death that I feel somehow different – a lot lost (including hair!) – but a good deal gained. I am shortly going to Bombay to write a book about India which ought to be a wow. India is a weird bag of tricks, mostly pretty bad ones. The United States have no idea of what is going on here. It is a conglomeration of utterly diverse races, mostly hating one another, doped with every religious perversity, and if we, the British, were to go, there would be unparalleled misery and chaos.

He gave as his address for correspondence the Ministry of Information, New Delhi.

Up to this point, though Beverley had met Indians of different ethnic backgrounds, religious beliefs and political opinions, he had only met two important leaders: Dr Ambedkar, leader of the Untouchables, and Mrs Sarojini Naidu, the first Indian woman to be elected President of Congress. She had only just been released from detention and apparently had little to say apart from proclaiming her hatred of British imperialism. Her son, Dr N.M. Jaisoorya, was present at the meeting, and, in a letter commenting on the book that Beverley wrote, appeared to confirm the lack of content in their discussion.

Dr Ambedkar, by contrast, was very forthright in his condemnation of Gandhi.

Beverley now had several discussions with Jinnah, the powerful leader of the Muslim league, who had always believed that self-government would be achieved by constitutional methods and had disassociated himself from Gandhi's policy of non-cooperation with the British from the beginning. In a letter to Gandhi written as far back as October 1920, he had pointed out that the methods employed by the Mahatma had already caused split and division in almost every institution he had approached. By the 1930s Jinnah believed that the Muslim population faced subjugation to the Hindu majority and must find its own destiny by collective political action. In 1940 this resolved into the demand for a separate state, Pakistan. One of the points he made was the separatedness of Indian Muslims: 'We are different beings. There is nothing in life which links us together [with Hindus]. Our names, our clothes, our food, they are all different – our economic life, our educational ideas, our treatment of women, our attitude to animals, we challenge each other at every point of the compass.' This was in contrast to the view of Congress summed up by Pandit Nehru in the *New York Times Magazine* of 19 July 1942: 'Except for a small handful of persons there is no difference between Hindu and Muslim in race, culture or language.'

Beverley was enchanted by Jinnah's sophistication and the cool logic of his argument as opposed to what he saw as the Hindu pot-pourri of religion, superstition and authoritarianism. He began to ask himself if Gandhi, with his deification of poverty and the maintenance of the status quo, was the tool of Hindu vested interests. Was his demand for freedom from Britain really in order to establish Hindu domination over India for all time, as Jinnah suggested?

Beverley decided to call his book *Verdict on India* and he began it with its conclusion firmly in mind – that the only solution to the Indian problem was partition. This was not the official British position. 'The one thing that keeps the British in India is the false idea of a United India as preached by Gandhi,' Jinnah had said. 'A United India is a myth which will cause endless strife. As long as that strife exists, the British have an excuse for remaining.'

Up to the last section of *Verdict on India* the book fulfilled all the demands of British wartime propaganda, although it was also written with the American reader as a prime target. (President Roosevelt, disappointed with the failure of the Cripps mission, had made no secret of his disapproval of the British stance and *Verdict on India* was designed to evoke sympathy with Britain.) From the beginning, Beverley made his anti-Hindu attitude clear. Echoing Jinnah, he accused Congress of being Fascist in intent and its anti-British tactics as supportive of the wartime enemy. The weakness of the book lay in its failure to present the Hindu point of view – it could be said that this was consistent with its purpose as propaganda, but on the other hand Beverley seemed genuinely unable to perceive that there was a Hindu point of view. Within its terms of reference the British case was made cogently, dramatically and with flair. However, Beverley also resorted to mockery. His chapters on Hindu art and particularly Hindu music displayed not only ignorance but also a destructive savagery; a diatribe against the Indian film industry, which he dubbed 'Hindu Hollywood', was both sarcastic and ludicrous; the chapter on Ayurvedic medicine was merely an updated version of Katherine Mayo, whose ghostly presence hovered over much of the book. But his strongest dose of vitriol was reserved for Gandhi whom he conjured up as a mixture of Hitler and Mussolini. He made it clear that he was not dealing with Gandhi the religious leader but Gandhi the politician, a distinction he found difficult to maintain, and emphasized that, unlike most Western writers, he did not propose to allow his criticisms to be modified by the qualification that

Gandhi was a 'saint': 'He seems to me a typical Hindu politician of quite inordinate vanity, narrow, ignorant and supremely intolerant.'

Beverley saw Gandhi's non-violence as 'weirdly muddle-headed'. Quoting a Gandhi definition of non-violence – 'If a man fights with his sword single-handed against a horde of dacoits armed to the teeth, I should say he is fighting non-violently. Supposing a mouse fighting a cat resisted the cat with his sharp teeth, would you call the mouse violent? In the same way, for the Poles to stand bravely against the German hordes vastly superior in number and strength was almost non-violent' – Beverley suggested that anyone who could say precisely what was meant by this would be a genius. Could it mean that violence against superior odds automatically became non-violence? That was a convenient theory, Beverley observed, which must be a perpetual solace to non-violent nationalists who 'so often poured non-violent petrol over policemen and lit it with non-violent matches' or 'battered British and Canadian boys to death with non-violent bludgeons'.

His strongest criticism was reserved for Gandhi's attitude to Japan at a time when it appeared that Japan was winning the war. Gandhi had suggested that Japan was anxious for peace and would only invade India if it was defended by the British: 'The presence of the British in India is an invitation to Japan to invade; their withdrawal removes the bait.' Beverley dismissed this as nonsensical self-deception, and castigated Gandhi and Congress for proposing civil disobedience at a time critical to the conduct of the war against Japan. Finally, he prophesied that, despite Gandhi's increasing irrelevance in solving the India problem, he would, when he died, be 'canonized and sit for ever among the myriad gods of the Hindu pantheon'.

Up to this point in *Verdict on India* Beverley had fulfilled his brief from the British government – if, indeed, he had a brief. He denied at the time that he had but, not surprisingly, he was disbelieved in India. After Beverley's death, Cyril Butcher said that Beverley was bound by the Official Secrets Act and could not tell the truth but 'of course he went to India under Government auspices.' Whatever the facts, in the final seventy pages of the book Beverley deviated dramatically from the British propaganda line and put the case for the creation of Pakistan with considerable force and skill, arguing that there could be only two reasons for opposing the policy: ignorance of the facts or denial of the principle of self-determination for 'a 100 million Muslims'.

Verdict on India caused a sensation when it appeared in 1944. It was a best-seller on both sides of the Atlantic, and its message also reached vast numbers of people through the pages of *The Reader's Digest*. It delighted the Muslim League, was hated by Congress, and did not much please the British government either.

With the passing of the years it would be easy to dismiss its significance, but at the time partition was a concept new to most of the public, and this was the first widely read publication to put the Muslim case. In 1982 Beverley said, 'I don't want to claim too much for it but I believe it played an important part and I am proud of it. It was written quickly and parts of it are poor but, overall, it was a workmanlike job and the conclusion was sincere, even if it did irritate some of the English hierarchy.' Asked about Gandhi, he replied, 'I take nothing back. He was a menace and his views were essentially Fascist, by which I mean he contrived to keep the peasants in their place and preserve the Hindu political status quo with the wealthy ruling class intact. Of course he was anti-British because he opposed any form of progess and, whatever else might be said about our rule, we gave India an idea of what it could become. We should have done much more, but look at India before we arrived. Politically, Gandhi was a disaster, and one day someone will have the guts to write the truth.'

Beverley appeared to be unaware that his criticisms of Gandhi the politician were being voiced by Indians themselves by 1982: perhaps the most trenchant book on the subject to date is V.S. Naipaul's *India, A Wounded Civilization* (André Deutsch, 1977).

· 19 ·

Sunlight and shadows

1945–1953

A T the end of the war in 1945, Britain was gripped by euphoric optimism; many believed that by some miracle a prosperous, fairer, happier society would emerge overnight. Discussing this over thirty years later, Beverley said, 'We wanted to make up for the lost years but when America suddenly cancelled Lend-Lease we were put in the most dreadful financial situation. Most people here did not realize that there had always been an undertow of anti-British feeling in the States. Look at Roosevelt: he thought better of the Russians, in some ways, than he did of us. I was very angry with America in 1945 and wanted to write a book but it was too soon. When I did write one a few years later, the loan was old news but the book was very critical of them and it flopped.'

Beverley was determined in 1945 to make the best of the years left to him and to compensate for time lost during the war. The controversy over *Verdict on India*, put him firmly back in the public eye, and it was characteristic that his next subject should be completely unexpected and unlikely – a story for children. It would be pleasant to report that he liked the company of children and enjoyed improvising stories to entertain them but this was not so. The only children with whom he occasionally came into contact were his nieces, Jill and Judy: Jill remembered that he was ill at ease with them, and far from telling them stories, found it difficult to talk to them at all. None the less, he began the book with complete confidence, weaving a plot combining satire, fantasy and magic, calling it *The Tree That Sat Down*. It was greeted with acclaim and became an international success, as it still is today. It was ironic that though he had almost given up hope of achieving literary esteem among his peers, he should see his new book placed in a class with *The Wind in the Willows* and *Alice in Wonderland*. He was later to remark: 'If I had only the children's books to my credit, I might be more highly thought of by the literary establishment.'

Among a host of characters his most innovative was a modern witch called Miss Smith. She was actually nearly 400 years old but, with the lavish use of cosmetics, a false nose and a series of wigs, she could transform herself from a frightening old crone into a pretty young lady – 'Just like certain actresses I have known,' Beverley commented. The unusual aspect of Miss Smith was that she was not a very successful witch: she had been a dunce at witches' school, always forgetting her spells and losing her dogs' tongues and newts' eyes. Children adored her despite, or probably because of, her wickedness – and they asked for more.

Over the next four years he wrote two sequels, *The Stream That Stood Still* (1948) and *The Mountain of Magic* (1950). In 1971, after a gap of twenty years, he wrote *The Wickedest Witch in the World* which starred – there is no other word for it – the redoubtable Miss Smith and her equally wicked friend and rival, the dreadful Miss Jones, her junior by 100 years. It was rather more sophisticated and frightening than the earlier books, taking account of the changing attitudes of children, and was well received. He later began another Miss Smith adventure with the provisional title, *Super Witch*.

One of the first things Beverley did after the war was to search for a country house. It was a dispiriting business for, although he had specified an eighteenth-century house with at least five acres of garden, estate agents bombarded him with particulars of everything from Victorian mausoleums to Tudor cottages. He hated the former and had fallen out of love with the latter. Frequently, misled by the glowing descriptions of estate agents' pamphlets, he travelled miles only to be disappointed and soon learned to decipher estate agents' prose. 'Easy reach of London' meant 'as the crow flies'; 'Georgian' meant early Victorian; 'excellent conservatory' more often than not turned out to be a ruin with most of the glass missing and a defunct heating system; 'outbuildings' meant anything from a roofless stable to a shed with a corrugated-iron roof and an advanced case of wet rot; 'well laid-out garden' meant nothing whatsoever.

At last he found exactly what he wanted – a Georgian manor house with the evocative name of Merry Hall, near Ashstead in Surrey. The four-acre garden was an overgrown ruin and the house itself, with twenty-two rooms, attics and cellars, was sadly neglected and needed complete redecoration. The magnificent staircase had been painted a lurid orange and hideous wallpaper had been used everywhere. What was worse, a previous owner had 'modernized' it between the wars, replacing many of the delicate fireplace surrounds with tiled monstrosities. To restore the house, let alone the garden, to anything resembling its former glory would require infinite patience, organizing ability, and a great deal of money.

Included in the purchase was a small bungalow complete with a 'protected' tenant, and Beverley had some difficulty in gaining possession of this for his own use. 'Looking back on it,' he said in 1972 in the foreword to *The Gift of a Home*, 'I now realize that the whole thing was not only merry but more than slightly mad. After I had paid the purchase price, I had barely enough to keep me, living modestly, for about six months. I had no rich relations but several poor ones. I had practically no furniture. I had no book on the stocks. All this, remember, shortly after the war, at a time when life was difficult enough for those who had money and almost impossible for those who hadn't.' His friends tried to dissuade him but the more logical their arguments, the more resolved he became to go ahead. As Arthur Diamond put it:

I think if we had all approved, he'd have dropped the idea at once. He was like that. But can you imagine taking on a great, rambling place in 1946 when everything was in short supply? It was sheer insanity and getting it straight nearly killed him, but he was determined, and in the end he was right because he got three books out of it and sold it at a good profit ten years later. Of course, half the attraction was the grandeur of the place. He always had big ideas and he liked showing off. So did Gaskin, and if he had been against it I don't think Beverley would have bought it.

Gaskin was freshly demobbed from the army where he had spent most of his time as general factotum to Oliver Messel, the stage designer, translated to Captain Messel, camouflage expert. It was Gaskin who said of the name of the house that 'it would look nice on the note-paper'. Beverley took him to look round it and far from being dismayed and appalled by the amount of work involved, he was enchanted by everything. Even the cavernous kitchens did not deter him: 'Give me room to move around,' was his verdict. Beverley once said of Gaskin that he really should have been head of a household staff in a stately home. 'He always reminded me of the butler in "Punch" opening the front door to a scruffy individual who announced that the revolution had arrived. "The revolution?" repeated the butler haughtily. "Kindly deliver it at the servants' entrance."'

The house at Ellerdale Close was put up for auction by Hampton and Sons who, in their prospectus, included extracts from *Green Grows the City* to tempt prospective purchasers. With the proceeds of the sale in the bank and the move to Merry Hall under way, Beverley went off to Cyprus for a holiday, leaving Gaskin and Cyril to sort things out at the house. Before he left, he wrote to Ray Harris in New York begging him to send a parcel of cooking fat and tinned butter – 'Gaskin will be your slave for life.' He wrote similar letters to other American friends, offering to reward them with books 'not necessarily my own'. In those days of austerity, such ordinary commodities were as rare as caviar and much more welcome.

He returned from Cyprus full of ambitious plans for the restoration of Merry Hall and the radical redesigning of the garden, and he soon discovered this would cost far more than he had anticipated. Caught between his fear of poverty and his love of extravagance, he threw himself into a programme of work as fierce as any he had undertaken when he was ten years younger. Money had to be made and it did not much matter how, so he accepted a proposal from James Drawbell to provide a weekly article for *Woman's Own*. There was, of course, nothing to be ashamed of in working for *Woman's Own*: it attracted some of the leading popular authors of the time including Somerset Maugham, Daphne du Maurier and A.J. Cronin; Monica Dickens, like Beverley, wrote a weekly piece for it. He knew nevertheless that this decision killed any remaining chance of his being taken seriously by the literary Establishment. He would have preferred work on a quality magazine or newspaper but consoled himself with the thought that *Woman's Own*, with its huge circulation, paid better than the upmarket press.

Browsing through old copies of *Woman's Own* is engrossing, for they provide a panorama of social change of every kind. When Beverley began writing for the magazine it had no more than twenty small pages, a reflection of the paper shortage at that time. By the end of the 1950s, eighty larger pages were packed with entertainment and colourful advertisements. Beverley wrote on every conceivable subject with an apparent spontaneity that belied the hard work that went into each essay. He contended that they required as much skill as writing a leading article for the *Sunday Times* – more, because he had to write simply, without condescension. Such was his success and that of his fellow columnist Monica Dickens that in 1949 Newnes published a hard-backed selection of their works called *Yours Sincerely*. Beverley was often ridiculed for his association with *Woman's Own*. Evelyn Waugh once remarked to him condescendingly: 'I hear you are reaching more housewives than ever before with your little pieces.' 'Yes,' Beverley replied, 'my little pieces make thousands of women happy, which is more than most men can say.'

On 17 February 1946 John Nichols died at Great Crosby, Lancashire, where he was then living with Paul. His last years were peaceful and unremarkable, but in his final months he went into a decline and refused to eat properly. In effect he died of self-inflicted malnutrition. Beverley, who had refused to have anything to do with him after his mother's death in 1939, attended the funeral, not out of respect but at Paul's request. If he believed that his unreasoning hatred would die with his father, he was wrong: over the years it intensified until he was haunted by a monster of his own creation.

In common with many writers, Beverley had a file full of ideas which one day might evolve into 'something'. He also had files on projects which had not reached fruition: one was a piano concerto which Leopold Stokowski planned to launch but for some reason did not; another was an operetta which he had begun in the late '30s and which may have been the work for C.B. Cochran that he had abandoned for *Cry Havoc!* The idea had come to him while he was dining on a terrace in Vienna: inspired by the clash of chimes when the clocks struck the hour, he scribbled a tune on the back of the menu card, but a gust of wind whipped it away into the street below. Suppose, he said to himself, it had been a song intended by a young composer for his lady love – and he drafted a scenario around the adventures of the composer trying to recover his lost song. He wrote a few numbers, called the show *Serenade* and forgot all about it.

Cyril Butcher liked the idea and during the longueurs of duty in the Navy began fleshing out the story. Beverley, infected by his enthusiasm, eventually completed the operetta in 1947, switching the location from Vienna to post-war Paris, and renaming it *A Song on the Wind*. He thought audiences might be in the mood for a heavily romantic confection which had nothing to do with reality, but London managements were not interested. There is no record of the show's being submitted to C.B. Cochran who, in any case, was in the throes of producing the A.P. Herbert–Vivian Ellis musical, *Bless the Bride*. Other managements had suffered badly with romantic shows: *Evangeline* starring Frances Day had been booed off the stage, and Noel Coward's *Pacific 1860*, which reopened the Theatre Royal, Drury Lane, failed despite its attractive leading lady, Mary Martin.

Cyril Butcher, who featured in both these shows, realized sooner than Beverley that *A Song on the Wind* was not strong enough for a London management to gamble on, and suggested sending it to BBC Television, then getting into gear again after its enforced closure during the war and hungry for material. The producer Eric Fawcett decided to do it.

In those early days, transmissions went out live from the studios at Alexandra Palace, a nerve-racking business for all concerned. Every detail had to be meticulously planned and rehearsed, for if anything went wrong there was no second chance. If an actor forgot his lines, the sound went dead while he was given a prompt and it was not unusual for the audience to catch a glimpse of a boom microphone or an arm moving a prop or piece of furniture. Lionel Harris remembered directing a drama when part of the set caught fire: he improvised his shots while the crew doused the flames, and the actors, ignoring the smoke whirling about them, carried on with apparent imperturbability.

The set for *A Song on the Wind*, designed by James Bould, was massive by television standards, with a Paris square, the streets leading off it, and several interiors including a café. The music was orchestrated by George Melachrino and the orchestra conducted by Eric Robinson. It had a cast of fourteen, a small chorus, and twelve ballet dancers choreographed by David Paltengi. The leading roles were played by Patricia Burke and Jack Melford, both well known in the West End at the time, and the show was so 'heavy', the rehearsal time was doubled. After all this preparation, it was seen only twice, on 5 and 8 November 1948, the viewers numbering thousands rather than the millions who watch today, for television was in its infancy and ownership of a tiny-screened set was still rare.

Whether viewers liked or hated the show is now a matter for conjecture: one viewer remembers it as 'quite pleasant' while another thought it 'pretty feeble'.

Although *A Song on the Wind*, billed as a 'musical fantasy' rather than as an operetta, was publicized as 'Prior to its stage production', this proved optimistic for it was never seen again. What is more, all trace of it subsequently vanished: not a script or a piece of music remains in the BBC archives. Even more curious is the absence of any trace of it among the Nichols memorabilia, except for a single page of manuscript which carries the melody of one of the thirty musical numbers. To add to the mystery, Beverley was firmly under the impression that copies of it were in his possession, and after his death Cyril Butcher, credited as co-author of the book, was startled to find it had disappeared.

Another of Beverley's projects was a novel, begun in the 1930s, about a middle-class, highly respected Edwardian family doing its best to conceal and cope with the father's alcoholism. He eventually abandoned this in favour of a dramatized version. The characters bore more than a passing resemblance to the members of his own family and while his father was alive he did not attempt to have it performed. As soon as John Nichols was dead, Beverley revised the play and sent it on its journey around the London managements under the title *Shadow of the Vine*. None of them displayed any interest in it, probably because they thought the subject too depressing for post-war audiences. Deeply disappointed and determined that it should not be lost, he persuaded Jonathan Cape to publish it in 1949. It sold well enough for a second edition to be printed a year later, but that, it seemed, was the end of it.

Meanwhile, between writing the children's books and beginning work on an autobiography, he went on a dollar-earning lecture tour to America. He was delighted to be back visiting old haunts and old friends, and revelled in the pleasures of plenty which contrasted so sharply with the poverty of Britain. He sensed a smug satisfaction among Americans that defeating Hitler had brought Britain low as well, and was dismayed by the lack of news about Europe, let alone Britain, in the American press. 'The American newpapers write as much about Britain as our papers write about the Isle of Wight,' he said afterwards.

What struck him most forcibly was how old-fashioned the 'New World' was by comparison to the 'old' where fundamental social change was taking place. Those who had any awareness at all about Britain expressed horror at the Labour government's mild version of socialism: 'Was England really going Commie?' they asked. His attempts to explain what was actually going on were greeted for the most part with bewildered disapproval. Their refusal to see the problems within their own society also alarmed him.

When he raised the question of black inequality in America, he was told he 'did not understand'.

As soon as he returned home to Merry Hall he began a serious study of contemporary America which was frequently ironical, harshly critical, and almost totally devoid of humour. It is impossible to do the contents justice by summarizing them but the chapters on his encounters with colour discrimination, whether in the North or South, remain horrifying, and when he compares the treatment of blacks with the treatment of Jews in Nazi Germany the parallel seems not wholly inappropriate. Equally disturbing in its implications is his account of the persecution of Charles Chaplin which was then at its height. His analysis of America, in short, is lively and provocative, but the public reaction to the book was a sad disappointment. 'I called it *Uncle Samson*, a title nobody understood. Perhaps it might have sold better if I had called it *Verdict on America*.' It was his last attempt at a serious work of social and political observation; for the next fifteen years, he stuck to subjects which were safe and easily digestible.

The reaction to his autobiography, however, was very different. Since it was a sequel to *Twenty-Five* he first proposed calling it *Fifty*, but on second thoughts he decided against this reference to his age and chose instead a phrase from Robert Browning, *All I Could Never Be*, which appealed to his sense of humour. It was a series of recollections, mostly light-hearted and unashamedly sentimental, and his large following found the book thoroughly to their liking. Even more to their taste was *Merry Hall*, an entertaining mixture in the manner of *Down the Garden Path*. The *Times Literary Supplement* described it as 'a piece of real and literary estate of the kind Mr Nichols knows so well how to develop and manage'. If he was repeating a past success, nobody minded and the book became a best-seller to prove it. Much the same applied to *A Pilgrim's Progress*, a new book on Christianity, which was *The Fool Hath Said* all over again.

Beverley still provided an element of controversy in his newspaper articles and, somewhat surprisingly, in the lectures he gave to audiences mostly consisting of his female devotees. The format was mostly warm and witty with more than a touch of show-business. Having entertained his audience, he would suddenly change mood in the final ten minutes and discuss the mistakes he had made in his life.

When I have been proved wrong, I have always admitted it, and I have done so, wherever possible, quite openly and without reserve. Perhaps it is for this reason that the critics, in addition to accusing me of illiteracy, have often accused me of inconsistency, because it is not profitable to admit one's mistakes; it is wiser to follow the example of those writers who lie low and say nothing, in the hope that the dust will gather on the library shelves and cover up their early follies. That, I think I can say in all honesty, has not been my way. The second thing I can say in my defence is that I have been consistent in one thing and that is my belief that the one unforgivable crime, indeed I would say the only true crime, is cruelty.

He ended with a dramatic plea for sexual tolerance.

Maybe the problem of sex is the greatest test of all. My own feeling is that, in matters of sex, we are still living in the dark ages. There is only one question to ask when you are sitting in judgement on a matter of sex and that is: is it or is it not cruel? In some cases, needless to say, the answer will be a very grim affirmative and when it is a question of an offence against a child, or any assault by violence, I would like to see the penalties not merely enforced but increased in severity. But in other cases where the answer is no, I fail to see why the sexual behaviour of others should be of the faintest concern to anybody but the people involved. There are hundreds of defenceless people shut up in prison for behaving as God made them. And it is not for society to pass judgement on God's creatures, even though society may not always understand them.

Other voices were, of course, saying similar things but to Beverley's audiences the final message came not only as a surprise but also, possibly, as a painful one; it was not what they expected to hear from a popular author. As he was a potential victim of the law then himself, it was brave and dangerous to speak out so uncompromisingly. He was one of the few famous men who happened to be homosexual who dared to do so, for the attitude towards them did not begin to change until the late 1950s.

On 12 December 1952, Beverley wrote in his diary that he had been given a ticket for the coronation of Queen Elizabeth at Westminster Abbey:

Only one ticket is allotted to the entire group of Kemsley Newspapers, which includes the *Sunday Times*, the *Sunday Chronicle*, etc. etc. and this ticket is to go to me.

I think this may be regarded as a feather in my cap. It is certainly a long way from my days when, as a beginner in Fleet Street, I stood on the doorsteps of burglars [sic], in the hope of interviewing them at two guineas per thousand words.

I also think Lord Kemsley is quite right to choose me. I shall probably make a better job of it than any living writer. Charles Morgan would be distinguished but dull. T.S. Eliot would be inhuman. Somerset Maugham's eyes would remain too dry. Neither Evelyn Waugh nor Graham Greene, even if they were not debarred by their Catholic faith, are good enough reporters.

My report will be syndicated all over the world. I propose to take endless trouble with it. I shall go to the Abbey early in the New Year to find out which seat I am to occupy. I shall sit in it soaking up the atmosphere. In short, I must do so much preliminary work that even if there was no Coronation at all, I should be able to write the article.

The piece he subsequently wrote was highly praised for its skill by Lord Kemsley.

Further excerpts from his diary provide a picture of the style of life Beverley enjoyed at this period.

16 December. Went to Noel's play [*Quadrille*] with Cyril. Supper with the Lunts afterwards [Alfred Lunt and Lynn Fontanne]. The critics had slashed Noel so mercilessly that we feared an embarrassing evening; it was not like that at all. It is not a great play, but it is a pleasant story with great dexterity; there were no longueurs and it had for me a charming 'patine' and a nostalgic fragrance.

The Lunts of course were superb. Lynn must be sixty, she looked a blooming thirty. They almost burst into tears when we told them we loved the play, and when they saw that we meant it.

A delicious supper at the house they have rented in Chapel Street. We had borsch and grouse and ice cream with little almond cakes that Alfred had made himself. He adores his food but is worried about his figure. Lynn made him try on the fancy waistcoat I was wearing, a very gay little number in claret-coloured silk. It became him, so she is going to get him one for Christmas.

I went to bed composing the letter I shall write to Noel tomorrow. 'Noel, my poppet, this is to tell you that all British critics are insane . . .' It is fun writing letters to Noel.

19 December. There were seven hundred people at today's Foyle's Luncheon at the Dorchester. I was chairman and had to stand shaking hands with all of them. It was very easy to shake but not so easy to unshake: some of the women clung to me as though one were a life-buoy. The luncheon was in honour of Aunt Aggie [Baroness Stoeckl] and Violet Stuart-Wortley, both of whom had written books.

21 December. Dinner at Coppins with the Duchess of Kent. She asked me to spend the day but I couldn't as I had guests of my own for luncheon at home. So I arrived at cocktail time.

Nobody else there at first except Princess Olga, Princess Alexandra and the young Duke [son of the Duchess]. The Duchess was looking lovelier than ever. She seems to have a way of wearing jewels which seems to give them an extra lustre.

When you wish to 'wash your hands' at Coppins there is a special convention to enable you to do so with the minimum of embarrassment. It is called 'seeing the statue of King Edward'. There is a large marble bust which stands just facing the door of the lavatory in the hall.

23 December. Cyril and I spent an enchanting Christmas week with the Bromley-Davenports at Capesthorne Hall in Cheshire. Half of Capesthorne is beautiful, half ugly. The ugly part consists of the main centre block which was rebuilt in 1860 after a disastrous fire. It looks like Euston Station. Let us hope there is a special corner of hell for Victorian architects. The rest of the building, about 1720, is simple and good. But it is all far, far too large. As for the gardens with their immense deserted conservatories, their endless acres of neglected lawns, their wide, wild lakes, one's heart sinks at the thought of tackling it.

What will happen to such places? What can happen? It would be understaffed with twenty servants; as it is there is a valet and his wife, a Spanish maid, an old nanny and a lady who cooks. The grounds need a dozen gardeners and half a dozen woodsmen; there is one gardener and an Italian labourer!

Walter [Bromley-Davenport], bless his heart, goes round switching off lights and seeing we do not burn too many logs on the library fire. I was so touched by this that I went out into the blistering cold and collected a huge pile of dead wood, so we were really warm on Christmas Eve.

Our celebrations were suitably feudal. I have memories of sitting after dinner while carol singers, thirty or forty at a time, came in from the neighbouring districts, pink with cold, to entertain us. And of a Christmas tree that stretched to the ceiling, hung with presents for 150 children of the tenants. Walter's son and heir, a blond young giant of seventeen with a most engaging grin, was Father Christmas. After the presents were given and a conjurer had performed, the party seemed to flag, so I went to the piano and organized musical bumps. It was fun.

5 January 1953. Today just as it was growing dark I saw Charles Graves standing in a bus queue outside the Piccadilly Hotel. He looked shabby, cold and antique. I surmise that he is not doing too well. He is no longer a star journalist. I wish I could say that I was sorry. I am not. In a sense, I launched Charles Graves for it was to him that I handed over *Isis* when I got bored with it at Oxford. He at once became bumptious. Two terms later (when I was President of the Union) he bounced into my room and offered me the job of dramatic critic on *Isis*, the paper of which I had previously been editor!

Graves was always jealous of me. Rightly. When I began the feature 'Page 2' on the *Sunday Chronicle*, he went to Jimmy Drawbell, the editor, and said, 'You've made yourself the laughing stock of Fleet Street. I give Nichols three weeks.'

Having written these words, I do feel sorry for Graves. He had many advantages that I lacked. The physique of a carthorse. Important. A small private income. Very important. An utterly 'normal' mind, all the right responses to women, wealth and wine. Most important of all. I have fluctuating health, no private means, none of the right responses. But there is a thing called charm.

8 January. Tomorrow I go into St Mary's Paddington for an operation. I am frightened. No, I am not frightened. Yes, I am. Anti-climax of anti-climaxes. Or should it be anti-climaces? The operation is only for varicose veins. But hospitals are hideously deterrent places, they are so cold, so originally antiseptic. As one walks down their corridors one feels that there are people dying behind every door. Also, nurses do humiliating things to one.

So I go to St Mary's to submit to the knife. For what? Not for actual pain; I am not in pain. Nor for acute vanity; I am not such an idiot as to imagine that the perfection of my left leg is the decisive factor in any possible romance.

Then why? God knows.

It will cost thirty guineas. It is being done by a nice man called Dickson Wright who, apparently, never stops doing it.

I must remember to smuggle in a bottle of gin.

In 1953, Beverley's second Merry Hall book appeared to good reviews and a highly satisfactory public response. It concentrated on the house as opposed to the garden, as its title *Laughter on the Stairs* suggested. Again he rejected the grim realities of restoration, as he had done in *A Thatched Roof*, although there is a passing reference to the difficulties of the time with its shortage and control of building materials, and the restoration of his Georgian home to its former chaste elegance appeared to be a relatively painless process. The real story of Merry Hall had enough drama in it to put any sane man off the purchase of old properties for ever, but the facts that the strain nearly drove Beverley mad and the cost almost crippled him financially were put to one side in his fictionalized account of the process of rehabilitation. The book blossomed into a series of integrated episodes woven around fictional characters descended from Jane Austen by way of E.F. Benson. In his foreword to *The Gift of a Home* (1972), the collected edition of the Merry Hall books, he wrote:

One of the characters who seems to have most interested people is Marius, the amiable scholar who wanders through the pages dropping little scraps of knowledge as lightly as if he were taking part in a sort of literary paper-chase. Since his outstanding characteristic is his erudition I feel some embarrassment in confessing that Marius is really only a fictional extension of an aspect of myself. Although this sounds conceited it was merely a technical device for introducing a quantity of unusual material which might have been tedious if it had been presented in the first person singular. As we go through life most of us accumulate quite a large collection of miscellaneous curiosa – literary, musical, botanical, historical – and though these might have been incorporated in the text, or collected in an appendix, it seemed more amusing to gather them together in the brain of another man, and let him play with them as he pleased. As soon as I had conceived this idea, Marius began to become very real to me, as somebody quite outside myself.

Another character who has aroused curiosity is 'Our Rose', largely because so many readers claimed to have met her in their own lives. Well, of course, they had met her, if they had ever belonged to a provincial Garden Club or taken a course in Flower Arrangement. 'Our Rose' is a distillation of those thousands of ladies who have transformed the gay and careless art of flower arranging into a grim and exacting science, with formal rules and strict taboos, and serried legions of passionate contestants, hotly arguing about the precise angle at which a lupin may be placed in its appropriate vase.

'Miss Emily' was a deliberate foil to 'Our Rose', but again, when the books were published there were many readers who claimed to recognize her. She was a very English type – well-bred, down-to-earth, not overburdened with humour, inclined to be bossy. You can still meet her in many a country lane, tramping home to a luncheon of roast beef and Yorkshire pudding, with an elderly spaniel at her heels. I should be the first to admit that neither of these ladies was of an amiable disposition, and neither had much feminine allure. But I have a fondness for them. To adapt the old song . . . 'They may have been a headache, but they never were a bore.' To me, at any rate.

It was now three years since the publication of *Shadow of the Vine* and Beverley had almost given up hope of its ever being produced, when Peter Cotes rescued it from oblivion. Cotes, a man of emphatic views on the place of theatre in society, had pursued excellence rather than commercial success, though he had enjoyed commercial success also. He was something of a pioneer in post-war theatre, one of those who prepared the way for newcomers like John Osborne. By 1953, he was making his mark as an innovator in the still relatively new medium of television. Beverley was overjoyed by his interest and readily agreed that he should adapt and produce the play for the BBC.

It was transmitted on 17 March 1953 with a fine cast headed by Arthur Young and Catherine Lacey, and its impact was electrifying. Letters of appreciation poured into the BBC, many from viewers who identified with the situation described in the play, some of the most moving from women who had believed themselves to be unique in coping with and keeping secret the problems of being married to an alcoholic.

Beverley was now convinced that *Shadow of the Vine* was a hot property, but London managements were still reluctant to take a chance on it. Then the Repertory Players, a company of actors including Sir Ralph Richardson and Dame Sybil Thorndike, dedicated to giving one-off productions of new plays, decided to present it. After its television exposure it was not, strictly speaking, a new play, but those concerned were so convinced of its merits that this seemed a mere quibble. Nearly a year after Peter Cotes's production, the curtain went up at Wyndham's Theatre on Sunday 14 February 1954 to a packed and excited house, word having gone round the West End that this was to be a theatrical event of some importance. The audience was not disappointed. The play, directed by Joan Kemp-Welch, had an unusually strong cast headed by Eric Portman and Barbara Couper in the roles Beverley had based on his father and mother. The supporting male lead, based on Beverley himself, was played by the young Alec McCowen. When the curtain fell at the end of the play, there was a moment of silence and then the audience roared its approval. Cyril Butcher said, 'It was sheer hell being in the same house as Beverley during the rehearsal period. He could not face the thought of it failing. He wanted a triumph and he got it. At the end, I thought he'd have a heart attack from sheer joy.'

Alec McCowen described it as: 'One of the most exciting evenings I can remember. As a young actor, it was a big step up for me at the time. But Eric Portman's performance as the father was an astonishing tour-de-force. In the scene where he has DTs, it was terrifying being on the stage with him. And the cheering at the end – I'll never forget it.'

The dressing-room area was soon packed with people offering congratulations all round and Eric Portman, whose own dressing-room resembled a bar, was holding court. There seemed to be no doubt at all that the play would open for a run as soon as arrangements could be made. Wyndham's Theatre itself was out of the question because it was home to *The Boy Friend*, Sandy Wilson's musical success. For the next few weeks, while details were being worked out, Beverley tried to immerse himself in other things but it was impossible for him to get the play out of his mind. 'Suppose', he said to Cyril, 'it is so successful that it is done on Broadway? Should I rewrite it, set it in Boston?'

He was playing with the cats in the garden one morning when Gaskin brought out the post. Among the letters was one from Eric Portman, explaining that he was withdrawing from the play. It had taken him a week to decide, following an incident in his personal life which mirrored the central situation of the play. He could not face the strain of re-enacting it while he was so emotionally upset. He hoped Beverley would understand and forgive him. Understanding for Portman was one thing, but Beverley never entirely forgave him for snatching away what he believed to be his last opportunity to establish his reputation as a serious playwright. Other actors, of course, were capable of playing the role, but none available had the star status necessary to attract the public to a 'problem play' of this type. Without Eric Portman, the deal collapsed.

It was some consolation when Peter Cotes produced the play again the following year with Richard Bird and Joan Miller, this time on the commercial television network. The production of a modern play on both BBC and Independent Television in so short a time does not appear to have happened since. Once again, the reaction was startling: Dick Vosburgh, the writer for theatre, radio and television, then newly arrived from America, recalled the production in 1989. If others might equate Beverley's name with cosy charm, he equated it with the play's searing examination of alcoholism. He said, 'It made stunning and startling television. I did not know who this guy Nichols was. I thought he must be some brilliant young playwright the BBC had just discovered.'

As Cotes has put it, the effect upon the ratings was electric. Viewers again wrote to Beverley in their thousands, mostly wives distraught about their husbands' alcoholic problems. One of these letters said: 'How did you know there was murder in my heart?' – a question that haunted him for years and sowed the idea for *Father Figure*. He continued to hope that the play would eventually be produced in London, saying in 1982: 'The problem of alcoholism does not date. If anything, it is now worse than it used to be, but I suppose the play cuts too deep and managements are still scared of it. Perhaps when I die it will be rediscovered by an ambitious young director.'

For the second TV production, Beverley composed a piece of piano music which generated so much interest among viewers that Lawrence Wright Music published it as 'The Shadow Prelude'. This, together with 'The Song of the Willow', written for Melba and sung by Mary Ellis in the television version of *Evensong*, were the last of his compositions to be published.

Eric Glass, Beverley's agent, recalls that the Comédie Française planned to do *Shadow of the Vine* until they discovered that the author was still alive, for under their rules only the works of dead playwrights could be produced. They had at first believed the play to be a British classic which they had rediscovered – and in a sense they were right.

One of the highlights of Beverley's social year was a party at Merry Hall to celebrate the Regale lilies grown in the garden and banked in glorious display around the house. Photographs taken at these parties show celebrities of the day in full evening-dress, the lilies much in evidence and Gaskin hard at work with a cocktail shaker. According to Beverley, Gaskin was in his element on such occasions, scrubbing, polishing, and preparing a vast array of food. He always insisted that Beverley wore tails, and hung the suit in the dressing-room with a starched shirt prepared with its Cartier links and studs. Once Beverley revolted against this formality and insisted on wearing his more comfortable dinner jacket, but Gaskin sulked so dramatically that he dared not do so again.

Beverley needed very little excuse for a party but not all of them were as innocent as those celebrating the lilies. Looking back, he was appalled by the risks he ran with some of these gatherings, for discovery could have led to public ruin and even imprisonment. It was, he admitted, the frisson of danger which added to their appeal, a danger which reflected the social mores of the time. In 1953 a witch hunt against homosexuals instigated by his old antagonist, Sir David Maxwell Fyfe, now Home Secretary, culminated in the prosecution of Lord Montague, Michael Pitt-Rivers and Peter Wildeblood, the diplomatic correspondent of the *Daily Mail* for homosexual offences, and all three were imprisoned. It has never been entirely clear why the case was brought in the first place except, perhaps, as a warning to others, but it prompted the publication of an interim report by the Church of England Moral Welfare Council, which had been studying the problem of homosexuality. This report called for a change in the law (which, it claimed, failed to act as a deterrent and encouraged blackmail, suicide and the corruption of the police) and for an immediate official enquiry. In the House of Commons, Beverley's old friend Bob Boothby, now Sir Robert, persistently pressed for a Royal Commission on the subject, which Maxwell Fyfe refused. Later, however, he was forced to agree, and thus began the long process which led to changes in the law.

Beverley, his crusading instincts aroused by the Montague case, secretly formed an unofficial action committee consisting of several well-known public figures, and proposed that homosexual and bisexual men in prominent positions should declare their sexuality in a full-page advertisement in *The Times* packed with their names. This plan was doomed to failure, for the Montague case had instilled terror among those he hoped to recruit; indeed, a number of them left the country. It was pointed out to him that his plan could prove counter-productive, and could lead to a nation-wide witch hunt even more repressive than Senator McCarthy's un-American horror circus which was than at its height. Beverley was determined to make a public gesture on his own account and damn the consequences, until Gaskin told him not to be a bloody fool. Brought down to earth by Gaskin's common sense and by the pleadings of others, he did not proceed further.

Merrily rolling along

1954–1956

EVERLEY was a fan of the English detective novel and often
contemplated writing one. Then fate presented him with an experience which sparked off an idea. After a holiday in the South of
France, and following a long last-night dinner-party with Rita Hayworth
and Aly Khan, he boarded a plane for Paris, feeling weary and liverish.
Anticipating an uncomfortable flight, he took two tranquillizers and fell
into a fitful sleep. When the plane landed, he hurried to the airport reception
area and enquired about taxis. The official seemed surprised: '*Vous allez en
ville, monsieur?*' Beverley replying that he was indeed, he was asked what part
of the town he was going to. Bewildered, he answered, The Champs-
Elysées. '*Mais Les Champs-Elysées, monsieur, c'est à Paris!*' Beverley stared at
the official in astonishment – was the man stupid? Then the man added, '*Ici,
monsieur, c'est Lyons!*' The plane had lost time against headwinds and had
landed in Lyons to refuel. Recovering his wits, Beverley reached the plane
just as it was about to take off.

This uncanny incident nagged at him. He could have sworn he had
landed at Paris – but then his half-awake state, the anonymity of airports
and the similarity of the general ambiance had deceived him. Suppose, he
asked himself, a killer planned a murder in location A but set up an alibi
with attendant witnesses in location B which had been dressed to look
like the place of the murder? Like all such ideas, making it credible to a
reader proved difficult, but he was determined to make it work. He
chose for his setting a nondescript flat in a dull back street of Chelsea, not
unlike the flat he rented for his sexual encounters with guardsmen. The alibi
was set in Portsmouth in a similar flat in a similar street, using a city
he knew well for identical reasons. In the plot, the important witnesses
drove from a third location and arrived in Portsmouth, convinced that
they were in Chelsea, an idea that eventually worked extremely well.
When he had finished his preparation for the book, every surface in his
work room at Merry Hall was a clutter of charts, timetables and biographies
of his cast of characters. Gaskin was forbidden even to think of dusting

until the book was completed.

Some of the characters he assembled were based on people he knew: Dame Nellie Melba appeared, thinly disguised, as did Benjamin Frankel and Cyril Butcher, the latter cast somewhat unexpectedly as the killer. The amateur detective who, as convention demanded, was always one step ahead of the police, was himself, enclosed in the short, fat body of a benign-looking, middle-aged man, Horatio Green. He knew that, as Stephen Sondheim was to say in another context, 'You gotta have a gimmick,' and he gave Mr Green an extraordinarily acute sense of smell, but in every other respect it was an idealized portrait of himself. Mr Green was a knowledge-able gardener and a lover of music and cats, had a sharp intellect without being an overt intellectual, a strong sense of humour, and was always even-tempered and mild-mannered, a perfect gentleman. It was a self-portrait with which not all of his acquaintances would agree.

He called his detective novel *No Man's Land* but later changed the title to *No Man's Street*. It appeared in 1954 and was successful enough for him to start work on a second. In all, he wrote five of them over six years: *The Moonflower, Death To Slow Music, The Rich Die Hard* and *Murder by Request*. All of them had a strong biographical content but *The Rich Die Hard* more than the others, its main characters being based on his friends Dorothy and Geoffrey Hart and the setting being their Sussex mansion, Wych Cross Place. Apart from any other interest this book may have, it evokes the style of life lived by the well-to-do in the 1950s which the prevailing austerity scarcely touched. Beverley was particularly close to Dorothy Hart and grew even closer after Geoffrey Hart's death. She was considerably younger than Beverley and he became something of an uncle-figure in her life. Later, when he was in financial need, she came to his rescue but, being a sensible businesswoman, with a properly structured loan rather than with an outright gift.

The detective novels were successful financially in Britain and overseas. Somerset Maugham described Beverley as one of the 'big five' British mystery writers, an opinion which was useful for publicity. But after the fifth book, Beverley, bored by the meticulous planning that each demanded, ran out of inspiration. It was not a literary genre that came easily to him, which was a great pity for, had he been able to continue, his financial position would certainly have been easier in the years to come. It appeared that Beverley had captured a new following with his mystery novels, but those readers showed no interest in his other work. Conversely, many who adored his home and garden books were indifferent to Mr Green. It was the price he paid for his versatility.

In January 1955 Beverley sailed, on the SS *United States*, for Jamaica where he was to be the guest of Edward Molyneux, the fashion designer. One of his fellow passengers was Evelyn Waugh with whom he had more than a passing acquaintance. He still retained a lingering suspicion that Waugh's *Vile Bodies* had been derived from his own success, *Crazy Pavements*, and knew from past experience that he could expect Waugh to be charming, or caustic, or patronizing, depending on his mood. Beverley, a self-proclaimed poseur, thought he recognized a fellow practitioner and dubbed him 'The Waugh of the Poses'.

In 1944 they had once found themselves staying together at Easton Court, an hotel in Devon to which they had retreated to write. Beverley was working on *The Tree That Sat Down* and Waugh on *Brideshead Revisited*. They shared a table at meal times and Beverley entertained Waugh with stories about Noel Coward, Somerset Maugham and Ivor Novello. The encounter gave him an anecdote about Waugh at his grandest. One evening, Waugh returned a fork that was not quite clean and remarked in all seriousness that he trusted the time would never come when his son had no servant to clean the silver. With the world in turmoil as war raged, Beverley thought the remark a grotesque pomposity. It encapsulated, he later said, both Waugh's weakness and his strength.

Waugh joined Beverley for dinner on the first night on SS *United States* and patronized him insufferably. He announced that he was going to stay with Lord Brownlow, and when Beverley explained that he was to stay with Edward Molyneux, exclaimed, 'The ladies' dressmaker!' in a tone reserved for tradespeople. He then asked if Beverley knew many dressmakers. As it happened, Beverley did: Chanel, Balmain, Schiaparelli, Hartnell and Balenciaga among them. 'One meets them from time to time,' he replied cautiously. 'Does one?' Waugh said drily. 'Do they stick pins in themselves, I wonder?' To Beverley's surprise, when the conversation turned to unemployment, it was clear that Waugh felt deeply on the subject; he spoke with knowledge and sincerity, although his contribution to the conversation was somewhat patrician, as if he were 'George V composing a note to his cabinet in the '30s'. Beverley, who also felt passionately about the unemployed, used the word 'underdog' which for some reason pained Waugh. Next day, when they met on deck just after Beverley had been below to see the animals who were leading a lonely life temporarily separated from their owners, Waugh enquired, 'Have you been to see the under-doggies?' He seemed delighted with his witticism and, from then on, dragged the 'under-doggies' into future conversations on the slightest pretext. 'I felt as if he thought of me as a figure of fun from one of his novels,' said Beverley. 'I not only wrote for the popular press which he apparently despised but I was also sentimental about dogs, not to mention cats.'

When Sunday came, Waugh, an ardent Catholic convert, went to Mass, or 'Marse' as he called it, while Beverley attended the Protestant service. Afterwards Waugh asked him sarcastically if he had said a little prayer for the 'under-doggies'. Beverley replied very firmly, 'Yes.' Waugh instantly changed his mood and said, simply and without irony, 'That was very nice of you.' For a fleeting moment Beverley thought he detected a hint of affection between them. However, Waugh then lectured him on the superiority of the 'Marse' as opposed to the Protestant practice, and for the rest of the voyage subjected him to what Beverley called Waugh's satiric genius. Afterwards Beverley claimed that he bore no resentment toward his tormentor – that despite it all, he actually liked him. In fact, the reverse was true.

Waugh's opinion of Beverley was uncompromising. In his diary entry for 21 May 1944, written at the Easton Court Hotel, he drew a lacerating pen-portrait of Beverley, describing him as, among other things, a 'flibbertigibbet'. In a letter written in 1955 on the SS *United States*, Waugh mentioned that there were several members of White's Club on board including Beverley, whom he dismissed as a poor old journalist, so vain that he wept with disappointment that the weather was too bad for him to acquire a suntan.

Beverley, of course, was not the only person subjected to Waugh's 'satiric genius', but he reacted badly to it. He often denigrated Waugh verbally, and after Waugh's death in writing also. His criticisms were not aimed at Waugh's capacities as a writer, for which he admired him, but for his failings as a man. The relationship might have been different if Beverley had stood up to him and tried a touch of grandeur and the 'satiric genius' of which he also was capable when he chose. The trouble was that he wanted to be liked and admired.

In 1982, Beverley said: 'Waugh imagined himself to be a grandee, always dreaming of marble halls and an aristocratic background. The joke was that he was physically miscast for the role. He was short, with a big bottom and a paunch, a stubby nose and clumsy workman's hands. A plebeian figure with aristocratic pretensions. He could be so unpleasant, as if being pleasant might lead him into sin. It took me years to realize he was a sad man. We might have been friends if he had not been so trapped in guilt. I don't mean about the book [*Vile Bodies*] but about his life. I suppose it had something to do with his brand of religion, or rather his interpretation of it.'

After a long interval, Beverley had begun to keep a detailed diary again.

Three a.m. Saturday 17 December 1955. If this diary is ever written at all, it will be because I suffer from insomnia. A few hours ago I was chasing around the kitchens of Kensington Palace holding a black kitten in my arms and explaining to Princess Olga of Yugoslavia the importance of providing it with a box of sand in order that it might powder its nose with propriety.

Upstairs in the drawing-room the Duchess of Kent was waiting to play

Scrabble. 'We shall have to go back,' said Princess Olga, 'and let it out into the garden.' 'You don't think it will get lost, ma'am?' 'No. And tomorrow I shall see it is provided with a box.'

So back we went and I opened the French windows. At length the kitten returned with great dignity and went over to the fire and sat on the rug of Queen Anne needlework and proceeded to wash its face. At last we could get on with Scrabble. It is a delightful game, the ladies played it extremely well. At any rate they beat me hollow.

We had spent the earlier part of the evening at *Richard III* [the film starring Laurence Olivier]. I called for the Duchess at seven and she showed me over the Palace. [She had only been living there a few weeks.] I thought she had done it with flair and imagination. 'This is the first time I have ever decorated entirely on my own,' she said. In the hall hangs a Laszlo portrait of the Duchess's mother, Princess Nicholas of Greece, painted as she was when I first saw her in Athens years and years ago. Even then, her eyes used to frighten me; she seemed to be staring into the future and to be seeing great tragedy ahead. Laszlo had caught that expression.

19 December. Well, I have delivered the kitten's present (a tree trunk mounted on a wooden block, on which it can scratch its claws. You can buy them at Harrods for fifteen shillings). And I hope it will be a success. I could not draw the card so George Anderson [a young Canadian artist and a close friend] drew it for me. He painted the kitten sitting on a cushion of royal purple, with a very grand crown on its head, inset with sequins. We tied the card to the scratch block with gold ribbon and I took it up to London in the car.

The policeman looked at me suspiciously when I drove up to the Palace. It is of course a private road. However he was most co-operative when he learned what it was all about. Bysouth, the butler, seemed delighted. The scratch block, he was sure, would help eliminate any cause of friction.

20 December. I seem to have been doing nothing but handing out £5 notes all day. Let me put them on record so that next year I can compare expenses.

Two to Gaskin £10

One to Ted [Edward Weston, Secretary]. £5

I feel I ought to give Ted more but I am going to give him a watch as soon as Hutchinsons pay the advance on *Death to Slow Music*. Also I have just given him my old television set.

One each to Judy and Jill [nieces] £10

One to Page [gardener]. I am also giving him a very nice
camellia.   £5
One to Miss Herridge. Again it is not very much but she has
recently had a legacy. So perhaps that excuses me.   £5
Three others to people I won't mention, not even in this diary   £15
That makes £50 in fivers alone, and in order to have £50 I have to earn
£150! That is only a drop in the ocean compared with all other Christmas
expenses. It really is dreadful and makes me wonder how long it can go
on. But unless I pension off Gaskin and go and live in a hut I do not see
how I can possibly cut down any more.

21 December. This morning a note arrived in the Duchess's handwriting
from the kitten of Kensington Palace to the cats of Merry Hall thanking
them for the wonderful claw-scratching log with many purrs and
presenting its 'relations' with the compliments of the season.

The Duchess's note with its reference to 'relations' established the
fact that the cats of Merry Hall are of the blood royal. Perhaps that accounts for the behaviour of 'Four' who refused to eat his morning's fish.

22 December. Christmas cards are arriving in stacks. I told Ted to count
them this afternoon. 633 – which must be a record. It makes me feel very
guilty, because I only send out 120 of my Cat Calendars. But even at the
wholesale price that means another £18, and it all mounts up.

How very Scroogy that sounds. However, it is written, so let it stand.
Perhaps one is really a Scrooge at heart.

A lot of the Christmas cards come from people to whom I never send
them. Aly Khan, for example. Why does Aly always send me one, when I
never return the compliment? I think he must have a secretary, with a list.
But that is being Scroogy again. Perhaps Aly really likes to send me a
Christmas card. Perhaps he even addresses it himself. This is an awful and
most guilt-making thought. Supposing Aly were sitting all alone, in the
splendour of the Château de l'Horizon, waiting and waiting for the
knock of the 'facteur' who would bring him my Cat Calendar . . . and it
never came? It makes me feel like rushing down to the post office and
sending an expensive telegram.

One should not assume – as I always do – that people who pay one
compliments, or do one kindnesses, are actuated solely by a motive of
pity. It is this damned inferiority complex that haunts me always . . . and
sometimes makes me behave outrageously. I am going to puff out my
chest and say 'Aly Khan sent me a Christmas card because he esteems
me.' 'Esteem' is a nice comforting word – a hot-water-bottle of a verb.

All the same, it is not a very nice Christmas card. It is a photograph of a
lot of horses winning something at Deauville. No – not something – the

Grand Prix. If the horses were frosted I should like them better.

The nicest Christmas cards come from people with lovely pictures . . . Gavin [Lord Faringdon] has sent a photograph of his Rembrandt and the Bromley-Davenports have sent a photograph of their Bicci di Lorenzo and Christabel [The Dowager Lady Aberconway] a photograph of her Cézanne, and Vivian Ellis . . .

Mais là . . . c'est une histoire!

1 January 1956. The commercial television people approached me today, asking me to sign up for another series of personal appearances. This time in the afternoon, and 65 guineas instead of 50 guineas. I turned them down, brusquely.

I do not see why I should be stuck on at these unearthly hours. If anybody wants to see me at all, which is improbable – inferiority complex again – they can damn well see me at a civilized hour, after the day's work, by their firesides, with a glass of something stronger than Bovril beside them. My first three appearances were at eleven-thirty in the morning, which is hardly the moment for a star. (One must pretend to be a star, to one's secret self, even when one knows one isn't.)

But seriously, it is depressing to go through all that – to be made up, to be rehearsed, to blink in the glare of lights – in the almost certain knowledge that all these antics are for the benefit of a smattering of personal friends, a handful of invalids, and a few stray people who have switched on their sets by mistake.

I felt this so strongly, on my second appearance, that I made an impromptu crack about it, which did not at all please the producer. I looked straight into the camera and began, 'When I think of the countless dozens of people who are watching me . . .' The camera men grinned; the producer didn't. It was the sort of remark that needs production. But then, everything and everybody needs production. The longer I live the more I realize the vital importance of production. You can take a moron and spot him or her in the right light, with the right music and, lo!, a star is born. It is a terrifying thought.

2 January. This morning I finished the fifth of my Preludes. In case I ever get bored with this diary and put it away in a drawer, and forget about it until I am an old man rummaging among a lot of yellowing documents, let me remind myself that I am engaged in writing Twenty-Four Preludes for the Pianoforte. The number, of course, is deliberately provocative; it is a challenge to myself, and a wide-open target for the critics, if any, who will eventually hear them. Chopin wrote 24 preludes; Beverley Nichols writes 24 preludes. The insolence of it!

I played the first four of them to Ivor Newton at Dorothy's [Hart] party. Ivor is not a great pianist, but he is a first-class musician, and most of the great singers of the past thirty years owe him a debt of gratitude for his exquisitely sensitive accompaniments. His reaction to the Preludes was almost embarrassing. He expressed it in German. He said he was 'begeistered'.

This was not the first public performance of the preludes. I had already played Number 3 on one of my ridiculous morning television programmes, about two months ago. I was so nervous that I made a complete hash of it. I got as far as the sixteenth bar and couldn't go on, so in sheer panic I modulated back to the beginning and began all over again. When I reached the sixteenth bar for the second time I stuck once more, like a horse jibbing to a gate. There was nothing to do but to improvise an entirely new development, on the spur of the moment, choosing phrases that would fit my trembling fingers. This, it seems, I managed to do, for at the end of the programme they all crowded round and said what a charming little piece it was, and asked me to repeat it. I don't think they believed me when I told them that I had not the faintest idea what I had been playing.

But it was a lesson – ye Gods! – it was a lesson! Never, never appear in public until your technique is one hundred and one per cent perfect. Ninety-nine per cent is not good enough, one hundred per cent is not good enough. You must have the extra one per cent – like Mr Micawber's extra penny [sic], or the result is misery.

3 January. Today I picked up a copy of the *TV Times* and saw an interview with Willie. It was headed 'Mr Somerset Maugham Looks at Life' – or something equally banal. I usually skip interviews with Willie; very few of the hundreds of reporters who pester him have the faintest idea of what sort of man he really is, or what he is really thinking. They don't even begin to understand what makes him tick, and they would probably be alarmed if they did.

In this interview Willie named me as one of the three masters of the detective story whose works gave him the most pleasure. At the risk of sounding ungrateful, I think that was the least he could do. When my last detective novel was published – *The Moonflower* – Willie wrote me an unsolicited letter in which he praised it in terms rather warmer than he recently employed for the works of Dostoievsky. Maybe that is an exaggeration, but he really went off the deep end about *The Moonflower*. That was very nice of him, and very encouraging, but when I wrote to thank him, and asked if I could possibly quote a phrase or two from his letter in advertisements, he wrote back 'No'. Which was neither nice nor encouraging. However, I suppose that Willie is always being asked for testimonials.

4 January. Eartha Kitt appeared on television for ten minutes last night, after a fanfare of Fleet Street trumpets which would not have been inadequate for the Day of Judgement. Perhaps, in a sense, it was a day of judgement. A nation gets the entertainment it deserves, and what we got last night was a young coloured woman with a husky voice singing 'I Wanna be Evil'. Miss Kitt has an adequate articulation, an effective command of gesture, and a limited but not utterly discordant vocal organ. She is neither pretty nor plain, and she looks as if she might be quite a good cook. This 'wanna be evil' is really an adolescent notion and the fact that it has swept the USA is only another proof that America is still an adolescent nation. It is when they start to sing 'I wanna be good' that we must look out for trouble.

One last word about Kitt. Apparently she reads 'the classics' and 'works of philosophy'. Maybe she does. For all I know, she may keep the Bhagavadgita in her bathroom. But I am getting a little tired of cabaret singers who are really terribly refined at heart. If, reaching the conclusion of Plato's Symposium, a girl's only impulse is to dress up in sequins and sing 'I Wanna be Evil', it is pardonable to conclude that some of the finer points of the Symposium may perhaps have evaded her.

5 January. This morning's 'Daily Express' carried a three-column splash 'DONALD MACLEAN'S BROTHER IN ROW AT CLUB'. With it went a large picture of Alan with the caption 'Travellers' Club member Alan Maclean . . . the Secretary was helped to a car.'

Poor Alan! It really is rather hard on him. Now everybody will go about saying 'Look at those mad Macleans – always getting into trouble – feckless, unstable, etc.' Yet from the 'Express' account it seems to have been a silly squabble in the hall in which somebody got kicked. It will brighten up the Travellers', and I only wish people would start kicking each other in the Garrick. We could do with a little light relief. I would pay the price of a stage box to see Charles Morgan take a running leap at J.B. Priestley. No, the price of two stage boxes. In fact, if it were a really hard kick on that complacent bottom, I'd buy the whole theatre.

I probably know more about the fabulous Burgess-Maclean mystery than most of the journalists who have made their fortunes out of it, for the simple reason that for over a year Alan Maclean took refuge in my little bungalow in the orchard and . . . well . . . we drank together of an evening and talked, and a journalist, if he is unscrupulous, can turn such occasions to good account. I saw no reason for doing so. I wasn't that hard up. And to me, the whole tragedy – or rather, my personal reaction to it – was conditioned by one remark which Alan made, on a December evening, sitting by the log fire in my music-room. He stared into the fire and then he turned to me. 'You see, Beverley,' he said, 'I loved my brother.' Some of the journalists who have pestered him and nagged him and persecuted his mother – an enchanting old lady – might have hesitated, before dipping their pens into their poisonous pots, if they had heard him say that.

One summer afternoon, Alan's mother came down to have luncheon with him at the little bungalow. Afterwards we all met in the orchard and made bonfires and burned grass, and I was intensely happy. A blue sky, charming people, and a dear, sad old lady, sitting on the trunk of a fallen apple tree, smiling at us with a smile that I felt was none too frequent nowadays.

12 January. Today I lunched at the Savoy with ten charming young girls from the provinces, who had been chosen by *Woman's Own* as typical of the ideal British girl – or something like that.

I am a fool about names. I sat next to a very charming woman who seemed vaguely familiar and it was not till I was driving home that I realized that she was Jeanne Heal [a household TV name at the time]. I wrote her the following letter:

Dear Jeanne Heal,
Driving home last night I did a double take – I suddenly realized who you were! It is best to be honest about it, for you must have thought me both stupid and impolite at luncheon.

How to account for this strange 'lapsus memoriae' I have no idea. One partial explanation may be that you do in fact look younger off the screen than on; another is that I am half-witted about people's names.

The strange thing about it is that I am, in fact, one of your most ardent fans; indeed, when I was last in New York I gave a long interview in which I named your programme the most intelligent and vital feature which British television had yet given us.

I hope this conduct doesn't mean that some awful mental decay is beginning.

I have one small consolation – and it is indeed a very small one – in the fact that you have never heard of my detective stories. There is no sort of reason why you should. However, as I believe you enjoy such trifles, I am asking my publishers to send you copy of *The Moonflower*, with my very genuine admiration.

And I shall quite understand if, on our next meeting, you cut me dead, or, even worse, address me as Mr Winn.

13 January. Today I lunched with Ava [The Viscountess Waverley] at her very pretty house in Lord North Street. Only two others – the French

Ambassador, Chauvel, and Ted Seago, the painter. We all arrived on the doorstep at the same time. Ava had been taking the ambassador to shop at the Caledonian Market. He had bought an opaline necklace (£2), a jet bracelet (15s), two Victorian glass vases for lamp shades (£1), and a papier-mâché powder box (12s). He seemed enchanted with these purchases, which he had carried away in paper bags.

Ava raised the question of foreign ambassadors and British charities. It seems that the energetic London ladies who arrange charity balls and concerts never cease pestering the ambassadors for subscriptions. She is very indignant about it. 'Whenever I am asked to organize anything,' she said, 'I tell them that I shall be delighted so long as I can be assured that none of the ambassadors will be asked to subscribe. I always get the same reply; they won't accept my conditions because the ambassadors are one of their chief sources of revenue. It seems to me quite monstrous. We have enough rich men of our own without dunning the representatives of other countries.'

Ted Seago said he was inundated with requests from charities to give them pictures. 'What's more,' he said, 'I am expected to pay for the frames, which cost about £20 apiece.' This made me feel that I was lucky only to be asked for books. All the same, I wish that these people would realize that authors have not an inexhaustible supply of their own books to give away. I get six copies of a book on its publication. After that, I have to pay cash for them.

26 January. With Ava to the ballet. John Waverley is one of the big noises at Covent Garden, so as usual we have the royal box. A very small party. Lord and Lady Moran and a charming lady of a certain age.

The royal box is wide and deep and behind it there is a small room where we dine during the intervals. This is a most agreeable way of seeing the ballet. A cocktail during the overture – then we take our places, just as the curtain is going up. Consommé and a glass of wine after the first act, chicken after the second, a sweet and coffee when it is all over. Perhaps it is for this reason that I saw *Coppelia* through rose-coloured spectacles.

The gentlemen's 'withdrawing rooms', attached to the royal box, are downstairs. There are two of them, and they have a heavy air of Edwardian luxury. In the further room, dominating it like a sort of sanitary cenotaph, is what might be described as the Private Toilet of King Edward VII. It is a remarkable piece of furniture, like a miniature corner cupboard, in mahogany, marble and china. Indeed, you would be excused for thinking it was a corner cuboard . . . until you stand on it. And then, hey presto, the doors of the cupboard slide open, and there is a hiss of water, and that is that. All very elegant and nostalgic.

When we had finished our supper, and the ladies were getting into their cloaks, I went back to the box to fetch my hat. The great theatre was still brilliantly lit. In its silence and desertion it was strangely impressive. I thought it as beautiful as a jewel. But it should have a chandelier – a giant affair like the one at La Scala. 'Why don't you put up an enormous chandelier?' I asked Lord Waverley. 'Because it would bring down the roof,' he replied tersely.

7 February. Dined with Vivian Cox, who produced the film 'Lost', which is now running at the Gaumont, Haymarket. His French colleague was also there.

He told me a good story about Somerset Maugham, when they were filming *Quartette* [sic], in which Maugham made a personal appearance as a commentator. The studio went to endless trouble to reproduce Maugham's study at the Villa Mauresque. They even got special artists to paint reproductions of Braque and Gauguin and Utrillo – very brilliantly too. They ransacked London for duplicates of rugs and fabrics. They painted a life-like reproduction of the view through the window. They made an exact copy of his desk, his chairs and all his paraphernalia. Then they waited breathlessly for his arrival, to know what he would think of it.

The old gentleman arrived on the dot and was conducted to the studio, where a crowd of technicians stood watching him in silence. He stared around him and blinked, but said nothing. Then he walked to the chair and felt the arms of it, which they had even made to appear worn with wear. Then he looked slowly all round the room and said one word – 'Christ!'

18 February. I dined with the Duchess of Kent at Kensington Palace. Alas! The little black kitten has disappeared. The Duchess was very sad about it, and hopes that it may come back one day. They had all grown very fond of it. However, it did not take to the scratching tree. She took it and scraped its paws down it, but it firmly folded its fists – if kittens can do that – and refused to co-operate. After dinner we played canasta with great concentration until one o'clock in the morning. We played for a penny a hundred. I had the Duchess as my partner, and at the end of the evening we had won 2s 2d, which was most satisfactory.

29 February. I went with Christabel [The Dowager Lady Aberconway] to *The Wild Duck* last night. Dorothy Tutin gave a heart-rending performance, and the whole production was most rewarding. Ibsen makes Shaw look very cheap. There is more brilliant characterization in this one play than in the whole of Shaw's work. Afterwards we went back

to North Audley Street for supper.

A very nice letter arrived today from Willie Maugham, in reply to one I had written to him about *Death to Slow Music*. It contained a remark which I think is vintage Willie . . . 'It doesn't matter who you sleep with, the important thing is who you wake up with.'

Now that I quote that, I am not so sure if it is vintage Willie, but it certainly might have come out of *Our Betters*.

6 March. Great gloom, and great worry about money. I make an income considerably larger than the Prime Minister of this country, but what happens? Nothing. It is impossible to save. Taxation takes it all. Today I signed a cheque to the Commissioners of Inland Revenue for £1,756 10s 11d. As I did so I had a sharp pain, just above the navel. Whether this is a sign of age, parsimony, or honest indignation I do not know. But really, it does seem monstrous. It means that during all those months when I was sweating over 'The Moonflower' I was really providing a lot of nasty little children – other people's children – with soft seats in charabancs on their way to school. I didn't go to school in a charabanc. I had to walk.

However, economies are being initiated. Last week I went through the wine accounts with Gaskin. It seems that we spend an astonishing amount on soda-water. So I rang up Geoffrey [The Hon. Geoffrey Cunliffe] and offered him £10 for his soda-water machine. This is a rather sinister object, a sort of immense cylinder, covered with rust, which he keeps in the stables. In spite of its appearance, it produces excellent soda-water . . . at least it has always done so when I have been up to his house for drinks. Geoffrey accepted the offer and the machine was installed. It took up a great deal of room in the kitchen, but it produced three delicious bottles of soda-water. They were so good that they demanded a great deal of whisky to go with them. I was just calculating that the machine would have paid for itself by 1961, when there was a tremendous explosion. I rushed out to the kitchen to find Gaskin in a shell-shocked condition, surrounded by broken glass, with three terrified cats balancing on the top of the plate rack. So much for economy.

14 May. Visit to Fort Belvedere. Gerald Lascelles told me that the Duke of Windsor had been so fond of the Fort that on some occasions when he had returned to England he had gone down, in secret, and prowled around the deserted gardens and through the overgrown shrubberies. It is a sad little picture, and more endearing than those he usually offers to the public.

On the same night I dined with Lady Aberconway. Talking of the Fort reminded her of when the Prince of Wales, as he then was, went to stay at Bodnant. He arrived at half-past six, having had a day that would have exhausted the ordinary man, beginning at nine o'clock without a let-up, opening exhibitions, receiving honorary degrees, etc. He walked round the gardens from 6.30 to 10.30. He then had supper and talked till 1.30. When he at last went to bed, to everybody's relief, he proceeded to walk up and down the bedroom for over an hour, practising the bagpipes. A pleasing example of the royal passion for the arts.

1 June. I went into the Garrick Club, which was as usual empty in the afternoon, and there I saw Alan Pryce-Jones, who is Editor of *The Times Literary Supplement*. He told me that he had put up Edward Hulton for membership, and that he had been asked to withdraw his name. This struck me as really monstrous. I'm not all that fond of Edward Hulton, but he is an intelligent man, he owns considerable interests in Fleet Street, and he happens to be a millionaire. As soon as I heard this, I went out into the hall and signed my name on his proposal sheet . . . which was already very amply covered with distinguished signatures. When I got home, I wrote a letter to him expressing my indignation. I told him that he was in very good company. Among the people who have been blackballed from the Garrick Club are Henry Irving, Bernard Shaw, Sir Charles Cochran, Noel Coward and a great many others.

4 June. I had a rather snobbish luncheon party here today. I don't know why I should call it snobbish, but it began with the Duchess of Grafton writing to me and proposing herself. She is great fun. Very tall, very alive to what is going on around her . . . she is one of those women who have antennae. Not embarrassing antennae . . . she does not send out tentacles into one's mind . . . it is just that you feel she is intensely sensitive to what is going on around her. That is why she is such fun to talk to. If one were an actor, and if one could fill the theatre with a thousand Duchesses of Grafton, one would have the time of one's life. A flick of the finger – if it were the right finger and the right flick – and it would bring down the house.

It had not rained for six weeks. Needless to say, on the morning of my luncheon party, the sky clouded over and the clouds burst. It was maddening. When one invites people down from London, and when a little party like this is something of an 'occasion', and when one has a garden which is a *point* with all sorts of coloured corners into which one has planned to lead one's guests, it is very debilitating to be obliged to receive them in drenching rain and bitter cold. I do not think only of myself, but of Gaskin, who has been decorating salads and whipping up mayonnaise and generally behaving as only Gaskin can. In spite of the rain I think the party was a great success.

6 June. I have been mouldering alone, walking up and down the room trying to think of clues for Mr Green, and generally disintegrating. So I thought I would go out tonight. There was a party at Fleur Cowles', who is a very remarkable woman. Middle-aged, pretty, brittle, ambitious, American and all that. At the same time a brave and generous person, who would be, I think, a damned good friend. Apart from that, she could not possibly be a bore.

She had collected about fifty people. As usual, I was at a disadvantage because of this ludicrous incapacity of mine for remembering names. Time and again people came up to me and said: 'Beverley darling, where have you been? And do you remember . . .?' To which I can only reply with a silly smile and a lot of vague conversation. This is a grave weakness on my part.

When he lived at Thatch Cottage, Beverley invited selected guests to 'sign the wall'. At Merry Hall, he invited them to sign the back of a door. Sometimes, to save embarrassment, those considered unworthy had to be included in this little ceremony but as soon as they had left their names were painted out. A photograph of the door taken by Cyril Butcher indicates that this occurred quite frequently. Among the fifty or so names, some of which are indecipherable, there are a few royals including Marina, Duchess of Kent, and a scattering of politicians such as Bob Boothby and Beverley Baxter. Most of the other signatories represent the arts: the Maughams – Somerset, Robin and Syrie – John Van Druten the playwright, Ram Gopal the Indian dancer, Frederick Ashton the choreographer, Vivian Ellis (who also appended the refrain of 'Spread a Little Happiness'), Oliver Messel the stage designer, Edward Molyneux the fashion designer and Rebecca West the writer. Actors are also prominent: there is Emlyn Williams, whose surviving letters to Beverley indicate a chatty intimacy which lasted into old age, the two Hermiones – Baddeley writ large and Gingold rather more modestly – Gladys Cooper, Douglas Byng, Jean Kent, Joan Miller, Mary Ellis, Alfred Lunt and Lynn Fontanne, Walter Pidgeon and Greer Garson. Among the 'unknowns' are Dorothy Hart, Barbara Back, still in Beverley's good books at the time, and his aunt and uncle, Blanche and George Nichols, from whom he had substantial financial expectations. Beverley, who happily acknowledged that he was a snob when it came to personalities in the public eye, used this photograph of the door, among others, to illustrate his lectures to American and British fans. Perhaps the photograph which impressed them most was of the Duchess of Kent, looking dazzling, posed at the entrance to the house.

In 1956, Merry Hall was sold – the story of Thatch Cottage with echoes of Cleave Court all over again. Beverley had done all he could with the house and had turned a ruined garden into something beautiful and impressive, but now he was bored with it. He was also suddenly obsessed with his old fear of poverty, but this time, with his sixtieth birthday looming not far ahead, his fear was justified. For a decade he had poured money into Merry Hall, and although the sale made him a profit on paper, he did not recover the true cost of his investment. He had also lived the life of a grand seigneur, and it was astonishing that, with soaring costs and taxation, he lasted as long as he did. In this respect, he was his mother's son, stubbornly clinging on when he should have unburdened himself years sooner. But if his lifestyle was financial folly, he extracted every ounce of pleasure out of living it. Merry Hall was merry in every sense of the word and, between them, he and Cyril Butcher entertained in a lavish manner with Gaskin doubling as major-domo and chef. The cuisine was of a superb simplicity that only skill and the best ingredients can provide, and was accompanied by the finest wines – indeed, the money spent on liquor alone would have kept a working-class family in modest comfort. On such evidence, his guests may have assumed that Beverley was a wealthy man but, apart from the house and its contents, his assets were now negligible and he had made little provision for his old age.

· 2 I ·

Stink pots

1956–1967

WITH the proceeds of the sale of Merry Hall in the bank, it was
suggested to Beverley that now was the time to join the
increasing numbers who had fled abroad to avoid the payment
of British tax. He refused. His reasons were a mixture of old-fashioned
patriotism and a deep love for anything English. When Noel Coward was
pilloried in the press for leaving the country for tax reasons in 1956, it
confirmed Beverley's decision and induced in him a contempt for tax exiles
exceeded only by his contempt for those who had run away from the war.

Economy was now the order of the day and, as if to emphasize the fact,
Beverley led his companions and three cats out of the spacious grounds and
twenty-two rooms of Merry Hall into the four cramped rooms of the small
bungalow in the grounds. 'He didn't exactly count the cornflakes but one
almost felt he might,' said Cyril. Beverley reported to his *Woman's Own*
readers that the cats treated the place with some disdain. It was only a
temporary home, a sort of purgatory prior to the comparative heaven of a
converted flat on the ground floor of a house in Fitzjohns Avenue,
Hampstead. This, Beverley hoped, would be his permanent home. Apart
from its geographical location, it is not clear why he chose it. Its only
potential asset was the walled garden. Beverley, whose ideas of making
economies rarely matched anyone else's, had it landscaped to his own
design at the then high cost of over £1,000. In a piece giving advice to
newly-weds, he had denounced as nonsense the old adage, 'Look after the
pennies and the pounds will look after themselves.' If you want a grand
piano, he argued, buy it – the so-called necessities will always materialize
somehow, but if you spend all your money on essentials, you may never be
able to afford the grand piano. At Fitzjohns Avenue the garden was his
equivalent of the grand piano. His next-door neighbours, the Coolings,
whose gallery in Bond Street was well known to art collectors, watched in
amazement as tons of fresh earth were delivered and a team of gardeners
carried out a transformation. The result was reminiscent of the temporary
displays at the Chelsea Flower Show. John Cooling remembered watching

with amusement while photographs were taken of Beverley poised with a pristine pair of gleaming secateurs, apparently in the act of cutting off a perfectly good branch of a cherry tree newly planted and in full bloom.

The flat proved to be a disastrous mistake. It might have been only a taxi-ride away from the West End but Cyril, Gaskin and Beverley all hated its gloomy atmosphere which the new decorations in pale colours did nothing to relieve. The cats showed their dislike by sulking and treating the fresh soil in the garden as an enormous litter tray. Cyril became convinced that the place was haunted by an evil force from the past. 'The room in which it was most noticeable was the one we used to eat in. Dinner parties, instead of becoming brighter as the port went round, seemed to die and ended with everyone depressed and argumentative. I told Beverley we had better get out before all our friends refused to come anywhere near us.'

While they were living in Hampstead, Beverley completed a reminiscence called *The Sweet and Twenties*, unashamedly cashing in on the awakened interest in the 1920s sparked off by Sandy Wilson's musical comedy *The Boy Friend*. The importance of its influence on popular taste has been submerged with time, but those who saw it originally remember the shocked surprise, turning into affectionate laughter, as the girls in their flat-bosomed, short-skirted dresses entered for their first number, 'We're Perfect Young Ladies'. With astonishing speed, everything to do with the period, which up to then had been regarded as ugly, became fashionable again. The show now ranks as the most performed musical of all time. Not surprisingly, then, one of the first people to whom Beverley wrote when preparing *The Sweet and Twenties* was Sandy Wilson, the provider, as it were, of the nostalgic feast Beverley had decided to share. When they subsequently met, Wilson was as intrigued by this encounter with the legendary figure from the past as Beverley was at meeting the young man who had created such a loving pastiche. In *The Sweet and Twenties* he commented: 'How so subtle and delicate a conceit managed to defeat the concerted stupidities of Broadway and St Martin's Lane is one of the unsolved mysteries of the theatre.'

His book was a combination of gossipy, sometimes malicious memories of personalities, together with reflections on the state of things in the '50s as opposed to the '20s. For example, he compared the melodies of the past with rock and roll which, he said, he hated. If the main attraction of this new musical form was due more to the sexuality of the performers than to their material, he suggested that time might be saved if, instead of opening their mouths, they merely stripped, though he suspected the results might prove disappointing. In more serious mood, he reflected upon the idealistic hope and trust of the young of his day in the League of Nations contrasted with the cynicism with which the United Nations was regarded: idealism had vanished and nothing had replaced it. The general impression given by the book was that of a man who, although he could still charm, entertain and provoke, did not conceal his growing bitterness or his impatience with contemporary life. His attitude crystallized in the assertion that, like men of promise who had failed (and here he cited Leslie Hore-Belisha and Oswald Mosley), he too had missed the boat. This might seem an odd claim from one who had enjoyed and continued to enjoy success, but it was not the last time that he would lay claim to personal failure. He ended with a reference to *Twenty-Five* in which he had quoted Browning: '*Grow old along with me, the best is yet to be.*' 'Even in those days,' he said, 'I secretly suspected that Browning was talking through his hat. Today, I know.'

The Sweet and Twenties, published by Weidenfeld and Nicolson, was launched at a party given at Lady Aberconway's London home, 12, North Audley Street, on 14 May 1958. The guests were invited to dress in '20s style but Beverley's only concession was to wear a straw boater with blazer and flannels. Sandy Wilson found it all rather bogus and escaped with fellow guest Nancy Spain to recover over dinner at the Ivy. His review of the book in the *Evening Standard* on 20 May concluded:

Certainly this book is a necessary addition to the library of anyone who has a taste for that period, and I personally never tire of reading about those horrific, vulgar old ladies who battled tirelessly with each other to become top hostesses . . . But I would love to read just one book on that era whose writer did not seem to be slightly ashamed of it. After all somebody must have thought cloche hats were charming. And I don't think it's necessary to assume any longer that we, in our generation, imagine that our counterparts in the 1920s were just a lot of Charleston-ing nincompoops. Or were they?

In his diary for 10 June 1958, Noel Coward wrote:

I have just read Beverley Nichols' new book *The Sweet and Twenties* in which, as usual, he says the most charming things about me, but alas the book is slipshod and full of minor inaccuracies which are most irritating. At one point the House of Commons listens to a motion with 'pursued' lips! A curious picture. Some of his anecdotes are witty, and his chaper on the Irish excellent, but there is a certain underlying bitchiness about quite a lot of it which I don't remember Beverley being guilty of before. He is incurably sentimental, of course, and always was, but I have a feeling that this wouldn't matter so much if only he wrote a little better. Too many years of journalism and his pervasive passion for barking up the wrong tree have spoiled his style. The whole book, which purports to be a light, gossipy recapitulation of the 'twenties, is ruined by his not very convincing moralizing and his typically journalistic habit of making comparisons. On finishing the book one is left with the impression that he has observed too much and understood too little.

After a few months in Fitzjohns Avenue, it was agreed that they must leave. The long search for a new home at a price Beverley was prepared to pay turned into a nightmare. A friend suggested Islington which, it was said, was 'coming up'. They saw several derelict properties which, while quite cheap, needed a fortune spent on them, and Cyril remembered one in particular which had antiquated gas stoves in every room and a communal sink on each landing, with just one outside lavatory. It had been a slum for years and the other houses in the street still were. Beverley said, 'By the time Islington comes up, if it ever does, I shall be deep down in my grave.'

Quite unexpectedly, fate offered the solution. A wealthy lady friend of Beverley's noticed that a pleasant-sounding property in Richmond was up for auction. Somewhat reluctantly, he agreed to go to see it, fully expecting to be disappointed. He was, on the contrary, delighted and amazed. In the late eighteenth century the Duke of Argyll had built a block of six cottages to accommodate workers on his estate, Sudbrook Park. At the western end, the sixth cottage was tucked away at the back of the block which then continued with stables to form a right-angled spur. This and the cottage on the corner had been knocked into one dwelling and christened Sudbrook Cottage. The Duke had not stinted on space and when a central staircase had been taken out and the rooms on either side of it combined, the result was a surprisingly large drawing-room. There were a further four rooms on the ground floor, together with a cloakroom, kitchen and a store-room fashioned from the stables, all in perfect condition. Upstairs were two bathrooms and four bedrooms.

Even better was the walled garden which was astonishingly large for a cottage, just under an acre, the size indicating that it might originally have been the vegetable garden for the 'Big House', or perhaps a paddock for horses. When Beverley first saw it, it was an uncompromising rectangle given over to grass with flower borders and dominated by a massive topiary bird hacked out of box. A similar creature, though not as large, dominated the small garden facing the road. These, Beverley decided, must go to leave a blank canvas on which a new garden could be designed. His mind raced ahead with possibilities – but how was he to acquire the property?

His wealthy friend came to the rescue. It was a Crown property with a lease of nearly forty years to run; she would buy the lease, and make it over to Beverley who would then repay her over a set period with minimal interest. Her only condition was that her action should not be made known publicly. At auction, bidding began at £3,000 and rapidly rose to £7,850. For a time, it was touch and go whether she would acquire it, but she had given her representative a free hand, and although Beverley's heart sank as the price went up, in the end he became, by her generosity, the owner.

In the summer of 1958, he left the hated Fitzjohns Avenue flat and moved into Sudbrook Cottage, which remained his home until his death. Cyril's and Gaskin's delight was only surpassed by that of the cats who, Beverley said, considered that they had now a home worthy of their status. Economy was forgotten as he began planning the new garden, helped by Kenneth Page whom Beverley considered to be the most knowledgeable gardener he had ever employed. Beverley provided the overall design and Mr Page interpreted it, supplying many suggestions of his own. After clearing the ground and ceremoniously burning the topiary monsters, the first step was to divide the garden in half, thus giving the impression that it was twice its real size. The second step was to make water an important feature, as at Merry Hall, but more informally, to suit Sudbrook Cottage. In the further section of the halved space a pond was dug and the earth dispersed to raise sections of the garden. Then, following another Nichols precept, they dug new curved beds so that the original straight lines of the rectangle were obscured. To mark the boundary between the two sections, two magnificent porphyry urns were placed on brick pillars. Several old fruit trees were left intact during the clearance, as well as a superb copper beech to one side of the ground. The new planting concentrated on colourful shrubs including rhododendrons; bedding plants were kept to a minimum and instead there was a liberal use of perennials.

All this cost a great deal of money and, following the publication of the final Mr Green adventure in 1960, Beverley faced the old problem of 'the next big thing'. His answer was a book about cats. It is surprising that he had never thought of it before. He called the book *Beverley Nichols' Cats A.B.C.* and such was its success that he wrote a sequel, *Beverley Nichols' Cats X.Y.Z.* which was published in 1961. The books were a concoction of sentiment, common sense, autobiographical reminiscence, wit and fiction, with cat drawings by Derrick Sayer.

Around this time, Beverley began a musical version for television of his children's book *The Tree That Sat Down*. After completing nine of the songs, he took them along to the London television company, Associated Rediffusion. Steve Race, then their light music adviser, was asked if Mr Nichols could use his piano to demonstrate the music. '[Beverley] sat down at the piano and began to hammer it unmercifully, in a way so criminal (to a pianist) that I was tempted to ask him to show the poor thing a little mercy. But I know how tempted one is, when playing through a composition for the theatre, to try and make it sound like a lusty chorus of twenty singers and a concert orchestra.' The songs were of the tum-te-tum variety, and Beverley sang them at the top of his voice with the sustaining pedal of the piano down. It is not difficult to imagine the effect, in a confined space, of 'Stink Pots', for example, with a chorus of toads yelling:

Stink pots, stink pots,
We're the stinkiest stink pots.
Each of our little smiles
Makes everyone swoon for miles and miles.
Stink pots, stink potty pots!

Whatever its other charms might have been, nothing further happened to
The Tree That Sat Down and Beverley added it to his store of uncompleted
projects.

In 1963 came the first book about the garden at Sudbrook Cottage.
Unlike the Thatch Cottage and Merry Hall books, it was primarily
concerned with the practicalities of gardening and in this respect may have
disappointed those readers who expected the usual dominating parade of
amusing characters and anecdotes. These were present, but very much in
the background. It seemed that Beverley now wished to establish himself as
a practical gardener and to kill off any impression that he was merely a
theorist 'playing at it'. He had previously disguised the fact that he had
avoided all the back-breaking chores but in his sixties he could concede that
others did the hard work while he confined himself (as he always had done)
to the lighter tasks. But in more than thirty years of gardening he had
acquired a sound knowledge, and even experts might learn a thing or two
from this book. Implicit in the title that Beverley chose, *Garden Open Today*,
was a challenge to his peers to come and see for themselves what he had
achieved in only a few years.

For the first time in his career, he included his views and advice on roses,
saying their omission in the past was because of their association in his mind
with a family tragedy which had overshadowed his childhood. He did not
explain what the tragedy was or its association with the Gloire de Dijon
rose – nor did he disclose that this particular variety grew riotously at
Sudbrook Cottage – but he did list others that he grew. In a significant
sentence, he admitted that he could never love roses as they should be
loved, an admission that would have meant nothing to his readers but that
signalled, to those close to him, his growing bitterness towards his father.

In the following year *Forty Favourite Flowers* was published. While not
claiming to be an addendum to *Garden Open Today*, for practical purposes
that is what it was. As usual, the text was entertaining and was packed with
advice, but the illustrations were in black and white rather than in colour,
which disappointed Beverley and, he believed, lost potential sales.

For several years he had been working on two books, both of which he
expected to be international best-sellers. The first, published in 1966, was
Powers That Be. In the past, he had often been successful in gauging the
public mood: *Down the Garden Path* and *Cry Havoc!* were, in their different
ways, examples of this. In the early 1960s he observed the growing interest

in mystic phenomena and the search for spiritual awareness as evidenced by the astonishing rise of cults such as Scientology. He himself believed in what he dubbed the 'X Force' which gave individuals the ability to heal, or to cause to happen things for which there were no logical explanations. (It was this belief which had prompted him to write his *Mesmer*.) In *Powers That Be* he examined several modern examples: Harry Edwards, a well-known 'spiritual healer' of the time, and Evelyn Penrose who could locate mineral deposits by the use of a map. The former had a host of witnesses to his powers and the latter was employed by drilling and mining companies. The book was an impressive record of such phenomena, written with conviction and rejecting sensationalism. In the final chapters, Beverley took various official bodies to task for not investigating these mysterious abilities which, he believed, might be of value to science and medicine. *Powers That Be* enjoyed a moderate success but it was probably not scholarly enough for one audience and not sensational enough for another. It was surprisingly successful in Germany and the paperback version did well in America. Reading it today confirms what Beverley said about it in retrospect: 'It was not good enough.'

The second book for which he had high hopes was a very different matter. Its origins went back to early 1962, when Somerset Maugham had completed a new volume of memoirs which he called *Looking Back* and which were known to contain a bitter attack on his ex-wife Syrie, who had died in 1955. It was also known that excerpts were to be serialized in the *Sunday Express* but there were no firm plans for the publication of the book. Barbara Back, always an avid gossip, mentioned to Beverley that following a quarrel between Maugham and his daughter Liza, Maugham had inserted a passage into the manuscript stating categorically that Liza was not his child but the result of an affair between Syrie and another man. Beverley, already angry about rumours of Maugham's defamation of Syrie, was enraged by this latest development and wrote of it to Rebecca West who at this time was in New York. She replied to him on 30 March, after her return, having already heard the story while she was in America. The previous evening she had called on Barbara Back and heard it again, though Barbara Back, who had previously been adamant that the allegation was in the final manuscript, was now less sure.

In her letter to Beverley, Rebecca West went into some detail. She had been a close friend of Syrie before the marriage and she was convinced that a woman as passionately in love as Syrie had been would not have been unfaithful to Maugham at that stage of their relationship. She reminded Beverley of a dinner party when Syrie, stung by a remark from Willie, had flashed back that it was at his request she had borne his child, accusing him of not wanting one at all, merely of needing proof that he could be a father. Liza was born in Rome on 6 May 1915 while her mother was still married to, but estranged from, Henry Wellcome. Following their divorce, Maugham married Syrie in Jersey City on 26 May 1917. At that time, he had no doubts about his paternity and his allegation over forty years later appeared to be purely malicious or, as Rebecca West suggested, the result of a senile fancy.

Looking Back so horrified Maugham's publishers, Heinemann, when they finally received the manuscript that they refused to handle it. As far as Syrie's reputation was concerned, however, the damage had already been done, for excerpts duly appeared in the *Sunday Express* in 1962, having already been seen by American readers in *Show* magazine. Maugham not only revealed details of his affair with Syrie and the illegitimate birth of their daughter, (hitherto not known to Liza) but also vilified his ex-wife in a shocking display which incensed many of his friends and those who had known and respected Syrie Maugham. The unwitting victim of all the publicity was, of course, Liza, now Lady Glendevon, whose distress was exacerbated when she was forced to prove that Maugham was her legal father in a French court action in 1963, following Maugham's attempt to supplant her by adopting his middle-aged secretary, Alan Searle.

Little had been said about Syrie Maugham following her death in 1955, but now her friends, led by Rebecca West, banded together to establish a memorial to her, which took the form of a bust of Catherine the Great by Shubin, presented to the Victoria and Albert Museum in 1964. Among those associated with it were Noel Coward, Sacheverell Sitwell, Diana Cooper, Cecil Beaton, Victor Gollancz, Lady Aberconway, Elizabeth von Hofmannsthal and Beverley Nichols.

Beverley, seething with anger over the entire business, decided to go further and write a book in defence of Syrie. There is no doubt that he was sincere, but whether he was wise is another matter. His old crusading instincts were aroused and, as so often happened before, he did not pause to consider the implications of his action, although he was not unaware that the book might do very well financially. He began work in 1965 and finished it shortly before Maugham's death in December of that year, by which time, publication had been arranged and serial rights organized. It is important to make this point because it has subsequently been said that he waited until Maugham was dead.

In December he handed Lady Glendevon a copy of the manuscript to read, expressing the hope that she would comment on the contents. In a letter dated 1 January 1966 she wrote at length, making three suggestions which she considered vital and adding others of lesser importance. In the same letter, she expressed her appreciation of his battle on her mother's behalf, and she signed herself, 'Love – Liza'. It was clearly understood from the outset that there was no question of her approving the book for promotional or any other purposes; she was, in any case, firmly under the impression that publication was a *fait accompli*, whatever she might have had to say. Beverley, on the other hand, later claimed he had said that if she disapproved he would 'destroy the manuscript and tear up the contracts'. It seems an unlikely promise to have given after so much work. He also claimed he had assured her that on no account would he disclose the fact that he had been in contact with her over the book, or that she had read it, or that she had made suggestions for revising the text. This assurance made him a hostage to fortune, as we shall see.

The core of *A Case of Human Bondage*, as he called his book, was his version of events during a weekend party in 1925 at the Villa Eliza, Syrie Maugham's home near Le Touquet. She had purchased the house using funds accumulated from her successful business as an interior decorator. The unpretentious dwelling was lifted out of the ordinary by combining French country style with brilliant use of colour. The salon walls were whitewashed, and the cement floor tinted beige, polished and covered with rugs of short, clipped sheepskin. The upholstery, of traditional design, was in tones of greyish brown. The curtains were of heavy peach-coloured silk bordered with twisted silk cord in old gold. Some, but not all, of the heavy old wooden furniture was bleached; the light-fittings were of black wrought-iron with peach-coloured shades; and the focal point of the room was a massive stone fireplace with niches for ornaments. Beverley, confusing this distinctive room with her sitting-room in Chelsea, described it as all white, with deep sofas of white leather, a carpet of thick, white sheepskin and, as the focal point, a screen of slated mirror reflecting bowls of white peonies. Such confusion might be a relatively minor point, but it did cast some doubt on his detailed recollection of events.

According to Beverley, Syrie had planned this particular weekend to fight one last battle with Gerald Haxton for Maugham's affections. If this is true, it was extremely foolish of her because the battle was already lost, her marriage in ruins and she could only suffer further humiliation. Haxton and Maugham had become lovers during the war. He was a young American with film-star good looks and boyish charm, and he gave an impression of candour which was deceptive. His life was dominated by sex and alcohol, and in both respects he was insatiable. Sexually he was versatile, with a taste for men, women and children. Maugham was so besotted with him that, after Haxton was refused further admission to England following a charge of gross indecency in a London hotel in 1915, he spent much time travelling abroad with him.

There has been a great deal of speculation about Maugham's reasons for marrying Syrie. The most obvious reason was his desire to do his duty by the woman who had borne his child, but it has also been suggested that he wanted the façade of social respectability that marriage would give him, and which was important to him as a man unable to escape entirely from the ethos of his class. But if he had expected Syrie to be a compliant wife and accept the homosexual side of his nature without demur, he badly misjudged her. She might, of course, have believed that she could 'reform' him, in which case her judgement was equally at fault. A more sinister reason has also been advanced: that she blackmailed him into marriage with the threat of exposing his homosexuality. The real reasons may have combined all these possibilities.

Whatever the explanation, simple or complex, they were two people doomed to incompatibility. Even if the sexual side of the marriage had been satisfying to both of them, their temperaments differed dramatically. She was an extrovert, surrounded by an entourage of talented people; he was essentially a recluse who wanted peace in order to write and, unlike Syrie, preferred to observe social life rather than participate in it. Syrie was deeply in love with him, despite his faults, and her love lasted until she died: according to Beverley, she never gave up hope that Willie would visit her for a last-minute reconciliation.

The other guests who were staying at the villa or who just 'dropped in' that weekend included Noel Coward and his new lover Jack Wilson, Lord and Lady Plunkett, Dudley and Doris de la Vigne, Gertie Miller an ex-star of the musical-comedy stage, and, inevitably, Barbara Back. The tensions, the covert and sometimes open hostility, the suppressed hysteria of Syrie, the self-satisfaction of Maugham and the arrogance of Haxton who called Beverley 'pretty boy' were all too much for Beverley, who may also have felt at a psychological disadvantage: his last book, *Twenty-Five*, had appeared three years before and the glow of his earlier success was beginning to fade. For all his charm and social acceptability, he was just a journalist who had yet to fulfil his early promise and so Haxton's derisive and patronizing 'pretty boy' bit deep. He felt so miserable that after Sunday lunch he told Syrie he had to return to London for business reasons. She promptly decided to leave with him and they crept out of the house without saying goodbye to anyone.

This, in essence, is the story he told in the book but what triggered his departure has never before been revealed. In the early hours of the Sunday morning, Jack Wilson, Coward's boyfriend, went to Beverley's bedroom and tried to make love to him. Suddenly Coward burst into the room looking like 'the wrath of a thousand Chinese gods'. In a cold fury, he ordered Wilson to leave and then accused Beverley of inviting Wilson to his room. Beverley used a very different version of this story in *A Case of Human Bondage*, substituting Haxton for Wilson and Maugham for Coward.

In a letter to Cole Lesley, dated 1 October 1976, in which he congratulated him on his biography of Coward, Beverley said:

> Did Noel ever tell you the true story of what happened between Jack and myself chez Syrie, when we were all staying at Le Touquet . . . or rather,

what did not happen? It is a very strange story and I have an uncanny feeling that it clouded my relations with Noel for the rest of our lives. At any rate, he never forgot it, nor did I – though my conscience is as clean as a newly polished whistle. Jack behaved like every variety of bitch.

Syrie poured out to Beverley her hatred of Haxton over dinner on the train to London. It was not simply a matter of the sexual angle, she explained: what did it matter whether one's marriage was destroyed by a man or a woman? What distressed her was that Haxton was a liar, a forger and a cheat. There was more talk in this vein; as she spoke, her voice became louder and her revelations caused an astonished reaction among the other diners. It was a startling climax to a bizarre weekend and Beverley was convinced that Syrie was teetering on the edge of a nervous breakdown. The point of her monologue, when she finally reached it, was that Haxton was poisoning Maugham's mind against her and that while she might put up with much else she could not tolerate that.

When he came to write *A Case of Human Bondage*, Beverley's anger completely unbalanced his assessment of the leading actors in his drama. He presented Gerald Haxton as a villain with no redeeming feature, and went on to ascribe to him the ability to manipulate Maugham into treating Syrie with contempt and hatred. His influence, Beverley asserted, as evidenced by Maugham's memoirs, *Looking Back*, extended from beyond the grave. The picture Beverley painted of Maugham was also an ugly one, although this was the man of whose friendship he had been so proud. The leading lady was, of course, Syrie, and Beverley's portrait of her was so idealized as to strain credulity. If Haxton had no redeeming features, Syrie had no faults. It was this lack of balance and objectivity, combined with an attempt to give trivial incidents an emotional importance they did not deserve, which landed him in trouble when the book was published in 1966.

In April of that year, Beverley sent a copy of the book to Robin Maugham (Viscount Maugham) and received a letter of acknowledgement dated 2 May. After a preamble relating to other matters, Maugham wrote:

And thank you for sending me *A Case of Human Bondage*. You really do flatter me by saying that I am a better story-teller than you are. It really isn't true. I have a deep respect and admiration for your work. But we both of us must be a little careful not to turn into a mutual admiration society! I think the book is technically excellent and well written, if I may say so, and is gripping throughout. You cannot expect me, under the circumstances, to make any comment on the central theme, because, of course, in my position as head of the Maugham family, that, you will admit, would be very difficult for me.

In his diary entry on 22 May 1966, Noel Coward wrote: 'Beverley Nichols has written a ghastly book purporting to defend Syrie's memory. He has been, rightly, crucified for it. It is vulgar, tactless and inaccurate. I have retitled it *I've Just Come Up From Somerset.*'

Coward's opinion was shared by many who saw *A Case of Human Bondage* as a slur on a great writer and a betrayal of friendship. Beverley was horrified by this. It had not occurred to him that his case for the prosecution might be countered by a case for the defence. He believed that it was Lady Glendevon's moral duty to make a public gesture to silence those who considered he had behaved irresponsibly; he failed to see that she was under no obligation to do anything, and that she had already generously read and commented on his manuscript. He had got himself into a mess. With hindsight, he must have seen that he had been rather stupid, but he never admitted this; on the contrary, he became angry and bitter about the adverse reaction, and was consoled only by those who, like Rebecca West, had always disliked Maugham.

Beverley would have been even angrier if he had read Noel Coward's entry in his diary for 6 July 1966, a footnote to the furore: 'I have finished the preface to Gar Kanin's book about Maugham. It really was difficult to do. Poor Willie was such an unadmirable character. Liza and John [the Glendevons] came to lunch yesterday and I read it to them and they seemed to be pleased. John, who loathed Willie, was afraid I was going to whitewash him, and Liza was dreading another essay in bitchiness like Beverley's.'

Beverley maintained his promise of silence (at least in Britain) until an item appeared in *The Times* in 1971 announcing that a biography of Syrie was being written by Richard Fisher 'with the help and approval of Syrie's daughter, Lady Glendevon . . . Mr Fisher is not interested in writing a scandalous biography. The last book about Syrie whose publication Lady Glendevon did nothing to encourage was Beverley Nichols' *A Case of Human Bondage.*' Enraged by the implications of this, Beverley wrote a letter to *The Times* which was published on 16 February. He gave his version of events and added:

When the book appeared, I was put in the pillory and accused of every crime in the moral and literary calendar. Time and again – this is the vital point – I was asked on television, on radio and in the press, why I had not consulted any member of the Maugham family about it. To all of these questions which were often phrased in the most insulting terms, I was obliged to answer 'no comment', for the simple and I hope honourable reason that I appreciated how reluctant Lady Glendevon might be to be personally associated with so unflattering a portrait of her father.

On 4 March, *The Times* published a reply from Lord Glendevon. In it, he pointed out that when Beverley approached his wife it was not for 'approval' of the book, as publication and serialization had already been agreed. He suggested that, under pressure and in good faith, Beverley had forgotten the exact course of events. He ended by hoping that the matter could now be left, as his wife had suffered enough unhappiness in the context of her father over the years.

Beverley did not intend to leave the matter and took legal advice. He was counselled to avoid litigation, the cost of which would have been enormous and the outcome in his favour highly doubtful. He decided to let the matter drop but it did not stop his festering resentment. Looking at the whole question after a due lapse of time, it is obvious that Lord Glendevon was correct in his assessment and Beverley completely unreasonable.

· 2 2 ·

Shading to black

1967–1970

WHEN *A Case of Human Bondage* was published, Beverley was at a low ebb following an operation, the first of a series related to cancer. The strain imposed by the adverse reaction to the book nearly resulted in his complete breakdown, but fortunately a lecture tour in America gave him the opportunity to escape. His previous tour had coincided with Maugham's revelations about Syrie in *Looking Back*, and Beverley had included in his lecture the following anecdote which involved Noel Coward.

> When he rang the bell, I found I was being followed by my beloved Siamese cat and so, when I opened the door, I said to Noel, 'I do hope you don't mind cats.' And Noel, with that incomparable technique, stepped forward, took up the cat, cradled him in his arms and said, 'My dear Beverley, I adore all animals to such an extent that I cannot see a water-bison without bursting into tears.' And then, when he entered my music room and noticed a photograph of Mr Somerset Maugham, he walked over to examine it and said, 'Dear Willie Maugham, the original Lizard of Oz.'
>
> In view of Mr Maugham's recent articles about his dead wife in which he speaks the grossest lies and slander about one of the most wonderful women I have ever known, I feel that the term lizard is too nearly a term of endearment. I won't say any more because I might run the risk of being rude. Mr Maugham's picture is no longer on my mantelpiece.

In his new version of the lecture, the Maugham story was expunged and, having explained why he had written *A Case of Human Bondage*, Beverley went on:

> If the truth must be told, I am pretty sick of this subject, for a number of reasons. Firstly, because there are circumstances connected with the writing of this book which, were I to make them public, would throw a

very different light on the whole matter and a very much more favourable
light on myself. However, these circumstances can't be made public, and
as long as I have anything to do with it they won't be. And that, I'm
afraid, must be that. But there are other reasons why I am sick of the
subject. And one of them is that the appearance of *A Case of Human
Bondage* caused such an uproar as has not been heard since the trial of
Oscar Wilde. When the British get these attacks of moral indignation,
they are very acute indeed and they get worse as the years go by,
presumably because Britain today is unquestionably the most immoral
country in the world and is apparently very proud of the fact. After all,
she's not got much else to be proud of at the moment.

Apart from this outburst, his lecture was similar to the one he had given
before – a rambling discourse on his gardens interspersed with anecdotes.
He told, for example, a story about Agatha Christie who had come to tea
and began speaking about her husband, a distinguished archaeologist: 'You
know, Mr Nichols, every woman should marry an archaeologist because
she grows increasingly attractive to him as she grows increasingly to
resemble a ruin.' Another story concerned a grand wedding reception
attended by Queen Mary:

> She was standing in a corner, holding court, and as usual she was dressed
> to kill in a gown of sheer silver with layers of diamonds and a cape of
> white ermine, and on top of her silver hair one of those remarkable
> toques, also of white ermine. Aldous Huxley, who was extremely short-
> sighted, looked over to the corner and dimly saw people circling round
> that glittering figure waiting to be presented. He blinked at me and said,
> 'What on earth's going on over there?' and I said, 'Why, that's Queen
> Mary, of course.' 'Oh!' he said. 'Indeed! I thought it was the wedding
> cake.'

In his lecture, Beverley included a section on flower arrangements upon
which he had decided views:

> Don't you think that in some of the more sophisticated circles of
> American society, this art of flower arrangement has possibly gone just a
> little bit too far? We have now reached the stage where, if one were to
> pick a bunch of daffodils and put them at random into a jam jar, one
> would be regarded as positively déclassé. Everything has to have
> significant form – a flower is no longer just a flower, it is a unit in a
> geometrical pattern. I don't like this sort of thing at all. But I must admit
> that it also strikes me as funny, particularly when you see it practised at a
> local flower show. The ladies are so very much in earnest. You see them

standing there in a sort of daze, with their arms full of flowers, and suddenly sticking a rather blatant hollyhock into a pinholder. And then stepping back five paces, squinting, and wondering how they are going to make it 'marry' with an obviously depressed lupin. When they have sorted out that little problem, you see them wondering how they are going to arrange, in the bottom left-hand corner, a bunch of rancid cabbage leaves into a 'composition' which will satisfy the eagle eyes of the adjudicating committee, and match up to the title, which will probably be something like 'Symphony of Summer'.

I am going to imagine that I am President of an American Garden Club charged with the duty of setting the subjects for the annual competition. And this is what you would read on your notice boards:

Class One. A flower arrangement in the style of the Dutch and Flemish painters of the seventeenth and eighteenth centuries.

Class Two. A flower arrangement in the style of the French Impressionists.

This idea which I have never seen even vaguely suggested by any of the so-called experts is completely revolutionary because it would compel every competitor to go back to the Classics and begin again. If you are going to arrange flowers in the style of the great masters of flower painting, you have to steep yourself in their art. And this is something not one person in a thousand ever dreams of doing.

This was the subject of his new book. When he returned to England, he completed work on *The Art of Flower Arrangement*, a beautiful, lavishly produced volume with decorative drawings by William McLaren and nearly sixty full-page colour plates. The text covered the history of the subject from early times until the present day, the tone was serious, and there was little of the usual Nichols sparkle about it: indeed, at times it was more like a textbook. If Beverley hoped it might become a standard work on the subject he was disappointed, for it has not appeared again. Perhaps the problem of reproducing it at an economic price might have something to do with that. It is one of the best books of its kind on the subject and certainly one of the best things Beverley ever wrote.

During 1967 Beverley's long association with *Woman's Own* came to an end. Since 1946, he had contributed a weekly piece and established a cosy rapport with millions of its readers. The loss of income was a shock, and nothing replaced it. This compounded the self-pity which had bedevilled him following the reaction to *A Case of Human Bondage*, and in a mood of 'to hell with it all', he left with Cyril in November for an extensive holiday beginning in South Africa. Here he was given VIP treatment by his white hosts but, despite the generosity of his welcome, he could not escape the sensation that, far from being 'abroad', he was caught in a time warp. It was as if South Africa was an extension of a bygone England with all the trappings of an Edwardian seaside resort, only the colour of the servants being different. As for apartheid, he found the arguments of both its supporters and opponents confused, and its practical application, of which he saw little, often ridiculous. From South Africa they sailed to Singapore to spend ten days with the Sultan of Jahore, an old friend from the '20s when, as the Crown Prince of Jahore, he had been one of the darlings of the bright young people in London, known to his chums as 'Buffles'. Following a detour to Penang during which Beverley was somewhat startled by the sight of an American soldier on leave from Vietnam having sex with his girl by the hotel swimming-pool, they flew to Australia.

It had been thirty-six years since *Evensong*, seen as a slur on their beloved Melba, had roused the Australian press to fury. Now, Beverley was greeted as a distinguished author and Melba was all but forgotten. The memory of the lady who had claimed with some justification that, as far as the arts were concerned, she had put Australia on the map, was not celebrated in any way, not even by a street name. Taking Cyril on a pilgrimage to her home at Lilydale, Beverley expected to find it a shrine to her genius, but it was locked up and they were given short shrift by a man they took to be a gardener. The taxi-driver who drove them there had not even heard of Melba. Beverley found it a distressing comment on the mortality of the famous, and held discussions with a leading television company about a documentary on her. After a heady start, with much talk of location shooting in Europe, the project suddenly died. Beverley was bitterly disappointed for he believed himself to be the only man alive who could do justice to the famous singer's story.

While Beverley was in Sydney, Cecil Beaton arrived on a brief visit. The local press made the most of the presence of these two figures from the '20s whom they described, in the terminology of the '60s, as the 'mod' men of their era and as 'leaders of the pack'. Both were asked similar questions. To a query about being typed in his profession, Beaton replied: 'You cannot type me,' while Beverley said that he had never found a niche so his name meant different things in different parts of the world: in Australia he was known as a writer on gardening, in Japan as a detective novelist, and in Scandinavian countries as a writer for children. Asked if he was happy to live in England, Beaton said, 'Yes, I'm delighted. London is still the best place for the exchange of ideas.' Beverley was gloomy: 'I don't really care for England much any more. I was asked to contribute a series of articles to *Queen* magazine beginning "England is . . ." I started off by quoting a six-year-old girl who, when asked to describe England after being shown a globe of the world, said, "England is a small, pink place." That's just what it is. The old grandeur and dignity seem to have gone.' Asked to name their favourite decade, Beaton gave the '20s, Beverley the 1890s. 'I wasn't born

then, but I'd love to have been a contemporary of Whistler and Beardsley.'
Did they like the revival of Art Nouveau and 1920s styles? Beaton was
enthusiastic, claiming he was largely responsible for it. Beverley disagreed:
'I hated the styles of the 1920s. I said so then and I still say so.' On the then
controversial subject of the Sydney Opera House, Beaton was again
enthusiastic: 'It makes other opera houses look like street kiosks.' Beverley
described it as looking like something that had crawled out of the sea and
was up to no good.

These replies say something about both men: Beaton was still very much
a man of the moment, Beverley was slightly sour and weary. It was
inevitable that there would be questions about *A Case of Human Bondage* and
Beverley was now at pains to emphasize that he had had the family's
permission to publish it. This was the first time that he had made such a
statement in public but, although he felt free to do so in Australia, he was to
maintain his silence in England for a little longer.

Beverley and Cyril had hoped to leave Australia in some style, but as their
funds were running low they were forced to book passages on a cargo boat
sailing to America, the final stop on their itinerary. It proved to be a
memorable journey, but for all the wrong reasons. Beverley, used to first-
class travel on luxury liners, found everything from the accommodation to
the food and the attitude of the officers and crew quite dreadful. Even Cyril,
used to the rigours of wartime service in the Royal Navy, was appalled,
describing the ship, in his usual forthright manner, as 'fucking awful'. One
of Beverley's favourite anecdotes concerning this journey was about the
lifeboat drill. He noticed that the emergency water supply was contained in
tins which had rusted up so they could not be opened in the way they were
intended to be. He enquired of one of the officers if a can-opener was
available, a question which produced great delight and the answer: 'Maybe
you'd better use your bloody teeth.' They left the ship at Panama and took a
plane to New York. Beverley, who had a collection of photographs
showing the state of the ship which in his opinion was almost unseaworthy,
was all for taking legal action, but after a few days ashore he thought better
of it.

This is not to say that his spirits were raised by New York; quite the
reverse. The city of which he was so fond now appeared to him drab and
unkempt, and the atmosphere tense and apprehensive. His impression was
underlined when a car in which they were travelling was caught up in a
street battle round Columbus University. He never forgot the hatred of the
rioters and the frightening ugliness of the scene, which seemed to him a
fitting comment on the so-called 'Swinging Sixties'.

It was with considerable relief that they eventually reached the calm of
Sudbrook Cottage, having been away for nearly six months. Looking back,
there were some happy memories of people and places but overall a feeling

of a world in the process of dramatic change. Beverley, asking himself whether the trip had been worth it, concluded that it would have been wiser to have stayed at home, but consoled himself with the thought that there must be a book in it. He had made notes and Cyril had taken hundreds of photographs; soon, he was planning what he intended to be a different type of travel book.

In the mean time, he completed work on a sequel to *Garden Open Today* called *Garden Open Tomorrow*. It was greeted with pleasure by garden-lovers when it appeared in December 1968 and it solved the problem of Christmas buying for many. Four years after this, it was republished in a special edition for the Country Book Club. It was very much the mixture as before – sound advice blended with familiar touches of satire, wit and sentiment, the pages again decorated with drawings by William McLaren. Fred Whitsey, the authority on gardening, reviewed the book for the *Sunday Telegraph*. 'I read it straight through because I couldn't stop,' he wrote, and ended, 'I added to my store of knowledge by way of the reportage of the author's own gardening experiences, and again and again I found myself nodding with that satisfying sense one gets from whole-hearted agreement.'

The travel book appeared in October 1969 under the title *The Sun In My Eyes* with the sub-title 'Or how not to go round the world'. The loyal Nichols reader might have anticipated a pot-pourri of encounters and incidents, perhaps even a little pontificating, put together with humour and felicity of style: in outline, this is what the reader got, but where once Beverley would have been controversial and outrageous, he seemed becalmed, and where once his wit would have had razor sharpness, now he resorted to cynicism or petulance. If the reader had glanced at the final chapter, he might not have bought the book at all, for there Beverley presented his apologia, as if aware he had not fulfilled expectations. It was salutary, he said, to remind those tempted to leave the increasing squalor and drabness of Britain of the disillusionments that awaited them. Three factors robbed foreign travel of its old magic. The first was television whose probing eye had diluted the element of surprise; indeed the reality often seemed an anti-climax. No longer could respect be summoned up for an erupting volcano when it had been seen on the screen filmed from a circling helicopter. The second was the 'permissive society': the red-light district of the East no longer elicited much reaction because England had its own equivalent. Somerset Maugham, he said, would have been at a loss for copy; Sadie Thompson today would be the toast of the ship and very likely writing her memoirs for the Sunday newspapers. Finally he blamed the tentacles of international commerce which were encircling the globe. Sooner or later, however remote the spot, one was likely to be confronted by posters for that ubiquitous liquid that had seeped over the entire surface of the earth: Coca-Cola. Added to all this was the transistor radio, for nowhere was safe from the monstrous intrusions of pop groups. To Beverley, it was the saddest aspect of all, that the natural music of the world was being slowly drowned in the uproar of synthetic sound. Perhaps, he concluded, one should never look over the garden wall to chronicle the outside world.

The Times Literary Supplement in its review gently mocked the author for, amongst other things, his frequent moan of distress because his spending power had been cut by the devaluation of the pound by the socialist government of Harold Wilson. The book, it said, managed to be full of the minutiae of travel and yet to be curiously uninformative. It was too full, of his encounters with the people he had met, many of whom were, frankly, boring. Even the fictitious characters that he introduced, presumably to brighten up the pages, were dull, as if he had lost the knack of humorous invention.

The South African section of the book provided the biggest surprise. The younger Nichols would have had firm views on apartheid, but Beverley merely recounted some of its more ludicrous consequences, such as being refused service in a 'blacks only' section of a liquor store and having to go into the 'whites only' section to buy a bottle of gin. He visited a black township, but he found it quite a pleasant example of modern housing development and said nothing about the segregation which had created it. He passed on, without comment, the information that all the whites he had met thought that, on balance, apartheid was a good thing. There was not the faintest hint of irony in his reportage.

Even allowing for Beverley's inconsistency and frequently violent changes of view, his neutrality on the subject of apartheid was odd because he was not as insensitive to the issue as he appeared to be. In private, he measured apartheid against the colour prejudice he had experienced in America in the late 1940s, and here it is useful to return to *Uncle Samson*, published in 1950, in which he had dwelt at length on what he described as America's greatest tragedy.

While he was in Washington, he had innocently invited a black singer to dine with him, and found the only place where, as a black man, his guest would be tolerated was the café at the railway station. Then Beverley invited a black professor of anthropology to visit him at his hotel; the professor, refused admittance at the main entrance, was directed to a back door and forced to use the baggage lift. Beverley had declared that these two incidents showed an outrageous state of affairs in the capital city of the world's greatest democracy, a city which claimed the moral leadership of the world in all matters of freedom and tolerance, and he began to investigate further for himself. Among a welter of official statistics he found that, every year, 30,000 light-skinned blacks crossed the 'colour-line' to begin life anew as whites. It was, he commented, as if America ran concentration camps from which thousands broke through the barbed wire to freedom. In the ghettoes, tuberculosis was eight times more likely to prove fatal than elsewhere. In Washington, hospital facilities for blacks were inferior to those for whites and a quarter of the hospitals barred blacks completely. Black doctors were excluded from all private hospitals and were not allowed to join the District Medical Association or the American Medical Association. A blacks-only school which had no outdoor recreation facilities whatsoever stood across the road from a large municipal playground with the warning sign: 'No negroes allowed.' All this was as nothing compared with conditions in the deep South where hatred for blacks was all too apparent. In the states of Mississippi, South Carolina, Alabama and Georgia, the blacks, who made up 40 per cent of the population, had had the right to vote since the end of the Civil War, but they were denied this right by 'violence, fraud, intimidation and skulduggery'.

It would be easy to dismiss what he had to say about America in 1950 as having no relevance to South Africa in 1967. The difference was that America claimed that all men were equal and had the vote when this was manifestly untrue at that time. Although progress had been made by 1967, the problem was by no means resolved, as the assassination of Martin Luther King in the following year showed. In South Africa, no claims were made at all. To Beverley, this was preferable to American hypocrisy, but it did not make apartheid any the less abhorrent to him. What stopped him from taking up the cause of black South Africans is not clear.

In Britain, however, in common with many others, he regarded the existence of colour prejudice with alarm. It was essential, he argued, that the 'black' races be given every opportunity to rise to important and influential positions in every aspect of national life, if dangerous confrontation were to be avoided. How this was to be achieved he did not know, but if only the problem were to be recognized, it would be a start.

He was therefore in a receptive frame of mind when an idea was put to him by Christopher Blackburn, the manager of the local theatre in Richmond. It was that a play should be produced with the male leading part, normally assigned to a white actor, to be played instead by a prominent black actor - hopefully Sidney Poitier. Such a proposition appeared startlingly innovative at that time. The play chosen was *The Voice of the Turtle* by John Van Druten, but it might equally well have been *Private Lives* or *Long Day's Journey Into Night*.

Beverley formed a company to produce the play and invited three peers, Robin Maugham, Gavin Faringdon and Patrick Kinross, to act as associates. He also approached his old chums John Betjeman and Mervyn Stockwood, the Bishop of Southwark, to whom he wrote on 19 August 1970: 'What I do care passionately about is that each of us, every man Jack of us, should try to play some role, however minor or limited, in narrowing the appalling gap between black and white.' In the end, nothing came of the scheme.

Later, he decided to write a book on the colour question, along the lines of *Cry Havoc!* He took as its starting point the West's preoccupation with the threat of Communism, which he believed was based on a false premise, for he was sure that the Iron Curtain and all it stood for would be destroyed by economic necessity, not by war. Instead of wasting vast resources on the Cold War, the major powers, including the Soviet Union, should be applying their might to solving the problems of black races everywhere. If the great powers continued to ignore them and did not help all blacks to achieve their rightful place in the world, there would be a confrontation in the twenty-first century of cataclysmic proportions.

In a conversation with Robin Maugham and his fellow writer Peter Burton, Beverley asserted that the contents of the book were so controversial that he had arranged for its publication only after his death. Later, in a brief paragraph in *The Unforgiving Minute*, he said he had taken this precaution because publication of the book in his lifetime would certainly result in prosecution under Britain's Race Relations Act. Following his death, his executors searched for the manuscript but could find no trace of it. Cyril Butcher concluded that Beverley had destroyed it, probably because he feared his prognosis would be ridiculed. Some readers may judge the prognosis to be the product of an over-active imagination, but Beverley's prophecy of the collapse of the Iron Curtain countries has proved to be correct – and who knows if he will also prove to be correct in his prediction of a black-white confrontation?

· 23 ·

Demonic possession

1970–1972

EVER since the 1930s, Beverley had determined that he would take revenge on his father, and the time came in the aftermath of his anger over *A Case of Human Bondage*. For all his protests about the reaction to the book, he had enjoyed the notoriety it had brought. At the age of sixty-nine he had been back in the headlines for the first time in many years. Like an old actor who cannot resist the lure of the limelight, he wanted to bask in its glare once more before his death, which he believed was not far away. Suddenly he saw that he might achieve his wish and his revenge on his father by writing a book even more sensational than *A Case of Human Bondage*.

In the mean time he wrote a new children's book, *The Wickedest Witch in the World*, which has already been mentioned, and which contained elements of cruelty and evil that had not been overt before. When this book was in the hands of his publisher, he began another adventure *Super Witch*. He said that he abandoned this because he was unwell, but it may have been because the plot, which dealt with the demonic possession of children's souls, developed into a tangled web; reading it today, one cannot see how he intended to resolve the plot without resorting to heavenly intervention. What the book lacks is the Nichols brand of fun which had delighted his young readers in the past and had obscured the stories' darker side.

He also edited the Allways and Merry Hall trilogies and wrote new introductions for the two volumes, which appeared under the titles of *The Gift of a Garden* and *The Gift of a Home* in 1971 and 1972.

Work on the 'revenge' book which, with irony he decided to call *Father Figure*, now began in earnest. Its genesis was the yellowing manuscript of the uncompleted, partly autobiographical novel he had written more than thirty years before, about a well-to-do, middle-class family called the Alders and the father's addiction to alcohol. It was the theme he had later dramatized in *Shadow of the Vine*. While the Alders novel dealt in graphic detail with the sordid effects of drink, it was also a compassionate study of the father. The incident of the yellow rose, for example, was told from his point of view. Alders has come downstairs after several days in his bedroom recovering from a monumental drinking bout. He has alarming memories of the scene in the dining-room, when, in a drunken rage, he had said the most terrible things to his wife Lilian and to his youngest boy Peter, while his other two sons looked on in horror. Now he stands looking down at Peter who sits at the table in the morning-room reading a book. In his hand, Alders holds a long-stemmed yellow rose.

'Hello, Peter. Just picked this.'
He held it out and it trembled with the shaking of his hand.
Peter bent lower over his book, but Alders did not move. Like a beggar asking for a crust he demanded some sort of word from his son. At this moment, he was suffering as acutely as it is possible for men to suffer. Apart from the throbbing of outraged nerves, apart from the feeling of degradation at being forced to appear loathsome in the sight of those whom he loved, he was really frightened. He knew what Peter was thinking, and though he was horribly afraid that he might put it into words, he was even more afraid of his silence.
That was the reason why he had picked the rose. It was a sort of white flag . . .
'Thought it was rather pretty.'
He could say no more. The room was swimming around him. He wanted to fall down at Peter's feet and to die. To pass out of this hell . . . He put his hand out quickly to steady himself. And at that moment Peter looked up and said, 'Yes.'
He said it with all the hatred that one can say so simple a word. His expression showed as much loathing as can be shown.

The story loses much of its biographical element at the point when Alders dies of a heart attack while desperately trying to restore the family fortunes following a stock market crash.
There are several sequences missing from the manuscript, among them the death of Lilian. It resumes when Peter has become a highly paid gigolo in Paris, where he is rescued by the pure love of a wealthy young woman. The story ends when he returns to his old home to find it has become a guest-house. He determines to buy it and restore it to its former glory, and an intriguing sequence in the final section of the novel has the authentic ring of autobiography. Peter stands in his old bedroom and remembers himself as a boy:

He saw the same wallpaper at which his young eyes had gazed – the sweet peas that tangled themselves in faded mauve around the ceiling and sprawled in a pale but abandoned pink over the walls' surfaces. He recognized the little chip in the mantelpiece over which he had so often smoothed his fingers before going to bed. The great mahogany mirror, too, was still there, on the opposite wall, and as he stared into it, it seemed that the vision blurred, that his reflected figure shed its years – shed even its clothes. For he saw himself as he had so often seen himself in years gone by, naked on a night of summer, white and slender, posing in a shameless ecstasy by the light of a serene and distant moon . . . twisting his arms above his head . . . posturing in the tense, ridiculous, but exquisite abandons of youth. Often, when the sky was a dark tray of diamonds, he had come to this mirror, and pressed his forehead against it, and gazed and gazed into his own eyes, trying to fathom their secret, in the precocious knowledge that he would never be able to fathom the secret of any others.

Beverley decided to revamp the novel as straight autobiography, but he knew that the story was not sensational enough. The only way to introduce the shock element was to let his pent-up hatred of John Nichols pour melodramatically on to the page. The danger of this was that it might appear merely as the neurosis of a homosexual son unless the character of his father was so blackened that the hatred became rational. He chose to do this, sweeping aside any hint of compassion and attributing evil motives to everything his father did. By the dextrous use of half-truths, omissions and speculation, he created a monster with few redeeming features. The allegations in *Father Figure* have already been dealt with in the course of this biography, the most difficult to counter being that of John's unremitting mental cruelty to Pauline. Paul denied it. He conceded that there were faults on both sides but he claimed that the two of them were interdependent and deeply fond of each other.

The only living person who could contradict Beverley's version of events was, of course, Paul whom Beverley rarely met. Before he began work on the book, he wrote to Paul at length, hoping to enlist his support, but the reply he received, dated 6 February 1969, was not encouraging, for Paul pointed out that, however sad the past had been, it was meaningless to speculate on what might have happened if things had been different. This did not suit Beverley, whose continuing complaints against his father were based on such speculation. The strongest of these was his belief that he could have been a successful composer of serious music; the schoolboy Chopin had not become the adult equivalent because his father had refused to pay for a musical education. It is worth remembering that John had paid for prep school and public school for all three sons and for university education for two of them. Beverley had not shown himself much of a scholar at Marlborough or at Oxford, as his diaries attest, and he had declined to study for the Bar, preferring to accept an offer from Fleet Street.

In his letter, Paul inconveniently reminded Beverley of the family's financial situation: 'There always seemed to be enough and he [John] appeared always to be generous financially.' Beverley covered himself in the text by including a sort of open letter to Paul, pointing out that they saw things differently and that their temperaments were entirely different as well. When the book appeared, Paul considered it beneath his dignity to enter into any controversy and he did not denounce the book until Beverley died. To make the case against his father seem even more dramatic, Beverley condemned the entire Nichols clan. One of his targets was his late Uncle George; Beverley had been very fond of him and his wife Blanche who had both treated him as a surrogate son. He believed, with reason, that he was their heir and, and after George's death, Blanche did not disillusion him, so he was furious when he learned that he was only a minor beneficiary in a new will made shortly before her death in 1970. In the book he vented his spleen on both of them but particularly on Blanche whom he blamed for turning the gentle and talented George into an ignoble and avaricious creature like herself.

Not even his brothers escaped, but his attack on Paul was catty rather than ferocious; praising him for his Christian forbearance he pointed out that Paul's ministry had been a failure. Paul was painfully aware of this: 'I see now, and have seen for many years that there was not in it any deep and true vocation.' By contrast Beverley had only admiration for his late brother Alan but he revealed that he had been an epileptic, up to then a well-kept secret. Although he did not say so in the book, he had helped Alan financially and also claimed to have paid for his nieces' education and he grumbled that neither they nor their mother had shown enough gratitude. By making Alan's condition public he caused them deep distress. He contended that Paul and Alan's misfortunes, like his own, were the fault of the evil John Nichols.

As a study in verbal patricide, *Father Figure* achieved its purpose. But did Beverley really believe what he wrote? Arthur Diamond was convinced that he did, but by the time he delivered this verdict, his love for Beverley had turned into dislike, and he was sure Beverley was deranged. Cyril Butcher, whose common sense was part of his charm, was not sure that he did believe it. 'Beverley never liked John much but it made a good story. I liked him. He was a jolly old gentleman with a sense of humour. Mrs Nichols was quiet but she could be quite sharp and witty at times. They struck me as being typical of elderly married couples.' Theatricality was in the air when, in the cosy surroundings of his home, Beverley spoke of John with intense hatred. Despite his apparent sincerity, it was as if he was playing a part. In mid-sentence, his expression would alter and with a twinkle in his eye and a witticism he would change the subject and dispel the atmosphere he had created. Once, in a reflective mood, he remarked of his father: 'He could be immensely kind and thoughtful, and he had charm and a sense of fun. He was only a beast when he was drunk.' But in answer to the direct question, 'Did you mean it?', Beverley replied with a smile, 'The reader must decide.'

In *Father Figure*, Beverley and his mother appear as the chief victims, but there is no suggestion of real closeness between them. He never discussed his hopes, dreams or achievements with her and he did not claim the special relationship which homosexual sons often have with their mothers. Perhaps there was none. We know of his affinities with other women – his cousin Cornie, for example, or Mrs Hart or even Miss Herridge – but he remained curiously detached from his mother. He also did her a disservice, for in his anxiety to portray John as a monster he pictured Pauline as a passive pudding of a woman when all the evidence suggests the contrary. In a passage which he cut from the final draft he described his mother as the most foolish woman he had ever known because she refused to leave John. Beverley could not acknowledge her love for her husband, which was just as strong as, if not stronger than, the love he praised in Syrie Maugham, and ascribed to Pauline a sense of misguided duty. He once said, in a moment of self-revelation, that he had never experienced true love for another individual in the whole of his life: obsession, tolerance, fondness, but never love. This may explain his lack of understanding of his mother's devotion to her husband.

In *Father Figure*, Beverley side-stepped any examination of the reasons for John's drinking by attributing it to demonic possession, a condition he had explored in the abandoned *Super Witch*. This, he said, also accounted for John's remarkable good health, his body apparently being unaffected by the massive intake of liquor. If he had sought a serious explanation, he would have had to look at John's history before the onset of alcoholism, and this would have meant admitting to the high esteem in which his father was generally held and to the fact that he was so successful that he was able to retire, a comparatively wealthy man, by the time he was forty.

What caused that abrupt departure from Bristol at the height of his powers, and the equally abrupt departure from Wissett after only two years? Perhaps John's political ambitions were so dashed that he gave up in disgust? But to go from so highly active a life to one of idleness in Torquay seems out of character. There would be little point in pursuing this but for a curious remark Beverley made a few days before his death. He had been discussing the structure of this biography when he suddenly changed the subject. 'Next time I must tell you the real story of my father, but now I am too tired and I must rest.' What did he mean by 'the real story'? His capacity for the unexpected, coupled with his hunger for publicity, leads one to suspect that the old showman still had a card or two up his sleeve, but whatever it was he had to say died with him.

It was more than a year later that a possible explanation began to emerge during a discussion with Paul. By this time the real John Nichols was beginning to surface, as layers of misinformation were stripped from Beverley's portrait of him. Paul refused to confirm or deny the theory of John's thwarted political ambition but it was obvious that he was holding something back. His discomfiture when questioned about the Wissett period suggested a different line of thought: suppose the entire matter hinged on a scandal within the Nichols family – but not one to John's discredit, which Beverley would surely have used in his own case against him. Suppose, however, it was Pauline who had precipitated a crisis? She was a beautiful, strong-willed young woman whose Shalders background was sophisticated compared to that of the Nichols clan. Could she have found life as the wife of a Bristol solicitor who was also heavily involved in politics dull, even lonely? Suppose she had formed an intimate friendship with the artistic, music-loving George Nichols? If John was cuckolded, or simply believed he was, might jealousy not have driven him to take decisions which later proved self-destructive? It is a theory which neatly explains why he refused ever to have anything to do with George after suddenly leaving Bristol. He even accused his brother, according to Beverley, of being riddled with syphilis, a condition which, at that time, caused as much horror as does AIDS today. It would explain why he called Pauline obscene names and referred to Beverley as 'the little bastard'; it would also explain Beverley's special fondness for George, which extended to exempting him partly from the treatment meted out to the rest of the Nichols family. It is, however, only a speculative theory. In discussion with Paul, it was inappropriate to voice it, but in answer to the question, 'Did the departure from Bristol and the move to Wissett have anything to do with Beverley?' Paul replied, 'I would rather not say.'

Father Figure depended as much on style as on content. The book is deliberately dramatic and written as if intended for performance: indeed, edited down, it would make a bravura one-man show. The theatrical drive of the narrative takes the reader from climax to climax, with the evil spirit of John soaking into every page. At last, the monster lies in his coffin, his face in repose, a smile on his lips. His work of destruction is complete but his evil influence continues to ruin the life of his youngest son: 'Father had won.' Slow curtain.

Beverley wrote an epilogue for *Father Figure* but it did not get beyond the form of a rough draft. He probably abandoned it because it would have weakened the dramatic effect of his story. The last paragraph reads:

> And I believe that the book was worth the writing, trusting as I do in the reality of the world to come, in the survival of each and every human personality. I have often asked myself, if there should be an encounter between us, how I should face my father, how I should explain it all. I

have a glimmering hope that there might be some rapport between us. In that hope lies another hope that at long last there would be forgiveness, not only for him, but for myself.

In the light of all we know about John Nichols, the reader might well wonder which of the two men suffered 'demonic possession', the accuser or the accused?

Father Figure created a sensation but not exactly as Beverley had planned. In January 1972 the *Sunday People*, a popular-style newspaper, splashed the stories of his attempts at murder across their front page. The source of their information was not disclosed. A few days later, Arthur Lewis, the Labour MP for West Ham North, demanded in Parliament that Beverley be prosecuted by the Attorney-General. The story was immediately taken up by the rest of the press. The *Daily Telegraph* in its report commented that, although the law could prosecute a self-confessed criminal, it was unlikely in this particular case because there was no corroborative evidence or testimony on oath. Their view proved to be correct as the Attorney-General, Sir Peter Rawlinson, QC declined to take proceedings.

Beverley's uneasy moments were balanced by his delight at the unexpected publicity. His publishers Heinemann promptly advanced the publication date from early March to mid-February and the *Sunday Express* advanced its excerpts of the book to the end of January. The free publicity was also boosted by television advertising featuring Beverley, and the usual interviews added to the hype. Critical reviews began to appear on Sunday 13 February. Predictably, their style reflected that of their newspapers. In a long, thoughtful review in the *Sunday Times*, Cyril Connolly confessed to being engrossed by the story, which was an extreme version of his own experience of an alcoholic father, and added: 'Homicidal ruthlessness must be added to my estimate of Mr Nichols's character.' In a summary of Beverley's career he recalled the 'amazing promise' he had displayed in the '20s, 'before he fell back on the herbaceous border'. He went on: 'Many young men of equal promise are totally eclipsed; others like Auden, Cecil Beaton, Evelyn Waugh, make the most of their talents. Pity those in whom a spark goes out and who carry on doggedly to regain in old age the position they once held so effortlessly.' This appraisal of Beverley's career can be said to reflect with deadly accuracy the literary Establishment's view of his work.

The critics of the *Daily Telegraph* and the *Scotsman* questioned Beverley's motive for writing this 'unpleasant' book. In the former, David Holloway did not equivocate: 'Clearly, his revelations will hurt the surviving members of his family,' and 'Equally clearly he stands to make a great deal of money out of this sorry and sordid tale.' He ended by commenting that, as in *A Case of Human Bondage*, 'the spiteful book he wrote about Somerset

Maugham', the author 'is a great hater . . . If it was his intention to pay off old scores, he has had his own back quite amply here.' In the *Observer* Maurice Richardson found it difficult to take the story as seriously 'as I am sure it deserves'. He placed the blame for this on Beverley's style: 'If it isn't as harrowing as it ought to be, that is because parts of it are too theatrically exhibitionist, over-written in popular novelist's style, even at moments reminding you irrevocably of the music hall and "Don't Sell No More Drink To My Father".' The *Financial Times*'s critic, Anthony Curtis, found it 'shockingly readable, every bit as much as Ackerley's "My Father and Myself"'.

On the whole, Beverley was pleased with the response but disappointed by the criticism of his literary style which he believed to be of a high order. His reaction was not unlike that which followed the publication of *Self* in 1922. In a letter to Robin Maugham dated February 1972, he commented; 'What I would like – apart from lots of money! – is that a few people, at long last, might try to assess it as a serious work of art apart from the sensational aspects.' He was to be somewhat consoled by the notice in the *New York Times Book Review* at a later date: 'He is a prose stylist of considerable skill, and tells his appalling story with detachment and humility.' Another critic, Hal Burton of the *Long Island Newsday*, added an American perspective. He emphasized Beverley's successful career and ended: 'It is a somewhat blood-curdling story. Somewhat, because the sweet smell of success, at least to American thinking, can overcome the stink of a dead body.'

· 24 ·

Sweet and bitter

1973–1980

T HE success of *Father Figure* brought a period of mental calm, almost contentment, to Beverley, marred only by the increasing evidence of his physical deterioration. He was full of ideas for new projects, one of which was for a book to be called *Every Picture Tells a Story*, in which he would weave tales around a selection of famous works of art. But there were no takers and he put the book aside. Then he thought of compiling a book of recipes, but he was sensible enough to realize that anyone could do this and a quick glance around the local bookshops suggested that an astonishing number did. His solution was to write two short books, back to back. The first told the story of Reginald Gaskin who had been in charge of the domestic side of his household from the 1920s to his death from cirrhosis of the liver (caused by chronic alcoholism) in the late 1960s. Gaskin, one of the last 'gentleman's gentlemen', was Jeeves made flesh and his contribution to Beverley's daily comfort was the envy of others less fortunate in their servants. Without him, Beverley was forced to fend for himself in the kitchen, and how he did this was the basis of the other book. Published together under the title *Down the Kitchen Sink*, and written with all his old lightness of touch, they provided a much welcomed antidote to *Father Figure*.

In July 1973, Beverley was arrested by the police for being drunk in charge of a vehicle. He had been out to dinner in Chelsea and it was while backing his car out of its parking place into the busy Fulham Road that he was apprehended for driving without lights. He was then breathalysed and found to be over the alcohol limit. Subsequently he was banned from driving for twelve months. He explained indignantly to his friend, Tom Corbett that he had only had two gins, several glasses of wine and three brandies. 'You can hardly call that drinking. They treated me like a criminal. Why couldn't they have let me play some Chopin to show I wasn't drunk?'

This incident resulted in an amusing piece for *Punch*, in which he described the awful consequences of being a 'breathalysee', not the least of which was learning how to use buses. In the mean time, his car stayed in its garage where he visited it and patted it on the nose as if it were a horse, or sat in it recalling their adventures together. He ended his piece: 'Roll on July 17th 1974,' the day the ban expired. But his car-driving days were over.

In March 1974 he was rushed into hospital following a sudden and massive haemorrhage. An exploratory operation revealed a deep-seated cancer and, two days later, it was removed in a second operation lasting six hours. Complications followed and for several weeks he hovered on the brink of death. Afterwards, he questioned the necessity for keeping alive someone for whom the span of life was nearly over. Given the choice, he would have preferred to slip away with dignity and, aided by medical care, with as little pain as possible. In the months that followed, he contemplated suicide rather than face further operations which he knew to be inevitable, but suicide, he discovered, was easier to imagine than to effect. Surely, he asked of those dearest to him, people in his condition should have the means to die?

A year of almost continual misery followed the operation, and the first piece of work he did was a fierce and emotional plea for the legalization of euthanasia. This appeared in the *Spectator* and evoked a flood of letters in agreement. After this, he supported the Voluntary Euthanasia Society by speaking on radio and television. He also signed a declaration in the presence of two witnesses requesting his physician not to maintain his life by drugs or any artificial means if there was no reasonable prospect of recovery from physical illness. It is ironic that, though he longed for death, he lived for another eight years, surviving four major operations, with their attendant treatments and side-effects. In addition, he had numerous lesser ailments which reduced the quality of his life even further. The body of which he had once been so proud now dismayed him, but his mental faculties remained unimpaired. The actor in him, however, refused to accept obscurity. He began work on a book intended to give comfort to those in circumstances similar to his own but abandoned it; he began a gardening guide but another operation intervened and he did not return to it.

During this period, Beverley's friends rallied round to divert him from moods of glum introspection. Sir Basil Bartlett, Bt., a rumbustious character, took him off to Tunis for a change of scene in November 1975. They had known each other since the early '30s when they had met at one of Barbara Back's social gatherings. Sir Basil was an actor and playwright, and a superb raconteur. 'When I was feeling particularly awful,' Beverley said, 'Basil would arrive with several bottles of wine and the makings of a delicious cold supper. I would listen through a haze of antibiotics and pain-killers while he told vividly funny stories of his eccentric relations. They made me laugh so much that I persuaded him to put them in a book which he called *Jam Tomorrow*. I wrote the introduction for it.'

It was not until 1976, following yet another bout of hospital treatment, that he found 'the next big thing' and some of his old spirit returned. In a letter to his agent, Eric Glass, he described it as 'My true autobiography. All those things I never said. At my age, it will take longer, I should say a year, but it will be worth it. I believe I have the perfect title, *Farewell Performance*.'

If the title implied a grand flourish and an exit to cheers and applause in the manner of Melba, it did not work out that way. The basis of the book was his earlier autobiography *All I Could Never Be* which had been written with all the assurance of a man who had found fame and financial success. The new version was, by contrast, haunted by self-denigration and self-pity. He dismissed much of his success as mere trumpery and bemoaned his lost opportunities. The monster he had created in *Father Figure* was resurrected to act as a scapegoat, but sometimes he blamed himself as well, claiming that he should not have prostituted his talent but rather have sold his body for the financial security he needed to be a serious composer. He blamed his inability to 'sell' his body on a fastidious dislike of going to bed with people who did not attract him sexually, and, on the subject of sex, deliberately ignored the dominating role it had played in his life, excusing this omission by averring that, 'When writers take down their trousers, I turn the page.' He went on at some length about the ugliness of it all, describing the act as 'clumsy and uncouth,' giving no hint of the fact that he had been sexually insatiable, had revelled in it and went on revelling in it well into old age. Despite the overriding gloom of the book, Beverley could never be dull. His opinions were penetrating, often witty, and there was a plentiful scattering of anecdotes about famous people.

Farewell Performance, as he had planned it, was never completed; instead, when the story reached 1939, he stopped and rounded it off by re-using the ending of *All I Could Never Be*. The sheer physical effort of writing had proved almost too much. He changed the title to *The Unforgiving Minute*, and promised a second volume to be called *Distance Run*, though it is doubtful whether he ever intended to write it. Both titles were culled from Rudyard Kipling's 'If' which Beverley considered a great poem, 'whatever the intellectual snobs may say about it'.

The Unforgiving Minute was a surprise when it appeared in 1978; it was disconcerting to read in it that he was a 'failure' when all the evidence showed him to be a success. The approach was, however, consistent with the strategy of the unexpected which he had followed throughout his writing career. When his claim to failure is analysed, it is difficult to know precisely what he meant by it. Although, for example, he invited sympathy for his period with the *Sunday Chronicle*, no one had forced him to renew his highly remunerative contract year after year. There is no doubt about his depth of feeling about his ambition to be a serious composer, but there was nothing, particularly in the years when he was a relatively wealthy man, to prevent him taking time off to prove his skill once and for all. Is it possible that he feared failure? Beverley had always enjoyed a self-indulgent lament when the mood was upon him, and once the mood passed it was as if it had never been. He certainly never described himself as a failure to his friends, indeed, he was far more likely to complain angrily of the lack of recognition of his success – an OBE, for instance, or, better still, a knighthood like Robert Helpmann or, of course, Noel Coward. 'They left it until Noel was nearly dead,' he said. 'If they leave me much longer, it will be too late.'

The press seemed disconcerted by the book. Robert Morley summed it up when he wrote in the London *Evening News*: 'Beverley Nichols has certainly taken a swipe at his own image.' Valerie Jenkins, in the London *Evening Standard*, agreed. 'Having to look back on a gilded youth and sort of downhill all the way, fifty books published, many of them, so he says, second rate, this, his fifty-first, is practically an Aristotelian tragedy, evoking pity and terror, horribly compelling, rivetingly awful.' John Mortimer had a high old time reviewing the book for the *Sunday Times*. 'At last a book with a genuinely funny central character as mercilessly observed and as comically drawn as the minor roles in Dostoievsky. In his latest work, Mr Nichols has given us "Beverley", a worthy addition to the long line of anti-heroes.'

Beverley was annoyed by the impression that many of the critics gave, that his career had ceased to prosper after 1939. 'Perhaps if you had finished the book?' Cyril Butcher ventured. 'They should read *Who's Who*,' Beverley snapped. In an interview for *Isis* shortly after publication, he corrected the misconception by giving examples of his later successes: 'So there hasn't been a total eclipse since the war.' The interviewer turned the conversation to modern art, and Beverley declared that the Trustees of the Tate Gallery should be drowned in the Thames in sacks along with the notorious pile of bricks exhibited there. When his interviewer suggested that perhaps the artist felt that his ideas were best expressed though the medium of bricks, Beverley retorted, 'Balls!' Asked what he considered to be the greatest danger to the modern world, he replied, 'Pop music. I consider the invention of the electric guitar was potentially more lethal than the invention of the internal combustion engine.' Over lunch, he regaled his young interviewer with an epigram: 'All things in life are too long, including life itself.' He sent him off with a word of advice, 'Always go to see the Pope when you are in Rome. Get a private audience,' and described his own audience with Pope Paul VI: '. . . he couldn't have been nicer.' Whatever impression *The Unforgiving Minute* might have given, this interview at least indicated that, at eighty, his mind was as lively as it had been when he had rejuvenated *Isis* after the First World War.

Those who attended the Foyle's Luncheon at the Dorchester Hotel in

January 1980 saw Beverley at his most urbane as its chairman. Seated at his right was the guest of honour, Dame Margot Fonteyn, and on his left was Princess Michael of Kent. On the top table were also three ambassadors, a scattering of titles as well as luminaries from the world of ballet, including Dame Marie Rambert, Dame Ninette de Valois and Sir Frederick Ashton who, to Beverley, was still the young man who had choreographed *Floodlight*. The lunch was to celebrate Dame Margot's book, *The Magic of Dance*, but, to Beverley, it was an acknowledgement of his status as an author and personality, and he revelled in it.

He badly needed the assurance that such an occasion gave him, for things were not going well for him. *The Unforgiving Minute* was not as successful as he had hoped and it had not produced any much-needed commissions. Although he did not have the stamina to write a full-length book, he could, for example, have coped with a column in a monthly magazine, and found it difficult to accept that his was not now a name which sprang to editors' minds. His finances were in a poor state: in 1979, for instance, his total income before tax was about £6,000. Although Cyril Butcher contributed and Sir Basil Bartlett came to the rescue with a gift of £700, it was not sufficient to maintain a fourteen-room house and a large garden. Beverley was the first to admit that he had not made proper provision for his old age when he was in a position to do so, but, with Micawber-like optimism, had always hoped that something would turn up. In the mean time, he economized where he could and shut his eyes to the effects of neglect in the house and the garden. The garden actually benefited from the lack of constant attention and he was pleased by its new, wilder appearance. He continued to entertain, and a frugal lunch in a freezing dining-room was offset by his ability to charm. He was fortunate in that Cyril's great friend, Peter Yan, was a superb cook and took over the kitchen when he could spare time from his own family's restaurant. The meals he produced echoed the great days of Gaskin, and guests on those occasions probably had no idea that Beverley's usual fare was simple and basic.

Only a few people knew the true financial situation; the rest assumed that Beverley was a wealthy man and he did nothing to disillusion them. The obvious answer to his cash-flow problem was to sell up and move on, as he had done in the past, but he could not face the upheaval or the loss of his garden. Curiously, it never occurred to him or to Cyril that the antiques they had collected over the years were of immense value. The sale of judiciously selected items could have solved the problem without impairing the comfort of the house. Cyril was amazed by the prices fetched by the furniture at auction after Beverley's death. On the subject of his finances, Beverley wrote in a lighter vein in January 1981:

I had an encouraging snippet last week. Dame Edna Everage [Barry

Humphries] sent me an Australian bookseller's catalogue with an item marked at £75, 'Rare signed letter from Beverley Nichols to a friend in London sent from Melbourne when he was staying with Dame Nellie Melba in 1924. Mint condition.' 'She' has actually purchased it. I told her she was a silly girl and that I would write any number of letters at half that fee!

In the mean time there was an occasional article for *Woman's Own* or a gardening magazine, but nothing of substance. Beverley was therefore particularly pleased when he was asked in 1980 to review for *Books and Bookmen* a biography of Somerset Maugham written by an American journalist, Ted Morgan. He had high hopes of it, but his anticipation turned to anger when he read in the 'blurb' on the book-jacket that Lady Glendevon 'who had hitherto refused to discuss her father with writers' was 'both candid and fair-minded in giving [this book] her support.' Thus an old wound was reopened.

In his review of Ted Morgan's book, Beverley told his story again. The following is a sample:

It is totally, indeed blatantly untrue to assert that Lady Glendevon had hitherto 'refused to discuss' her father with other writers for the simple reason that she had not only discussed but corrected, approved and encouraged my own book, *A Case of Human Bondage* which was the work originally responsible for inspiring a ceaseless flood of Maugham revelations of which Mr Ted Morgan's book is the latest, the least excusable and most unpleasant. She knows this, Lord Glendevon knows this and Spencer Curtis Brown [Maugham's literary executor] knew it.

He was further angered by a description of himself in Morgan's book, some of whose phrases had a familiar ring. He surmised that these had come from Cecil Roberts's autobiography, *Half Way*, published in 1930; Roberts, a friend of Beverley's until his death, had written a long analysis of him which, read today, is shrewd, full of fun, and ultimately full of praise. It concluded that Beverley's delight in being Beverley had been shared by all those he met. There was little praise, however, in Morgan's description, which spoke of Beverley as facile, a Byron without the talent. Beverley was also not best pleased when he found Cyril Butcher was described as 'a hard-drinking clerk turned actor.' Neither was Cyril amused: 'I was never a clerk, hard-drinking or otherwise and, as a struggling actor, there was never enough money to pay for essentials, let alone drink.' There was, too, a reference to Barbara Back's letters to Maugham, describing the sexual involvements of the two young men. Cyril commented: 'She knew nothing, but her lively imagination made up for it. Not a very pleasant lady, as it turned out.' This opinion was endorsed by Rebecca West in her letters to Beverley.

All in all, Beverley's review was, to say the least, uncomplimentary. In one of the milder passages, he wrote:

> No professional writer who is prepared to wallow so deeply in the gutter and to report so pitilessly upon his findings could fail to emerge with something that is, at least, readable. Even so, I find it inexplicable that Maugham's literary executor endeavoured to foist this stuff upon the world as the 'final and definitive portrait'. It is to be deplored not only for what it puts in but also for what it leaves out. There is no serious attempt to assess Maugham's position as an artist, or to judge his standing in relation to his rivals. What is more inexplicable is that the book should have met with the approval of the Maugham family or the few remaining men and women who were associated with him in friendship or in business.

The first sentence in this passage referred to an occasion, described in the book, when Sir Malcolm Bullock and the art critic Douglas Cooper called on Maugham, who, now senile, popped up from behind the sofa and, having defecated on the rug, scooped up a handful of faeces. *Books and Bookmen* subsequently published a letter from Douglas Cooper denying all knowledge of the story and pointing out that he never visited Maugham with Sir Malcolm Bullock who was, in any case, not a friend of his. He also said that he had had no correspondence with Ted Morgan and had no idea where he had obtained this nonsensical story. Beverley read the letter gleefully and said, 'What did I tell you?'

Beverley forbade his friends to read the book, which probably had the reverse effect, and he simmered for weeks afterwards. 'I do not think Mr Morgan understood Maugham. He certainly does not empathize with him. There is no trace of Willie's sense of humour, probably because Mr Morgan appears to lack one himself. Humour is so important in a biographer. So is objectivity. This is all so unsophisticated and bereft of a sense of period. As for the writing style, it would have horrified Willie.'

· 25 ·

Finale

1980–1983

B EVERLEY was not afraid of death – indeed he prayed for it. 'It won't
be long now, no more pain, no more vertigo [his latest affliction]
and someone else can pay the gas bill!' His lack of fear was due to his
belief in an after-life where he would find fulfilment not attained in his
earthly life. In two books, *The Fool Hath Said* and *A Pilgrim's Progress*, he
had expressed views which were not in keeping with orthodox Christianity
and, as he grew older, he became more unorthodox.

Christ, to me, is vividly alive. Admittedly, there is much in His story, as it
has been handed down to us, that is sheerly incredible. As for the manner
in which His doctrine is interpreted by the Churches, that is often sheerly
wicked. Of all the phrases that have ever clouded men's thoughts and
befuddled their innate sense of right and wrong, the orthodox Christian
phrase 'born in sin' is the most pernicious. It is like a hideous scar slashed
across the face of humanity.

Sin is being untrue to oneself. I base my definition of sin on the
fundamental assumption that the 'self' is good, because it is of God. So
being untrue to oneself is being untrue to God, deadening the pity with
which He has charged one's heart, stifling the instincts with which He
has directed the movements of one's body and neglecting the talents with
which He has stored one's mind. It irks me to be told, even by
implication (in sermons) that, when I swim with the stream of my own
nature, I am ipso facto swimming towards a cesspool. It irks me even
more to be urged to swim against the stream, as though the river of life
could only cleanse you if you fought it.

Your nature may not be the conventional Nature, and the type of man
or woman that you are may not conform to the composite type that
various societies of the world have been obliged to create for their own
convenience in order to codify their laws, to protect their property and to
simplify the functions of the police. You may be a total rebel but as long
as you are true to your 'self', you need have no spiritual concern.

Beverley had expressed these views in a book which he had begun in 1960 but never completed. In old age, he saw no reason to change them. In a sense, he was returning to a period in his adolescence during which he had rejected Christianity, when his great confidante was his cousin Cornie. In letters to her he had let his thoughts tumble out in a confusion of emotion. Writing when he was seventeen, he once explained that his views had been influenced by his study of Shelley and in particular the notes on 'Queen Mab', from which he quoted:

> The plurality of worlds, the indefinite immensity of the universe is the most awful subject of contemplation. He who rightly feels its mystery and grandeur is in no danger of seduction from the falsehoods of religious systems.

He ended the letter with a poem he called 'Credo'. It concluded:

> My altars are the hills,
> My incense the sweetest flowers that scent the skies,
> And I am the eternal soul.
> These are my creeds,
> Nature's immensities.

He enjoyed debating the matter in his final years with a small number of people including John Betjeman. When arthritis prevented him from playing the piano, he returned to poetry as a means of creative expression, and much of his verse had a strong spiritual basis. The task gave him a shape to his day, for, in the absence of other work, he followed the discipline of a lifetime and spent several hours each morning writing. He found the work demanding, but ultimately almost as satisfying as composing music. The recurring theme of his verse was not dissimilar to that of 'Credo'. In his poem describing his reaction to a drop of water seen through a microscope, revealing 'a world of monsters hot from hell', he ends:

> How do we meet such most disturbing mysteries?
> Fall on our knees? Yes – if we must
> And if it helps, recite some pious article of trust.
> But in the end, it's better to arise
> And face the sun to find our grace
> For then the pattern falls into its proper place.
> We see it all with different eyes
> And realize, when all is said and done,
> The sun itself is but a particle of dust.

He was so pleased with his work that he sent examples to John Betjeman, seeking his comments and advice on publication. In his reply, dated 4 September 1980, Betjeman avoided expressing an opinion on the quality of the verse. He advised Beverley to hire a hall or give a party and read his work aloud. By doing this a number of times, he would deduce from audience reaction what was best left in or what was best taken out, for he feared the verses were too long. Beverley was infuriated by this and guessed that Betjeman did not like his efforts, but far from being discouraged he worked even harder, determined to see his poems published, 'if it's the last thing I do, which it probably will be.' As for hiring halls or giving parties, he dismissed this with, 'I can't afford to.'

Once he had completed *Twilight*, as he called his collection of verse, there was nothing in prospect. He had to concede that, at the age of eighty-two, he had retired, and he did not like it. The void left by the lack of work was filled with the minutiae of daily domestic routine which achieved an importance it did not, in his opinion, justify. He found it ironic that so much energy was needed to live when he would have preferred to be dead. Most evenings, he played cards, a favourite pastime, but without the stimulus of 'the next big thing' he succumbed to a form of mental weariness. In effect, he was a prisoner in his own house and met few people beyond his immediate coterie of friends. This did not help for, as he remarked ruefully, love them as he might, he knew them too well and they held no surprises for him.

The months dragged slowly by until, early in 1982, he received a proposition to make a long-playing record of his words and music. For years, he had been mildly astonished to receive small cheques for royalties from radio broadcasts of songs recorded in the 1930s, and now he was pleased and flattered by the idea. The company concerned wished to supplement his published songs with others whose lyrics existed but whose music had been lost. The reconstruction of the music was a relatively simple matter since Beverley could hum all the tunes, but he saw it as an obstacle. It was explained to him that assistance could easily be provided, but he prevaricated and the whole project was put into the pending tray.

In the mean time, several other matters took his attention. First, he was commissioned by *Woman's Own* to write three articles to celebrate the Golden Jubilee of the magazine. Second, he was asked to do a series of three programmes for BBC Radio 4, and last, the publication date of *Twilight* was announced by its publishers, Bachman and Turner. The book was to be launched at a party at the English-Speaking Union in Mayfair on 2 December, at which he was asked to read some of his verse. In preparation, he learned the poems by heart and rehearsed them until he was satisfied with every inflection. He rehearsed his linking dialogue as well so that the overall impression would be one of artless spontaneity. In a note to a friend, he wrote, 'I feel groggy and I am dreading it,' but once he had settled in front of his audience, his stage-fright left him. The years had done little to impair his voice or his charm, and it was easy to imagine him at the height of his powers as a public speaker.

The old showman had a surprise for his audience as a climax: a long poem called 'Memories of Chopin' which, he said, had been inspired by a friend and fellow-musician of Chopin named Julius Celinski. Over the years, Celinski had communicated with Beverley, first at a séance and then directly on several occasions. 'Perhaps it is only my intense love of Chopin's music which makes me feel that Celinski had anything to do with them, but as I transmitted the verses from time to time, the details have been so vivid that I find it difficult to believe I invented them.' The message was an assurance to Beverley that his life after death would fulfil his yearning to compose. Any cynics in the audience probably thought it nonsense, or a gimmick to attract press publicity, but those who knew of Beverley's lifelong study of religion, philosophy and the paranormal may have accepted that his story, even if it was not real to them, was certainly real to him.

Twilight made little impact on the public. Beverley sent a copy to John Betjeman, fearful of his reaction after his comments two years previously, but in a letter dated 14 February 1983 Betjeman said he found the verses arresting: 'Their sincerity rings through them all like a bell.' He thought the satirical poems particularly good and original. Such praise from the Poet Laureate was an accolade Beverley had not expected.

The activity and renewed interest in him was a boost to his self-esteem but the effort it required was physically debilitating. To his close friends he appeared precisely what he was, a very frail old man, and in the last months of his life he grew frailer still. Nevertheless, he was still capable of an astonishing transformation for the benefit of people outside his immediate circle. In June, he invited an old business acquaintance from New York, Elliott Graham, who had handled the promotion of many of his American books, to visit him. Graham had retired as Director of Publicity for the New York publishing house, Dutton, but he was still retained by them as consultant. He had not met Beverley for some years and he was apprehensive, but when he arrived at four o'clock on Saturday 11 June he was delighted to find Beverley in sprightly mood and apparently in good health. He was given a tour of the garden with his host supplying a running commentary: 'That myrtle is descended from a sprig that came from Queen Victoria's wedding bouquet. I gave a cutting to Princess Alexandra on one of her visits.' Beverley apologized for name-dropping – 'one of my faults' – but when the two men settled down to tea on the terrace, he continued to mention the famous in a torrent of reminiscence. Much of what he said was familiar to Graham but he was more fascinated by Beverley's technique as a raconteur than by the subject matter of his conversation. One Noel Coward story was new to him.

It concerned Beverley's last meeting with Coward shortly before the latter died. As he was leaving, Beverley said soulfully, 'It's awful at our age to say goodbye. One runs into old friends and promises to contact them soon and almost the next day, one reads their obituaries in *The Times*.' Coward eyed Beverley up and down and remarked pointedly, 'I consider myself lucky if they last through luncheon.' Beverley went on, 'I miss Noel dreadfully. Now Cecil [Beaton] has gone, too. Osbert Sitwell called me the first of the bright young people and I am the last of them.'

After Graham had left for a dinner engagement, Beverley, exhausted by his efforts, went to bed. His guest, unaware that a performance had been put on for his benefit, later spoke of Beverley's astonishing vitality, and commented on the style in which he lived, assuming, as most people did, that he was a wealthy man. On learning of Beverley's death three months later, he talked about the Nichols publications he had handled: 'He worked brilliantly on a small canvas and his writing was always graceful.'

On the morning of 9 September, Beverley's eighty-fifth birthday, he was working on a new poem when something, apparently, caught his attention in the garden and he stood up to see what it was. Exactly what happened next is not known – possibly he had an attack of vertigo – but he was found lying on the floor unable to get up. He was rushed to Kingston Hospital and for several days Cyril Butcher believed that there was no cause for alarm. Beverley, though weak, was mentally alert, chatting as vividly as ever and complaining about the refusal of his doctor to allow him coffee. He instigated changes to his will but before these could be implemented, he died peacefully on 15 September.

The poem he was writing on his birthday and did not complete gives, perhaps, some clue as to his state of mind. In an explanatory note, he said that his mother had told him that he had been born in the late afternoon 'when the lamps were being lit'.

Lamplight

It was the hour when shadows flit across the lawn
When blinds are drawn
Against a deepening sky,
When solitary stars like silver sentinels
Take up their watch.
It was the season when September roses fade
When life gives way to death,
And then begins again.

When little boys are born
And lamps are lit.

If I had stood above myself, in that first hour
With hands outstretched,
With powers of life and death
To strangle and to end the feeble breath,
How would I answer if I had the choice?
With nothing but a date
Upon a modest monument
To mark my insignificance?
To weep or to rejoice?

On the following Friday, the funeral service was held at St Andrew's Church on Ham Common, and the cortège went on to Mortlake Crematorium for the final ceremony. Beverley's ashes were later scattered in the grounds of the church at Glatton, better known to his readers as Allways.

On 16 November, with copies of the fiftieth anniversary edition of *Down the Garden Path* on sale in the shops, a celebration, as Mervyn Stockwood described it, took place at St Paul's, Covent Garden, the 'Actors' Church'. Apart from the religious aspect of the occasion, Ned Sherrin had arranged a programme of Beverley's work. Patrick Ryecart read from the preface to *Twenty-Five*, Liz Robertson sang 'I Will Pray', Derek Jacobi read 'A Bluebell' from *Twilight*, and Michael Hordern read from the new preface to *Down the Garden Path*. The address, full of warmth and humour, was given by Alfred Shaughnessy. The event had begun with 'The Shadow Prelude' and it ended with a recording of John Mills and Frances Day singing 'Little White Room' from *Floodlight*. It was a cheerful and highly theatrical occasion and, as Cyril Butcher commented, 'He would have been pleased there was a full house.'

Conclusion

I N *Enemies of Promise*, the influential critic Cyril Connolly provided a standard of literary merit: any book that survives in print for ten years must
have some quality that not only transcends initial success but that also
improves with time. If Connolly was correct, over twenty of Beverley's books
are of distinct literary value. Of these, the children's books can claim a life of up
to forty-five years, and the detective novels over twenty years. Of his earlier
work, *Twenty-five* lasted more than sixty years. (Five books continue to grace the
lists of publishers as I write.) Seventeen of Beverley's longest-selling works were
written after *Down The Garden Path*, and twelve of them had nothing to do
with homes and gardens, which refutes Connolly's contemptuous dismissal of
Beverley's career as having ended in the herbaceous border or stranded up the
garden path.

Unfortunately Connolly's sneer haunted Beverley and was taken up by others who asserted, somewhat pompously, that he had not 'fulfilled his early promise.' If his career had fizzled out, as so many do after a bright start, the accusation
might have made sense, but Beverley's work attracted admiration, popularity
and commercial success beyond the wildest dreams of most writers. Ironically,
this was taken by some as evidence of artistic failure! So whatever he did, he
could not win the approval of his detractors however much he tried to. Of
course, Beverley's passion for self-publicity at any cost no doubt led many to
conclude that he was not to be taken seriously.

As J. W. Lambert of *The Sunday Times* observed in his obituary, Beverley
suffered his share of denigration when 'a comparable talent exercised in diligent
obscurity would have earned approval.' This is borne out by reference guides to
English Literature, beloved of universities, which celebrate writers known only
to a tiny coterie of academics, but exclude others with popular approval such as
Beverley. In other words he, and many of his contemporaries, remain victims of
intellectual snobbery.

Today his books, including the recently re-issued 'Merry Hall' series, continue to enlighten and entertain readers around the world; but how long will

this last and what of his future literary reputation? In his diary for 3rd January 1956 he wrote: 'It will be a hundred years before my own work finds its proper level. I have a shrewd idea of what that level will be. I shall be on the same shelf as Jane Austen, Mrs Gaskell, Hazlitt and Lewis Carroll.' It might be thought that to predict his own literary survival was audacious and his choice of shelf companions presumptuous, but it was typically ambitious and characteristic of him. Who knows? He may prove to be right. After all, who in 1932 could have guessed that *Down The Garden Path* would still be on sale nearly seventy years later?

Bibliography

WORKS BY BEVERLEY NICHOLS

I wish to thank Roy C. Dicks for his invaluable assistance in revising and updating the bibliography that appeared in the 1991 edition of this book. Gratefully acknowledged, also, is the bibliography prepared for the Nichols entry in *Contemporary Authors*, New Revision Series, Volume 17 (Gale Research 1986).

Titles are arranged chronologically. United Kingdom publishers are listed first; United States, if any, second. All entries refer to original editions; subsequent paper editions or reprints are not included.

Books by Beverley Nichols

Novels
Prelude (Chatto and Windus 1920)
Patchwork (Chatto and Windus 1921; Holt 1922)
Self (Chatto and Windus 1922)
Crazy Pavements (Jonathan Cape 1927; Doran 1927)
Evensong (Jonathan Cape 1932; Doubleday 1932)
Revue (Jonathan Cape 1939; Doubleday 1939)

Mysteries
No Man's Street (Hutchinson 1954; Dutton 1954)
The Moonflower (Hutchinson 1955; Dutton 1955 as *The Moonflower Murder*)
Death to Slow Music (Hutchinson 1956; Dutton 1956)
The Rich Die Hard (Hutchinson 1957; Dutton 1958)
Murder by Request (Hutchinson 1960; Dutton 1960)

Short stories
Women and Children Last (Jonathan Cape 1931; Doubleday 1931)
Men Do Not Weep (Jonathan Cape 1941; Harcourt 1942)

Children's novels
The Tree That Sat Down (Jonathan Cape 1945)*
The Stream That Stood Still (Jonathan Cape 1948)*
   *These two titles were published in one volume by St. Martin's in 1966.
The Mountain of Magic (Jonathan Cape 1950)
The Wickedest Witch in the World (W. H. Allen 1971)

Autobiography
Twenty-Five (Jonathan Cape 1926; Doran 1926)
All I Could Never Be (Jonathan Cape 1949; Dutton 1952)

The Sweet and Twenties (Weidenfeld and Nicolson 1958)
A Case of Human Bondage (Secker and Warburg 1966; Award Books 1966)
Father Figure (Heinemann 1972; Simon and Schuster 1972)
Down the Kitchen Sink (W. H. Allen 1974)
The Unforgiving Minute (W. H. Allen 1978)

Gardens and homes

Down the Garden Path (Jonathan Cape 1932; Doubleday 1932)*
A Thatched Roof (Jonathan Cape 1933; Doubleday 1933)*
A Village in a Valley (Jonathan Cape 1934; Doubleday 1934)*
   *These three titles form the Allways trilogy about Nichols's Tudor cottage in Glatton,
   Cambridgeshire. *The Gift of a Garden*, a condensation of the three, along with a new
   introduction by Nichols, was published by W. H. Allen in 1971 and Dodd in 1972.
How Does Your Garden Grow? (Allen and Unwin 1935; Doubleday 1935)
   A collection of four radio essays by Nichols plus essays by Compton Mackenzie,
   Marion Cran and Vita Sackville-West.
Green Grows the City (Jonathan Cape 1939; Harcourt 1939)
Merry Hall (Jonathan Cape 1951; Dutton 1953)*
Laughter on the Stairs (Jonathan Cape 1953; Dutton 1954)*
Sunlight on the Lawn (Jonathan Cape 1956; Dutton 1956)*
   *These three titles form the Merry Hall trilogy about Nichols's Georgian manor house
   in Ashtead, Surrey. *The Gift of a Home*, a condensation of the three, along with a new
   introduction by Nichols, was published by W. H. Allen in 1972 and Dodd in 1973.
Garden Open Today (Jonathan Cape 1963; Dutton 1963)*
Forty Favourite Flowers (Studio Vista 1964; St. Martin's 1965)*
Garden Open Tomorrow (Heinemann 1968; Dodd 1969)*
   *These three titles form the Sudbrook trilogy about Nichols's late-eighteenth-century
   attached cottage in Richmond, Surrey.
The Art of Flower Arrangement (Collins 1967; Viking 1967)

Politics

Cry Havoc! (Jonathan Cape 1933; Doubleday 1933)
News of England; or a Country without a Hero (Jonathan Cape 1938; Doubleday 1938)
Verdict on India (Jonathan Cape 1944; Harcourt 1944)
Uncle Samson (Evans 1950)

Religion

The Fool Hath Said (Jonathan Cape 1936; Doubleday 1936)
A Pilgrim's Progress (Jonathan Cape 1952)

Travel

No Place Like Home (Jonathan Cape 1936; Doubleday 1936)
The Sun in My Eyes (Heinemann 1969)

Drama

Failures (Jonathan Cape 1933)
   A collection of three plays: *The Stag, Avalanche* and *When the Crash Comes.*

Drama (continued)

Evensong (Samuel French 1933)
   Written with Edward Knoblock.

Mesmer (Jonathan Cape 1937)

Shadow of the Vine (Jonathan Cape 1949)

Miscellaneous

Memories and Melodies (Thornton Butterworth 1925; G. H. Doran 1926)
   Nichols 'ghost-wrote' this 'autobiography' of Dame Nellie Melba. The 1980 reissue of this title in Australia (Thomas Nelson) and in London (HamishHamilton) acknowledged Nichols's authorship.

Are They the Same at Home? (Jonathan Cape 1927; Doran 1927)*

The Star-Spangled Manner (Jonathan Cape 1928; Doubleday 1928)*
   *These two books of celebrity sketches were published, together with *Twenty-Five*, as *Oxford—London—New York* by Jonathan Cape in 1931, with a new introduction by Nichols.

For Adults Only (Jonathan Cape 1932; Doubleday 1933)
   A satire on parental advice manuals.

Puck at Brighton: The Official Handbook of the County Borough of Brighton (Brighton Corporation Publicity Committee 1933)
   Annual tourist guide to which Nichols heavily contributed.

A Book of Old Ballads (Hutchinson 1934)
   Compiled and annotated by Nichols.

Yours Sincerely (George Newnes 1949)
   A collection of Nichols's columns from the popular weekly *Woman's Own*, including those by fellow columnist Monica Dickens.

The Queen's Coronation Day: The Pictorial Record of the Historic Occasion, with the Eyewitness Account of Her Majesty's Crowning (Pitkin Pictorials 1953)

Beverley Nichols' Cat Book (Thomas Nelson 1955)

Beverely Nichols' Cats' A. B. C. (Jonathan Cape 1960; Dutton 1960)*

Beverley Nichols' Cats' X. Y. Z. (Jonathan Cape 1961; Dutton 1961)*
   *These two titles were published together as *Beverley Nichols' Cats' A to Z* in 1977 by W. H. Allen.

Powers That Be (Jonathan Cape 1966; St. Martin's 1966)
   An overview of paranormal phenomena.

Twilight: First and Probably Last Poems (Bachman and Turner 1982)

Books introduced or prefaced by Nichols

The Faro Table, or The Gambling Mothers by Charles Sedley (Nash and Grayson 1931)

The Making of a Man: Letters from an Old Parson to His Sons by Albert Victor Baillie (Nicolson and Watson 1934)

Cats in Camera by Jan Styczynski (Deutsch 1962)

In an Eighteenth Century Kitchen: A Receipt Book of Cookery, 1698 (Woolf 1968)
   A reprint of the original that Nichols found boarded up in his Glatton cottage and described in *A Thatched Roof.*

So Brief a Dream by Rafaelle, Duchess of Leinster (W. H. Allen 1973; John Day 1973 as
  The Dutchess from Brooklyn)
All About Cats (Orbis 1975)
Jam Tomorrow: Some Early Reminiscences by Basil Bartlett (Elek 1978)

Published Music and Lyrics by Beverley Nichols

Published by Warner-Chappell:
From *Cochran's 1930 Revue:*
  'Selection'
  'The Little Things You Do'
  'Since Eros Went Away'
Cabaret number 'My Heart Is Out of Work' (1934)
From *Floodlight* (1938):
  'Artificial Flowers'
  'Birds of Dawn'
  'Dancing with the Daffodils'
  'I Will Pray'
  'Little White Room'
From TV Production of *Evensong* (1953): 'The Song of the Willow'

Published by Lawrence Wright Music:
Cabaret number 'Another One Gone' (1935)
From TV production of *Shadow of the Vine* (1958):
  'The Shadow Prelude'
Included in *Father Figure* (1972): 'Piano Etude'

Recordings (Music and Lyrics by Beverley Nichols)

Selection from *Cochran's 1930 Revue*, including 'The Little Things You Do', piano solos by
  Billy Mayerl, Columbia DB 117.
'The Little Things You Do' was also recorded by 'Hutch', Leslie Hutchinson, on Parlo-
  phone R 639
'The Little Things You Do' was included in the 1986 LP and the 1990 CD *The Song Is—
  Richard Rodgers and Lorenz Hart*, to whom it was incorrectly attributed, Living Era
  AJA 5041.
Piano Selection from *Floodlight* (1938) played by Beverley Nichols, HMV BC 443. Also
  from this revue, 'Artificial Flowers' sung by Frances Day and 'Little White Room' sung
  by John Mills and Frances Day, HMV B 8590. This song was included in the 1970 LP
  Revue 1930–1940, EMI Parlophone PMC 7154, when the entire score of *Floodlight* was
  incorrectly attributed to Vivian Ellis.

Other songs by Beverley Nichols were recorded by performers including Dame Clara
Butt. Unfortunately, archive material is incomplete or information had been lost.

SELECTION OF OTHER BOOKS CONSULTED

Amory, Mark (Ed.). 1973. *The Letters of Evelyn Waugh.* Weidenfeld and Nicolson.
Aronson, Theo. 1973. *Grandmama of Europe.* Cassell.
Bennett, Daphne. 1984. *Margot.* Victor Gollancz.
Bolitho, Hector. 1954. *Jinnah.* John Murray.
Boothby, Robert, Raymond Massey (and others). 1977. *My Oxford.* Robson.
Burton, Peter. 1985. *Parallel Lives.* GMP.
Calder, Robert. 1989. *Willie.* Heinemann.
Connolly, Cyril. 1938. *Enemies of Promise.* Routledge and Kegan Paul.
Core, Philip. 1984. *Camp.* Plexus.
Cotes, Peter. 1949. *No Star Nonsense.* Rockcliffe.
Curtis, Anthony. 1974. *The Patterns of Maugham.* Hamish Hamilton.
Davie, Michael (Ed.). 1982. *The Diaries of Evelyn Waugh.* Weidenfeld and Nicolson.
Drawbell, James. 1963. *The Sun Within Us.* Collins.
Ellis, Vivian. 1953. *I'm On A See-Saw.* Michael Joseph.
Falk, Bernard. 1933. *He Laughed In Fleet Street.* Hutchinson.
Fisher, Richard B. 1978. *Syrie Maugham.* Duckworth.
Flanner, Janet (Ed. Irving Drutman). 1984. *London Was Yesterday.* Michael Joseph.
Forbes, Bryan. 1977. *Ned's Girl.* Elm Tree Books.
Fyfe, David Maxwell (Lord Kilmuir). 1964. *Political Adventure.* Weidenfeld and Nicolson.
Graves, Charles. n.d. *The Cochran Story.* W. H. Allen.
Graves, Robert and Alan Hodge. 1940. *The Long Week-End.* Hutchinson.
Griffiths, Richard. 1980. *Fellow Travellers of the Right.* Constable.
Hadfield, John (Ed.). 1961, 1963, 1964. *The Saturday Book.* Hutchinson.
Harding, James. 1986. *Agate.* Methuen.
Hart-Davis, Duff. 1986. *Hitler's Games.* Century.
Hassall, Christopher. 1959. *Edward Marsh.* Longmans.
Hetherington, John. 1967. *Melba.* Faber and Faber.
Holman-Hunt, Diana. 1974. *Latin Among Lions—Alvaro Guevara.* Michael Joseph.
Jog, N. G. 1945. *Judge or Judas?* Bombay: Thacker.
Kee, Robert. 1984. *The World We Left Behind.* Weidenfeld and Nicolson.
Kunitz, Stanley J. and Howard Haycraft (Eds.). 1950. *Twentieth Century Authors—A Biographical Dictionary of Modern Literature.* New York: H.W. Wilson.
Lean, Garth. 1985. *Frank Buchman.* Constable.
Lees-Milne, James. 1980. *Harold Nicolson.* Chatto and Windus.
Lesley, Cole. 1976. *The Life of Noel Coward.* Jonathan Cape.
Mackenzie, Compton. 1966/67. *My Life and Times* (Octaves 5 and 6). Chatto and Windus.
MacQueen-Pope, W. 1957. *Give Me Yesterday.* Hutchinson.
Margetson, Stella. 1974. *The Long Party.* Saxon House.
Massey, Raymond. 1979. *A Hundred Different Lives.* Robson.
Maugham, Robin. 1972. *Escape from the Shadows.* Hodder and Stoughton.

Mayo, Katherine. 1927. *Mother India.* Jonathan Cape.

Maxwell, Elsa. 1964. *The Celebrity Circus.* W. H. Allen.

McKnight, Gerald. 1980. *The Scandal of Syrie Maugham.* W. H. Allen.

Mills, John. 1980. *Up in the Clouds, Gentlemen, Please.* Weidenfeld and Nicolson.

Monk, L. A. 1976. *Britain 1945–1970.* G. Bell and Sons.

Montgomery, John. 1957. *The Twenties.* Allen and Unwin.

Morgan, Ted. 1980. *Somerset Maugham.* Jonathan Cape.

Morley, Sheridan. 1969. *A Talent To Amuse.* Heinemann.

Mosley, Oswald. 1968. *My Life.* Nelson.

Muggeridge, Malcolm. 1940. *The Thirties.* Hamish Hamilton.

Nicolson, Harold and Nigel Nicolson (Eds.). 1966. *Diaries and Letters 1930–1939.* Collins.

Palmer, Geoffrey and Noel Lloyd. 1988. *E. F. Benson.* Lennard.

Patmore, David. 1960. *Private History.* Jonathan Cape.

Payn, Graham and Sheridan Morley (Eds.). 1982. *The Noël Coward Diaries.* Weidenfeld and Nicolson.

Pearson, John. 1978. *Façades.* Macmillan.

Roberts, Cecil. 1930. *Half Way.* Hutchinson.

Seeley, Robert and Rex Bunnett. 1989. *London Shows on Record.* General Gramaphone Publications.

Shaughnessy, Alfred. 1978. *Both Ends of the Candle.* Peter Owen.

Shirer, William L. 1960. *The Rise and Fall of the Third Reich.* Secker and Warburg.

Short, Ernest. 1942. *Theatrical Cavalcade.* Eyre and Spottiswoode.

Sykes, Christopher. 1975. *Evelyn Waugh.* Collins.

Vickers, Hugo. 1985. *Cecil Beaton.* Weidenfeld and Nicolson.

Waller, Jane (Ed.). 1977. *A Man's Book.* Duckworth.

Whistler, Laurence. 1985. *The Laughter and the Urn.* Weidenfeld and Nicolson.

Wildeblood, Peter. 1957. *Against the Law.* Penguin.

Wilson, Sandy. 1975. *Ivor.* Michael Joseph.

Index